I0896064

The politics of gender and sexuality in modern Ireland: a reader

The politics of gender and sexuality in modern Ireland
A Reader

Jennifer Redmond & Mary McAuliffe

EDITORS

FOUR COURTS PRESS

Set in 11.5pt on 13.5pt Centaur by
Carrigboy Typesetting Services for
FOUR COURTS PRESS LTD
7 Malpas Street, Dublin 8, Ireland
www.fourcourtspress.ie
and in North America for
FOUR COURTS PRESS
c/o IPG, 814 N. Franklin St, Chicago, IL 60610.

© The various authors and Four Courts Press 2024

A catalogue record for this title is available from the British Library.

ISBN 978-1-80151-139-1

All rights reserved. No part of this publication may be reproduced, stored in or introduced into a retrieval system, or transmitted, in any form or by any means (electronic, mechanical, photocopying, recording, or otherwise), without the prior written permission of both the copyright owner and publisher of this book.

Printed in England
by CPI Antony Rowe, Chippenham, Wilts.

This book is dedicated to the members of the
Women's History Association of Ireland,
of which we are both proud to be past Presidents
and especially in memory of Dr Margaret MacCurtain,
an inspiration in the field.

Contents

Acknowledgments

We would like to acknowledge the assistance of librarians and archivists in providing access to the historical materials and secondary sources in this volume. All researchers, especially those in the arts, humanities, and social sciences, owe a debt of gratitude to those who dedicate their lives to preserving the history of under-represented and minority groups. Without those records, we would not be able to present the rich histories contained in this collection. We acknowledge the dedication and patience of our contributors who stoically awaited updates amid numerous delays – we truly are grateful to you for entrusting your fantastic research to us. We would also like to thank the members of the Women's History Association of Ireland, past and present, the forum that first brought together many of the authors in this collection, including our original collaborators Professor Sonja Tiernan Hall and Dr Sandra McAvoy. Both scholars have done much to enrich our understanding of the politics of gender and power in Ireland's history.

We are deeply grateful to Professor Maria Luddy, an inspirational leader in the field of women's history in Ireland, for writing our Afterword. We recognise the difficulty of this task but did not doubt her abilities to produce her searingly insightful piece, reflective of the research she is renowned for.

We also extend thanks for the practical assistance of Lorna Fagan, MA student in Maynooth University, for helping us to prepare the final manuscript. Her quick work and positive attitude helped to get the final manuscript together and we are really grateful for this essential assistance. Thank you to the Department of History, Maynooth University, for providing funding for this invaluable support. Special thanks to Alan Hayes for last minute citation help – we owe you a drink! This collection grew out of, and expanded on, the histories of gender, sexuality and the body discussed in *Sexual politics in modern Ireland* (2015) published by Irish Academic Press.

Jennifer would like to thank her family and the FFC (you know who you are!) for the collegial support in all her endeavours and the sympathetic ear provided while facing the challenges of producing this book. Mary would like to thank 'the Drs' (you know who you are), her partner Julie, and her family for their continuing advice, love, and support.

We would like to thank UCD, through its OBRSS Research Support Scheme, for funding the index to the collection. We appreciate the hard work of Conor Reidy in producing that index. We gratefully acknowledge the Research Development Office, Maynooth University, for their support for Jennifer's time in producing the final version of this volume. Our sincere thanks, finally and most emphatically, to Martin Fanning and the team at Four Courts Press who helped us bring this collection to press after many setbacks. Míle Buíochas!

Introduction

Jennifer Redmond and Mary McAuliffe

Issues of gender and sexuality have occupied the Irish public for decades and this is unlikely to end any time soon. This collection offers historical reflections and analyses of contested and often hidden histories related to sexual politics and gender identities in Ireland in the nineteenth and twentieth centuries. *The politics of gender and sexuality in modern Ireland: a reader* adds to the body of literature produced on Irish women's and gender history by a lively community of scholars over the last five decades. The chapters vary in focus but are united in examining conceptions of bodies as political terrain, in essence the politicisation of gender and sexuality, in various ways. As Judith Butler has argued, bodies do matter; the materiality of the body has an intimate connection to the performativity of gender and hence the treatment of those bodies by the law, in the public sphere and in our conceptions of masculinity, femininity and otherness.[1] This collection follows upon the tradition established in Irish women's history since 1978 with the ground-breaking publication of *Women in Irish society: the historical dimension,* edited by the renowned and much-loved Margaret MacCurtain and Donncha Ó Corráin, in bringing together new research by established and emerging scholars in the field.[2] The 'agenda' for Irish women's history laid down by Margaret MacCurtain, Mary O'Dowd and Maria Luddy in 1992 is rightly pointed to as a turning point in the historiography of women's history in Ireland.[3] Indeed, in the special issue of *Irish Historical Studies* dedicated to the thirtieth anniversary of the piece, guest editors Frances Nolan and Bronagh Ann McShane acknowledge the plethora of additional primary sources that have been made available through published collections, digitised repositories, databases and archival practice itself, which has allowed for 'the debate around women's and gender history' to move on 'to a point where both approaches co-exist and overlap productively, allowing for a greater dimensionality in scholarship'.[4] Building upon seminal collections, this book offers fresh insights

1 Judith Butler, *Bodies that matter: on the discursive limits of 'sex'* (New York and London, 1993).
2 Margaret MacCurtain and Donncha Ó Corráin (eds), *Women in Irish society: the historical dimension* (Dublin, 1978). 3 Margaret MacCurtain, Mary O'Dowd and Maria Luddy, 'An agenda for women's history in Ireland, 1500–1900', *Irish Historical Studies,* 28:109 (May 1992), pp 1–37.
4 Frances Nolan and Bronagh Ann McShane, 'Introduction: a new agenda for women's and

in the field of gender and sexuality in modern Ireland from scholars examining themes of love and intimacy, political activism, migration, the incarceration of women in mother and baby homes on the island, the world of work, debates on sexual education and more.

The book considers gender and sexuality in historical perspective, going beyond the binary of male and female heterosexual experience to explore LGBTQI+ histories, the treatment of intersex persons in Ireland, the history of trans people and activism in Ireland, and strategies used to resist patriarchal, heteronormative constructions of sexual and gender identities. Recent trends in historical research have been emphasising personal experiences that were marginalised, suppressed or ignored in the major historical works on modern Irish history and this volume contributes both individual and collective experiences that will add to our knowledge of the cultural and social milieu of Ireland in the last two centuries. Indeed, the pace of social change in Ireland in recent decades has been fast, marked by the referenda on marriage equality (2015) and abortion (2018) and investigations into the treatment of unmarried mothers and their children captivating the country and bringing old issues into a new light.

One such issue is the privileging of domesticity for married women. The ideal of marital motherhood was embedded in the Irish Constitution, written in 1937. Article 41.2, commonly called the 'woman in the home' article, asserts that by her life within the home, 'woman gives to the State a support without which the common good cannot be achieved'. It further states that mothers 'shall not be obliged by economic necessity to engage in labour to the neglect of their duties in the home'. As soon as the draft of the Constitution was released feminists, many of whom had participated in the suffrage battles, rejected this article as 'sinister and retrogressive', and that opinion has not altered among feminist activists and most women to the present day, while that article remains in the Constitution.[5] Over the last three decades since the constitutional review of 1996, which recommended that these 'dated' provisions be either deleted or 'replaced with a gender-neutral provision', governments have promised a referendum on the issue. Following recommendations from a Citizens' Assembly on Gender Equality (2020–1) and a Committee on Gender Equality (2021), the government proposed a referendum for 8 March 2024 which would remove the 'women in the home' article and replace it with Article 42B, which read 'the State recognises that the provision of care, by members of a family to one another by reason of the bonds that exist among them, gives to society a

gender history in Ireland', *Irish Historical Studies*, 46:170 (2022), pp 207–16. 5 Maria Luddy, 'A "sinister and retrogressive" proposal: Irish women's opposition to the 1937 draft Constitution', support without which the common good cannot be achieved, and shall strive to support such provision'. A further Amendment, the Thirty-Ninth, known as the family amendment, which would have expanded the definition of family outside of the marital family, was defeated by 73.93%. Initial analysis suggests that what new rights this expanded definition would give to families based on 'durable bonds' was not well explained by the government.[6] Despite having based the referendum on the recommendations of the Citizens' Assembly for the Fortieth Amendment (dealing with the 'woman in the home' article), it was defeated by 67.69%.[7] It also failed to include the more expansive wording provided by the all-party Oireachtas Joint Committee on Gender Equality which referred to 'care within and outside the home and Family'.[8] Many disability activists regarded the final wording as ableist and campaigned against its insertion. As we write, the sexist article 41.2 remains in our Constitution and will do so for the foreseeable future.

Mary Cullen's observation on the importance of understanding male and female experiences in history remains a stark warning to the omission of gender perspectives: 'The absence of gender analysis in the writing of history deprives men and boys, as well as women and girls, of an important part of their group and individual memory'.[9] This holds true a decade after the publication of her seminal collection of essays reflecting on a lifetime of inspirational work in gender and women's history. Yet while modern Irish gender history has moved beyond the simple process of recovery of women in the past to innovative work in masculinities, same sex relationships and lesbian and gay activism, these histories often remain marginal as the subject is taught and written in many contexts, making it necessary to continue to revisit the past and our understanding of men and women's roles. We have noticed a continuous demand for histories beyond the traditional accounts of high politics and war from university students, eager to see themselves reflected in what is remembered and taught about our past. We hope this book appeals to all those curious to know more about the dynamics of gender, power, identity, sexuality and in many cases,

Transactions of the Royal Historical Society (2005), pp 175–95. 6 Results information available from the Electoral Commission website https://www.referendum.ie/ (accessed 19 March 2024). 7 The suggestion from the Citizens' Assembly was that Article 41.2 of the Constitution should be deleted and replaced with language that is not gender specific and obliges the state to take reasonable measures to support care within the home and wider community. See *Report of The Citizens' Assembly on Gender Equality*, p. 53, available https://citizensassembly.ie/wp-content/uploads/2023/02/report-of-the-citizens-assembly-on-gender-equality.pdf (accessed 19 March 2024). 8 For further detail see Maeve O'Rourke, 'A right to care and the Care Referendum on 8 March', https://maeveorourke.medium.com/a-right-to-care-and-the-care-referendum-on-8-march-9d6bdc7834ba (accessed 19 March 2024). 9 Mary Cullen, *Telling it our way: essays in gender history* (Dublin, 2013), p. 21.

shame, in Ireland's recent past. We had in mind, in particular, the scholar of gender history in modern Ireland who would like to learn more through case studies, different methodologies ranging from primary source analysis to interviews and the blending of theoretical work on gender with standard historical accounts. There are chapters that describe how the research has been conducted as well as those that offer threads for future research in areas where it was previously difficult to access sources.

The first section on sexuality and relationships compares and contrasts the narratives of heterosexual and homosexual relationships through two case studies provided by Maeve O'Riordan and Mary McAuliffe respectively. Although both relationships described developed in the same historical era, we can see the mores and values of the period operating very differently on the basis of sexuality. Yet both accounts reveal the sincerity of the intimacy and bonds of affection held between Dermod and Mabel and Kathleen and Madeleine. In order to preserve their social and class position, intermarriage was, for the landed elite, with their strong ties of identity, religion, culture and politics, very important. Although a small cohort of eligible singletons existed, love and romance could develop. In her chapter O'Riordan explores the romance and engagement of Dermod O'Brien and Mabel Smyly, offering an alternative perspective on sexuality and propriety among their class, providing a rare glimpse of the personal and sexual desires of young men and women in this era through a series of letters they exchanged prior to their marriage. She highlights the passion, both physical and emotional, that emanated from Smyly and was reciprocated by O'Brien. Although constrained by societal expectations of women of her age, class and status Smyly's desires and feelings, as expressed in her letters, run contrary to the Victorian stereotype of 'the angel in the house'. The gendered double standards that cast women as both passive recipients and controllers of men's desires were paradoxically embraced and rejected by Smyly, at times rhetorically playing the temptress, yet at others wishing to be consumed and controlled by O'Brien.

Mary McAuliffe's chapter also looks at relationships between women whose upper middle-class status should have played a similar role in their lives, but, born a generation later than Smyly, they could and did make different choices. Dr Kathleen Lynn, daughter of a Church of Ireland clergyman, educated in Alexandra College for Girls and a qualified medical doctor, made the political journey from being a self-declared unionist to being a militant suffrage, socialist and republican activist. Madeleine ffrench-Mullen, daughter of a Royal Navy surgeon, made a similar journey, one which brought the two women in contact with each other in 1914, at a Cumann na mBan first aid training session. From 1914, until ffrench-Mullen's death in 1944, the two women made their lives, professionally, politically and personally, together. Using Lynn's diaries as the source, their lives together, and their interconnected network of activist women, are considered through a queer lens. Irish queer histories are a new but vibrant and growing sub-discipline; however, queer femininities remain somewhat marginalised within this area of research. This chapter makes the argument that a deep analysis of Irish revolutionary women provides us with a new history of same sex relationships between women during this period of radical activism and radical lives. McAuliffe's work on the diaries further evidences Senia Pašeta's observation that these women did not expect to be forgotten:

> they chronicled their own experiences as they lived them [and] ... they were acutely aware of how they, and Irish women more generally, might be remembered. The many memoirs, reminiscences, rough lecture notes and half-finished autobiographical sketches which survive remind us of both the vibrancy of the world they lived and of their own sense that their experiences were worth remembering in and of themselves and in the context of the wider national narrative.[10]

The following section on gender and institutionalisation features work that spans the nineteenth and twentieth centuries when the incarceration of 'problematic' citizens increased dramatically with devastating consequences. Jim Smith's work on 'the containment culture' surrounding sexuality, sexual behaviours and sexual norms resonates in each of the three chapters in this section.[11] Conor Reidy's work on women treated in Clare for alcoholism shows the gendered basis of the treatment and the moral attitudes that informed such incarceration. Unlike the first section where we hear the women's voices in their own words, Reidy points to the silence that hangs over the women themselves as their voices were not recorded and their perspectives on their treatment are absent from the historical record. Leanne McCormick, John Privilege and Sean O'Connell's piece reflecting on the Northern Ireland report into mother and baby homes gives an insight into the work of the historian doing this sensitive research. Their work attests to the delicate approach needed to represent the experiences of those who were in institutions for unmarried mothers and their children, and while there are commonalities in both parts of the island in terms of how such women and their children were treated, the formal inquiries and the final reporting on this history is markedly different. The outraged reception given to the final report of the Commission of Investigation into Mother and

10 Senia Pašeta, *Irish nationalist women, 1900–1918* (Cambridge, 2013), p. 1. 11 James M. Smith, *Ireland's Magdalen laundries and the nation's architecture of containment* (Indiana, 2007).

Baby Homes (COIMBH) in the Republic of Ireland rightly stands in stark contrast to the most positive reception given the Northern Ireland Mother and Baby Home and Magdalene Laundries Research Report.[12] The exclusion or minimisation of survivor testimony in the report on the republic makes its conclusions untenable for many historians.

Caitlín O'Neill and Jennifer Redmond investigate the contested history of just one of the institutions examined in the COIMBH report, Sean Ross Abbey. At a time when many of the religious orders have yet to pay their full financial share into the government scheme for survivor compensation, this chapter reveals multiple ways in which one order, the Congregation of the Sacred Hearts of Jesus and Mary, were generating funds at the time of its operation: state support, profitable activities, donations from those wishing to adopt children and money, often directly demanded, from the families of girls housed in the institution.[13] It is also one of the institutions that has featured in a legal case taken by survivor Philomena Lee whose claim that the government misrepresented her consent for the adoption of her son Anthony was upheld in the High Court in November 2021. While the COIMBH report has been criticised for its approach and its partial scope, O'Neill and Redmond's chapter reveals its potential to create critical narratives using its evidence, a recourse taken of necessity as many of the original records held by congregations are unavailable to the public.

The politics of bodies section includes chapters that directly reflect on the ways in which people's bodies have been defined, debated and distrusted throughout Irish history. Often this is as a direct consequence of their gender. Jennifer Redmond examines the rhetoric surrounding female emigrant bodies in post-independence Ireland, which focused almost exclusively on Irish women's

12 The final report of the Commission of Investigation into Mother and Baby Homes and Certain Related Matters (COIMBH in this text) was produced in January 2021. It covered only some of the many institutions in which unmarried women were incarcerated in Ireland including the following: St Patrick's/Pelletstown, Navan Road, Dublin 7, The Tuam Children's Home, Tuam, Co. Galway, Bessborough mother and baby home, Cork, Manor House, Castlepollard, Sean Ross Abbey, Co. Tipperary, Árd Mhuire, Dunboyne, Bethany Home, Dublin, Denny House, Dublin, Miss Carr's Flatlets, Dublin, The Regina Coeli Hostel, Dublin, The Castle, Newtowncunningham, Co. Donegal, The County Clare Nursery, Kilrush, Co. Clare, Belmont Flatlets, Dublin and St Gerard's, Dublin. The Commission comprised of Judge Yvonne Murphy (chair), Dr William Duncan, and Professor Mary E. Daly. The details of the Commission and the report can be seen at https://www.gov.ie/en/publication/316d8–commission-of-investigation/, accessed 21 February 2024. 13 According to Irish government information on the redress scheme, 'The purpose of the Mother and Baby Institutions Payment Scheme is to provide financial payments and an enhanced medical card to defined groups in acknowledgment of suffering experienced while resident in Mother and Baby and County Home Institutions'. Information taken from https://assets.gov.ie/204595/b3a52e17–ae0c-4897–8a3e-9ae7a6e59d08.pdf, accessed 21 February 2024.

sexuality and behaviour (presumed and actual). Their bodies were central to this thinking: bodies were the site of sin, the literal embodiment of transgressive sexual behaviour through pregnancy, and thus control of them was essential in order to diminish what was seen as a significant moral problem. Opinions on women's sexual practises as emigrants was also based on partial evidence of the phenomenon of unmarried mothers, and the opinions of religious charitable institutions in Britain, which found themselves assisting in 'hiding Ireland's shame'. Women emigrating were often castigated as sexually profligate, immoral, or excessively naïve and susceptible to sin and accused of bringing shame to the nation. Unsurprisingly, there was no such similar commentary on male emigrants.

Tanya Ní Mhuirthile highlights the legal position, historically and in the present, of intersex people, a group often overlooked in binary categorisations of citizens yet, as this chapter shows, there are clear signs of evidence in the past that we have always known about non-binary identities. As Ní Mhuirthile writes, historically the law recognised three types of bodies as conferring legal status: male, female and hermaphrodite. However, by the Victorian era, despite increased specialisation in medical knowledge about hermaphroditic conditions, legal provisions governing the registration of persons notably excluded intersex. This coincidence of events is analysed and seen to signal the beginning of the erosion of intersex people from legal consciousness. This analysis is further strengthened by an examination of the case law that has directly addressed the categorisation of bodies as either male or female. Presently, Irish law does not actively protect or ensure the vindication of the rights of people with intersex variations. Ní Mhuirthile's work is a clear example of where future research in legal and historical narratives of non-binary citizens may develop.

Reflecting on a lack of attention paid to violence against women during the conflict in Northern Ireland, Theresa O'Keefe's chapter focuses on how and why wartime sexual violence has been marginalised as an issue. She concentrates here on the weaponisation of strip searching in women's prisons and the responses to this from among divided feminist groups in Northern Ireland and in the Republic. O'Keefe vividly describes the women in Armagh's resistance through hunger strike, no wash protests and other methods, the abusive gendered regime to which they were subject. The feminist responses to the treatment of these women were fractured along ideological lines. The importance of recognising the experience of wartime sexual violence from the State and its policing arms, and its impact on feminist politics, is central to this chapter.

In her chapter Sinéad Kennedy reflects on an Ireland of the not-too-distant past and yet a place where the controls and judgements placed on women's bodies could prove fatal as in the tragic case of Ann Lovett. Using a critical and gendered lens, Kennedy argues that gender, and women's bodies, are central to understanding the polices of that decade, offering a framework to understand the backlash to the gains, however limited, of Irish second wave feminism in the 1970s. Using Susan Faludi's concept of 'backlash' as not necessarily against the limited rights gained by women, but against the possibility that equality might be achieved, Kennedy outlines several of the landmark cases in the 1980s. The successful campaign, in 1983, by pro-life campaigners to insert the anti-abortion Eighth Amendment into the Irish Constitution, the Ann Lovett and Joanne Hayes stories, and ending with the 1992 case of Miss 'X', reveal the impact and legacies of the advance of the right in its battle against equality and the fightback, by embattled but ultimately resurgent, feminist and civil liberties campaigns in the 1990s. The fortieth anniversary of Lovett's death this year (2024) has created a new interest and curiosity about an Ireland that is within 'touching distance' and yet seems like another world to many younger generations.

The two chapters in the next section on women and work offer new evidence on the world of women's work in nineteenth- and twentieth-century Ireland, a time when the continued pressure in the public sphere for women to remain in the home was in tension with an economic need to contribute to the family wage and the increasing expectations from women to be part of working life. Antonia Hart's exploration of women's self-employment through pawnbroking business reveals a rich landscape of gendered entrepreneurship in what was regarded as a somewhat appropriate business for women to be involved in, especially in urban centres such as Dublin. Deirdre Foley reflects on the world of work for mothers in the period that encompassed Ireland's shifting economic priorities and our entry into the European Union which transformed maternity leave and the rights of working parents. The persistence of the marriage bar in Ireland was closely connected to the traditional ideal of the male 'family wage' or what has been termed the 'male breadwinner' model, which was also preserved by a poor system of maternity leave. From the 1960s onwards, the practice of the marriage bar was gradually giving way to a 'maternity bar' as women were excluded from work due to pregnancy, and had difficulty maintaining work or re-entering the workforce once they were mothers. While discrimination against parents in the workforce is outlawed in modern employment legislation, there are still pressing issues in access and affordability of childcare and options for flexible parental leave which mean this chapter is not simply a historical reflection on a closed chapter but informs present debates.

In the next section, the sexual politics of debate and activism, Elizabeth Kiely's chapter on the fierce debates around school-based relationships and sexualities education is another example of a living history or an issue that continues to inspire debate and controversy. Although media has taken different forms, what is clear from examining radio contributions, blog posts or newspapers is that the Irish public has always been interested in sexuality and the most appropriate ways for knowledge of sexual identities and relationships to be communicated to young people. The use of letters to the editors of major newspapers as a way to explore the 'culture wars' around appropriate sex education in modern Ireland provides a fascinating glimpse into how the debate continues to play out among those, especially parents, outside of politics and education. Mary Muldowney's chapter on the struggle for abortion rights and pro-choice activism in Ireland between 1983 and 2018 suggests that the changes in Irish attitudes to abortion were significant and the silence about abortion was of a very different nature in 2018 than it had been in 1983. Drawing on a variety of sources, Muldowney's piece is an important chronicle of the history of reproductive activism in Ireland and the shifting mores and values that characterise Ireland in the last few decades.

Personal reflections and new directions, the last section of the volume, contains the two final chapters, which are placed here to inspire new histories and further research, written by activists and collectors of those histories. While LGBTI+ histories are receiving deserved attention in recent decades, much of the work concentrates on national groups and their activism, most based in Dublin, while lesbian and gay histories elsewhere have been somewhat sidelined. Orla Egan's chapter, 'The Cork LGBT Archive and lesbian activism in Cork, 1970–2000', looks at both the history of lesbian lives and activism in Cork, and her own decades-long involvement as an archivist of those histories. Dublin may have had the national organisations, but Cork has an equally long, rich, and sometimes more radical LGBTI+ history. Lesbian activism especially was prominent in Cork LGBTI+ histories in a way it hasn't been written in Dublin-based narratives. Egan gives us an insider view of Cork's lesbian history, as a lesbian activist and a devoted collector and founder of the Cork LGBT Archive. As she outlines, lesbian collectives, bookshops, lesbian line, the Women's Place, the left wing, queer inclusive and the Quay Co-op, were among the spaces in which lesbian activism grew and flourished. Cork's famous Women's Fun Weekend drew lesbian, dykes and queer women from all over the country. As Egan's chapter also shows terms such as dyke, sometimes considered a slur, were reclaimed by Cork lesbians as an empowering act of self-construction. Cultural and activist events were often termed 'dyke night', or 'dyke march'. This was similar to such processes in America, where the radical origins of dyke have been reclaimed to demonstrate a sense of history and continuity within lesbian communities.[14] Egan's chapter is also a demonstration of living histories as she

14 See Clare Forstie, 'Disappearing dykes? Post-lesbian discourse and shifting identities and communities', *Journal of Homosexuality*, 67:12 (2020), pp 1760–78.

continues to collect for the Cork LGBT Archive, curate exhibitions and publish on her own activism and from the archival collection, which, as the Cork LGBT Archive's masthead says, makes Cork's queer history impossible to ignore.[15]

In her chapter, 'Out is a very dangerous place to be: the emergence of the trans movement in Ireland', trans activist Sara R. Phillips gives an insider/participant reflection on the modern emergence of the trans rights movement in Ireland. While academic histories of LGBTI+ activism, especially those looking at the emergence of the Irish sexual liberation movement and lesbian and gay identity politics activism, have access to archives such as the Irish Queer Archive, now deposited at the National Library of Ireland, to write those histories, trans histories are often marginalised both within collections and in the histories they have produced. Phillips provides a reflective piece on the long history of the modern Irish trans movement as well as indicating the existence of a long and varied Irish trans history yet to be researched and analysed. The contemporary Irish trans activist movement began, like the modern Irish feminist and sexual liberation movements, in the 1970s and gathered pace from the 1990s and continued into the twenty-first century. Phillips pays homage to activists such as Dr Lydia Foy whose long campaign to have her gender recognised on her birth certificate was, after several court cases, successful in 2015 with the passage of the Gender Recognition Act. Phillips outlines the many decades of activism to achieve the Act, through the campaigns of individuals and of NGOs such as Trans Equality Network Ireland (TENI). She ends her piece on the importance of building a trans archive in Ireland, to truly broaden histories of LGBTI+ to include the complexities and questions of trans histories and identities.

Finally, the Afterword by renowned historian of modern Ireland Maria Luddy draws together many of the themes in *The politics of gender and sexuality in modern Ireland* in a reflection on the histories that have been recorded, the ones that are possible to retrieve and the ones that may be lost without greater vigilance on the part of historians, information professionals and the public. This piece rounds out the volume, an appropriate ending to a collection dedicated to histories of sexuality, gender and power, many of which have been helped and inspired by Luddy's outstanding work in the fields of gender and social history. As Luddy states in the 'Afterword', the chapters convey 'the varying ways relationships of power and dominance have shaped Irish society'. It is our sincere hope as editors that we inspire further investigations into power and dominance so that the shame so wrongly attributed to women, children and other marginalised groups may be exorcised for good.

15 See Cork LGBT Archive webpage at https://corklgbtarchive.com/ accessed 21 February 2024.

SECTION ONE

SEXUALITY AND RELATIONSHIPS

CHAPTER 1

Elite courtship: the case of Mabel Smyly and Dermod O'Brien, 1901–2

Maeve O'Riordan

Marriage has always been an essential feature of upper-class life in Ireland; it ensured the safe passage of property from father to legitimate son and tied socially and politically compatible families together. It was common for intermarriages to occur between the children of the landed gentry and the professional classes.[1] These predominately Anglican members of elite Irish society valued their shared sense of identity, status and ideals, and were unwilling to accept marriage partners from a lower social class or of a different religion. For women, the choice of partner had significant bearing on their lifelong economic comfort, and for men, a wisely chosen bride could enhance their career through connections and status. Even with such social and economic incentives to marry within a circumscribed sphere of eligible singletons, marriage partnerships could be based, partly at-least, on sexual attraction and love.[2] This chapter will explore the pre-marital relationship of Dermod O'Brien (1865–1945)[3] and Mabel Smyly (1869–1942) which culminated in their marriage in 1902. This relationship was one characterised by sexual desire combined with an adherence to the patriarchal social structure of the day.

The relative importance of love, money, social position, security, and the desire for a legitimate heir in men's and women's minds as they chose or accepted a marriage partner has been the topic of historians' interest for several decades. Studies across various time periods for Britain and Ireland have observed a shift towards individualism and affection in marriage partners for the elite. Lawrence Stone argued that by the end of the eighteenth century 'complex calculations of scheming parents and artful lawyers took second place – and willingly so – to the dictates of the heart'.[4] Judith Schneid Lewis placed the change later,

1 Maeve O'Riordan, 'Home, family and society, women of the Irish landed class, 1860–1914: a Munster case-study' (PhD, University College Cork, 2014), Tables 5 and 6, pp 144–5. 2 Maeve O'Riordan, *Women of the country house in Ireland, 1860–1914* (Liverpool, 2018). 3 Bridget Hourican, 'Dermod O'Brien', *Dictionary of Irish biography*, https://doi.org/10.3318/dib.006460.v1 accessed 22 February 2024. 4 Lawrence Stone, 'The law and custom of marriage' in *Road to divorce: England,*

arguing that by 1860 it was deemed necessary to be 'perfectly in love' with one's partner.[5] How much that perfect love was influenced by economic and other factors is still being determined by historians. Romantic love has recently come under scrutiny as a cultural construct. For Katie Barclay, 'love was manifested in behaviour, which, in turn, was expected to conform to rank-appropriate patriarchal gender norms. As a result, love reinforced male authority and female subordination'.[6] Her work on marriage in Scotland (1650–1850) provides a model on how to read the system of patriarchy into marital love and relationships. When marriages have been closely analysed using correspondence between the couple there have been consistent examples of affection and even lust between couples dating back to the Middle Ages. Pat Jalland has provided clear examples of marriages that were both economically appropriate and sexually fulfilling in her study on marriage in political and academic circles at the end of the nineteenth century.[7]

Studies of Irish marriages have treated on the combined, if not competing, desire for an economically and emotionally suitable match across the eighteenth, nineteenth and early twentieth centuries.[8] Caitriona Clear observed that 'pragmatism could, and can, co-exist with sexual attraction, friendship and joy in one another's company', while Deborah Wilson illustrated how the financial aspect of elite marriages worked in practice, as families circumvented misogynistic property law for their daughters through marriage settlements.[9] The role of patriarchal social structures and romantic considerations in the brokering of Irish marriages across the social classes has been comprehensively explored in Luddy and O'Dowd's *Marriage in Ireland, 1660–1925*. They too observed a degree of continuity in marital attraction among the elite across the centuries as 'patriarchy was usually diluted by the circumstances as well as the personalities of individual husbands and wives',[10] while also noting a growing freedom in choice of marriage partners by the 1900s, observing that 'love was

1530–1987 (Oxford, 1990), p. 59. 5 Judith Schneid Lewis, *In the family way: childbearing in the British aristocracy, 1760–1860* (New Brunswick, 1986), pp 31, 30, 36. 6 Katie Barclay, *Love, intimacy and power: marriage and patriarchy in Scotland, 1650–1850* (Manchester, 2011), p. 103. 7 Pat Jalland, *Women, marriage, and politics, 1860–1914* (New York, 1986). 8 Leanne Calvert, '"Do not forget your bit wife": love, marriage and the negotiation of patriarchy in Irish Presbyterian marriages, *c.*1780–1850', *Women's History Review*, 26:3 (2017), pp 433–54; Leanne Calvert, '"He came to her bed pretending courtship": sex, courtship and the making of marriage in Ulster, 1750–1844', *Irish Historical Studies*, 42:162 (2018), pp 244–64; Lindsay Earner-Byrne, 'The family in Ireland, 1880–2015' in Thomas Bartlett (ed.), *The Cambridge history of Ireland*, vol. 4 (Cambridge, 2018), pp 641–72; Diane Urquhart, *The ladies of Londonderry: women and political patronage* (London, 2007). 9 Caitriona Clear, *Social change and everyday life in Ireland: 1850–1922* (Manchester, 2007; 2013), p. 85; D. Wilson, *Women, marriage and property in wealthy landed families in Ireland, 1750–1850* (Manchester, 2009; 2013). 10 Mary O'Dowd and Maria Luddy, *Marriage in Ireland, 1660–1925* (Cambridge, important to individuals in courtship'.[11] For the wealthy in society, choice did not lead to dramatic changes in partner selection as head and heart combined to make socially acceptable choices. Adelman and O'Neill's innovative article explores the sexual script of 'male pursuit, female refusal, and eventual consent' followed by a genteel (albeit unequal) Victorian Dublin couple.[12] Attraction without economic compatibility was not enough to lead someone down the aisle. Marriages rarely took place between partners from dramatically different social backgrounds; the potential for loss of face and income was too great for the wealthier party.

Provided they enjoyed a companionate rather than abusive marriage, there was some scope for elite wives to circumvent patriarchal structures designed to keep them in a subordinate position. K.D. Reynolds used the concept of 'incorporated wives' to explore 'the significance of a subordinate role [of wife], accepted and even enjoyed by its players, whose priorities were different from those of late-twentieth-century women'.[13] As Peterson observed in her study of upper-middle-class English families:

> … these were not 'dual careers' … These were 'single career families,' but both husband and wife partook of that single career. And among family, friends, and co-workers the wife's contribution was known and acknowledged.[14]

Still, the legal options for escaping abusive or unhappy marriages were virtually nil,[15] and as Diane Urquhart has shown birth families rarely did anything to protect women after their marriage. Even in companionate marriages, the wife was largely dependent on her husband to manage the family size.[16]

THE SMYLY AND O'BRIEN FAMILIES

The Smyly–O'Brien marriage can be viewed as a relatively typical upper-class marriage with family approval, an engagement period of less than one year, an expression of love by both parties for the other, and broad financial equality. Both were a little above the average age at first marriage, Dermod was thirty-six when he proposed to Mabel, who was thirty-two. Mabel's father was a knighted

2020), p. 227. 11 O'Dowd and Luddy, *Marriage*, pp 145, 157, 144. 12 Juliana Adelman and Ciaran O'Neill, 'Love, consent, and the sexual script of a Victorian affair in Dublin', *Journal of the History of Sexuality*, 29:3 (2020), pp 388–417. 13 K.D. Reynolds, *Aristocratic women and political society in Victorian Britain* (Oxford, 1998), p. 155. 14 M. Jeanne Peterson, *Family, love and work in the lives of Victorian gentlewomen* (Bloomington, 1989), p. 184. 15 Diane Urquhart, *Irish divorce: a history* (Cambridge, 2020). 16 Sandra McAvoy, 'The regulation of sexuality in the Irish Free State, 1929–1935' in Greta Jones and Elizabeth Malcolm (eds), *Medicine, disease and the state in Ireland, 1650–*

doctor and honorary surgeon to the viceroys, queen, and later the king in Ireland and left a personal estate valued at £7,324 on his death in 1904.[17] The O'Briens, as landholding magnates,[18] were in decline, but they maintained a comfortable nomadic existence between Ireland, London, and continental Europe, moving in artistic and creative circles. Dermod's father left several properties and inheritances on his death in 1909 with a gross value of £9,153.[19] Dermod's own income as an artist was supplemented by inherited wealth, estate rental and eventually the sale of land.[20] In 1901, he decided to set up his studio in Dublin, away from the heavier competition of London.[21] This move coincided with the escalation of his relationship with Mabel, and perhaps his decision to 'settle down'.

Mabel, aside from a couple of months in Italy, had lived her unmarried life in Dublin's Merrion Square with her parents and siblings. The Smylys were actively involved in philanthropic activities.[22] Mabel helped run the (sometimes controversial) Smyly schools established by her grandmother, gave classes, and sat on committees. Both Mabel and Dermod were religious, but she wore her Protestantism more outwardly, and defended proselytising.[23] Dermod had familial ties to important nationalists[24] whereas Mabel was staunchly unionist. They shared a love of music, though Dermod's more liberal upbringing meant he had a wider knowledge of classical music. He lamented to his stepmother that Mabel had an 'upbringing among Hymns & the lowest church people' but insisted she had 'any amount of the right stuff in her'.[25] Both were interested in languages; Mabel's Italian allowed her to translate Dante.

FAMILY APPROVAL

Dermod received universal praise when he announced his engagement. The benefits of gaining a wife were so widely held, that his friend wrote: 'I am very

1940 (Cork, 1999). **17** Her maternal uncle was 4th Baron Plunket, Anglican archbishop of Dublin. Anon., 'Sir Philip Crampton Smyly, MD, DUH, obituary notices', *Journal of Larynology, Rhinology and Otology*, 19:6 (June 1904), pp 286–7. 'Will of Sir Philip Smyly', *Irish Times*, 14 June 1904. **18** They were a junior branch of the Inchiquin baronetcy of Dromoland, with an estate at Cahermoyle, Co. Limerick. The family estate was sold in 1919. **19** 'Mr Edward William O'Brien's will', *Irish Times*, 24 March 1909. **20** Lennox Robinson, *Palette and plough: a pen-and-ink drawing of DOB* (Dublin, 1948), p. 54. **21** Ibid., p. 71. **22** Oonagh Walsh, *Anglican women in Dublin: philanthropy and education in the early twentieth century* (Dublin, 2005), p. 53. **23** Dermod O'Brien (DOB) to Mabel Smyly (MS), 16 November 1901, O'Brien of Cahermoyle Collection, National Library of Ireland, NLI/MS/36/694/2. **24** His grandfather was Young Irelander leader William Smith O'Brien, his cousin was Mary Spring-Rice of the *Asgard*, and his sister was Nelly O'Brien who attempted to establish an all-Ireland church. **25** DOB to Julia O'Brien, 14 October glad, I was beginning to fear that you would not marry at all ... I think I should have been glad, whoever you were marrying.'[26] His father was 'heartily glad' Dermod was forsaking the life of 'old bachelordom', believing that it was 'no small point' to the success of the marriage that he was 'to marry into so very nice a family'.[27] Dermod's step-mother, Julia, went 'off her head' with joy at the news, believing a wife, and 'this wife' in particular, would provide him with 'not only the happiness ... but the added power, confidence in yourself, freedom of will and action ... for your aims will be hers, she will stand between you & hindrances and make you have your own life more abundantly.'[28] Dermod also believed his work would improve once married.[29] Even Dermod's father stressed the importance of love and attraction, and was 'delighted' to see that 'in spite of all the women you have met & (if I may say so) flirted with you are just as much in love as if you were 21'.[30] He reassured his son there was little 'danger that the flame will burn itself out'.[31]

The perceived benefits of marriage for Dermod's fiancée were even stronger. She would enter a state of more complete existence. Greater respect was shown to married women, even when they were younger than their single relatives.[32] Mabel could still be 'sent' to bed, and her activities and acquaintances were vetted. At the age of twenty-six, she was still reprimanded for not observing the Sabbath in a suitably sombre way.[33] She consistently wrote, and most likely believed, that she was becoming more complete by marrying, and especially by marrying a man she loved:

> Somehow I feel as of then [marriage] I shall be more of an identity, more myself from being part of you ... I have all my life submitted more or less, rather more than less, to other people's stronger wills and views, partly from a sense of duty, partly from policy, partly because it seemed too much trouble to resist, and partly I think because I find it very difficult to put my feelings into words. With you I think it will be different because I feel you don't only want to make me a shadow of yourself but to bring out what is in me, good or bad, and make the best of it. I wonder what you will make of me in the end: but I have a great trust in you.[34]

1901, NLI/MS/36/778/10. 26 Arthur Cane to DOB, 4 December 2014, NLI/MS/36/797/3. 27 Edward O'Brien to DOB, 7 December 1901, NLI/MS/36/773/7. 28 Julia O'Brien to DOB, 7 December 1901, NLI/MS/36/777/2. 29 MS to DOB, 25 February 1902, NLI/MS/36/699/3/. 30 Edward O'Brien to DOB, 7 December 1901, NLI/MS/36/773/7. 31 Ibid., 15 December 1901. 32 Anon., *Manners and rules of good society: or solecisms to be avoided*, 33rd ed. ([1911], London, 2004). See also Gerard, *Country house life*, p. 32. 33 Ellen Smyly to MS, 5 December 1896, NLI/MS/36/784. 34 MS to DOB, 22 December 1901, NLI/MS/36/699/1.

TIMELINE OF THE RELATIONSHIP

Dermod and Mabel's relationship began when Mabel was a guest of Dermod's elder sister, Nelly, at a house party at his family seat of Cahirmoyle, Co. Limerick, in 1901.[35] The party facilitated romance as guests consisted of married and unmarried members of their own generation. Chaperonage was light. The couple enjoyed talking while leaning together against a secluded gate.[36] When the party broke up, Dermod went to London, and Mabel returned home. The courtship of letters then began. This courtship correspondence survives almost completely intact. He proposed on 3 December 1901, and they married just over three months later on the 8 March 1902. Rarely did he allow a day to pass without writing a letter, or two. By the eve of their wedding, he had written 165 surviving letters, totalling 600 pages. Mabel was less prolific, and only managed eighty-seven letters, totalling 300 pages, between 1 October and 7 March. These 900 pages of correspondence can be divided into three stages. The first, and shortest, took place between September and October when Dermod was in London, and still addressed Mabel as 'Miss Smyly'. In mid-October, he dropped the 'Miss Smyly', and his letters became more flirtatious, while she continued to uphold polite social conventions, acting as the moral police of the relationship.[37] These letters caused her mother to go into 'a state of fizzle', and were only permitted because Mabel had 'attained to years of discretion'.[38] With such differing expectations of male and female sexual desires, the role of moral watchdog fell heavily on Mabel who was vigilant in protecting her reputation, especially before their official engagement. She was cautious not to write him more letters than her view of propriety allowed, and passed on invitations from her mother, rather than offering them herself (thus demonstrating her mother's approval). In the month before their engagement, Dermod consistently tried to spend time alone with her out shopping, at art galleries, concerts, or at his home. Mabel would not countenance such plans. Mabel, and her family, were already stretching propriety by accepting Dermod's almost daily correspondence for two months before he proposed.

The last, and longest, phase began on 3 December 1901 when his proposal was accepted, and both parties perceived themselves to be married in spirit.[39] From this time, the letters became more explicit, longer, and more frequent, on both sides demonstrating a growth in trust, and the significance of the engagement period as a distinct stage in the making of a marriage. Throughout

35 DOB to MS, n.d., NLI/MS/36/694/2. 36 MS to DOB, 16 January 1902, NLI/MS/36/699/2. 37 See Adelman and O'Neill for discussion of sexual scripts; Luddy and O'Dowd, *Marriage*, p. 119. 38 DOB to MS, 25 January 1902, NLI/MS/36/694/7, MS to DOB, 25 January 1902, NLI/MS/36/699/2. 39 DOB to MS, NLI/MS/36/694/4–8, MS to DOB, NLI/MS/

this written relationship, there is a sense that the couple perceived themselves a modern couple, enjoying a passionate love not experienced by everyone. Their letters reveal they believed they were stretching, rather than breaking with, existing sexual norms.

ENGAGEMENT EXPERIENCE

Before their engagement, physical contact was minimal. On visits to Mabel's home, Dermod was tantalised by the proximity of her body but limited himself to touching the lace of her sleeve 'when no one was looking', holding her bracelets while she played the piano, presenting her with flowers to wear in her blouse, turning the pages of music while she played the piano so as to look at her neck, and holding her arm briefly when he was permitted to lead her into supper.[40] Mabel wrote of her surprise at the depth of her own sexual arousal during the engagement period. She subscribed, or at least felt it proper to appear to subscribe, to the contemporary notion that respectable women were incapable of the same levels of sexual desire and fulfilment as men. By the time the wedding arrived, she felt free to express her physical yearning and wrote of her annoyance at a music stand for physically separating them.[41]

This correspondence illustrates that male and female sexual desire was a significant aspect of the engagement period. *Manners and rules*, a successful etiquette manual, condemned the 'strict ideas' held by some parents who would allow their daughters no private time with their beaux.[42] M. Jeanne Peterson has convincingly argued that broken engagements were so shocking during the Victorian period because extensive sexual experimentation during this time was the norm.[43] Peter Gay's microhistory of the diary of the American bourgeois Mabel Loomis Todd, who went to her marriage only 'technically a virgin', had the same conclusion.[44] Recent scholarship on the early twentieth century in Ireland demonstrates that liberated sexual views and practices were not entirely unknown.[45] Luddy and O'Dowd have summarised the paradox that 'while young couples had more freedom to choose a partner by the 1900s, they had less freedom to spend intimate time with each other'.[46]

Dermod had feared 'conventions' would prevent them from seeing each other privately, but his fears were unfounded. They were permitted to spend increasing amounts of time alone, with Mabel sitting on his lap, kissing, and caressing each

36/699/2–3. 40 Ibid., 9 December 1901, NLI/MS/36/694/4. 41 MS to DOB, 23 February 1902, NLI/MS/36/699/3. 42 Anon., *Manners*, p. 250. 43 Peterson, *Family, love and work*, pp 75–7. 44 Peter Gay, *The bourgeois experience: Victoria to Freud* (Oxford, 1984), pp 80–1. 45 For example, see Leeann Lane, *Rosamund Jacob: third person singular* (Dublin, 2010). 46 O'Dowd and other. They were frequently interrupted, however, and by 30 January, Dermod wrote to his 'poor compromised little maid' that 'people are always bursting in on us, your hair down your dress with a lappet unhooked hair pins strewn around gaps twixt body & soul & my hair combed proper but unnatural'.[47] When discussing their sexualised contact in letters after the fact, Dermod played into the convention that he was taking from Mabel and that she was permitting his advances, rather than acting as an equally knowledgeable participant. She was the 'compromised' one. He wrote of his nerves when they first shared a chair, and he attempted an embrace.[48] Mabel found she hungered for physical contact and enjoyed seeing him get into 'heat'. She liked to hug and kiss while he wrapped them both in his coat, or to 'ram [her] chin into [his] neck', and to see 'illuminations' light up in his eyes. Their relationship was obviously passionate and Dermod often disturbed her hair pins in his fervour, and occasionally partially opened her dress to kiss her throat.[49] On one walk home, he was forced to go to his club 'to cool down'. He wrote enigmatically: 'you have me fair bewildered with your arts called in from improper French novels. To think of your doing such a thing & I who looked on you as an innocent guileless creature'.[50] What this thing was, we do not know, but it was important that Mabel remained outwardly guileless, even as they enjoyed such activities. The engagement period remained preliminary to marriage, and they both agreed that the step from female virginal state to marriage, 'should be a big step, that it is not quite right to make the transition gradual'.[51] Dermod repeatedly addressed Mabel as a 'maid' and expected that if he died before the wedding, she would be a 'virgin widow'.[52]

This behaviour was implicitly permitted by Mabel's conservative family who left the couple alone, suggesting even the most 'respectable' engaged couples could practice sexualised behaviour in private.[53] By the final weeks of their engagement the couple had almost complete freedom to be seen together in public and private. Before their engagement, and despite his 'pretended ignorance', she reprimanded him: 'we are strong on propriety in our village and I neither could nor did invite you to come and buy tools for the carving class in company'.[54] By 25 February she could luxuriate in the experience of shopping for pillows writing 'it feels very married to go around shopping with you'.[55]

Luddy, *Marriage*, p. 157. **47** DOB to MS, 30 January 1902, NLI/MS/36/694/7. **48** Ibid., 8 January 1902, NLI/MS/36/694/6. **49** Ibid., 30 January 1902, NLI/MS/36/694/7, MS to DOB, 10 January 1902, NLI/MS/36/699/2. **50** Ibid., 6 February 1901, NLI/MS/36/694/8. **51** DOB to MS, 27 February 1901, NLI/MS/36/694/8. **52** Ibid., 27 January 1901, NLI/MS/36/694/7. For discussion on the wider community, see Luddy, *Matters of deceit*, p. 35. **53** *Manners and rules* advised newly engaged couples to spend little time in public together. **54** MS to DOB, 5 Nov. 1901, NLI/MS/36,699/1. **55** Ibid., 25 February 1902, NLI/MS/36/699/3.

Family support for their relationship continued, and there was even an openness regarding their future married life. Mabel tried on her new, rather short, nightgowns in the drawing room and was jokingly told it was 'improperly transparent' by her brother.[56]

Dermod's attraction to Mabel was influenced by the still popular 'angel in the house' motif. He held a very strict patriarchal view of gender and did not want a wife who would overtly defy social conventions. He was physically attracted to her small frame and compared her favourably to his clumsy aunt (the humanitarian campaigner Charlotte Grace O'Brien) for her ability to 'softly & silently vanish from a room'.[57] He consistently reprimanded her, sometimes severely, for taking on so much philanthropic activity. He constantly commented on her health and feared she might fall ill from the most innocuous activity. When she did get a cold, he could not but find her weakness a further attraction and likened her to 'some pure ethereal spirit'.[58] A generous read of these critiques of her lifestyle would allow that his own mother had died young as a result of tuberculosis, while a sceptic might wonder if he was attempting to control and reduce her world in advance of the wedding.

Practical and organised Mabel did not always like to be idolised in this way: 'don't put me on a pedestal, the doormat position is much more in my line'.[59] Contemporary views on male domination and female submission were so ingrained in society, that she often lapsed into expressing a desire to be dominated and physically overpowered. She thought it was 'wonderful' to think of herself as 'little and weak', and Dermod as 'big and strong', with the ability to 'crumple [her] up into nothing if he chose'.[60] On 10 January 1902, she wrote: 'I like to feel that you are my master and that there won't be any question about who is to command'.[61] This language did not fully reflect the reality of their relationship as Mabel felt confident in arranging plans for their future home. The physical domination did not always run in the same direction either, and Dermod liked to visualise Mabel in different guises as 'dainty beguiler, torment of [his] life, heart's easer & smoother of cares'.[62] Sometimes she acted the baby, sometimes the submissive maid, but occasionally the indulgent mother. She liked him to lie with his head on her lap while she rocked him to sleep, pretending he was the child 'little D'.[63] He readily submitted.[64]

56 Ibid., 22 February. 57 DOB to MS, 2 November 1901, NLI/MS/36/694/2. 58 Ibid., 11 December 1901, NLI/MS/36/694/4. 59 MS to DOB, 5 November 1901, NLI/MS/36/699/1. 60 Ibid., 14 December 1901, for example. 61 Ibid., MS to DOB, 10 January 1901, NLI/MS/36/699/2. 62 DOB to MS, 28 January 1902, NLI/MS/36/694/7. 63 MS to DOB, 2 January 1902, NLI/MS/36/699/2. 64 DOB to MS, 2 November 1901, NLI/MS/36/694/2, and MS to DOB, 10 December 1901.

Their attitudes towards their previous relationships reflected the very different opportunities, and standards, afforded to unmarried men and women. Mabel's most significant previous relationship had been a one-sided longing where she 'did truly care for some one [*sic*] else for a long time ... There was never any explanation or point to the whole affair but [she] went through a very bleak time'.[65] Despite the apparently trivial nature of this relationship, Mabel felt compelled to confess it to Dermod as she was 'rather ashamed'. Dermod, who would never need to protect his reputation in the same way believed that 'to care for a person or love them is a fine thing', and magnanimously wrote: 'I see no difference in that between a man & a woman ... all of us make mistakes, but ... it is better to do so than never risk anything'.[66] Dermod had more considerable relationships in his past, and told his fiancée about his relationship with Stella (Duckworth, 1867–97, half-sister of Virginia Woolf).[67] He felt no shame in his past experiences and once blithely remarked that he had been in love with another woman, before she married his friend, for whom he was best man.[68] As a man, Dermod was free to share that he could engage in sexual activity without the tie of love or marriage writing that though he did not want anyone else, he 'might feel tempted by a strange shoulder or nape in a kind of speculative way'. He took a light-hearted view of his 'casual kisses' which 'are mostly impersonal and mean only a conjunction of opportunity & desire'.[69]

Physically, the courtship took place in Mabel's childhood home, on her occasional visits to his house (their future marital home), and on outings in Dublin. The land of letters was just as important a part of their sexual relationship as any of these physical spaces. The letter travelled where the author could not and allowed for many fantastical sexual encounters to occur. In one of his early letters from London, Dermod introduced the topic of sexualised behaviour by describing a couple he had seen at the theatre who were 'holding each other's hands and rub[bing] their shoulders together like two cats'.[70] He would not get the opportunity to discuss such subjects in person for some time, as he was confined to general group conversations on his early visits to her home.[71] He once wrote to her while she sat 'close pressed' against him, and used it to tell her that he was 'longing all the time to fling down the pen & just enfold [her] body & soul'.[72]

65 MS to DOB, 5 December 1901, NLI/MS/36/699/2. 66 DOB to MS, 5 December 1901, NLI/MS/36/694/4. 67 MS to DOB, 5 December 1901; see also Robinson, *Palette & plough*, p. 84. 68 DOB to MS, 19 February 1901, NLI/MS/36/694/7. 69 Ibid., 26 January, NLI/MS/36/694/6. 70 Ibid., 7 October 1901, NLI/MS/36/694/1. 71 Ibid., 22 October 1901, NLI/MS/36/694/1. 72 Ibid., 11 December 1901, NLI/MS/36/694/4.

Dermod wrote most of his letters late at night when he imagined Mabel was asleep, playing into the trope of active man and passive woman. Before they were engaged, he repeatedly enquired into the location of her bedroom. When she was sick, he used the medium of the letter to picture her 'sitting up in bed'.[73] By 6 January he had grown braver and wrote that he had 'no sense of decorum' and imagined himself invading her room to look at her and kiss her while she slept.[74] Two weeks later he allowed himself to imagine she was awake:

> I find you thinking of me & welcoming me with your eyes & I kneel by your bed & put my arms about you despite all conventionalities & draw your small night clad person 'sweet as boughs of May' close up against me; oh I make you blush too, for I insist on undoing a top button that I may kiss your throat & play at drawing the cough out of it.[75]

While he luxuriated in these images, he had no intention of performing such activities in reality, for he believed a 'girl's [even a woman of over thirty's] room at all times is a sacred temple'. When he finally stepped inside her bedroom he became shy 'to see the place where you have spent so many hours of your life … dressing & undressing'.[76]

While Mabel initially deflected his enquiries as to the location of her room, after the engagement she was happy to imagine he had 'crept up quite quietly last night and kissed the cough out of [her] throat'.[77] As the wedding day drew nearer, and marriage settlements[78] were drawn up, both Mabel and Dermod's thoughts, and letters, turned increasingly towards the subject of sex.

EXPECTATIONS OF MARRIED LIFE

Despite her attraction to Dermod, Mabel occasionally felt a sense of panic at her impending marriage.[79] When she thought of their longed-for future 'shadow children', she admitted that with the 'mystery and happiness', she felt 'a little thread of fear' at how they might be produced.[80] She found it difficult to discuss their future children face-to-face in Dermod's house, where such children would likely be conceived, and preferred to put her thoughts in writing while sitting in her girlhood home.[81]

73 Ibid., 13 November 1901, NLI/MS/36/694/2. 74 Ibid., 6 January 1902, NLI/MS/36/694/6. 75 Ibid., 20 January 1902, second letter. 76 Ibid. 77 MS to DOB, 1 January 1902, NLI/MS/36/699/2. 78 Marriage settlements were legal documents drawn up in advance of elite marriages, which arranged for the control of the couple's property and inheritance. 79 MS to DOB, 24 December 1901, NLI/MS/36/699/1. 80 Ibid. 81 Ibid., 26 February 1902, NLI/MS/36/699/3.

Such ignorance and fear of sex was not unique among middle- and upper-class women of the era. Margaret Cousins, the middle-class suffragist, married in 1903. The marriage never promised much sexual attraction but ignorance also contributed to the utter repugnance she felt on her wedding night. Her biography demonstrated just how uneducated a woman might be on consummating her marriage, leaving her 'ashamed of humanity and ashamed for it'.[82] Luckily for Mabel, she was attracted to her husband, and preliminary sexual activity suggested her marital experience would not be so shocking. Dermod was conscious his fiancée felt '[a] little more shyness about looking into the future & its possibilities'.[83] He assumed that she, as a woman, would have a lower sexual appetite, and knowledge and in the weeks before marriage took on the role of sexual mentor. He hoped she would not be shocked when he argued that sex was natural, and love was not 'entirely made up of that fine essence of the unity of soul with soul, but it is indefinably mixed up with desire of one body for the other, only the finer elements make it permissible'.[84] He looked forward to going to bed with her kisses on his lips and 'the pulse of [her] being trilling [him] through body & soul.'[85]

In these efforts, Dermod relied on Mabel's faith, and not just her lust, to reassure her about sex, and to elevate it in her eyes. He prayed that they 'may have courage to dare & strength to perform such acts as [they] may be impelled to by His Holy Spirit.'[86] It is possible that Dermod, or at least Mabel, believed that sex, within marriage, for the purpose of conceiving children was an act of God. Peterson noted that such a linkage 'was the natural outcome of … deep religiosity'.[87] Mabel's faith was at the heart of her relationship with Dermod. She believed they were each 'God's gift to each other'.[88] Even the act of going to church with Dermod and to 'kneel side by side in God's house' made Mabel feel 'more one' with him.[89] On the night before the wedding, Mabel wrote to Dermod saying 'let me tell you that I love you very dearly and that it is a great joy to me to think that my little being is going to be merged in your big one … make me a good wife to you, in real earnest now, not in play any longer'.[90] Her faith was also a tool which allowed her to keep some autonomy despite the female marital vow of obedience, as she told him:

> It is hard to argue about what cannot be. If you wanted me to do what I thought was wrong you would come upon the Puritan rock in me which

82 James Cousins and Margaret Cousins, *We two together* (Madras, 1950), p. 108. 83 DOB to MS, 27 February 1902, NLI/MS/36/694/8. 84 Ibid., 4 February 1902. 85 Ibid., 3 February 1902. 86 Ibid., 16 February 1902. 87 Peterson, *Family, love and work*, p. 76. 88 MS to DOB, 16 December 1901, NLI/MS/36/699/1. 89 Ibid., 2 March 1902. 90 Ibid., 7 March 1902.

> cannot move, but as I know you never would and my trust in you is absolute, I cannot see how the question would arise.[91]

This strong faith ratified the physical desire she would allow herself to act on within marriage. There was also the welcome prospect of children. Dermod accepted that however pleasurable sex might be, it would ultimately cause Mabel the pain of childbirth, but reverted to gender stereotypes to reassure himself 'that every woman would joyfully undertake them for the subsequent blessings'.[92]

CONCLUSION

Mabel and Dermod got to know each other's personalities, and bodies, better during the engagement period and letters were important in the process. Through letters, Dermod tried to mould Mabel's opinions and take her away from her 'low church' past by discussing Darwin and the theatre. He also used his letters to describe his opinions on how women should behave. Meanwhile, Mabel defended her philanthropic and proselytising activities. She took great care to demonstrate her beliefs on the perfect marriage, where a wife was not an ornament, but a supportive partner.[93] Like Dermod's stepmother, Mabel believed a wife could contribute positively to the success of her husband's career by being his confidant and helper. As the wedding day drew nearer, Mabel reflected on the social conventions which restricted her activity more than Dermod's, without a sense of injustice:

> Of course, times change but I suppose it is the individual actions of people like ourselves that make them change. I am very glad that our lot is cast in a generation where it matters more to be true and honest than to be orthodox and conventional. Not that I want to break away from either orthodoxy or conventions but to use them instead of bowing down to them.[94]

These letters demonstrate that despite the sexual double standard and the culture of patriarchy prevalent at the time, individual couples were able to conduct themselves in a manner which, if not equal, was negotiated to where they both felt respected. Dermod was surprised and delighted his outwardly puritan fiancée was capable of the arts found in improper French novels, and

91 Ibid., 16 December 1901, NLI/MS/36/699/1. 92 DOB to MS, 16 February 1902, NLI/MS/36/694/8. 93 MS to DOB, 1 January 1902, NLI/MS/36/699/2. 94 Ibid.

he was determined to provide her with a positive sexual experience. Mabel was careful to keep a distance from Dermod before he proposed, when she trusted him enough to display the depth of her sexual desire. There was an accepted contradiction between their respect for propriety and their private activities and words. Despite Mabel's fears at the unknown mysteries of married life, and for all the lip service she paid to the ideal of the submissive wife, she viewed this marriage as an opportunity, and it was. She would have more independence and freedom of expression and action by marrying. She would gain a sense of partnership, households to manage, as well as, hopefully, sexual fulfilment, and eventually motherhood. Both Mabel and Dermod appear to have been happy with this socially and personally compatible match. They married on 8 March 1902 and conceived a son almost immediately. During their first separation of married life, Dermod addressed Mabel as the 'best of wives', while she missed tousling his hair.[95] Thanks to an intense courtship of correspondence and physical exploration, Mabel really 'would rather be a little bit of [his] empire than a small independent province of [her] own'.[96]

95 DOB to MS, 28 October 1902, NLI/MS/36/694/9, MS to DOB, 14 September 1902, NLI/MS/36/699/3. 96 Mabel O'Brien to DOB, 16 Dec. 1901, NLI/MS/36/699/1.

CHAPTER 2

Queer Irish female revolutionaries: a case study of the diaries of Dr Kathleen Lynn

Mary McAuliffe

In discussing the English militant suffrage and activist female couples who are the focus of her research, Emily Hamer wrote that 'if a relationship looks like that of lovers, it usually is that of lovers ... lesbians in history are recognizable through the lesbian lives that they have led'.[1] She and others have reclaimed many same sex couples in British suffrage histories using 'records and documents already in the public domain ... [as] ... it seems that there is a lot of lesbian history waiting to be discovered'.[2] In Ireland, Roy Foster, in his study of early twentieth-century radical and activist culture, discussed the potential of 'consciously lesbian lifestyles' among some Irish revolutionary and suffrage women, 'which was embraced by many of their contemporaries in feminist circles in England'.[3] At least one activist, Eva Gore Booth, sister of revolutionary and socialist activist, Constance Markievicz, bridges the gap between activist women in Ireland and England who had same sex relationships. A poet, playwright and radical political activist, Gore Booth, born in Ireland, shared her life, in England, with suffrage campaigner Esther Roper. As her biographer Sonja Tiernan has written, all aspects of their lives together suggest that they were a couple; 'they lived together for thirty years, jointly purchased property, and arranged to be buried in the same small plot after they died'.[4] A previous biographer of the women actively sought to 'prove that Eva and Esther were not lovers', but were instead platonic friends.[5] However, Tiernan has shown how Gore Booth's sexuality had a profound influence on her life and how her relationship with Roper was 'intense, passionate, and uncompromising; their lives centred on each other'.[6] Similarly, this author's biography of militant nationalist, feminist and trade union activist, Margaret Skinnider, uncovered her

1 Emily Hamner, *Britannia's glory: a history of twentieth-century lesbians* (London, 1995), p. 3. 2 Ibid. 3 R.F. Foster, *Vivid faces; the revolutionary generation in Ireland, 1890–1923* (London, 2014), p. 133. 4 Sonja Tiernan, 'Challenging presumptions of heterosexuality: Eva Gore-Booth, a biographical case study', *Historical Reflections*, 37:2 (2011), pp 58–71, p. 65. 5 Ibid., p. 60. The previous biography mentioned is that by Gifford Lewis, *Eva Gore-Booth and Esther Roper: a biography* (London, 1988). 6 Tiernan, 'Challenging presumptions of heterosexuality', p. 68.

lifelong relationship with fellow revolutionary activist Nora O'Keeffe.[7] As with Gore Booth and Roper, there were attempts to obscure the shared life of Skinnider and O'Keeffe, when, on Skinnider's death, her executor burned her diaries fearing that 'her private life would make it into the history books'.[8] These marginalisations or occlusions of the private lives of political women who shared their lives with other women are receiving some correctives as Irish scholars, influenced by a turn towards researching sexualities in Irish histories, begin to look at the public and private lives of these women.

In this chapter the diaries of Dr Kathleen Lynn are used to consider the reality of an Irish suffrage, revolutionary and queer life. Her relationship with fellow activist, rebel, and social reformer, Madeline ffrench-Mullen, is considered through the lens of Lynn's diaries, and more broadly, this chapter looks at what the diaries reveal about an interconnected cohort of feminist, republican women who had relationships with other women, in early to mid-twentieth-century Ireland. Lynn and ffrench-Mullen, often referred to as 'life-long partners', first met when they were both involved in revolutionary politics in Dublin.[9] While Lynn does not begin her diary until 1916, she mentioned her first meeting with ffrench-Mullen in her Bureau of Military History (BMH) witness statement.[10] As chief medical officer of the militant workers militia, the Irish Citizen Army (ICA), she gave lectures on first aid to that organisation and to the women's militant, nationalist organisation, Cumann na mBan, after it was founded in 1914. It was, as she recalled, at the Cumann na mBan headquarters at 6 Harcourt St where she first encountered 'Miss French-Mullen [*sic*] who became my closest friend'.[11] Soon after that meeting they moved in together and lived at No. 9 Belgrade Rd, Rathmines, 'for 30 years – until her [ffrench-Mullen's] death'.[12] Her diaries give a sense that Lynn was a very practical woman not given to sentimentality, however, another version of their first meeting indicates an instantaneous connection. Medb Ruane, in her short biography of Lynn, interviewed several people who knew them both. A description from one of the interviewees, May Cummins, paints a picture of ffrench-Mullen 'as a robust young woman who fell off a chair and collapsed with laughter' at a first aid meeting Lynn was conducting.[13] Lynn is said to have helped her up and the

7 Mary McAuliffe, *Margaret Skinnider* (Dublin, 2022). 8 Ibid., personal communication from Skinnider descendants. 9 See Mary McAuliffe and Harriet Wheelock, *The diaries of Kathleen Lynn: a life revealed through personal writing* (Dublin, 2023). 10 The Irish Bureau of Military History was established in January 1947 to allow individuals to record their own experiences of the fight for Irish independence. Lynn was interviewed twice in late 1947 about her revolutionary experiences. 11 Kathleen Lynn, Bureau of Military History (BMH), witness statement, WS 357, 1–2, Irish Military Archives (IMA). 12 Ibid. 13 Medb Ruane, 'Kathleen Lynn' in Mary Cullen and Maria Luddy (eds), *Female activists; Irish women and change, 1900–1960* (Dublin, 2001), p. 69. May

two became firm friends.[14] Between 1914 and 1916 both became very involved in trade union activism, feminism, and militant nationalism, often collaborating together in the same organisations. Both were active in preparing for the 1916 Rising and, although Lynn said, 'I never drilled, I had no time for that sort of thing', like most of the senior women she knew the Rising 'was coming off altho' we did not know the exact date'.[15]

On Easter Monday 1916 both women were sent with Irish Citizen Army (ICA) groups to outposts, Lynn to Dublin Castle (although they took City Hall instead) and ffrench-Mullen to St Stephen's Green; this group ended up in the Royal College of Surgeons.[16] A witness statement from ICA member Rosie Hackett gives us a sense of how worried Lynn was about ffrench-Mullen. Hackett said the only instruction she got from Lynn was 'that I would be with Miss French Mullen … wherever Miss French Mullen [*sic*] would go, I was to be next to her'.[17] Lynn and her group lasted a day in City Hall, after which they had to surrender, were arrested, and spent the rest of the week in Ship Street barracks. ffrench-Mullen was among those who surrendered at the end of the week and was one of the seventy-seven women arrested and imprisoned in Kilmainham gaol. At that stage neither woman knew where the other was, and both were very worried. There is a short diary ffrench-Mullen kept of her experiences in Kilmainham gaol, where she was sharing a cell with Helena Molony and Countess Plunkett. On 1 May 1916, she wrote, 'we had heard various stories that the doctor was arrested, missing and the Countess and I feared we would not see her again'.[18] The following day she was relieved to write 'met the doctor going for water, had her to breakfast hip, hip'.[19] On 4 May she discussed the terrible conditions and the fact that each morning they could hear the condemned leaders of 1916 being 'shot in cold blood' in the prison yard, but she and 'the doctor settled down to life and agreed that as long as we were left together prison was somewhat bearable'.[20] Lynn's diaries reflect a similar happiness at finding ffrench-Mullen in Kilmainham: On 2 May she wrote:

> Saw M.ffM early this mg. Greatest joy. Emer, she & I have cell together, such joy, cheerfully we do with one basin of water for washings, hog wash of cocoa & dog biscuits for b.fast.[21]

Cummins is often mentioned in Lynn's diaries. 14 Lynn, WS 357, p. 2. 15 Ibid. 16 The Irish Citizen Army (ICA) was an armed workers militia formed in the aftermath of the 1913 Lock-Out strike by socialist James Connolly. Most of the left leaning, radical women joined the ICA as they were welcomed as members on a more egalitarian basis. Both Lynn and ffrench-Mullen joined the ICA. 17 Rosie Hackett, BMH, WS 546, p. 5. Hackett would spend the Rising in the same outpost as ffrench-Mullen. 18 Madeleine ffrench-Mullen documents in the Brother Allen Archival Collection IE/AL/MFM/, Irish Military Archives (IMA). 19 Ibid., 2 May 1916. 20 Ibid., 4 May 1916. 21 Kathleen Lynn diaries (1916–55), ACC/1997/2, are housed in the Royal

Their reunion in Kilmainham was not to last long. They were separated when Lynn was moved to Mountjoy jail, where she wrote on 10 May, 'Mtjoy clean & comfortable, but I'd give £10,000 for Kilmainham & Madeline'.[22]

Lynn and ffrench-Mullen were finally reunited in the autumn of 1916. Both had resumed their political, feminist and nationalist activities and in 1919, as Lynn records, 'she and I with the help of others – mostly republicans – founded St Ultan's Hospital – Teach Ultain – for infants'.[23] A 1934 report in the *Irish Press* on the rise and success of St Ultan's regarded it a 'great romance'.[24] It was 'the fortunes of war' that brough Dr Lynn and Miss ffrench-Mullen, 'the present secretary of the hospital', together when 'both of them took an active part in Easter week'. While both would remain involved in work for women's rights, workers' rights, and republicanism for most of their lives, it was St Ultan's, their great project, which took most of their energies. Over the next 36 years Lynn would keep an (almost) daily diary of her life. As well as her political and feminist activities, the diaries cover her medical work, including her work during the 1918–19 flu pandemic, the establishment of the hospital, the innovative medical practices for infants they sought out and introduced in St Ultan's and the role of members of the hospital staff in the fight against TB in Ireland. Lynn, along with St Ultan's colleagues such as Dr Dorothy Stopford Price, fostered research into tuberculosis eradication and, in 1937, St Ultan's became the first hospital in the British Isles to introduce the BCG (Bacillus Calmette-Guerin) inoculation, which prevented TB.[25] The diaries also demonstrate her commitment, and that of ffrench-Mullen, to social reforms, including better housing and education for all, particularly those caught in the vicious cycle of poverty in the Dublin slums.[26] They also reveal the difficult road these radical political women forged in the new Irish Free State, which viewed women through the constraining lens of marriage, motherhood, domesticity, and respectability. They show the supportive networks of political women, many of whom worked together for social and political change long after the revolution was over. One of their closest friends was Helena Molony, the radical revolutionary, suffragette and socialist, who had been with Lynn at City Hall in 1916, and whose commitment to women's and workers' rights and unruly private life is well documented in the diaries. It was Molony who brough Lynn into

College of Physicians, Dublin, https://heritage.rcpi.ie/Projects/Dr-Kathleen-Lynn, hereafter KLD. KLD, 2 May 1916. 'mg' means morning. Emer is the name used in the diaries for their friend Helena Molony. **22** KLD, 10 May 1916. **23** Lynn, BMH, WS 357, p. 2. **24** *Irish Press*, 9 June 1934, p. 5. **25** *Dictionary of Irish biography*, Kathleen Lynn, https://www.dib.ie/biography/lynn-kathleen-a4964, accessed 22 February 2024. **26** Both women were active local councillors on Rathmines Urban District Council for many years, serving on the public health and housing militant nationalism, as recorded by Lynn herself, who said that Molony, 'a clever and attractive girl', converted her 'to the national movement'.[27]

By the time she met Lynn, Molony already knew ffrench-Mullen and all three would remain close in their private and public lives. For instance, on 22 September 1918, Lynn describes an 'Inignie [sic] protest meeting for women prisoners. Mrs S.S., M & Emer taken & released in 2 hrs. Poor M. much mauled by police'.[28] This meeting at Foster Place in Dublin was held to protest the treatment of female prisoners, Kathleen Clarke, Countess Markeivicz and Maud Gonne McBride, who were all in Holloway jail, arrested in May 1918, as part of the so called 'German plot'.[29] Both Sheehy Skeffington and Molony were speakers and when the Dublin Metropolitan Police (DMP) baton charged the meeting, they along with ffrench-Mullen were arrested, although all were released shortly after. This short entry demonstrates the interconnected relationships between the couple and many of the people and events of the revolutionary period, 1912–23. The diaries also cover Lynn's family and personal relationships. Born in Co. Mayo, with two sisters and one brother, she was close to her family, although they found her radical politics difficult to accept. A visit from her father (Fardie), Robert Lynn, a Church of Ireland clergyman, and her sister Anne (Nan) when she was imprisoned in Mountjoy in 1916 was fraught: 'Fardie & Nan were here, oh, so reproachful, they wouldn't listen to me & looked as if they would cast me off for ever'.[30] Despite their misgivings they never did 'cast her off' and she remained in contact with them. She reconciled somewhat with the family in 1920 when, after an anxious wait when she didn't 'know yet if I can go home for Xmas', a letter arrived on 24 December, 'to say I may go home for Xmas if I won't have demonstrations (do they picture bands?) or see people who are not their visitors'.[31] After a rather tense visit she was happy to begin the journey back to Dublin where 'M met me, she & I are glad I'm back'.[32]

committees. 27 Lynn, BMH, WS 357, p. 2. Molony was also involved in a close relationship with another woman for many years. 28 KLD, 22 September 1918. 'Inignie' was Inghinidhe na hÉireann, the feminist, separatist, militant organisation founded by Maud Gonne McBride in 1900, who also features in the diary. Mrs S.S. is Hanna Sheehy Skeffington, founder of the Irish Women's Franchise League (1908) to which Lynn and ffrench-Mullen both belonged. M is ffrench-Mullen and Emer is Helena Molony, who had been an organiser with Inghinidhe na hÉireann and editor of its newspaper *Bean na hÉireann.* 29 'The German plot', so called as the British viceroy to Ireland, Lord French, claimed that there was evidence of a treasonable plot between Sinn Féin and the German military, and those presumed to be involved in the 'plot' were to be arrested. These included three women, Countess Markievicz, Maud Gonne MacBride and Kathleen Clarke. 30 KLD, 12 May 1916. 31 KLD, 23–5 December 1920. This visit home to Mayo was during the War of Independence when there were atrocities committed by both sides, the crown forces and the IRA. Revd Lynn obviously supported the policing arm of the crown forces, the RIC. 32 KLD, 27 December 1920.

Her sisters were also disapproving of her politics and seem to have had a civil but distant relationship with ffrench-Mullen. Lynn always visited them by herself, while on the other hand she was very friendly with, and integrated into, the ffrench-Mullen family. Ffrench-Mullen's brother Douglas was a regular visitor and guest in their home over the years, while there are numerous mentions of tea with Madeline's mother. For instance, on 14 November 1921, Lynn notes that she 'went first to Mrs ffM, saw Douglas, first time since he came back. He is working now, D.G.'.[33] While many other family, friends, neighbours, feminist and revolutionary comrades, medical personnel at St Ultan's, and others with whom she interacted are mentioned in the diaries, it is her partner in life and in work, 'M' or 'M ffM' (Madeline ffrench-Mullen), and very occasionally 'Madeline', who is mentioned on an almost daily basis.

Writings on queer female histories, cultures, language and definitions from Martha Vicinus, Joan Scott, Joan Nestle, Laura Doan, among others, has helped define, complicate, and elaborate on the difficulties of historicising the lesbian, or indeed, of defining the lesbian. As Martha Vicinus commented, 'the lesbian is a popular subject for scrutiny – she exists, but how are we to define her history, who do we include and when did it begin?'.[34] In Ireland, research on queer femininities, mostly by literary scholars, has concentrated on the concept of romantic friendships, homosocial groups, or female couples in so-called 'Boston marriages'.[35] As Smith Rosenberg has argued we should view female sexuality on a continuum which heterosexuality at one end and homosexuality at another and 'between, a wide latitude of emotions and sexual feelings'.[36] Her research revealed intense, loving, devoted, sensual, often lifelong female friendships which were possibly but not necessarily always platonic. Couples in Ireland who fit with this type of historicising include the eighteenth-century couple, the ladies of Llangollen, and, from the nineteenth century, couples such as Somerville and Ross.[37] A recent biographer of Somerville and Ross argues that 'the erotic potential of the bond [between the women] should be foregrounded', but sought neither to deny or promote 'the possibilities of lesbian attachment, and thus avoids the empirical investigations of sexuality' which she argues 'have consistently marred critical attempts to explicate the

33 KLD, 13 November 1921. 'D.G.' is Deo Gratias/Thank God. 34 Martha Vicinus, *Lesbian subjects: a feminist studies reader* (Indiana, 1996), p. 1. 35 'Boston marriages' were considered romantic unions between women that were usually monogamous but not necessarily sexual. 36 Carroll Smith-Rosenberg, 'The female world of love and ritual: relations between women in nineteenth-century America', *Signs*, 1:1 (1975), pp 28–9. 37 The ladies of Llangollen were cousins, Eleanor Butler and Sarah Ponsonby, who eloped from Kilkenny and set up home in Llangollen, in north Wales in 1780, where they lived together for the rest of their lives. E.Œ. Somerville and Martin Ross, pseudonyms of Edith Anna Oenone Somerville and Violet Florence Martin (respectively), were

nature of Somerville's and Ross' authorial and sentimental bond'.[38] This wide latitude allows the researcher to queer intense same sex relationships, although studies of these presumed asexual, homosocial female friendships, while useful to a degree, do serve to obscure the existence of women who desired, and had, intimate relations with women.

Unpacking and understanding the world of intimacy between women can create a 'lesbian like' or queer history based on a 'sexualised, or at least reasonably eroticised, relationship with another woman'.[39] Sexual intimacy and self-representation are included as valuable subjects of research; Vicinus, for instance, focuses on intimacy, love, and the erotic, rather than the sexual, in her study of women in same sex partnerships.[40] Understanding that lesbian history is not separate from or isolated within women's histories is also important. Questions of family, heterosexual marriage, childbearing and rearing, class, race, politics, as well as revolutions and radical politics arise, and means that historians need also to consider the ways in which lesbian sexuality has intersected with other lived categories and identities. As Morgan argues, 'historical lesbian watching ... privileging the visible' has given way more recently to 'more open ended and fluid understanding of female sexual subjectivity alongside various radical deconstructions of the hetero-homo binary'.[41] While historical challenges emanating from the 'formation of historical identities, the ambivalence of historical evidence and authorial intention' remain, the most provocative challenge is to 'deconstruct the hidden meanings of historical silences and omissions ... that characterises so much of lesbian history'.[42]

These historical challenges are central to researching sexuality and same sex relationships among Irish revolutionary women. A central question is to see beyond a heteronormative history and, as Judith Bennett has argued, reexamine the history of single women, women like Lynn and ffrench-Mullen, and how they are often depicted 'through a heteronormative lens ... pathetic, sexless and lonely failures in a game of heterosexual courtship and marriage'.[43] Leeann Lane in her biography of Rosamund Jacob, a heterosexual revolutionary women, writes of the interior life of a woman, who although she never married, 'never stopped longing to find love, companionship, and, marriage', and who described in a secret addition to her daily diaries her sexual relationship with republican Frank Ryan.[44] Sources such as these reveal that there were spaces, often secret

life companions and writing partners. 38 Anne Jamison, *E.Œ. Somerville and Martin Ross: female authorship and literary collaboration* (Cork, 2016), pp 67–8. 39 Ibid. 40 See Martha Vicinus, *Intimate friends: women who loved women, 1778–1928* (Chicago, 2002). 41 Sue Morgan (ed.), *The feminist history reader* (London, 2006), p. 25. 42 Morgan (ed.), *The feminist history reader*, p. 25. 43 Judith M. Bennett, '"Lesbian-like" and the social history of lesbianism', *Journal of the History of Sexuality*, 9:1–2 (2000), pp 1–24, p. 23. 44 Leeann Lane, *Rosamund Jacob: third person singular* (Dublin, 2010), pp 173–91.

and/or dangerous spaces, in which heterosexual women could have sexual relationships outside of the expected marital and procreative. For other revolutionary single women however, the phrase 'she never married' or 'she died unmarried' can be used as an obscuring term when discussing their histories of intimacy and relationships. Several women who are mentioned in Lynn's diaries and who appear to have had same sex partners are referred to as 'unmarried' in the *Dictionary of Irish biography* (*DIB*) for instance. Lynn's entry in the *DIB* refers to ffrench-Mullen as a 'close friend' and a 'confidante', while in ffrench-Mullen's entry they are described as living together and as each other's 'lifelong friend and collaborator'.[45] None of these phrases do justice to their lifelong relationship. Ostensibly single women, heterosexual (Jacob) or lesbian (Lynn and ffrench-Mullen), could, Bennett argues, have rich lives devoid neither of 'sexual possibility or emotional richness'.[46]

In studying the intimate lives of queer women scholars have tackled the question of what constitutes lesbianism and cautioned against 'ahistoricism by distinguishing between questions which concern us now (the urge and desire to know for sure) and what the historical record allows us to conclude (what might never be known)'.[47] Historical subjects 'conceptualised sexuality differently than we do' and may have 'expressed unusual desires or committed certain acts, but did not acquire a sexual identity'.[48] In that case we need to consider the usefulness of sexual identity as an 'analytic category for historians of sexuality'.[49] If, as Doan argues, we construct histories of modern sexuality around individuals who self-defined themselves in ways we recognise, then it is likely that 'those histories will be limited and skewed'.[50] What about all those women who lived private lives with other women but never self-defined or perceived their identity or sexuality as a thing apart? Doan and Jane Garrity argue that it may not be necessary to know for sure if they did or did not self-identify.[51] There is only a need to clarify the possibilities or suggestibility of sapphism, and to speculate on what that means.[52] They argue that late nineteenth- and early twentieth-century public knowledge of the term sapphic/sapphist and the term sexual inversion was much wider than previously thought, often 'bound up with the circulation or medical and sexological knowledge ... [following the] publication of Richard von Frafft-Ebing's *Psychopathia sexualis* (1886) and Havelock Ellis's *Studies in the psychology of sex*, vol. II (1897)'.[53] Closer to home, in

45 Kathleen Lynn, https://www.dib.ie/biography/lynn-kathleen-a4964 Madeline ffrench-Mullen, https://www.dib.ie/biography/mullen-madeleine-ffrench-a6039. 46 Bennett, 'Lesbian-like'. 47 Laura L. Doan, 'Topsy turvydom: gender inversion, Sapphism and the Great War', *GLQ: A Journal of Lesbian and Gay Studies*, 12:4 (2006), pp 517–42, at p. 526. 48 Ibid. 49 Ibid., pp 536–7. 50 Ibid., p. 537. 51 Laura Doan and Jane Garrity, 'Introduction', *Sapphic modernities; sexuality, women and national discourse* (London, 2006), p. 6. 52 Ibid. 53 Ibid.

1916, Eva Gore Booth founded the magazine *Urania,* which she and Roper edited for many years and which was read in radical feminist and educated women's circles. *Urania* 'challenged mainstream feminism medical sexology and society's gender norms … [it was] a radical challenge to the system of presumed heterosexuality [and] portrayed female same sex relationships as superior'.[54]

As a medical doctor, Kathleen Lynn would have been familiar with *The Lancet,* a widely read medical journal, in which an entry for the term 'sapphist' appears as early as 1901, and it is not beyond the realm of possibility that she knew of and read *Urania,* published as it was by her distant cousin Eva Gore Booth. There are what seems to be coded hints in Lynn's diaries of such 'queer' knowledge. On 5 January 1931, she remarked that 'M ffM reading Sophie Jeck's [*sic*] life with joy', and on 8 January, 'M ffM finished Sophie [*sic*] Jex Blake, she wasn't forthcoming but fine for Anglo Saxon'.[55] Sophia Jex-Blake (1840–1912) was one of the first Scottish women doctors; she was also, like Lynn, a diarist. Her diaries detail very close friendships with women, including an intense relationship with the social reformer Octavia Hill (1838–1912). Jex-Blake and Hill separated in 1861, and she later settled down with a fellow woman doctor, Margaret Todd. Jex-Blake died in 1912 and Todd published a biography, *The life of Sophia Jex-Blake,* in 1918. It is most likely that this was the book which ffrench-Mullen was reading, which included entries about the relationship between Jex-Blake and Hill. An entry for 31 December 1861 describes a trip taken by 'Octa and I':

> The few days (Thursday to Tuesday) pure unmixed heart sunshine. Purer and deeper if possible than that of Wales … Never seemed our love truer, deeper, purer … I know though *now* that mine *could* be all three.[56]

Both were then recalled to London and separated for five months, which Jex-Blake wrote was 'hard it seemed then, but painless – heaven – to what came after', that is the pain of their split.[57] In the biography Todd refers to Jex-Blake's relationship with Hill as a 'strange unearthly friendship'.[58] Perhaps ffrench-Mullen 'wasn't forthcoming' because of the tragedy at the centre of the biography, the ending of the relationship, that 'strange unearthly friendship' (so like her own with Dr Lynn). Jex-Blake and Hill split in late 1861 and Todd wrote that until the eve of her last illness she (Jex-Blake) would not extinguish the

54 Sonja Tiernan, '"Engagements dissolved": Eva Gore-Booth, *Urania* and the radical challenge to marriage' in Mary McAuliffe and Sonja Tiernan (eds), *Tribades, Tommies and transgressives: histories of sexualities; Volume I* (Newcastle, 2008), pp 128–44, p. 128. 55 Scottish physician Sophia Jex-Blake (1840–1912) devoted her life to the advancement of women's rights in the field of medicine. 56 Margaret Georgina Todd, *The life of Sophia Jex-Blake* (London, 1918), https://www.gutenberg.org/files/54215/54215–h/54215–h.htm accessed 2 February 2023. 57 Ibid. 58 Ibid.

hope that 'even in this life' the friendship might be renewed.[59] This was not to be as Hill had moved on, living and working, for thirty years, with Harriet Yorke; they are buried together in the churchyard at Crockham Hill, Kent.

It is not only in Lynn's own diary that we get references to her relationship with ffrench-Mullen. The close friend of the couple, suffrage and republican activist, Rosamond Jacob, wrote, in her own diary, of a conversation she had about sex, in October 1919, with fellow suffrage activist, Hanna Sheehy Skeffington. Sheehy Skeffington, she noted, was glad to be 'through with sex & regarded it as rather a nuisance'.[60] Sheehy Skeffington, she continued, imagined a romance between Jacob and a man named Ben, but also that she imagined Jacob could perhaps be 'like Dr Lynn & Madeline, having no use at all for men'.[61] It is obvious that Jacob knew what Sheehy Skeffington was averring to as an entry a few days later is about another conversation she had about sex, with her male friend Ned. Jacob was worried that her admiration of the male form rather than the female form was unnatural and unlike most women, who, she wrote, admired the female form. This was a new idea to him and he asserted that those women 'must be homosexual', like Sappho of Lesbos who practised 'vice with other women', hence the term lesbianism.[62] Later in her diaries, Jacob, who often visited Lynn and ffrench-Mullen in their home in Rathmines, described a domestic scene, of the two women, who, when she called to see them, were breakfasting in bed together, 'as was their custom'.[63]

Of their relationship, Margaret Ó hÓgartaigh, Lynn's first biographer, wrote that 'while there was no evidence of sexual activity between Lynn and ffrench-Mullen, clearly they were very intimate'.[64] She also noted that a neighbour who was intrigued with the women reported that 'they wore collars and ties and hats like men' and indeed photographs of both women indicate a very practical, almost mannish, sense of dress.[65] She said little more about their relationship and the biography concentrates mainly on Lynn's public life. Marie Mulholland, in her short biography of Lynn, argued that it should be the task of the biographer to examine the relationship as 'not only did they mirror each other's politics, but they also established a partnership that went beyond a shared political ideology and extended to every aspect of their lives'.[66] In this she is agreeing with Hamer who argued that 'lesbianism is not, and has not been, a separate part of women's lives but an inalienable part of the fabric of their

59 Ibid. 60 Lane, *Rosamond Jacob*, p. 107. Sheehy Skeffington's husband Francis had been killed during the Easter Rising 1916. 61 Ibid. 62 Rosamond Jacob diaries, National Library of Ireland (NLI), MS 32,582/36, 6 November 1919. 63 Rosamond Jacob diary, 21 September 1920, NLI MS 32,582, 37. 64 Margaret Ó hÓgartaigh, *Kathleen Lynn: Irishwoman, patriot, doctor* (Dublin, 2006), p. 4. 65 Ibid., p. 3. 66 Marie Mulholland, *The politics and relationships of Kathleen Lynn* (Dublin 2002), p. 38.

experiences and of their choices', and with Tiernan who wrote that 'we cannot simply ignore sexuality in a biographical subject'.[67]

If we follow on from Doan and Garrity in accepting that it may 'not be necessary to know for sure' about self-identity or sexual activity, the Lynn diaries do give an intimate and very personal portrait of a committed, lifelong relationship between two women, which as Foster states had 'all the hallmarks of a marriage'.[68] In the more than thirty-one years they shared together, and for the twenty-nine years Lynn kept her diary, until ffrench-Mullen's death in 1944, rarely a day went by when 'M ffM' was not mentioned. They lived together, gardened together, worked together, had many friends, mostly women, in common, campaigned together, went on holidays together, ran St Ultan's together, loved their holiday home in Glenmalure in Wicklow equally, admired each other, and missed each other when apart. They cared for each other, worried about each other, argued and made up, took care of friends, loved pets together and when she died ffrench-Mullen left most of her money to Lynn to continue her work in St Ultan's.

A selection of extracts below emphatically demonstrates this point. On 5 December 1916 Lynn wrote, 'M. coming home to me to-morrow' – ffrench-Mullen had had a serious operation for a thyroid condition and Lynn was anxious to have her home.[69] On 4 March 1921 she says that it is 'v. lonely in no. 9 without Madeline', who was away on holiday.[70] Lynn often wrote of missing ffrench-Mullen when she was away from their home; on 7 January 1926 she was 'so lonely without Madeline. I miss her every turn' and on 25 April 1933 when she delightedly wrote, 'M ffM home. Hip Hip. I realise more how lonely it was', while on 30 December 1937, 'Joy of Joys, M ffM was back abt. 11 o/c & a great cloud rolled away'.[71] She obviously disliked not knowing ffrench-Mullen's whereabouts as several times she worried when 'M ffM' was not home on time, including on 27 August 1924 when she awoke and 'got fright abt. Madeline who never turned up till 1 a.m. I had been asleep, got up to look for her. Not at 63'.[72] The following day on 28 August she wrote, 'M v. penitent, went off with some Americans to Miss Cranwill's & forgot time'.[73] On 29 December 1926 she marked the years she and ffrench-Mullen had been together: 'Madeline's birthday tomorrow, we are living together nearly 11 years now'.[74] While work took up much of their time, and both were very involved in ensuring the smooth running and survival of St Ultan's, they also had time for fun and enjoyment as

67 Hamer, *Britannia's glory*, p. 10; Tiernan, 'Challenging presumptions of heterosexuality', p. 68.
68 Doan and Garrity, 'Introduction', Morgan, *The feminist history reader*, p. 2 and p. 6; Foster, *Vivid faces*, p. 133. 69 KLD, 5 December 1916. 70 KLD, 4 March 1921. No. 9 was their home, 9 Belgrade Rd, Rathmines. 71 KLD, 7 January 1926, 25 April 1933, 30 December 1937. 72 KLD, 27 August 1924. 73 KLD, 28 August 1924. 74 KLD, 29 December 1926.

on 5 May 1933 when 'M ffM went to 8.30, we had b.fast late, she & I are in our 2nd childhood, after b.fast catching tadpoles to put in with waterlilies'.[75] Their favourite place was their cottage in Glenmalure, Co. Wicklow, where they spent as much time as possible; 12 June 1933, while on a visit there, she wrote, 'M & I shoughed to heart's content & were warm & happy after it'.[76] Even at home they enjoyed their garden and each other's company; on 5 October 1933, Lynn recorded that 'We slept like little sleepers & still not ausgenschlafen. V. busy all day. … M fM wonderful but must rest'.[77]

In April 1944 ffrench-Mullen was beginning to experience very bad health and Lynn wrote of caring for her. On 18 April 1944 she wrote, 'we just had M ffM in the chair when the Reids arrived. I had them to dinner while M. had hers in drawing room. They were nice & didn't tire her'.[78] By 11 May, ffrench-Mullen was in need of more care and Lynn was preparing for the St Ultan's annual fund-raising festival, so she went to a nursing home for some respite. Lynn recorded that she brought her to 'Miss O'Reilly's Home at 6 in ambulance & went again at 9.30 & stayed till she was almost asleep. D.V. the change will be good for her'.[79] However, it was not to be and on 28 May 1944 Lynn wrote that the nursing home rang to say, 'dear M dying, but she had gone quite suddenly a few moments before'.[80] Two days later she took her final farewell of her partner; 'beautiful day, got some wee flowers in garden & bunch of yellow roses & went & said good bye to the earthly M ffM & sat there a while in the stillness, the yellow roses make the coffin so sweet'.[81] At the funeral Lynn was treated similarly to a bereaved widow by many present and recorded, poignantly, that a relative of ffrench-Mullen's said to her that 'they were relations, but she belonged to me'.[82]

She always missed ffrench-Mullen and every so often, for the next ten years, a mention is made, for instance on 6 June 1944 she noted that she was 'So so lonely for dearest M ffM', or 11 October 1947, 'how I miss dear M ffM on a Sat. Office closed, all gone by 1 o/c so diff MffM always stayed & worked in peace Sat. aft'.[83] She was always happy to see old friends who knew ffrench-Mullen, as on 12 March 1955, six months before she died, she wrote, 'yesterday went to C. O'Loughlin's & saw him & a friend & we had a great pow wow over old times. Refreshing to talk to someone who remembers dear M ffM.'.[84] These selected snapshots from Lynn's diaries demonstrate the centrality of ffrench-Mullen to her public, private and emotional life. The diaries reflect all their work and play and, taking a queer lens, we can also discern a more intimate life.

75 KLD, 5 May 1933; 'going to 8.30' indicates ffrench-Mullen went to 8.30 Mass. 76 KLD, 12 June 1933 – 'shoughed' probably means smoked. 77 KLD, 5 October 1933; ausgenschlafen – German, to sleep in, lie in. 78 KLD, 14 April 1944. 79 KLD, 14 May 1944. 80 KLD, 26 May 1944. 81 KLD, 28 May 1944. 82 KLD, 31 May 1944. 83 KLD, 6 June 1944, 11 October 1947. 84 KLD,

Birthdays were special and several times Lynn uses the word 'grussen' on those occasions: 28 January 1921, 'M grussed [*sic*] me as the clock struck last night' and again on 28 January 1932, 'M ffM grussed [*sic*] me at midnight, 58th birthday & it was nice, got several things, big cake, record, basin & jug, grapes & so on'.[85] Both women were interested in German language and culture and use of German words occurs, in the diaries, at moments on intimacy between them. Grüssen means to greet, however here, I would argue, given the special dates on which it is used by Lynn, it can be read as a coded term for something more special, more intimate. Mulholland also argues that there is 'something special about this "greeting" … and requires a special word, a covert word to distinguish it from the usual form of greeting'.[86]

In addition to providing a view into the intimate and emotional life of the couple, the diaries also reveal their friendships with many of the leading feminist and revolutionary women of the time. Helena Molony appears regularly, both for her activism, which Lynn admired, and for her struggle with alcohol addiction which worried the couple constantly. In the 1930s Molony formed a relationship with Dr Evelyn O'Brien with whom she lived until her death in 1967. They also knew Kathleen O'Brennan who had a relationship, while in the United States, with the socialist and suffrage activist, Irish American Dr Marie Equi. ffrench-Mullen had fought the 1916 Rising in the company of Margaret Skinnider at the Royal College of Surgeons, and entries indicate that Skinnider later visited their home. She had overseen a lifesaving operation on Skinnider when she was wounded, and who, from 1919, lived in Dublin with her lifelong partner, Nora O'Keefe.[87] Both knew Ella Young, a well-known cultural nationalist and feminist and later professor at Berkeley College, California. Young, a close friend of Maud Gonne McBride, also had lesbian relationships. They knew Eva Gore Booth and her partner Esther Roper, and Lynn kept in touch with Roper long after Gore Booth's death. They also knew and worked with Louie Bennett, head of the Irish Women Workers Union (IWWU), and her lifelong partner Helen Chenevix. There is an occasional reference to Miss O'Farrell, that is 1916 rebel, feminist, and republican Elizabeth O'Farrell, who lived with her lifelong partner, Julia Grenan. As Fearghal McGarry argued, it has to be asked if there was 'an influential network of lesbians prominent in overlapping feminist, socialist, trade union and republican circles whose sexuality has remained largely hidden from history?'[88] How influential they may have been is open to question, but there does seem to have been a small cohort of Irish

12 March 1955. **85** KLD, 28 January 1921, 28 January 1932. **86** Mulholland, *The politics and relationships*, p. 38. **87** McAuliffe, *Margaret Skinnider*. **88** Fearghal McGarry, 'Helena Molony: a revolutionary life', *History Ireland*, 4:21 (July–August 2013), https://www.historyireland.com/helena-molony-a-revolutionary-life/, accessed 14 January 2023.

feminist, socialist, trade union and republican women who lived their lives with other women, and among them were Dr Kathleen Lynn and Madeline ffrench-Mullen.

Reading the Kathleen Lynn diaries with a 'queer eye' allows a hidden or marginalised history to emerge. This is an answer to the provocative challenge as put by Morgan to historians to 'deconstruct the hidden meanings of historical silences and omissions' and allow the 'historicisation of the unspoken'.[89] In the writing of early twentieth-century Irish history, archival source materials are subjective and often read only, in terms of women activists' histories, to explore the centrality of economic independence, higher education, or to see their capacity to be involved in activism, be those suffrage, socialist or revolutionary movements. Rereading these same sources allows us to see there was space for same sex relationships to flourish in revolutionary movements, where new ways of living, desiring, and being with other women existed. There is a further compelling reason to revisit archives, to 'read against the grain' in search of lesbian lives in all contexts, as Vicinus has argued that ideas matter and history changes lives 'because it had changed ours. Faced with a fierce backlash against homosexual rights, this history has become even more necessary today'.[90]

89 Morgan, *The feminist history reader*, p. 25. 90 Martha Vicinus, 'The history of lesbian history', *Feminist Studies*, 38:3 (2012), pp 566–96, p. 589.

SECTION TWO

GENDER AND INSTITUTIONALISATION

CHAPTER 3

Shameful women, violent men: the criminal inebriate in Ireland, 1900–18

Conor Reidy

The second half of the nineteenth century brought new focus on the drunkard as an abandoned psychiatric patient rather than as an individual marked largely for their boisterous and disruptive nature.[1] The State Inebriate Reformatory was a reincarnation of previous institutional concepts and combined detention as a form of treatment and punishment. Treatment was intended for habitual addiction to alcohol and punishment was for any one of a long list of drink-related criminal offences. Citing studies on the inebriate reformatory in Scotland, Warsh describes how it became an institution for women convicted of prostitution and child cruelty.[2] There is considerable merit to this statement, but it by no means paints a complete picture. There were several women whose occupations were registered as being a 'prostitute' on entry to the State Inebriate Reformatory for Ireland, located in Ennis, Co. Clare, and some of their cases will be considered in this chapter. While there was only limited disquiet about their sexual behaviour, there was a greater concern with the threat they posed for their children, their immediate community and to society as a whole. The courts and agencies of intervention showed little sympathy for the women or for the circumstances that led them to their immoral lifestyle.

Studying the inmates of the state reformatory reveals another reality about women in Irish society but not individuals detained inside those walls. The case histories of numerous men detained in Ennis expose an undercurrent of violence toward women in their lives. Ironically, these violent attacks were not always the cause of their detention in the reformatory and so went unpunished. While society judged and condemned so-called 'prostitute' inmates of these reformatories, it tended to ignore the plight of other women, wives, mothers and daughters, whose only 'crime' was to be trapped in a household with a violent male figure. The State Inebriate Reformatory for Ireland was unique

1 Cheryl Krasnick Warsh, '"John Barleycorn must die": an introduction to the social history of alcohol' in C.K. Warsh (ed.), *Drink in Canada: historical essays* (Quebec, 1993), pp 3–26. 2 Ibid.

among institutions operated by the General Prisons Board (GPB) for Ireland. It was the first one mandated to reform as well as punish its inmates. Usefully, it was the only institution during the board's fifty-one-year tenure for which comprehensive before and after 'histories' of inmates are recorded. This allowed reformatory administrators and, by extension, historians, to understand the lives of these individuals in ways that were not otherwise possible. This understanding is expanded by newspaper court reports, which exposed their flaws of character and behaviour, thereby fuelling a public loathing and greater than ever isolation of the inebriate.

TRACING THE LEGISLATION

From the early nineteenth century alcohol was recognised as an enormous societal challenge with unquestioned links between drink, poverty and escalating crime. Barton underlines a view, held by many in the so-called 'respectable classes', that women were particularly susceptible to the debasing influences of drink.[3] Following decades of legal and scientific discussion that saw the establishment of committees, homes for drunkards and increasing attempts at medical understandings of their problems, the first major legislative breakthrough came in Britain in 1879 with the passing of an Act to Facilitate and Control the Cure of Habitual Drunkards. This defined an habitual drunkard – male or female – as one who 'not being amenable to any jurisdiction in lunacy, is notwithstanding, by reason of habitual intemperate drinking of intoxicating liquor, at times dangerous to himself or herself, and his or her affairs'.[4]

The Inebriates Act 1898 was the final and most significant step in a century-long quest to understand and address some of the social consequences of excessive drinking. Initially designed only to establish a system in England, Scotland and Wales, on its second reading it was extended to Ireland.[5] It provided for the establishment of three new institutions for the reform and/or punishment of habitual drunkards, the majority of whom committed criminal acts associated with their addiction. The first, the inebriate retreat, was the only institution of voluntary admission; one did not have to have committed a criminal act to be treated there. Once admitted, the managers had powers to

3 Alana Barton, 'Wayward girls and wicked women: two centuries of "semi-penal" control', *Liverpool Law Review*, 22 (2000), pp 157–71, at p. 165. 4 Cited in Leon Radzinowicz and Roger Hood, *A history of English criminal law* (London, 1986), p. 299. 5 Beverly A. Smith, 'Ireland's Ennis inebriates' reformatory: a nineteenth-century example of failed institutional reform', *Federal Probation*, 53 (1989), pp 316–49.

detain them for a fixed time to try and exact some level of reform.[6] The only Irish inebriate retreat opened in Belfast in 1902 under the management of the Irish Women's Temperance Union.[7] It accepted only Protestant women of the better working classes. The second institution under the 1898 Act was the certified reformatory. Established privately, it was licenced, supervised and part-funded by government.[8] There were two certified reformatories in Ireland. One opened in Waterford in 1906, catering for men, while a women's reformatory was established in Wexford in 1908.[9] The third was the State Inebriate Reformatory. While less hardened criminal drunkards were sentenced to the certified reformatory, the regime at the state institution was more in line with that of a local prison. With its national catchment area, the Irish State Inebriate Reformatory opened in the old county gaol at Ennis, Co. Clare, where it began receiving inmates in 1900.

At the time, Ireland was served by a network of local prisons, bridewells and convict prisons. Local prisons met the needs of the geographical region directly surrounding each institution and that could be one or more counties depending on the next closest prison. Trends in criminality represented in each institution were reflective of that locality rather than any other part of the country. Ennis inebriate reformatory was not at all parochial and did not solely represent trends in drunkenness and criminality in county Clare and its surrounding counties. A national institution, in its lifetime it housed only eight inmates from Clare.[10]

The gender composition of state inebriate reformatories has been well debated among historians. The higher number of females in detention was as much a trend in Ireland as it was in Britain. Between 1900 and early 1918, 126 males and 204 females were detained at Ennis.[11] In Britain, at least 80% of inmates of the broader inebriate reformatory system were female indicating, according to Hunt, Mellor and Turner, that significant and powerful elites perceived women as reproducers in danger of passing on their own unfortunate characteristics to their children.[12] This concern for a generation perhaps yet unborn was matched by a reluctance to send men to inebriate reformatories where they would be detained for longer than they might be at a local prison. Morrison points out that, as men were primary breadwinners, long periods of detention would leave families dependent on local rates and might damage future employment prospects. Additionally, institutional treatment was not

6 George Bretherton, 'Irish inebriate reformatories, 1899–1920: a small experiment in coercion', *Contemporary Drug Problems*, 13 (1986), pp 473–502. 7 Ibid., p. 479. 8 Smith, 'Ireland's Ennis inebriates' reformatory', p. 58. 9 Bretherton, 'Irish inebriates' reformatories', p. 484. 10 General Prisons Board (GPB), Ennis inebriate reformatory, *Register of inmates*, 1900–18. 11 GPB, *Register of Inmates*, 1900–18. 12 Geoffrey Hunt, Jenny Mellor and John Turner, 'Women and the inebriate reformatories' in Lynn Jamieson and Helen Corr (eds), *State, private life and political change* (London,

considered necessary for male drunkards as alcoholism among men was often considered to be a disease of the will. As men were believed to have greater willpower than women, it followed that they would be able to cure themselves.[13] There was little outward concern for the well-being of women as individuals or the physical and physiological dangers posed to them by a drunken lifestyle. Another factor in historical debates surrounding higher female inebriate detention rates is contemporary attitudes to the contrasting mental states and abilities of men and women. Though as many as three-quarters of those apprehended for drunkenness were men and more likely to qualify as habitual drunkards, late Victorian society conceptualised the problem as a gendered one, associated mainly with women.[14] Nineteenth-century social reformers and penal authorities considered it essential to control young, sexually active women. By the end of the century many non-statutory bodies cared for, rehabilitated and controlled women, focusing first on sexual activity but expanding to female criminality and drunkenness.[15] C.F. Marshall, a surgeon at the British Skin Hospital, stated in 1910 that many prostitutes turned to alcohol 'to attain temporary oblivion from the misery of their deplorable existence' and that alcohol was not a cause but the result of prostitution.[16] In somewhat of a contradiction, women were seen as dangerous and vulnerable, corrupting and corruptible: capable of asserting influence over others, but susceptible to external influence themselves and therefore in need of care and protection.[17]

Contemporary opinion during the late nineteenth century complained of the ongoing economic burden regular imprisonment of drunken women imposed. It cited maintenance in prison cells, cost of police surgeons, accommodation in prisons, policing costs, property damage and repeated cost of transportation between court and prison.[18] Most of this expenditure would also have applied to males but with deviant and drunken behaviour perceived as more acceptable among men, great offence was taken at the burdens caused by women. Zedner notes that women were assumed to be 'morally superior to men', with expectations of higher standards of behaviour. They were thought less inclined to dishonesty, perjury, stealing or cheating and less in danger of committing sexual crimes because they were, by nature, more chaste.[19] Such

1990), pp 163–82. 13 Brownyn Morrison, 'Controlling the hopeless: re-visioning the history of female inebriate institutions, *c.*1870–1920' in H. Johnston (ed.), *Punishment and control in historical perspective* (London, 2008), pp 135–58. 14 Morrison, 'Controlling the hopeless', p. 138. 15 Russell P. Dobash and Pat McLaughlin, 'The punishment of women in nineteenth-century Scotland: prisons and inebriate institutions' in Esther Breitenbach and Eleanor Gordon (eds), *Out of bounds: women in Scottish society 1800–1945* (Edinburgh, 1992), pp 65–88. 16 C.F. Marshall, 'Alcoholism and prostitution', *The British Journal of Inebriety*, 8:1 (1910), pp 29–31. 17 Barton, 'Wayward girls and wicked women', pp 157–71. 18 Morrison, 'Controlling the hopeless', p. 143. 19 Lucia Zedner, expectations of higher standards of behaviour fed into greater levels of outrage when women deviated from these societal norms. McCormick points out that the word prostitute was probably employed in many cases where women were not working in the profession but may have had some fringe involvement or gave that appearance.[20] Nineteen women whose occupations were registered as a prostitute were detained at Ennis reformatory between 1900 and 1918. They ranged in age from 19 to 65 years old; nine women were in their 30s, five in their 40s, three in their 20s, one in her 60s and one in her teens. Twelve were married or widowed while seven were single. Four were convicted of attempting suicide, a crime common across the institution. Four were convicted of malicious damage, three of child neglect, three of assault, to each of drunk and disorderly behaviour and being drunk on a public highway. Just one was convicted of larceny. All inmates in the state inebriate reformatories of Ireland and Britain were convicted of being habitual drunkards – this was a condition of entry. Seven give Dublin as their last place of residence, by and large reflecting the overall population composition of the institution and the reality that urban settings provided the best opportunity for prostitution. Five were from the city of Derry or Londonderry as it was variously described on the register of inmates. Two were listed as having no fixed address while Galway, Sligo, Antrim, Kildare and Belfast provided one inmate each listed as a prostitute.[21] The following case studies of inebriate prostitutes have been selected at random but largely based on the best, most complete, primary sources.

When sentenced to two years at Ennis, in October 1903, Annie A. had a lengthy list of convictions dating back to 1887. A 43-year-old single woman from Derry, her next-of-kin was her mother whose address was a workhouse in the city. Almost all her convictions were for vagrancy, but recent charges included attempted suicide and indecent exposure. Her prison record indicated that she was a prostitute.[22] In the early twentieth century, women named as prostitutes or prosecuted for that offence were often convicted for a range of other crimes such as larceny and theft, indicating, perhaps, that prostitution did not provide a sufficient living for these women.[23] And she had a further twenty-nine convictions for minor offences such as drunkenness. In total, she had accrued 152 short prison sentences.[24] The annual reports of the GPB showed that it was inmates such as Annie that penal administrators and prison staff most despaired of because they had become so familiar with the system that it ceased to be a threat or, by extension, a deterrent.

Women, crime, and custody in Victorian England (London, 1991), p. 23. 20 Leanne McCormick, *Regulating sexuality: women in twentieth-century Northern Ireland* (Manchester, 2009), p. 16. 21 GPB, *Register of inmates*, 1900–18. 22 Ibid. 23 McCormick, *Regulating sexuality*, p. 29. 24 GPB, State

By comparison with other female inmates at Ennis, Annie was at the higher end of the scale both in terms of prior detentions and character description. A 'woman of the unfortunate class', she reportedly spent the greater part of her life in prison often becoming suicidal when drunk. She once attempted to strangle herself while detained in a police cell. Apart from her mother, described as a drunkard and a prostitute, she had no other known relatives. Physically, Annie was a malnourished snuff addict and prone to headaches when deprived of it. All her bodily organs were healthy, and she menstruated regularly. This latter medical detail appears only in notes relating to prostitutes. Mentally she was violent, possessed a 'vile temper' when drunk and often displayed it in prison. In a telling summation, Annie's institutional case history described her as having been a prostitute from childhood.[25] Annie was discharged from Ennis in October 1905 having served her full sentence. A March 1906 first progress report came from one J. Heatley, an unknown supporter who clearly had some influence over her post-release well-being. Heatley declared that Annie was 'doing wonderfully well' and gave more hope every day. While 'uncertain in her moods', he believed she was trying her best, that she was 'just a little cracked' and her most promising feature was that when her temper rose she did not succumb to alcohol. Since the money earned in the institution ran out, she had become 'self-supporting', although he does not spell out in what way. Every Monday night, unprompted, she brought her earnings to Heatley to hold and pay her rent. An April 1908 report, however, shows that there was some inaccuracy in this forced account of Annie's post-discharge life. A local RIC sergeant reported that between November 1905 – one month after her release – and January 1908, Annie had appeared drunk in court thirty-four times on charges including drunkenness, being drunk and disorderly and vagrancy.[26] Clearly, between October 1905 and March 1906, Heatley was either unaware of Annie's conduct or trying to protect her from further prosecution. By April 1910 she had accrued a further nineteen drunk and disorderly convictions and eight more by February 1911. This final report described her as doing very badly.[27] Nothing was recorded in the after history of her moral conduct and so it cannot be ascertained whether the authorities continued to deem her a prostitute.

The label of living a moral or immoral life was attached to many inmates of the inebriate reformatory, particularly to women. Galway woman Bridget P. was twenty-two years old, single and living in Dublin when convicted of assault and being an habitual drunkard at the Dublin city sessions on 20 March 1911. Her occupation was recorded as a prostitute, but she was not convicted of prostitution on this occasion. She was sentenced to eighteen months in Ennis.[28]

Inebriate Reformatory, Ennis, *Casebook*, 1900–18. 25 Ibid. 26 Ibid. 27 Ibid. 28 GPB, *Register of inmates*, 1900–18.

Bridget's father was described as a labouring man from Lawrencetown in Galway, where she grew up. At fifteen she was employed as a domestic servant and began keeping company with a former soldier. It was alleged that at this time she began leading an immoral life and became addicted to alcohol. She and her sister Mary were denounced by the local parish priest and both left Galway for Dublin.[29] This to some extent reflects a pattern postulated by Walkowitz in her study of British prostitutes in Victorian society that saw the women drawn to the nearest big city where they would eke out a precarious living in the job market.[30] Two years later Bridget returned to Galway, to Ballinasloe, where her employment in domestic service was terminated due to her alcoholism. She moved in with a woman accused of keeping an immoral house, was arrested for larceny of a watch in 1908 and was sentenced to three months in prison. For two years prior to March 1911, she lived in Dublin, working as a prostitute and accumulating twenty convictions for assault and drunkenness. Bridget's parents were described as respectable, industrious and sober but she, her sister Mary and her brother were apparently fond of having their own way.[31] Every aspect of her physical and mental health suggested that Bridget was in a good state, perhaps reflecting her youth. She was discharged from Ennis on 19 September 1912 having served her full sentence.[32]

Prior to her release, there was clearly some apprehension about her return to Galway. An individual described as her parent's employer, J.E. Kenny, wrote to the reformatory governor on their behalf asking that some employment could be found for Bridget away from Galway, possibly in Ennis. The inquiry questioned whether a home existed for such discharged girls or if, perhaps, she could be employed in a laundry. Kenny, having obviously received a negative response to the query, wrote again four days later to state that it was unfortunate no such solution could be devised as Bridget would be no credit to her family in this part of the country. Her parents did agree to take Bridget into their home as they felt it was most important that she had somebody to look after her upon release.[33] Representations such as the one made by J.E. Kenny were not uncommon in these situations where those from the so-called labouring classes did not have the confidence to address or lobby the authorities themselves. The first formal report on Bridget's post-discharge progress came from a local police constable in Galway and it was not positive. On 9 November 1912, two months after her release, Constable Mollaghan reported that, though not coming to police attention in his district, she had been canny and carried on her social

29 GPB, State Inebriate Reformatory, Ennis, *Casebook*. 30 Judith Walkowitz, *Prostitution and Victorian society: women, class and the state* (Cambridge, 1982), p. 15. 31 GPB, State Inebriate Reformatory, Ennis, *Casebook*. 32 GPB, *Register of inmates*, 1900–18. 33 GPB, State Inebriate

activities, namely her drinking, in the sub-district of Eyrecourt where she was convicted of being drunk and incapable on 1 October 1912. Constable Mollaghan believed that Bridget consumed alcohol 'on the quiet' to conceal her behaviour from police.

A January 1913 report recorded that she had departed Galway, apparently for Dublin. It appeared that she was drinking all the intoxicating drink she could get, and the police claimed that her moral conduct was again questionable. This is borne out by at least two appearances by Bridget in Mountjoy prison registers in August 1914. Listed as having no fixed address, she was convicted of soliciting and sentenced to seven days imprisonment and a fine on each occasion. In September 1914 she was sentenced to a month in Mountjoy for threatening behaviour and, within days of her release, she served a further week for soliciting. In November 1914, at the Dublin Metropolitan Police Court, she was sentenced to a month in prison for being drunk and disorderly. January 1915 saw her receive a one-week sentence for soliciting, with Meath Place, Dublin, listed as her most recent address.[34] By 6 March 1915, Bridget had come to the attention of John Bolton of the Dublin Discharged Prisoners' Aid Society (DDPAS) who described her as a questionable character. She had no fixed residence and ten convictions during the previous two years, mainly related to drunkenness. A February 1916 report recorded charges including soliciting for prostitution and, in a final report, one year later, Bolton revealed that Bridget had not since come to his attention mainly because he could not trace her whereabouts.[35] It clearly caused no difficulty for an individual of the age, good health and acumen of Bridget to disappear in a city such as early-twentieth-century Dublin. A month after this final 1917 report, however, Bridget appeared in the Dublin city police court and was given two weeks in Mountjoy for soliciting. In June of the same year, she received two different seven-day sentences for the same offence and another fourteen days in July.[36] This was the final time Bridget appeared on the Mountjoy prison register and her ultimate fate is unknown. Evidence of her activity as a prostitute is clear and the failure of her reform at Ennis is without question.

Edith C, aged thirty, posed a threat to the middle-class sensibilities of her husband's family when she was detained in Ennis in August 1900. Sentenced to eighteen months for malicious damage and being an habitual drunkard, Edith held seventy-six prior convictions for various offences including assault and soliciting.[37] Like many of the prostitutes detained at Ennis, concerns around Edith did not focus on that aspect of her life but on her being a disruptive and

Reformatory, Ennis, *Casebook*. 34 GPB, *Register of inmates*, 1900–18. 35 GPB, State Inebriate Reformatory, Ennis, *Casebook*. 36 GPB, State Inebriate Reformatory, Ennis, *Casebook*. 37 GPB, potentially violent force in the lives of those around her. Once a children's governess, in the ten years since a divorce from her medical student husband, she had lived a 'loose and immoral life'. Her marriage ended because of her adultery, and she had allegedly succumbed to a 'desperate and dissipated existence' and became a continual source of aggravation for her husband's family. In advance of her release from Ennis on 31 January 1902, the authorities frequently repeated that Edith had conducted herself badly while in detention, with Governor King declaring that 'there is no prospect of reformation in the case of inmate Edith [C]'.[38] Extraordinarily, it emerged that in the months prior to her release, Edith's former father-in-law, George O'C, of Lansdowne Road, Dublin, travelled to Ennis in an attempt to persuade Governor King to prevent her return to Dublin. He believed that she would prove a continual source of annoyance to him and his family, although he had assisted her in every way. In a follow-up letter to Governor King shortly before her release, George revealed his family's heightened anxiety at her possible reappearance in Dublin. The family had moved house, but he was worried that she would return to their previous residence and attempt to do damage. In a pointed reference to his family's connections with officialdom, George revealed that David Harrel, the undersecretary for Ireland, had assured him that every precaution possible will be taken to have the woman watched. By early 1903, when the first post-release report was sent to Ennis, Edith was in a lunatic asylum where she died in 1910.[39] This case probably raises more questions than many others, not merely because of the involvement of the official apparatus of state at higher levels than would normally be appropriate. Her estranged husband's family demonstrated no concern for her career as a prostitute and were instead concerned with her propensity for violence. The question arises as to whether this latter concern masked a fear that her immoral lifestyle might pose some hazard to their standing in society. Significantly, there must be a question over the family's role in Edith's committal to a lunatic asylum within a year of her release from Ennis. With no record of *her* voice, it is difficult to ascertain the extent to which she was a victim or a perpetrator.

VIOLENT INEBRIATE MEN AND THEIR VICTIMS

Indeed, the voice of women, inside *and* outside the reformatory, is often absent when they are faced with the violent outbursts of male inebriates. While this chapter does not attempt to define or redefine violence, it is necessary to point

Register of inmates, 1900–18. 38 GPB, State Inebriate Reformatory, Ennis, *Casebook*. 39 GPB, State Inebriate Reformatory, Ennis, *Casebook*.

out then that while the male offender cases put forward here all feature *physical* violence of some sort, those other non-physical forms, that Aitken correctly defines as violent nonetheless,[40] were very heavily foisted by the men of Ennis reformatory on the women in their lives. Who were the women in their lives? It is important to dispel any accidentally-held assumption that the male-on-female violence was restricted to the marital domain – it was not. Writing in 1914, J.W. Astley Cooper, the medical superintendent, Ghyllwood Sanatorium for Inebriates, Cockermouth, Cumberland, argued that the male inebriate was typically a person lacking in initiative who, although surrounded by many occupational opportunities, will not do anything when left to his own devices. This man will complain loudly of having little to do, and so, with an unoccupied mind and body, he will 'soon get into some mischief or other, while his physical and mental health will soon suffer'.[41] Cooper may as well have been profiling James G, a 25-year-old from Tullamore who described himself as a stonecutter by trade, when he was sent to Ennis for assaulting police in 1906.[42] James was addicted to alcohol for eight years and worked in 'fits and starts' and drank anything he earned. He was prone to extreme violence, and he had several epileptic fits. James had twenty-four previous convictions for assaults 'on both civilians and the police'. He was also convicted of attempting suicide, for which he earned three months in prison. While in the army he received 112 days for a 'military offence'.[43]

After his release from Ennis in 1909, like every other discharged inmate, James was subjected to close monitoring. During the initial months of his freedom, he fared well, staying away from alcohol and physical violence. Around a year later, however, in December 1910, the police were summoned to his father's house by his sister Teresa. The constables arrived to find the house in disarray with broken delph, six panes of glass broken across various windows, and James being restrained by three men. In the struggle, he lost his shirt, vest, coat and boots. He was in a furious state and lashed out at the police as they attempted to take over his restraint. His elderly father was hiding outside the house. In their report to the governor at Ennis, the Tullamore police confirmed that James eventually worked himself into a fit. When he recovered they removed him to their cells and he was subsequently prosecuted.[44] The lack of impulse control exercised by James was a common trait among almost all of the Ennis inebriates, male or female. His propensity for extreme and uncontrollable violence was a

40 Jo Aitken, 'The horrors of matrimony among the masses: feminist representations of wife beating in England and Australia, 1870–1914', *Journal of Women's History*, 19:4 (2007), pp 107–31.
41 J.W. Astley Cooper, 'The care and control of inebriate men', *The British Journal of Inebriety*, 11:4 (April 1914), p. 186. 42 GPB, *Register of inmates*, 1900–18. 43 GPB, State Inebriate Reformatory, Ennis, *Casebook*. 44 GPB, State Inebriate Reformatory, Ennis, *Casebook*.

somewhat rare dimension. R.W. Branthwaite, the Inspector for the Inebriates Act in England, noted that poor impulse control, however, was not rare. Using 1908 medical and psychological understandings, he linked brain development to impulse control. He argued that 'a well-developed brain causes a man to hesitate before he strikes to avenge an insult'.[45] The only record of violence against a woman comes two years after his discharge from Ennis when he was convicted for striking his sister Teresa. His entire post-release career was littered with convictions for assaulting his father, the police, anybody in his vicinity. This was an extremely violent individual and he is one of these cases where it was clear that his violence was not targeted toward one gender.

William C was a 42-year-old stonecutter from Cork city and had been addicted to alcohol for eight to ten years when he was sent to Ennis in 1900 for assaulting a peace officer.[46] He had twenty-three prior convictions, mostly for assault. A feature of his life during that time was the frequent assaults upon his sisters who ran a public house. He apparently believed that he had some ownership right to the property, but he had none. Such was his rage towards his sisters and his theft of alcohol from them, by force, it was alleged that their lives were hardly worth living.[47] The alleged cause of his alcoholic rage fits, albeit imperfectly, a narrative set forth by Hammerton whereby the notion of the man as a breadwinner was threatened by the cheaper, less-skilled labour of women. This led to fears of undermining the familial authority of the male.[48] After leaving Ennis he was initially reported to be 'doing very badly'. He was very quickly sent to prison for some unrecorded offence and in subsequent reports up to 1907, he was still attracting negative attention from the forces of law and order. By 1911, he turned his life around, was employed and 'a change for the better' had come over him.

Hammerton pointed out that many wives were reluctant to prosecute their violent husbands, even after calling the police and taking out a summons to stop a severe beating. This could stem from wives' fear of further violence after the conviction, from anxieties about jeopardising an already marginal family income or a genuine wish not to punish the husband.[49] This theory can safely be applied to many cases at Ennis. William M was a 49-year-old gardener from Dublin, convicted of neglecting his children in 1904.[50] He was married with six children and had no previous convictions. He 'was constantly making use of the worst and lowest language to his wife and children'.[51] Aitken argues that in these

45 R.W. Branthwaite, 'Inebriety: its causation and control', *The British Journal of Inebriety*, 5:3 (January 1908), p. 118. 46 GPB, *Register of inmates*, 1900–18. 47 GPB, State Inebriate Reformatory, Ennis, *Casebook*. 48 A. James Hammerton, *Cruelty and companionship: conflict in nineteenth century married life* (London, 1995), p. 13. 49 Hammerton, *Cruelty and companionship*, p. 40. 50 GPB, *Register of inmates*, 1900–18. 51 GPB, State Inebriate Reformatory, Ennis, *Casebook*.

contexts, violence against wives is not restricted to broken bones and bruises. In fact, feminist understandings extend the definition to underline links between physical violence and emotional, economic, or sexual abuse. These work in tandem to project male power and control.[52] A year before his conviction William was charged at Kingston station by his wife of cruelty to her and their children. Ten years after his discharge from Ennis he was back living with his family, and rarely drank, and even when he did there was no further drunkenness or violence.[53] This outcome, though obviously not excusing any previous behaviour, was actually quite common in these situations. The fact of a family's dependence on the husband's wages was recognised by E.D. Daly speaking to the Statistical and Social Inquiry Society in 1897 when he noted 'a poor man's wife has no redress if a drunken husband makes off with her wages and spends the money on alcohol'.[54] William's family was fortunate that he was one of those few who happened to mend his ways.

The voice of the female victim of male inebriate violence is seldom heard in these inebriate institution records. Hector M was twenty-nine years old when he was sent to Ennis. He was the son of an Australian medical doctor. He had nine previous convictions and twelve fines. He had been drinking since the age of thirteen or fourteen and had fallen into gambling and pawning his mother's property. He was arrested many times for violence towards his mother and also took money from her by force. She had him arrested on three separate occasions for assaults and threatening language 'and on each of these occasions he was a total wreck from drink'. He was married 'to a girl supposed to be of immoral character' but she left him to live in Canada with another man. He was on record of saying that when he had spent the family money, he would kill his mother and himself. At one of his court proceedings, Hector's mother swore that he had spent around two thousand pounds on drink alone.[55] His was the type of violence alluded to earlier by Aitken: it was usually non-physical, constructed instead on threat, menace and a relentless climate of fear. A month after discharge in late-1914, he was arrested at 11.30 p.m. after his mother was forced to leave the house due to his drunken threats. His mother, described as a 'kind old lady' by authorities, wrote to the governor at Ennis and implored him to give her son another chance as it would 'break her heart' if he was returned to custody. We seldom hear the voice of the victim of the violent inebriate but in this case, she wrote:

52 Aitken, 'The horrors of matrimony among the masses', p. 109. 53 GPB, State Inebriate Reformatory, Ennis, *Casebook*. 54 E.D. Daly, 'The struggle between the state and the drunkard', *Journal of the Statistical and Social Inquiry Society of Ireland* (February 1897), pp 275–6. 55 GPB, State Inebriate Reformatory, Ennis, *Casebook*.

> I beg to appeal to your clemency in favour of my son. He has unfortunately given way to drink but if you will kindly allow him another chance he is firmly resolved to abstain from it in future. He is at present confined to bed very ill and Mr Godfrey is attending him and has given him strict orders to remain in bed. Sir, I do pray you will overlook it as I am desolate and utterly friendless.[56]

Hector was given another chance at the time but was ultimately returned to Ennis. He was again released and joined the army, where he accrued many offences for drink-related violence. He continued his career of violence inside the army, subjected to arrest, court martial and most forms of discipline that the military seemed to have had in its armoury.[57] Interestingly, Hector does not fit a stereotype sketched by Aitken of a working-class male named in (her analysis, marital) household. Generally, that individual was of a higher profile in the courts, and newspaper reporting, because community and police surveillance was more enhanced in working-class districts.[58]

Conflict arising from any issues could be expressed in a variety of forms but for the working class, it was most likely through domestic violence. The violence most often emerged from men and was often the concluding act following other events, grievances and arguments. Owen O was 56-year-old and from Limerick when he was convicted of assault in 1903. In recent years, Owen had taken to drink and his language toward his family was 'foul and vile' and he alleged his children were 'bastards'. Three of his children had to leave home and his wife frequently sought refuge in a neighbour's house because of his violence. At one moment he was quiet and calm, the next he was 'shouting like a maniac'. In general, he was haughty and stubborn and would accept neither advice nor remonstrance. His after-history reports were fairly positive except for one entry about two years after his discharge: a discharged prisoners' aid society officer noted that 'he has not been as violent towards his wife and family as he used to be before treatment'.

CONCLUSION

Martin Joel Weiner writes that while historians have taken note of gender, it has usually been to target the stigmatisation and control of women, such as prostitutes or unmarried mothers. In virtually all times and places, males have accounted for a very disproportionate share of physically aggressive behaviour.

56 Ibid. 57 Ibid. 58 Aitken, 'The horrors of matrimony', p. 113.

Drunkenness, 'the leading stimulant of violence', was less likely to mitigate one's responsibility for disorderly conduct.[59] Both Victorian anti-drink campaigns and Victorian feminism drew much of their emotional force and moral authority from the denunciation of male violence, particularly against women and children. One of the key considerations that must be applied to the analysis outlined in this chapter is that the State Inebriate Reformatory, while a significant experiment, also represents a small physical sample of the wider problems related to alcohol in Ireland between approximately 1900 and 1918. The incidences of alcohol-related crime were much greater in number than could be facilitated in this institution. Likewise, the scale of drunkenness convictions was also quite vast. What the State Inebriate Reformatory has always offered, in my view, is a microcosm, something that is representative of the large problem: it offers an imperfect window into a world of pain, poverty, degraded mental health, abuse, neglect, violence – a world of broken lives.

59 Cited in Barry S. Godfrey and Paul Lawrence, *Crime and justice, 1750–1950* (Devon, 2005), pp 104–5.

CHAPTER 4

Mother and baby institutions in Northern Ireland: telling a forgotten story

Leanne McCormick, Sean O'Connell and John Privilege

Following recommendations from both the United Nations Committee on the Elimination of Discrimination against Women and the United Nations Committee against Torture in 2013, the Northern Ireland Executive established an inter-departmental working group (IDWG) in 2016–17 under the auspices of the Department of Health to consider whether any action should be taken in relation to historical mother and baby institutions and Magdalene laundries in Northern Ireland.[1] It was decided that given the lack of information available about the institutions and before any decisions would be taken regarding issues such as a Public Inquiry, which organisations such as Amnesty International were suggesting, twelve months' research would be commissioned. This was to produce a report that considered the archival records relating to the institutions as well as carrying out oral history interviews with victims and survivors and others involved in the operation of the institutions. The Northern Ireland Executive was influenced by the establishment in the Republic of Ireland of the Commission of Investigation into Mother and Baby Homes (COIMBH) in 2015, initially for a three-year period, but which was extended several times before a final report was published in January 2021.[2] There had also been a Report commissioned in the Republic of Ireland on Magdalene laundries. It was published in February 2013, commonly known as the McAleese Report after Senator Martin McAleese, the chair of the inter-departmental committee who produced the report.[3] The Department of Health and the IDWG based their terms of reference and the research requirements on those drawn up for the COIMBH. Moreover, by commissioning a research report overseen by an IDWG, the authorities in Northern Ireland adopted a similar structure to those for the McAleese Report.

1 Northern Ireland was established following the partition of the island of Ireland in 1921. The Northern Ireland Executive is the devolved government of Northern Ireland established under the terms of the Northern Ireland Act 1998, following the Good Friday Agreement. 2 *Final report of the commission of investigation into mother and baby homes (COIMBH)* (Dublin: Department of Children, Equality, Disability, Integration and Youth, 2021). 3 *Report of the inter-departmental*

Following a public procurement exercise, Professor Sean O'Connell, Queen's University Belfast, and Dr Leanne McCormick, Ulster University, were awarded the funding to carry out the research. This commenced in March 2018 and two research assistants, Dr John Privilege and Dr Ida Milne, were recruited, with Dr Livi Dee replacing Dr Milne in September 2018. The researchers were asked to report on: entry and exit pathways; living and working conditions; mortality rates and causes; and post-mortem practices in the institutions. The nature and extent of state involvement in each institution was examined and the institutions placed in a wider historical context. A literature review, a review of archived records and oral accounts of those with experience of the institutions were also to be included. Under examination were four institutions under the category of Magdalene laundries: three St Mary's Homes run by the Good Shepherd Sisters in Belfast, Derry and Newry, and an Industrial Home operated by the Salvation Army in Belfast. Eleven mother and baby institutions fell under the research remit, three Catholic institutions, the Good Shepherd Sisters-run Marianville in Belfast, and Marianvale in Newry, and Mater Dei, the Legion of Mary's institution in Belfast. Protestant-operated institutions included Malone Place Maternity and Rescue Home, Hopedene House, Kennedy House (Church of Ireland) and Thorndale (Salvation Army). Deanery Flats (Barnardo's) and the state-funded Mount Oriel were also considered, as were workhouses, as places where unmarried mothers gave birth and boards of guardians were involved in the boarding out and fostering of children. Sixty oral history interviews were carried out, including twenty-nine with women who had spent time in the institutions and sixteen relatives of such women. The other interviews were with individuals who had been involved with the institutions, including two nuns and one woman who had worked in Good Shepherd institutions, two priests, a retired midwife, a retired doctor, three retired social workers, three retired probation officers, a retired PSNI officer (who subsequently withdraw their testimony) and an individual who lived close to one of the institutions. The report was submitted in August 2019. Following revisions and a Maxwellisation process the report was published in January 2021.[4] This chapter focuses on the findings in the *Mother and baby homes and Magdalene laundries in Northern Ireland, 1922–1990 report* (hereafter *MBHML Report*) with a focus on mother and baby homes.[5] It will also consider some issues involved in writing the report with a particular emphasis on access to records and archives.

committee to establish the facts of state involvement with the Magdalene laundries (Dublin: Department of Justice, 2013). 4 Maxwellisation is the name given to a process whereby those discussed in a public report have an opportunity to respond before publication. Institutions or legacy organisations were given relevant chapter(s) and could respond to these. The researchers met with

Scholarly research has focused predominantly on mother and baby institutions in the Republic of Ireland.[6] That similar institutions operated in Northern Ireland throughout the twentieth century has often been neglected in academic and popular discussion.[7] Until the publication of the *MBHML Report* there was relatively little known about the institutions, particularly post-partition.[8] However, the same issues existed across the island of Ireland with regards to the lack of tolerance within society for unmarried mothers. As Lindsey Earner-Byrne and Diane Urquhart have argued, both states placed a 'high premium on sexual "purity"' and 'shame and secrecy formed fundamental bulwarks' of societies which were intolerant of sex outside of marriage and shunned unmarried mothers.[9]

The establishment of mother and baby institutions in Northern Ireland followed a slightly different pattern to the Republic of Ireland where the majority of institutions specifically catering for unmarried mothers and their children were established in the 1920s and 1930s. These included county homes which were former workhouses; institutions operated by religious orders and lay Catholic groups as well as a number of Protestant-run institutions. The final report of the COIMBH focused on eighteen of these institutions. When it was published, in January 2021, it met with considerable criticism, from survivors, activists and academics, particularly for the way it dealt with oral testimony

the Department of Health to review and agree any changes to the Report. 5 Leanne McCormick, Sean O'Connell, Olivia Dee and John Privilege, *Report into mother and baby homes and Magdalene laundries in Northern Ireland, 1922–1990* (Belfast: Department of Health NI, 2021), pp 58–9, https://www.health-ni.gov.uk/publications/research-report-mother-and-baby-homes-and-magdalene-laundries-northern-ireland, accessed 22 February 2024. 6 See, for example, Lindsey Earner-Byrne, *Mother and child: maternity and child welfare in Dublin, 1922–60* (Manchester, 2007); Maria Luddy, 'Unmarried mothers in Ireland, 1880–1973,' *Women's History Review*, 20:1 (2011), pp 109–26; Eoin O'Sullivan and Ian O'Donnell, *Coercive confinement in Ireland: patients, prisoners and penitents* (Manchester, 2012); Paul Garrett, 'Unmarried mothers in the Republic of Ireland,' *Journal of Social Work* 16:6 (2016), 9708–27; Sarah-Anne Buckley and Caroline McGregor, 'Interrogating institutionalisation and child welfare: the Irish case, 1939–1991', *European Journal of Social Work*, 22:6 (2019), pp 1062–72; James M. Smith, 'Knowing and unknowing Tuam: state practice, the archive, and transitional justice', *Éire-Ireland*, 55:1 & 2 (2020), pp 142–80. 7 Exceptions to this include, Christopher Shepard, 'The legion of Mary, unmarried mothers and the expansion of the welfare state in Northern Ireland, 1945–55' in Sarah O'Connor and Christopher Shepard (eds), *Women, social and cultural change in twentieth-century Ireland: dissenting voices* (Cambridge, 2008), pp 124–47; Alexandra Tierney, 'Partition, women and social policy, 1921–1939' (PhD, Trinity College Dublin, 2018), chapter 2. 8 For institutions, in what was to become Northern Ireland, pre-partition see Maria Luddy, *Prostitution and Irish society* (Cambridge, 2007), chapter 3; Leanne McCormick, *Regulating sexuality: women in twentieth century Northern Ireland* (Manchester, 2009), chapter 2; Diane Urquhart, 'Gender, family and sexuality, 1800–2000' in Liam Kennedy and Philip Ollerenshaw (eds), *Ulster since 1600: politics, economy and society* (Oxford, 2011), pp 248–9. 9 Lindsey Earner-Byrne and Diane Urquhart, *The Irish abortion journey, 1920–2018* (London, 2019), p. 11.

provided by victims and survivors.[10] However, the Irish government decided not to review the final report of the COIMBH due to 'significant legal complexities'. It argued that the government did not have the right to 'retrospectively alter or interrogate the independent commission's findings or methodology'.[11] Roderic O'Gorman, Minister for Children, Equality, Disability, Integration and Youth, speaking in October 2022, instead outlined proposals to create a centre for research and remembrance where survivor testimonies would be gathered and held, possibly located at the site of a former Magdalene laundry in Sean McDermott Street in Dublin.[12] In addition, a redress scheme is being established by the Irish government which will pay €5,000 to every woman who spent time in a mother and baby institution, with an increasing rate determined by length of stay and requirement to work while in the institution.[13]

In the north of Ireland before partition several organisations focused on unmarried mothers. These included the Belfast Midnight Mission/Malone Place, a non-denominational Protestant-run institution established in 1861 as a rescue home for women involved in, or at risk of becoming involved in, prostitution. By the early twentieth century it had expanded its remit with a maternity home for unmarried mothers, also providing beds for fee-paying maternity patients. The Church of Ireland Rescue League operated a home for unmarried mothers from 1912 which became Kennedy House in 1947. The Salvation Army opened a maternity home, Thorndale House, in 1920 but had been admitting unmarried mothers to its rescue home from the early 1900s. Hopedene, a Protestant-run home with close links to the Church of Ireland, opened in 1943. Catholic-run institutions were established later than most of the Protestant ones, with the Legion of Mary opening Mater Dei on the Antrim Road in north Belfast in 1942 and the Good Shepherd Sisters opening Marianville (Belfast) in 1950 and Marianvale in Newry in 1955.

For unmarried mothers without support from family or friends or for those who could not afford private nursing home fees, the workhouses provided

10 See, for example, Statement from Clann Project, http://clannproject.org/wp-content/uploads/Clann-Press-Release_17–12–21.pdf; Catriona Crowe, 'The Commission and the survivors', *The Dublin Review*, 83 (2021); *Mother and baby homes commission of investigation report*: draft alternative executive summary, https://www.tudublin.ie/media/website/news/2021/main-news/ Draft-September-24.pdf; Ciara Breathnach, 'A dark, difficult and shameful chapter', https:// www.historyworkshop.org.uk/mother-and-baby-homes-report/ (accessed 22 February 2024). 11 Joint Committee on Children, Equality, Disability, Integration and Youth, 4 October 2022. https://data.oireachtas.ie/ie/oireachtas/debateRecord/joint_committee_on_children_equality_disability_integration_and_youth/2022–10–04/debate/mul@/main.pdf (accessed 22 February 2024). 12 Ibid. 13 https://www.gov.ie/en/publication/0c637–mother-and-baby-institutions-payment-scheme/, accessed 22 February 2024.

another option. They continued to operate in Northern Ireland until 1948 and the establishment of the National Health Service.[14] The workhouses, established by the Poor Law (Ireland) Act in 1838, were one of the few institutions that provided for unmarried mothers and their children. They viewed unmarried mothers as 'immoral' and women with more than one child born outside of marriage were categorised alongside prostitutes and separated from 'more respectable inmates'.[15] Large numbers of unmarried mothers entered the Belfast workhouse to give birth or to use the workhouse to board out their children. Doing so, perhaps enabled some to avoid the more rigorous moral restriction of the religious-run institutions.[16] The *MBHML Report* estimated that over 10,500 women entered mother and baby institutions between 1922 and 1990 in Northern Ireland. However, this number excludes the unmarried mothers who gave birth in workhouses between 1922 and 1948 and further research is necessary to determine a final number. In addition, there is a cross-border element to be considered. Significant numbers of women from Northern Ireland entered institutions in the Republic to avoid local scrutiny; a pattern repeated in the opposite direction.

Like many voluntary philanthropic organisations, mother and baby institutions provided separate provision for Protestant and Catholic women. There was a long-standing tradition of denominational provision across the island, and within Northern Ireland, financially challenged local and national authorities looked to voluntary and religious organisations to provide services.[17] In addition the state, north and south, justified handing over care of unmarried mothers and their children as a pastoral issue on which Churches were best placed to provide suitable, denominational care.[18] The institutional records highlight how these separate provisions were sometimes used by families who wanted to ensure secrecy around a pregnancy and felt this could be achieved by using a home of a different religious persuasion.[19] There were concerns about proselytisation and in some cases action was taken to ensure women were in an institution that matched their religious background. In the Salvation Army's Thorndale mother and baby home, the records reveal a number of instances

14 *MBHML Report*, pp 58–9. 15 Maria Luddy, 'Unmarried mothers in Ireland, 1880–1973', *Women's History Review* 20:1 (2011), p. 111; Virginia Crossman, *Poverty and the poor law in Ireland, 1850–1914* (Liverpool, 2013), p. 111. 16 Olwen Purdue, 'Surviving the industrial city: the female poor and the workhouse in late nineteenth century Belfast', *Urban History* 44:1 (2017), p. 89. 17 Nicholas Acheson, Brian Harvey and Arthur Williamson, 'State welfare and the development of voluntary action: the case of Ireland, north and south', *Voluntas: International Journal of Voluntary and Nonprofit Organisations* 16:2 (2005), p. 195. 18 James Smith, 'The politics of sexual knowledge: the origins of Ireland's containment culture and the Carrigan report (1931)', *Journal of the History of Sexuality*, 13:2 (2004), pp 208–33, p. 211. 19 *MBHML Report*, p. 70.

where Catholic organisations made contact with Catholic unmarried mothers to persuade them to transfer to a Catholic institution.[20] This reflected wider concerns about children being adopted by parents of a different religion rather than necessarily concerns about the spiritual well-being of the mother.

It is important to note that only a quarter of women who were recorded as giving birth to 'illegitimate' children in Northern Ireland entered mother and baby institutions. These were women without support during a pregnancy, who may have personally wanted to keep a pregnancy a secret, or more commonly were urged to enter by their families, members of the clergy or other professionals. The shame and stigma associated with a pregnancy outside of wedlock and the fear of the loss of respectability this brought to a woman and her family permeate both the written records and the oral testimonies. 'JP' who entered one of the Good Shepherd mother and baby institutions when she was seventeen, in the mid-1970s, recalled how when her father found out she was pregnant he 'went mad' and told her to 'get the eff out that door and don't come back, you've brought nothing but bloody shame and disgrace'.[21] 'AB' who entered Thorndale as a 15-year-old in the 1970s described how, 'You felt as if you were the lowest of the low and a sinner, the biggest sinner there was because you had this baby out of wedlock'.[22] As late as 1988 in Marianville in Belfast, five women were admitted without their family's knowledge.[23] Female relatives, mothers, sisters, aunts, often kept the secret of a pregnancy from male relatives. In the case of one woman who entered Mater Dei in 1968, her parents thought she had gone to stay with her sister in England.[24] The border also operated as an effective way of keeping a pregnancy secret. A number of women were admitted into Marianvale in Newry from the Republic of Ireland to avoid anyone from their local communities finding out. The Good Shepherd Sisters had a payment scheme negotiated with health authorities in the Republic where payment for women who entered Marianvale could be claimed from their local Health Board through the Good Shepherd Convent in Dunboyne, Co. Meath. Sometimes assumed names were used or names were replaced with numbers to further preserve anonymity in communication or billing. In two examples in the 1970s the Catholic Protection and Rescue Society in Dublin organised for women to be admitted to Marianvale, identified only by number with their fees paid by their local Health Board through Dunboyne.[25]

Marriage before or very swiftly after the birth of a baby was often seen as the preferred option for unmmaried mothers. However, for many women in mother and baby institutions, marriage was not an option for several reasons.

20 *MBHML Report*, pp 83–4. 21 *MBHML Report*, p. 379. 22 *MBHML Report*, p. 477. 23 *MBHML Report*, p. 86. 24 *MBHML Report*, p. 165. 25 *MBHML Report*, p. 72.

In some cases, the religion of the putative father was the issue. As one academic noted in 1996, in Northern Ireland 'the overall attitude of the Catholic and Protestant churches to one another has been negative, even antagonistic, and this has carried over into their views on mixed marriage'.[26] There was a 'long history' of a 'commitment to raise children of a mixed marriage in the Catholic faith' and after the papal *Ne Temere* degree of 1908 this became obligatory in any mixed marriage solemnised by a Catholic priest.[27] The impact of *Ne Temere* reduced mixed marriages in Ireland and subsequently Protestant and Catholic churches discouraged them. When they did occur both denominations were keen to 'retain allegiance' of members and ensure children from such marriages were brought up in their church.[28] In the records of the mother and baby institutions the statement 'father is a Protestant/Catholic' was effectively a statement that a marriage would not go ahead. One woman who entered Mater Dei in 1942 had been advised by her parish priest not to marry the Protestant father of her child. In another case from 1949 it was noted that the Protestant putative father 'thinks he might convert and marry her', but the woman's family 'would prevent it if they knew'.[29] A mixed marriage was considered a worse option than the shame of a child born outside marriage for many families.

For other women the putative father was already married, as in the case of a woman who entered Marianville in 1957 who had gone 'wrong with a married man – a Protestant'.[30] For others their pregnancy effectively ended the possibility that a marriage might occur, as their situation would bring shame to the families involved. Stark statements in the case notes remarked, 'marriage out of the question now' or 'no hope of marriage now'.[31] The young age of a number of girls who entered the institutions also precluded marriage. The youngest recorded admission was a 12-year-old girl in Marianville, Belfast. In Hopedene, 20.2% of those admitted, where age was recorded, were under the age of consent, which was raised to 17 in Northern Ireland in 1950. Across all the institutions, a significant proportion of those who were admitted were below the age of consent. However, there was limited discussion of this or the fact that a crime had been committed in the institutional records. In some cases, it was noted that women admitted to the institutions were pregnant as a result of sexual crime, including incest, rape or unlawful carnal knowledge and, occasionally, that the authorities were aware of this. In Hopedene in 1954 and 1964, two 13-year-old girls were admitted with references to ongoing court cases.[32] However, in other situations the references to incest raise questions as

26 Valerie Morgan et al., *Mixed marriages in Northern Ireland: institutional responses* (Coleraine: University of Ulster, 1996), Section 3. 27 Maria Luddy and Mary O'Dowd, *Marriage in Ireland, 1660–1925* (Cambridge, 2020), p. 47. 28 Ibid., p. 46; Morgan, *Mixed marriages*, Section 3. 29 *MBHML Report*, p. 166. 30 *MBHML Report*, p. 84. 31 *MBHML Report*, p. 86. 32 *MBHML Report*, p. 217.

to whether the authorities were as involved as they should have been. For example, the case notes of a 15-year-old girl in Marianvale, whose brother was the father of her baby, record how the family did not want Social Services involved as this would mean the police had to be notified. It was noted that Social Services had advised this would be the case, but it is unclear what action was taken.[33] In Marianville, two teenage girls, who arrived in 1952 and 1962 respectively, were both pregnant as a result of incest. Their case notes record they were subsequently 'confined' and 'sent' to the 'laundry'. This was the St Mary's Home, the Magdalene laundry, which was on the same site as Marianville and also operated by the Good Shepherd Sisters. This course of action was totally inappropriate in the cases of teenage victims of incest.[34] In these examples, innocent victims were held responsible and 'confined' as a result of sexual abuse they suffered. The men involved were very rarely condemned for their behaviour, even where criminal offences had taken place. Girls who had been abused by family members had their pregnancy recorded as 'father of baby was X's brother' or more shockingly, 'father/daughter union'.[35] Similar practices operated on both sides of the border and the final report of the COIMBH also identifies women who were in institutions as the result of rape and incest.[36] The institutionalising of victims of rape and incest had a long tradition as Sarah-Anne Buckley has shown and as Diarmaid Ferriter suggests, the 'incarceration' of those who had been sexually abused highlighted the 'degree to which the victims had to pay a heavy price, despite having been criminally wronged'.[37] Following the publication of the *MBHML Report,* the Police Service of Northern Ireland (PSNI) launched an 'investigation into allegations of possible criminality involving Mother and Baby Institutions, Magdalene Laundries and Workhouses'.[38] In January 2023 they had received over 80 reports.[39] While the nature of the reports or if they will lead to prosecutions is not known, the PSNI investigation, Truth Recovery Independent Panel and Public Inquiry, will undoubtedly lead to wider discussion of issues of abuse and sexual assault.

The process of admitting women and girls to the institutions involved a variety of people and organisations. The role of religious organisations and clergy, Protestant and Catholic, was of considerable importance in encouraging families to put their daughters in mother and baby institutions: around 50% of admissions to mother and baby institutions in Northern Ireland were referrals

33 *MBHML Report,* p. 70. 34 *MBHML Report,* p. 88. 35 *MBHML Report,* pp 88, 69. 36 *Final report of the COIMBH,* 8.70; 19. pp 171–80. 37 Sarah-Anne Buckley, *The cruelty man: child welfare, the NSPCC and the state in Ireland, 1889–1956* (Manchester, 2013), pp 162–5; Diarmaid Ferriter, *Occasions of sin: sex and society in modern Ireland* (London, 2009), p. 228. 38 https://www.psni.police.uk/safety-and-support/advice-and-information/investigation-mother-and-baby-institutions-workhouses, accessed 20 October 2022. 39 *Belfast Telegraph,* 2 January 2023.

from religious organisations and clergy.[40] It was often priests or ministers who explained the existence of the institutions to families, provided introductions and, on occasion, transported women to the institutions. All denominations were clear in their emphasis on moral standards and behaviour and within a society of high church attendance and adherence this encouraged and maintained a view that pregnancy outside marriage brought shame. For example, Cardinal MacRory's (Catholic archbishop of Armagh) 1931 Lenten Pastoral lamented the 'lowering of the moral tone' in which 'an increased number of young girls have brought shame and ruin on themselves, and shame and sorrow on their families'.[41] Clergy were also clear about the need for mother and baby institutions, as Revd McGonigle explained to the Church of Ireland Armagh Diocesan Synod in 1951 when discussing the work of Kennedy House: 'We clergy know just how often we have to fall back on the help of the House in these matters. It is a credit to the Church of Ireland and must be maintained'.[42]

General practitioners, often the first individuals to know about a pregnancy, made up around 11% of referrals and state welfare authorities around 23%.[43] The majority of women funded their stay through welfare benefits. Local authorities supported the operation of the mother and baby institutions by grants and other forms of funding. For the years before the late 1970s only fragmentary written evidence exists relating to statutory inspections of mother and baby institutions that should have taken place. While it is difficult to determine the involvement of the authorities in overseeing the institutions, they clearly provided a service that local and national authorities, across the island of Ireland, were content to support.

It is difficult to determine a great deal about the living conditions and experiences within the institutions from archival records themselves and it was the oral testimony of those who had been in the institutions that was crucial in providing detail. Many of the testimonies described cold and unsympathetic institutions where they were made to feel guilty about their situation.[44] Having to work, often carrying out cleaning and domestic tasks, right up to delivery dates, were also common across the institutions. Some women did offer more positive experiences, finding the institutions a safe place from their home environment.[45]

Unlike in the majority of mother and baby institutions in the Republic of Ireland, in Northern Ireland only Thorndale and Malone Place operated as maternity homes. In most cases women went to a local hospital or sometimes

40 *MBHML Report*, p. 24. **41** *Derry Journal*, 16 February 1931. **42** *Portadown News*, 20 October 1951. **43** *MBHML Report*, p. 24. **44** *MBHML Report*, p. 25. **45** A number of the oral testimonies can be found in full at https://quote.qub.ac.uk/mother-and-baby-homes-and-magdalene-laundries-oral-history-project/, accessed 30 November 2022.

a private nursing home to give birth. This experience of giving birth was described by many women as isolating and lonely. Women were unprepared for the experience of giving birth and were often made to feel ashamed of being unmarried.[46] Young women in the institutions were also particularly vulnerable to predatory sexual behaviour in relation to their medical care. Three separate women offered testimonies which made serious allegations about 'internal examinations' carried out by Sister Z in one of the Good Shepherd mother and baby institutions in the mid-1970s–early 1980s.[47] The oral testimonies also revealed the trauma and mental health issues women who spent time in the various institutions experienced. These issues are particularly prevalent among those whose babies were adopted. Many women felt they had not consented fully to the adoption process, were given no option on what should happen to their baby and had subsequently been hindered in their attempts to access their records.[48]

A major difference between mother and baby institutions across the island of Ireland was the longer periods of time women spent in the institutions in the Republic of Ireland. Moreover, a mother or child could remain in institutions there after the other party had left.[49] In Northern Ireland women in general entered institutions in their third trimester and spent only a short period of time there after giving birth. This was often around six weeks, which was the earliest point adoption consent papers could be signed legally. This regulation was introduced in the Adoption of Children Act (Northern Ireland) in 1950. Mothers did not generally remain in institutions without their babies, when a mother left so did a baby and vice versa. Across all the institutions in Northern Ireland 32% of babies left to be placed in baby or children's homes, 23% of babies were recorded as having been adopted and 15% were fostered. In 26% of cases, babies left with their mothers. It is not known if they stayed with their mother or were subsequently placed for adoption or put into care. Some babies remained with their mother outside of family support networks. In other cases they returned to family homes where, in some cases, babies were passed off as children of other family members.[50] This is something that occurred across the island of Ireland and as in the cases of women who migrated either before or after having a baby, we will never know the extent of these practices.[51]

The destinations for babies when they left the mother and baby institutions was one of the areas which was identified in the *MBHML Report* as needing further investigation. Some additional research was carried out on St Joseph's

46 *MBHML Report*, p. 26. 47 *MBHML Report*, p. 26. 48 *MBHML Report*, p. 25. 49 See for more on this *Final report of the COIMBH*, executive summary and chapters on specific institutions. 50 *MBHML Report*, p. 27. 51 Ferriter, *Occasions of sin*, pp 252–3, and p. 438.

Baby Home in Belfast, operated by the Sisters of Nazareth, which indicated concerning mortality rates.[52] In the 1920s, for example, death rates were particularly high with 50 babies dying in 1925, 46 in 1927 and 50 in 1928. As there were 298 recorded admissions to St Joseph's in those three years, these figures indicate one death for every two babies admitted.[53] As one of the major issues surrounding mother and baby institutions in the Republic of Ireland related to the high mortality rates of children, it is necessary that further work is carried out to determine the outcomes for babies who entered other institutions upon leaving mother and baby ones in Northern Ireland.

Similarly, the issue of cross-border movement and adoption of babies born in mother and baby institutions in Northern Ireland requires further research. Nearly 500 babies were identified as being moved across the border from four of the mother and baby institutions.[54] The real figure is undoubtedly higher as the calculations were based on specific references to cross-border movements within the records. In these cases, the largest number of babies were placed in a baby home in Fahan, Co. Donegal, run by the Sisters of Nazareth. A significant number were sent to the Sisters of Clare in Stamullen, Co. Meath. Smaller numbers went to a variety of institutions or were moved to families by adoption organisations in Dublin. There were also a number of babies taken across the border by individuals with addresses in the Republic, but it is not clear what, if any, relationship they had with the baby. This situation is further complicated by the fact that at least seven of the babies who went to Stamullen and Fahan were then adopted in the United States. The issues surrounding how this process operated are illustrated in the case of 'KO' who was born in Marianvale in Newry in the late 1960s and adopted through the adoption agency associated with Stamullen by an American couple. 'KO' has three birth certificates, issued in Northern Ireland, the Republic of Ireland and the US. The legality of these movements is questionable given that in the Republic of Ireland between the 1940s and 1970s there were 'hundreds if not thousands' of mostly 'illegitimate' children who were sent to the United States 'in illegal adoptions organised by Catholic Agencies'.[55] The MBHML researchers had no access to adoption records, and this is an area that will require further investigation to determine whether the correct legal procedures were followed in the cross-border movement of babies.

52 *MBHML Report,* chapter 17. See also research carried out by *The detail,* https://www.thedetail.tv/articles/lost-lives-the-43–babies-who-died-from-malnutrition, accessed 7 January 2022. 53 *MBHML Report,* pp 340–1. 54 *MBHML Report,* pp 30–1. 55 Buckley, *The cruelty man,* p. 32; see also Moira Maguire, 'Foreign adoptions and the evolution of Irish adoption policy, 1945–52', *Journal of Social History,* 36:2 (2002), pp 387–404; Mike Milotte, *Banished babies: the secret history of Ireland's baby export business* (Dublin, 1997).

In terms of the archival material for the MBHML report there were two major problems that needed to be overcome: access and time. With no powers to compel organisations and institutions to grant access to their records, the process of securing permissions was a delicate and protracted one. It was over six months into the project, for example, before permission was secured to examine the records of the Good Shepherd Sisters, which could only be accessed in the offices of their solicitor. For both the Good Shepherd records and the relevant records held by PRONI, as they are 'closed', the use of digital photography was forbidden. In the case of the Good Shepherd records, this along with the need to anonymise records meant information had to be recorded manually onsite. This slowed the process of gathering data and tightened the timeframe considerably. It also necessitated the sampling of data rather than the capturing of the full dataset.

In addition to the records relating to the institutions themselves, research was needed to be carried out on public records including those of local authorities across Northern Ireland and government departments and ministries such as, Labour, Commerce, Home Affairs, Health and Local Government, Health and Social Services and Cabinet records. The process of determining what records might be relevant, and the fact that in a series of records some might be open and some closed, made for slow and painstaking work. While the volume of records was overwhelming in some areas, it is also evident that many institutional records either no longer existed or were not made available to the researchers. When institutions closed, the records were vulnerable to loss and destruction. For example, records relating to Mater Dei, which had been used by a historian fifteen years ago, could not be located while the research for the MBHML report was being undertaken.[56]

Comparing the Good Shepherd records the COIMBH viewed for Dunboyne, Co. Meath, with what was provided for the Good Shepherd institutions in Northern Ireland there are marked differences. The COIMBH recorded over 2,000 scanned pages and in addition to notes on admissions and departures, there was extensive financial information, correspondence and internal documentation such as the Good Shepherd's Annals of the Convent and Chapter Books.[57] For Northern Ireland, the researchers were given admission records and very limited financial information. In relation to the mother and baby institutions, the financial details only covered a few years in the 1960s detailing payment plans for some women who were in Marianvale. No internal documentation relating to the operation of the Convent was provided.

56 Minute books relating to the Mater Dei home used by, Shepard, 'The legion of Mary'.
57 *Final report of the COIMBH*, chapter 24.

For Bethany Home in Dublin, a Protestant home operated on similar lines to Hopedene, minutes of the management committee were kept and held in the Church of Ireland Representative Church Body Library. However, no such records appear to exist for Hopedene.[58]

Of major concern to the research team was the condition of many of the records. With the exception of the material held in PRONI and the Salvation Army Heritage Centre in London, the records are not held in appropriate archival conditions. Those responsible for the records do not have the facilities necessary for the preservation of records. They are held variously in cardboard boxes in cupboards or in filing cabinets and are vulnerable to damage. Some of the records relating to Hopedene have already been lost in a fire. The Truth and Recovery Design Strategy Panel, which was set up after the publication of the *MBHML Report* and reported in October 2021, recommended 'immediate action' by the Northern Ireland Executive to 'create a statutory requirement on all relevant record holders to preserve and not destroy any information' relating to the various institutions. They also recommended legislation be progressed to establish 'a dedicated permanent independent repository of all personal and administrative records relating to historical practices within a range of social care institutions'.[59] Legislation relating to the preservation of documents relating to workhouses, Magdalene laundries and mother and baby institutions was passed in May 2022.[60] This makes it an offence to destroy, alter or remove records, and requires custodians to ensure they are not stolen, lost, destroyed or damaged. While the legislation is welcomed, it is problematic in that it does not indicate who is responsible for identifying the location of records or how it will be determined whether they have been destroyed or removed.

With the establishment of a Truth Recovery Independent Panel in April 2023 work has begun on identifying, locating and preserving records.[61] The Independent Panel will also record testimony in a non-adversarial way and will feed into a statutory public inquiry. A redress scheme is also being established, but it is evident that the lack of a functioning Northern Ireland Executive for extended periods has slowed down the overall process. It can only be hoped that for the more than 10,000 women who entered mother and baby institutions in Northern Ireland and for their children and families the future will bring truth, justice and redress.

58 *Final report of the COIMBH,* chapter 22. 59 Deirdre Mahon, Maeve O'Rourke and Phil Scraton, *Mother and baby institutions, Magdalene laundries and workhouses in Northern Ireland: truth, acknowledgement and accountability report for Northern Ireland Executive* (Belfast: Northern Ireland Executive, 2021), pp 15–17. 60 https://www.legislation.gov.uk/nia/2022/26/contents/enacted. 61 https: //truthrecoverystrategy.com/independent-panel/, accessed 21 November 2023.

CHAPTER 5

'The unmarried mothers in the institution are admirably dealt with': Sean Ross Abbey, 1931–69

Caitlín O'Neill and Jennifer Redmond

> Sean Ross mother and baby home opened in 1931 and closed in 1969. During that time, 6,414 women were admitted there and 6,079 children were born or admitted there. It was owned and run by the Congregation of the Sacred Hearts of Jesus and Mary. The public assistance/health authorities paid for the vast majority of the mothers and their children while they were living in Sean Ross but there were a small number of 'private' patients.[1]

> They actually tied me, because I was in pain, I thought I am going to die. They tied me down with some, I don't know, stuff to the bed. It was like the bed was on the floor because it was in case I fell out I suppose, I don't know, and it was absolutely horrific, but anyhow once it is over and I was told I suppose, this will teach you, offer it up for the sins you committed and all that. You felt that too, that that is why you got more pain maybe than maybe another one, you know. There were no painkillers in those days I don't think, I don't know whether there was.[2]

INTRODUCTION

The stark difference in the above quotations in tone and content about one mother and baby home, Sean Ross Abbey, exemplifies the competing narratives within the final report of the Commission of Investigation into Mother and Baby Homes and Certain Related Matters (hereafter, the Commission or COIMBH).[3] In many cases the voices of women did not feature or were not

1 Commission of Investigation into Mother and Baby Homes and Certain Related Matters (hereafter COIMBH), *Final report*, chapter 19, p. 1. The quote in the chapter title (cited in the same report, p. 9) is taken from 'Notes from the secretary of the North Tipperary Board of Health', May 1934. 2 Testimony of Resident A, COIMBH, *Final report*, chapter 19, p. 61. 3 The COIMBH was established in 2015. The chairperson was Judge Yvonne Murphy, with commissioners Professor Mary E. Daly and Dr William Duncan. The COIMBH produced seven

represented accurately in the report creating deep hurt among survivors and has led to several court cases to date. In a rare, frank insight into the birthing practices, 'Resident A', a rape survivor, recounted in her testimony the physical discomfort and the shame that imbued her experience. According to the Commission's report, 89.4% of women admitted to Sean Ross stayed and gave birth there.[4] While we do not know all of their stories, it is possible other women had similarly traumatic birthing experiences. The order in charge of Sean Ross, the Congregation of the Sacred Hearts of Jesus and Mary, was also singled out by the Commission in its fifth interim report for its apparent amnesia over its own practices in another infamous home it ran, Bessborough: 'The Commission finds it very difficult to understand that no member of the congregation was able to say where the children who died in Bessborough are buried'.[5] It seems when compassion and care were most needed, this order were found wanting, even by the COIMBH, which has been critiqued by many as being overly fair in its judgement of religious orders.

This chapter will use Sean Ross as a case study to explore the vista of mother and baby homes in Ireland and to compare the individual, lived experience with that reported in the official government investigation. There are just four women from Sean Ross whose testimony is included in the report in any way. While these women are not identified by name, one survivor of Sean Ross, Philomena Lee, took a case against the findings of the COIMBH. In December 2021 the Irish High Court determined the rights of survivors were breached when they were not given a draft of the final report of the Commission of Investigation into Mother and Baby Homes prior to its publication in January 2021, breaching the Commission of Investigation Act (2004) and denying them the opportunity to correct statements they have identified as erroneous.[6] Lee said this after the High Court's ruling:

> The commission's findings are deeply hurtful and troubling to me. Those findings deny what we lived. They deny the truth. I call on the government to denounce this report now, and to open up the commission's archive of documents to survivors and adopted people so that they can access information still withheld to this day. The secrecy and obstruction by State and church must end. It has gone on for far too long.[7]

interim reports, between 2016 and 2020. The final report was published in January 2021. 4 COIMBH, *Final report,* chapter 19A: Sean Ross statistical analysis, p. 7. A further 8.4% were admitted with their baby having given birth elsewhere and 2.2% of admissions left the home before giving birth. 5 COIMBH, *Fifth interim report,* p. 8. 6 *Philomena Lee and Mary Harney v. the Minister of Children, Equality, Disability, Integration and Youth.* As the Commission has been dissolved, the challenges were brought against the Minister for Children, the government, Ireland and the attorney general. 7 Philomena Lee's story inspired the book *The lost child of Philomena Lee* by

As Anne Enright commented, the Sacred Hearts have only opened their records 'on their own terms' leaving many more questions than answers.[8] Among a litany of errors, one was identified as the Sean Ross Chapter (paragraphs 19.195–19.203), putting Sean Ross at the centre of serious allegations of misrepresentation of the women's experiences. This led to a permanent statement detailing the errors found in a review of the report on the government website hosting the Commission's report and in the Oireachtas library.[9] Sean Ross is also one of the institutions that had its burial practices significantly investigated and the archaeological reports on graveyards are contained in the COIMBH final report.[10]

MOTHER AND BABY HOMES IN IRELAND: A CARCERAL VISTA

Magdalene laundries and mother and baby homes are often confused, as although they are similar, they were not the same. Magdalene laundries were institutions for women who had affronted Irish society. They mostly, but did not always, have a commercial laundry attached to them and beyond infancy, children were not allowed in these institutions. Mother and baby homes were institutions for both unmarried mothers and their children. Mother and baby homes were not, as many believe, an exclusively catholic, twentieth-century phenomenon. The first institution established was the Leeson Street Magdalen Asylum, in 1765, a protestant philanthropic endeavour initiated by Lady Arabella Denny as a rehabilitative asylum for women. Despite the common rule of a two-year stay, Redmond uncovered that by 1919 women in the Leeson Street Asylum stayed just six months on average.[11] Between 1765 and 1918, only two mother and baby homes were established, however between 1919 and 1940 an additional eight were founded.[12] Mother and baby homes were not uniquely Irish as they appeared in a range of countries, for example, Kunzel stated women in the

Martin Sixsmith (London, 2010) and the movie, *Philomena* (2013). Lee quoted in O'Riordan, 'Rights of eight mother and baby home survivors breached'. **8** Anne Enright, 'Antigone in Galway: Anne Enright on the dishonoured dead' in Katherine O'Donnell, Maeve O'Rourke and James M. Smith (eds), *Redress: Ireland's institutions and transitional justice* (Dublin, 2022), p. 28. **9** Statement available on Irish government website here: https://www.gov.ie/en/press-release/b981a-settlement-of-applications-for-judicial-review-of-final-report-of-commission-of-investigation-into-mother-and-baby-homes/, accessed 9 March 2022. **10** The COIMBH fifth interim report also stated: 'There is no evidence that any record of burials was kept by the Congregation of the Sacred Hearts of Jesus and Mary in respect of burials in Castlepollard and Sean Ross' despite a canon law requirement (p. 7). Furthermore, there is no certainty where children in these institutions were buried (p. 8). **11** Jennifer Redmond, *Moving histories: Irish women's emigration to England, from independence to republic* (Liverpool, 2018), p. 106. **12** COIMBH, *Final report*, executive summary, pp 25–41.

United States were subjected to 'benevolent incarceration' in maternity homes in a similar time period.[13] However, Ireland likely admitted more unmarried mothers to these institutions than anywhere else in the world.[14] These institutions operated alongside County Homes which grew out of the workhouse system and continued to 'play the largest role in the institutionalisation of unmarried mothers throughout the 1930s, 1940s, and 1950s'.[15]

SEAN ROSS, THE SACRED HEARTS AND THE STATE

The Sisters of the Sacred Heart of Jesus and Mary (hereafter Sacred Hearts), ran three mother and baby homes in Ireland: Sean Ross Abbey, Bessborough, and Castlepollard.[16] They are described by the COIMBH as 'extern institutions' as 'they were not owned by the local health authorities but the local authorities could send people who were eligible for services to them. The local health authorities who sent mothers to these homes paid a capitation rate in respect of each resident'.[17] In 1929, the Department of Health asked Mother Laurence to establish their second mother and baby home in Ireland.[18] The COIMBH *Final report* states the Mother General of the congregation along with Mrs Croft, a senior inspector from the Department of Local Government and Public Health visited 'several dioceses and spoke with several bishops' about establishing a new home.[19] The congregation's original idea was to set up a mother and baby home in Dublin, but Archbishop Byrne of Dublin would not allow it, an example of the power held by the hierarchy of the Church in twentieth-century Ireland. When an estate in Roscrea came on the market in the early twentieth century, it was seen as an ideal second choice for the Sacred Hearts' plans. This may seem like an insignificant detail, but it is important to understand the state's role in these homes – they were not passively providing funding to an institution out of their control but rather they played a fundamental role in Sean Ross from its very establishment. Sean Ross, like the

13 Regina G. Kunzel, *Fallen women, problem girls: unmarried mothers and the professionalisation of social work, 1890–1945* (New Haven, 1993), p. 92. 14 COIMBH, *Final report*, executive summary, p. 12. 15 Lindsey Earner-Byrne, *Mother and child: maternity and child welfare in Dublin, 1922–60* (Manchester, 2007), p. 183. 16 Bessborough operated between 1919 and 1998, Sean Ross from 1931 to 1969, Castlepollard 1935 to 1971, COIMBH, *Final report*, executive summary, pp 28–31. This religious house at Roscrea started life in Ireland as the Brigidines but were accepted into the Sacred Hearts in 1842 when the latter order needed additional support to staff a school founded in Roscrea in 1823. See Micheál Breathnach, 'A notable centenary II', *The Irish Monthly*, 827 (1942). 17 COIMBH, *Fifth interim report*, paragraph 3.1, p. 22. 18 Rosemary Clerkin, *A heart for others*, p. 86. Available at http://www.sacredheartsjm. org/sites/default/files/documents/A%20Heart%20for%20Others%2C%20R.%20Clerkin.pdf (15 March 2024). 19 COIMBH, *Final report*, chapter 19, p. 4.

other mother and baby homes, was different from the County Home as women from all over Ireland could be sent to the former. This worked to the advantage of some unmarried mothers as they could gain a sense of anonymity by being sent far from their homes. It also shows how these homes were viewed, not as a provision for county poor relief, but closer to a national moral rehabilitation facility for destitute unmarried mothers. Despite this, there were limitations on what 'kind' of mother could be admitted to Sean Ross. For example, the Clare BOH (Board of Health) considered sending unmarried mothers who fell pregnant more than once because they were 'a dangerous type to have roaming through the country'; this request was not granted.[20]

The refusal to admit women who fell pregnant more than once outside of marriage is in line with Sean Lucey's assessment that '"repeat offenders" were viewed as the most problematic and subject to the harshest attitudes.'[21] This contempt is evident among those BOH officials but they also admitted they did not have the 'legal power' to detain.[22] This does not seem to have been widely understood by the women who found themselves admitted to Sean Ross or other mother and baby homes, although in fact there were no laws introduced which allowed local authorities to incarcerate unmarried mothers. Instead, the Clare BOH concluded they could detain mothers through 'obligations on the inmate are that she must take her child with her, and that prevents a number of them from going out'.[23] This grey area created between legislation and social obligations was used against unmarried mothers which, as James Smith has argued, contributed to the architecture of containment in Ireland.[24] Realistically, without any support from family or the state, there were few options for women who found themselves in an institution like Sean Ross.

The Irish Free State played a significant role in promoting institutions such as Sean Ross. This can be seen in a Dáil debate on 1 May 1930, when Richard Mulcahy was Minister at the Department of Local Government and Public Health (DLGPH). In this debate, Prof. James Craig claimed 'their parents in many cases do not want to have them back in their homes', a clear explanation as to how so many unmarried mothers became destitute. Cumann na nGaedheal's Patrick Walter Shaw believed that although it was 'an unpleasant subject' the current County Home system left 'very little hope for their reformation' due to the mixing of first-time unmarried mothers with 'professional bad characters', an allusion to prostitution Luddy has explored in

20 'Clare Board of Health to send children to Sean Ross Abbey', *Nenagh Guardian*, 5 March 1932. 21 Donnacha Sean Lucey, *The end of the Irish poor law? Welfare and healthcare reform in revolutionary and independent Ireland* (Manchester, 2015), p. 86. 22 'Clare Board of Health to send children to Sean Ross Abbey', *Nenagh Guardian*, 5 March 1932. 23 Ibid. 24 James M. Smith, *Ireland's Magdalen laundries and the nation's architecture of containment* (Indiana, 2007), p. 54.

detail.[25] Institutions like Sean Ross absolved the government from dealing with the 'unpleasant subject'. Tipperary's *The Nationalist* noted in 1931 the minister at the DLGPH asked for the women to be transferred from Tipperary's County Home to Sean Ross 'at once'.[26] Yet despite this promotion of Sean Ross, which was not a state-run institution, there are no inspection reports to be found for the home until 1944, a full ten years after the Maternity Home Act was passed which gave the state the authority to carry out inspections.[27] It could be argued that state support for these homes was strong because of their devotion and trust in the Catholic Church, and their simultaneous disregard for women who had transgressed the social norms. Tom Inglis has argued, 'the distinctive combination of religious orthodoxy, family-based production, and the Church's unrivalled prestige and legitimacy, resulted in the goals of state policy being by and large those of the Church'.[28] Or as Beatty has framed it, 'it is rarely clear where the church ends and the state begins in modern Ireland'.[29] It is also worth noting the clear absence of any discourse around paternal obligation. Ann-Marie Graham argued 'the putative fathers were generally forgotten about and rarely required to confront their responsibilities'.[30] This is because, as Maria Luddy has concluded, throughout most of the twentieth century 'the church and the state made the mother primarily responsible for the maintenance of her child'.[31]

The controversial Illegitimate Children (Affiliation Orders) Act of 1930 did little to redress the imbalance. Although purportedly designed to create an obligation for the father 'to contribute to the support or otherwise in respect of such child and for the enforcement of such obligation', *The Bell* reported in 1941 that only 'in 2 out of 200 cases before the courts over a certain period was paternity successfully established – and the man solvent'.[32] Throughout the 1930s, at least three Affiliation Orders were brought to court by local authorities on behalf of women in Sean Ross, and, unsurprisingly, all were dismissed. In July 1933 the South Tipperary BOH attempted to get an order made against a man on behalf of a woman in the institution and her baby. This case had two witnesses who saw the pair 'keeping company' on multiple occasions, but the

25 Dáil Éireann debate – Thursday, 1 May 1930 – In Committee on Finance. – Vote 40 – Office of the Minister for Local Government and Public Health (Resumed), [1327] (https://www.oireachtas.ie/en/debates/debate/dail/1930–05–01/10/). See also Luddy, 'Moral rescue and unmarried mothers'. 26 'Unmarried mothers', *The Nationalist*, 22 July 1931. 27 COIMBH, *Final report*, chapter 19, p. 20. 28 Tom Inglis, *Moral monopoly: the rise and fall of the Catholic Church in modern Ireland* (Dublin, 1998), pp 254–5. 29 Aidan Beatty, 'The strange career of R.S. Devane', available at https://aidanbeatty.com/2017/03/29/the-strange-career-of-r-s-devane/ (15 March 2024). 30 Graham, 'Unmarried mothers', p. 14. 31 Luddy, 'Unmarried mothers in Ireland', p. 110. 32 Illegitimate Children (Affiliation Orders) Act, Minister for Justice, 17 June 1930, http://www.irishstatutebook.ie/eli/1930/act/17/enacted/en/print and Diarmaid Ferriter, *Occasions of sin: sex and society in modern Ireland* (London, 2009), p. 271.

Judge believed 'disaster might befall a defendant' if he were to rule in favour of the BOH.[33] The judge's words imply concern over damaging the father's reputation and that this, therefore, was too grave a decision to make. Hence, despite the Act's intention to force the fathers of illegitimate children to take responsibility, it was very difficult for a woman to prove and successfully force a man to provide maintenance, even when the case was taken by a local authority.

Over Sean Ross Abbey's 38-year span, 6,414 women were admitted and a further 6,079 children were either born or admitted there.[34] There were more women than babies admitted/born in Sean Ross, therefore some women must have been admitted for reasons other than pregnancy. Sean Ross, began accepting expectant mothers in 1931 and did not cease until 1969.[35] The Sacred Hearts admitted 21,154 into the three homes along with 19,576 children during the course of running the three institutions.[36] Sean Ross was the second largest of the Sacred Heart homes, with more admissions than Castlepollard but less than Bessborough.

At a Clare Board of Health (BOH) meeting in 1931, a proposal was presented by a board member on opening a mother and baby home in Roscrea. This discussion arose due to the poor state of repair of the County Nursery. The move had the additional advantage of saving the ratepayer 3 shillings per week for the care of each unmarried mother and their child, reducing the cost from 24 shillings to 21 shillings. According to the officials present, opening this home would provide 'hope for prevention of a recurrence of the disease'; the disease referred to was illegitimate children.[37] The testimony from the meeting is loaded with judgement about unmarried mothers, with Roscrea being touted as a beacon of hope for those that wished to embrace the training: 'The idea of the training at Roscrea is to bring out the best that is in the patient. It is certainly worthy of an experiment and if we succeed in saving only one of these unfortunate creatures it would be worth a great deal'.[38]

Finances appear to have been at the forefront of minds at the establishment of Sean Ross and an analysis of state support for the order reveals a significant financial investment in their work, without proper oversight. Figure 5.1 displays the capitation grants awarded from local authorities for the women in Sean Ross for each decade, from its opening to its closing, an estimated £327,814.9 or a modern equivalent of several million euro.[39] This is in conjunction with other grants received, worth £48,164, also worth exponentially more in today's figures.[40]

33 'Decision in affiliation order application', *Nenagh Guardian*, 29 July 1933. 34 COIMBH, *Final report*, executive summary, p. 12. 35 Ibid. 36 Ibid. 37 'Sean Ross Abbey an advantage', *Nenagh Guardian*, 7 November 1931. Recorded testimony of Mr O'Grady. 38 Ibid. 39 CPI inflation calculator – Central Statistics Office (https://www.cso.ie/en/interactivezone/visualisationtools/cpiinflationcalculator/) (22 March 2021).

Figure 5.1 Total amount of capitation grants given to Sean Ross Abbey, 1930s–1960s.

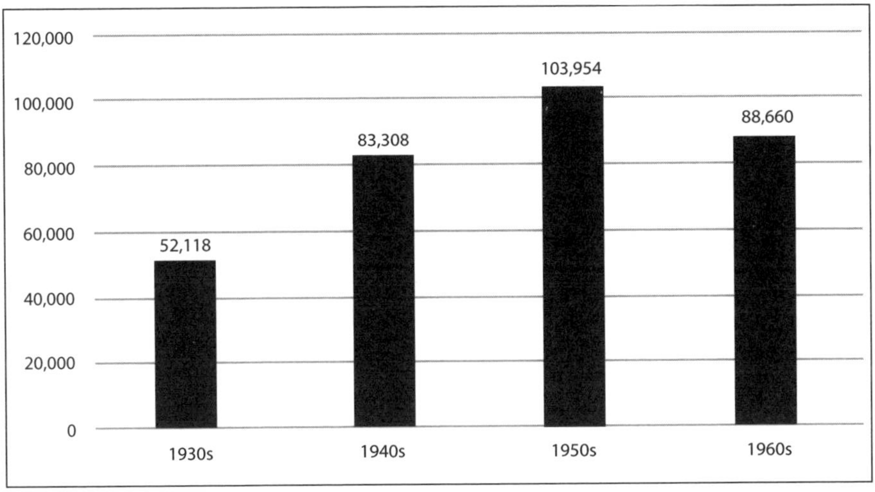

Source: COIMBH, *Final report*, chapter 19B, p. 5, graph 1.

It is disputed as to whether the Sacred Hearts were also receiving donations in exchange for arranging adoptions, but even if this is not true, they were most likely receiving general charitable donations and bequests. 'Resident C' stated she was once asked to count money with Sister Winifred as it was being transferred from biscuit tins into a new safe. In her own words, she described the contents of the tins: 'All notes. Money I had never seen before which looked like dollars [...] She finally counted it and then it was registered in the book ... I mean but there was quite a lot of tins'.[41] This could have been a collection of money from general donations from America, or solicited for adoptions, it is impossible to state for certain, but there was enough money on site to justify purchasing a safe. Another example of money garnered by the order is heartbreaking: as 'Resident C' remembered, she 'bought clothes for her baby for the day that she would leave the home' but was subsequently informed her baby 'was in a nappy and blanket' when received at her adoptive home.[42] 'Resident C' believes the nuns resold the same set of baby clothes to the women for their children. Furthermore, 'Resident C''s daughter stated her adoptive mother 'got letters regularly from them [the congregation] asking by the way how they were and how was the baby and she always sent a donation'.[43] 'Resident D''s son was adopted to America and she was informed by his adoptive sister and another

40 Ibid. 41 COIMBH, *Final report*, chapter 19, p. 64. 42 Ibid. 43 Ibid. A thorough analysis of adoption practices, including the critical issue of consent, is beyond the scope of this chapter but is alluded to throughout the COIMBH report. Women in Sean Ross and other institutions

person 'that the American couple that adopted her baby paid a significant sum of money to Sean Ross Abbey' and annual sums after this.[44] The allegation that a 'donation' was required before an adoption was reported by women in many different mother and baby homes throughout Ireland, not just in Sean Ross.[45]

Despite a lack of documentary sources, there is oral evidence from the congregation that donations received were sizable. Sister Hildegarde told a social worker in 1995 that:

> donations coming back from American adopters had constituted the largest single source of income for Sean Ross Abbey in the period when the adoptions were in full swing. She also admitted to removing and destroying documents from individual adoption files which related to these American payments.[46]

This interview was not included in the COIMBH findings; perhaps if it had been, it could have given further credibility to survivors who firmly believe the adoption of their children resulted in monetary gain for the congregation. Even if the COIMBH did not wish to include a second-hand interview it is significant the nun in charge of adoptions admitted to destroying files. The neutral judgement of the COIMBH is based on a discounting of direct oral evidence given to them and other similar sources and a lack of documentary material, an attitude prevalent throughout the report as illustrated by the following quote: 'She ['Resident B'] said that she never actually saw any couple handing money over to adopt a child from Sean Ross and that she had "no evidence whatsoever" that this happened but believes that this was a regular occurrence'.[47] 'Resident B' testified married couples came to the orphanage and chose children to adopt, estimated the fee charged to US couples and quoted an 'exit fee' amount (more below) for her to leave, yet because she did not have receipts her testimony was discounted.[48]

have repeatedly claimed they did not consent to adoptions and were not made aware of the full import or contents of documents they were required to sign. 44 Ibid., p. 67. 45 Ibid. 46 This interview with Sister Hildegarde by a social worker is quoted in Milotte, *Banished babies*, p. 137. 47 COIMBH, *Final report*, chapter 19, p. 63. 48 The Commission made this comment which is indicative of the attitude taken to survivor testimony: 'The Commission has no doubt that the witnesses recounted their experiences as honestly as possible. However, the Commission does have concerns about the contamination of some evidence. A number of witnesses gave evidence that was clearly incorrect. This contamination probably occurred because of meetings with other residents and inaccurate media coverage', ibid., p. 12. Yet a few pages earlier, this is stated: 'As is clear from the report, many witnesses had never discussed their experiences with any other person; this included witnesses who had not told family members such as their husbands and/or their other (now adult) children' (p. 9). A total of 550 people gave evidence to

All of this is important to consider when examining the history of Sean Ross Abbey because the COIMBH *Final report* alleges 'At various times, it is clear that they [the congregation] struggled to make ends meet and their members were not always paid for their work',[49] that they were late in payments and rates were 'not overly generous'.[50] It is unclear if they are referring to nuns or supplementary staff. When Sean Ross opened in 1931, they had on-site a dairy and poultry farm, and a bakery, all of which they intended for the women to work in for educational purposes.[51] In addition, Sean Ross had a commercial laundry which has led to confusion over whether Sean Ross was a mother and baby home, or a Magdalene laundry but although the women were obligated to work in the laundry it is still categorised as a mother and baby home. Claims have been made that profit was gained from these enterprises, as alleged by Philomena Lee, that the order took in laundry from 'the town of Roscrea and surrounding villages, hospitals, and state boarding schools'.[52] Therefore, the financial usefulness of women to the order should not be underestimated and may be the reason why the home 'was already crowded' a few months after opening.[53] It also explains why objections were made by the Matron of the County Nursery, Kilrush, in 1931 to moving five unmarried mothers to Sean Ross as they would have to be replaced by five paid employees.[54] Such overcrowding was part of the experiences of women at Sean Ross which will be examined next.

'A LESSON TO THEM NOT TO COME AGAIN': THE TREATMENT AND EXPERIENCES OF WOMEN IN SEAN ROSS ABBEY

The four women quoted in the COIMBH report who resided at Sean Ross all recounted being given an alternate name to go by, working in various roles, living in dormitories or in close quarters with other women and witnessing distressing scenes such as women handing over children. Food is recounted as scarce or of poor quality.[55] 'Resident C' reported having her incoming and outgoing letters censored and when caught complaining about the food, 'one of the nuns read her letter in the dining room and then made her eat it'.[56] 'Resident D' stated on one occasion she was forced to 'go down on my knees' to publicly apologise to

the Confidential Committee with a further nineteen giving evidence to the Commission directly.
49 COIMBH, *Final report*, chapter 25, p. 2. 50 COIMBH, *Final report*, executive summary, p. 12. 51 COIMBH, *Final report*, chapter 19, p. 9. 52 Sixsmith, *The lost child of Philomena Lee*, p. 25. 53 COIMBH, *Final report*, chapter 19, p. 5. 54 Ibid. 55 This finding is also asserted more widely in the report of the Confidential Committee. COIMBH, *Final report, confidential committee*, p. 45. 56 COIMBH, *Final report*, chapter 19, p. 64.

a nun. This was 'just another part of the humiliation and shame' she was subjected to every day. The nuns constantly reminded her she had 'committed a mortal sin' and 'her shame would be eternal'.[57] The Confidential Committee confirmed the ubiquity of such behaviour by the religious:

> Witnesses reported being called 'sinners' 'dirt' 'spawn of Satan' or worse. They related similar, sometimes identical stories from time spent in institutions where the type of work and living conditions, although based throughout the country in widely spaced geographical locations, seemed to be the same.[58]

The Commission acknowledged that 'little kindness was shown' to the women, going on to explain that 'large institutions were regimented and they were inadequately staffed until the later decades'.[59] Would more staff have meant an increase in compassion? It seems doubtful.

Demographic data is unavailable for all women admitted to Sean Ross, but for a third of women (2,071) we know spent time there, 82.5% were domestic servants or unskilled workers.[60] Aside from this, 9% of women were working in the home or on a farm, 6% were employed as a civil servant/teacher, and there was 1% described as unemployed or a full-time student.[61] The COIMBH noted 721 women as private patients, representing 11.2% of all admissions appearing from 1933, although their numbers increased dramatically in the early 1960s.[62] This profile suggests the vast majority had little resources and came from lower socio-economic backgrounds.

The average age of women admitted to Sean Ross was 22 years old, with the oldest being a 52-year-old woman; however the records also show the youngest was 12 years old, with a quarter of the cohort being 18 and under, evidence of an alarming rate of assault against minors.[63] 'Resident A' was 15 in the mid-1950s when admitted and described the circumstances of her pregnancy: 'There was two lads and they pulled me into the bushes and whatever happened, it happened, and I didn't even know that that is where babies come from or anything. So, I didn't know. It was rape I suppose you would call it'.[64] This case illustrates that even if sexual assault was acknowledged it did not 'excuse' the pregnancy, the girl was still cast out from the family home and wider community. 'Resident A' also assumed 'she would be in Sean Ross for her whole life', thus proving the point, made by Earner-Byrne, that 'in the absence of

57 Ibid., p. 66. 58 COIMBH, *Final report, confidential committee*, p. 42. 59 COIMBH, executive summary, p. 5. 60 COIMBH, *Final report*, chapter 19B, p. 12. 61 Ibid. 62 COIMBH, *Final report*, chapter 19A, p. 3. 63 Ibid., p. 10. 64 Ibid., chapter 19, p. 59.

Figure 5.2 Age of women on admission to Sean Ross (N=6,414)

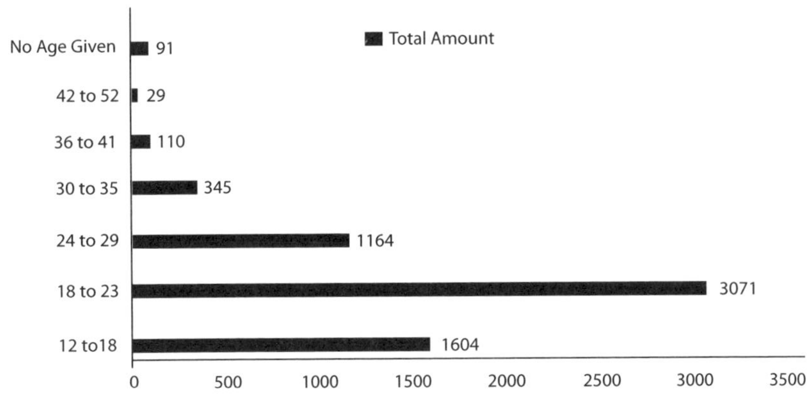

	12 to 18	18 to 23	24 to 29	30 to 35	36 to 41	42 to 52	No Age Given
Percentage of overall	25.08%	47.88%	18.15%	5.38%	1.71%	0.45%	1.45%
Total Amount	1604	3071	1164	345	110	29	91

Source: COIMBH, *Final report,* chapter 19A, p. 10, Graph. 1.

policy guidelines and legal safeguards, unmarried mothers were literally at the mercy of society, the County Home or the religious mother'.[65] 'Resident B' was assisted to enter Sean Ross by an aunt she was living with when her pregnancy at the age of 21 was discovered at seven months.[66] Interestingly, 'Resident B' preferred her time in Sean Ross to that at her aunt's home where she had been 'treated as slave labour'.[67] 'Resident C''s admission was arranged by the Catholic Protection and Rescue Society of Ireland who also arranged the adoption of her baby, despite the existence of the Order's own Sacred Heart Adoption Society. The COIMBH *Final report* found 'several instances of women turning up unannounced at Sean Ross or another of the special homes, having been dispatched there by an English Catholic charity', illustrating the well documented connection between migration and unplanned pregnancy in modern Ireland.[68] For 'Resident D', a family member took her 'to a doctor who recommended that she be admitted to Sean Ross'.[69] This nexus of medical, religious, familial,

65 Earner-Byrne, *Mother and child,* p. 190. 66 COIMBH, *Final report,* chapter 19, p. 62. 67 Ibid. 68 COIMBH, *Final report,* chapter 7, p. 5. For more on the connection between migration and unmarried motherhood see Jennifer Redmond, 'In the family way and away from the family: examining the evidence for Irish unmarried mothers in Britain, 1920s–40s' in Elaine Farrell (ed.), *'She said she was in the family way': pregnancy and infancy in modern Ireland* (London, 2012), pp 163–86. 69 COIMBH, *Final report,* chapter 19, p. 65.

Figure 5.3 Average length of stay per decade for public patients at Sean Ross (N=6,322)

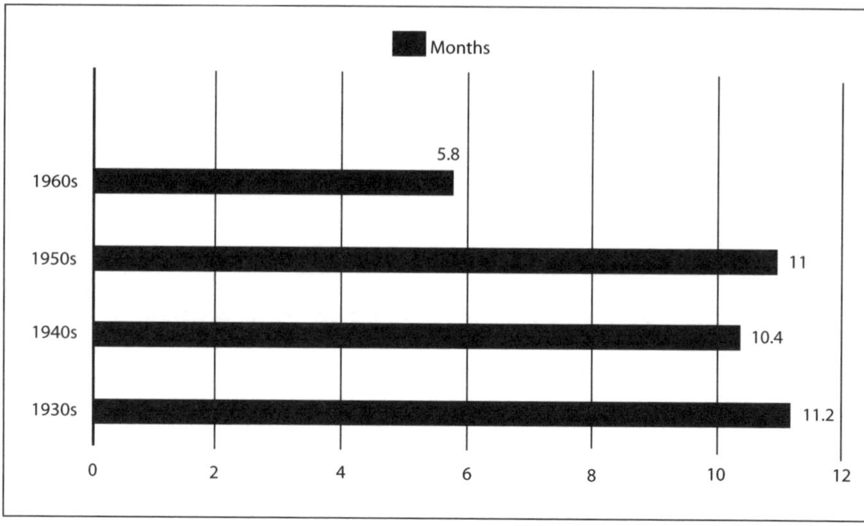

Source: Data derived from COIMBH, *Final report,* chapter 19A, p. 9.

charitable and social work organisations and individuals demonstrates there were many routes into Sean Ross (and other similar institutions) without clear paths to exit. As Paul Michael Garret has suggested: 'Although nuns were in charge of the day-to-day management of the establishments, it was men, particularly those laden with "symbolic capital" such as priests and doctors, who referred women to the homes and acted as gate-keepers'.[70]

Once in the institution, the length of stay appears to have varied, although overall it reduced over the decades of the institution's operation and was found to be shorter for private rather than public residents, an unsurprising finding when resources and external supports are considered.[71] By the 1960s just 3% of privately funded women spent more than two years in the home.[72] In contrast, publicly funded women stayed an average of 150 days in the same decade, itself a decrease from 298 days average stay in the 1950s.[73] Privately funded women also

70 Paul Michael Garrett, 'Excavating the past: mother and baby homes in the Republic of Ireland', *British Journal of Social Work,* 47(2), pp 358–74, at p. 363. 71 One peculiarity of the data presented in the chart ('Sean Ross mother's length of stay after birth', chapter 19A, p. 9) is that the categories are titled 'A to 'F', but 'E' is absent. This may have been a typo, but it may indicate that there was previously another category that possibly narrowed the final category which simply states 'over 700 days'. Having this information would be a huge benefit in understanding the extent of power held by the religious orders over the lives of women in their care. 72 COIMBH *Final report,* chapter 19A, p. 9. 73 Ibid., p. 8.

reported more positive experiences of the conditions as noted in the report of the Confidential Committee: 'Their stays in mother and baby homes (while being far from luxurious or easy) were by all accounts less punishment prone or humiliating than those whose families could not pay and found themselves in the front line of fire'.[74] As Figure 5.3 shows, between the 1930s and 1960s the period of incarceration almost halved on average for public patients.

'Resident B' claimed she could have left Sean Ross immediately if she had paid the sum of £105 but she appears to have wanted to stay in an attempt to keep her baby; unfortunately this plan did not work out because of her boyfriend's reluctance to claim her and the child, and the baby was subsequently adopted locally.[75] The exit paths reveal a variety of experiences, with most returning home but some experiencing further institutionalisation:

> Information relating to exit pathways from Sean Ross was available for 5,857 women (91.3% of admissions). Institutional records show that most women (69.8%) returned home or were discharged to a private address; 21.85% were discharged to employment; 4.46% transferred to hospital; 1.88% were discharged to a Magdalen Laundry; 1.45% were placed in situations by the Congregation of the Sacred Hearts and 0.44% transferred to another institution under the Commission's remit (generally Kilkenny County Home).[76]

Even those placed in 'situations' by the order were within the power of religious and not entirely free. The situation for some women appears to have improved over time: 'in 1951 around one in ten women were discharged directly to employment; by 1969 over one in seven were discharged in this manner' and 54% of women who returned to the family home in this period took their babies with them.[77] What stories were told about these children is undetermined, but it is hoped some comfort was gained by keeping them within the family. However, this is not to forget the 46% of women who returned to the family home while their babies remained in Sean Ross. In 1951 the average stay for children born/admitted that year was 367 days which declined to 44 days on average for children born/admitted in 1969 and, unsurprisingly, children funded privately 'spent considerably less time in the home than children born to public patients'.[78] Unfortunately, 1,090 children born in or admitted to Sean Ross died

74 COIMBH, *Final report, confidential committee report*, p. 45. 75 COIMBH, *Final report*, chapter 19, p. 63. 76 COIMBH, *Final report*, chapter 19A, p. 14. 77 Ibid., p. 15. 78 Ibid., p. 20.

in infancy or early childhood.[79] Twenty-seven women are recorded as dying in Sean Ross according to the Commission's report, two of whom were buried in the children's graveyard.[80]

CONCLUSION

Women from every single county in Ireland (including from Northern Ireland with the exception of Derry) were admitted to Sean Ross over its near forty-year operation, thus it is an important case study to consider in examining histories of abusive practices towards unmarried mothers on the island of Ireland.[81] The ongoing legal cases associated with the COIMBH report attest to the discrepancies between survivor's experiences and the official record produced by the government inquiry, which in many cases ignored testimony or failed to regard it as seriously as documentary evidence produced by the state and the institutions. Some of these cases relate to Sean Ross. Interestingly, among the limited number of direct quotations given from personal testimony (as opposed to third person narratives based on oral evidence) is the one included at the outset of this chapter from a Sean Ross survivor. It is one of the most damning pieces of evidence in the report as to the inhumane treatment of young women giving birth in such institutions. It is unclear why this quote, and not others, was chosen as meeting an undefined threshold of belief by the COIMBH to be regarded worthy of inclusion, but if the occurrence was replicated even once in testimony by other women it suggests a truly horrifying birth experience for vulnerable women in modern Ireland. This is not to excuse the harsh societal attitudes that condoned confining women to these institutions. As one woman interviewed by Sharon Lambert noted, 'If a girl has a child and she wasn't married they treated her worse than if she had took a gun and murdered half a dozen people'.[82]

The discrediting tone of the Commission towards oral evidence, even when it is presented multiple times by women in different institutions who may never have met each other, is hard to fathom. It is also in direct contrast to the 'central place' testimony from sixty survivors is given in the comparative report into

79 Ibid., p. 25. **80** COIMBH, *Final report, forensic archaeological investigations at Sean Ross Abbey, mother and baby home children's burial ground*, p. 91. **81** There is no reason provided as to why Derry was the exception. However, the other counties in Northern Ireland had extremely low rates of admission: Down (0.11%), Antrim (0.05%), Fermanagh (0.05%), Tyrone (0.03%) and Armagh (0.02%). COIMBH, *Final report*, chapter 19A, p. 13. **82** Sharon Lambert, 'Irish women's emigration to England, 1922–1960: the lengthening of family ties' in Alan Hayes and Diane Urquhart (eds), *Irish women's history reader* (Dublin, 2004), pp 152–67, p. 156.

institutions for unmarried mothers in Northern Ireland.[83] The COIMBH conclusion on money obtained for adoptions is a classic example of the primacy given to documentary evidence and the dismissal of oral testimony:

> A number of witnesses spoke about donations they believed were sent by their adoptive parents following on from their USA adoption. Again, no concrete evidence was provided. Such donations would not have been illegal and could not be described as unethical unless the adoptive parents were trying to adopt another child.[84]

The Commission referred to the expense of inter-country adoption and does not clarify why it would be unethical to donate in relation to the adoption of a second child. It clearly believes the lack of documentary evidence is proof of some kind that adoption fees *were not* charged, but the sworn testimony of an unidentified number of witnesses is not to be trusted. It is this kind of commentary that has drawn much ire towards the COIMBH's findings.[85]

Upon the vindication of claims by survivors Philomena Lee and Mary Harney that the Commission had breached legal procedures and inaccurately represented survivor testimony in 2021, Mary Harney has claimed: 'This time our voices have been heard in terms of justice'.[86] Despite ongoing issues related to the state's legislative response to the report, it can only be hoped the voices of survivors continue to be heard.

83 Leanne McCormick, Sean O'Connell, Olivia Dee and John Privilege, *Report into mother and baby homes and Magdalene laundries in Northern Ireland, 1922–1990* (Belfast: Department of Health NI, 2021). 84 COIMBH, *Final report,* chapter 32, p. 137. 85 This is referred to in multiple media reports as well as O'Donnell et al., *Redress,* p. xiv. 86 O'Riordan, 'Rights of eight mother and baby home survivors breached'.

SECTION THREE

THE POLITICS OF BODIES

CHAPTER 6

'Terrible risks to soul and body': the sexual politics of female emigrant bodies

Jennifer Redmond

> In a nation seeking to define and assert its own unique voice, sexuality was an unmentionable subject that lurked beneath every conversation. In a society preoccupied with establishing and maintaining order, sexuality constituted a principle of chaos.[1]

Historians of modern Ireland have argued that sexual behaviour and its regulation became a national obsession post-independence in an effort to prove decency, respectability and capability as hallmarks of an independence. In Howes' analysis above, sexual matters were 'lurking' within discourses ostensibly outside sexual matters. What was lurking, however, was proscribed according to the mores of the time and rooted in a Catholic analysis of the situation in Ireland, one that conceived only of heterosexual relations; there was little public commentary or censure of lesbian relationships, for example, so far were they outside the norms of post-independent Ireland.[2] Hill has pointed to the difficulty in identifying same-sex relationships in the past, given the public censure on openly discussing 'female sexual identity in even a general way', and our evidence from literature and the archives suggests those in homosexual relationships may have felt 'that they could not publicly acknowledge them'.[3] Although this may seem like an obvious point, it is important to acknowledge so as not to simply replicate the discourses in which same-sex relationships have been silenced. The point is to highlight the limits of contemporary discourses – moral concern was directed at 'illicit' sexual behaviour by cis males and females in a heterosexual context for, as Tanya Ní Mhuirthile has outlined in this collection, those who did not fit clearly defined gender binaries were not considered by successive stakeholders in modern Ireland.

1 Marjorie Howes, 'Public discourse, private reflection, 1916–70' in Angela Bourke et al. (eds), *The Field Day anthology of Irish writing: volume 4: Irish women's writing and traditions* (Cork, 2002), pp 923–30, p. 923. See note 24 for the source of the quote in the title of this chapter. 2 The terms independent Ireland, Free State and Éire are used in this chapter to signify Ireland's post-1922 names. Ireland became a republic in 1949. 3 Myrtle Hill, *Women in Ireland: a century of change*

While moral concerns also preoccupied the Church of Ireland community at this time, there does not seem to be the same volubility and panic over a perceived decline in moral standards as existed in the Catholic Church, expressed in Lenten pastorals and newspaper articles. In the context of this chapter, the migration of young Catholic women appeared to heighten fears about modern sexual behaviour; emigrants, no longer under the watchful eye of family and community, were at risk of sexual transgression once the bonds of propriety exercised so strongly on them at home were gone. Lest we forget the consensual, religious nature of the state and Catholicism, this was not a case of the Catholic Church imposing its values on an unwilling, bohemian population ready to embrace modern values and free love after the revolution. As Kennedy has posited, 'the Irish desired and received from their clergy a very strong emphasis on the dangers and sinfulness of sex among single persons'.[4] Elsewhere I have emphasised the single status of female emigrants as being at the heart of the concern for their behaviour, particularly of a sexual kind.[5]

Extending this analysis, this chapter seeks to build upon the scholarship of those who have contributed to our knowledge of Ireland's past sexual mores, including Earner-Byrne, Luddy, Ferriter, McAvoy, Ryan and Valiulis, in highlighting the ways in which the body was conceptualised as particularly problematic. Emigrant bodies, what they did or had done to them, concern over the dangers and perils of leaving their normal environments, was at the heart of much of the negative discourses about women emigrants. This was, in short, the reason they were consistently posited as needing guidance of a moral nature. J.H. Whyte argued that the preoccupation of the Catholic Church with issues of sexual behaviour arose from 'objective signs of a decline in moral standards' such as increased illegitimacy rates.[6] What can be added to this observation is that it was in women's bodies that these 'objective signs' could be read and hence why women were continually imbued with 'deviant' sexuality in religious discourses. As Luddy has highlighted, the 'rise in illegitimacy levels was attributed to a loss of parental control and responsibility during the period of the war of independence and civil war. That parental control, it was argued, had never been restored'.[7] A small minority of births in Ireland were officially registered as illegitimate: in the period 1921–3, illegitimate births accounted for 2.6% of all births; this rose to 3.5% in 1933–4 and to 3.9% in the years 1944–6.[8]

(Belfast, 2003), p. 32. 4 Robert. E. Kennedy, *The Irish: emigration, marriage and fertility* (Berkeley, 1973), pp 14–15. 5 Jennifer Redmond, '"Sinful singleness"? exploring the discourses on Irish single women's emigration to England, 1922–1948', *Women's History Review*, 17:3 (2008), pp 455–76. 6 John H. Whyte, *Church and state in modern Ireland, 1923–1970* (Dublin, 1971), p. 31. 7 Maria Luddy, 'Sex and the single girl in 1920s and 1930s Ireland', *The Irish Review*, 35 (2007), pp 79–91, p. 82. 8 Whyte, *Church and state*, p. 31. Note that Whyte's figures are taken from the *Annual reports*

Even allowing for the fact that reported figures are probably lower than the actual rates, they do not suggest an 'epidemic of immorality in modern Ireland'.[9] Thus, as Whyte posited, some 'have suspected that the Irish Catholic preoccupation with sexual morality is subjective rather than objective in origin: that it is motivated not by evidence that this [illegitimacy] is a serious problem in Ireland, but by some kind of inner necessity that obliges Irish people to harp on the subject'.[10]

Reactions to sexual immorality could be broadly similar across the confessional divide and the political border, the perception being that standards were slipping, requiring a religious response. Concern regarding promiscuity and illegitimacy was therefore not confined to the Irish Free State or to Catholics. Bishop John Hind's pamphlet, *Welfare work in the Church of Ireland*, detailed the endeavours of the Moral Welfare Committee in the six Northern Ireland dioceses to combat promiscuity, extra-marital relations, unmarried motherhood, and the increased use of contraceptives which prevented married couples from fulfilling their duty of producing a family.[11] The Committee employed a full-time moral welfare worker and supported a number of homes for unmarried mothers in the Belfast area. It is interesting to note that those dealing with unmarried mothers tended to perceive the problem in crisis terms. Given the influence and power of the Catholic Church in independent Ireland, it is unsurprising that moral concerns received prominent attention and legislative responses on Catholic principles.

Sandra McAvoy has identified three broad areas of moral concern in the Free State: access to contraceptives and information on sexuality; the 'problem' of unmarried mothers; and sexual crime and public morality, including prostitution.[12] All of these matters are inherently concerned with women's bodies and the ways in which they could become problematic for the state. Concerns resulted not only in a discursive preoccupation with these topics, but also the official investigation of sexual behaviour and the enactment of specific legislation. Hence the convening of investigative committees such as the Committee on Evil Literature (which included the examination of birth control literature) and the Carrigan Commission to investigate matters related to sexual behaviour.[13] Both enquiries led to the adoption of legislation that limited access to information about sexual reproduction in 1929 and banned the importation

of the registrar-general. 9 Ibid. 10 Ibid. Whyte suggests that, while the preoccupation with sexual morality in Ireland may have been extreme, it is also the case that such attitudes could be seen all over the world. 11 Bishop John Hind, *Welfare work in the Church of Ireland*, pamphlet based on a paper read at the Clerical Society, A. Nelson, Belfast [no date, *c*.1944]. 12 Sandra McAvoy, 'The regulation of sexuality in the Irish Free State, 1929–1935' in Elizabeth Malcolm and Greta Jones (eds), *Medicine, disease and the state in Ireland, 1650–1940* (Cork, 1999), pp 253–66, p. 253. 13 The Carrigan Commission is the more commonly used name for the Committee on the Criminal Law of contraception in 1935. This environment led to an intense focus on women rather than men illustrating the sexual double standards of the time. As Spivak has argued, there are value codings assigned to the body in society that make them become gendered, and in the Irish context, it appears that values rooted in women's bodies codified them as pure but vulnerable to sexual sin.[14] Indeed there is a connection between Irish women's bodies and the nation that is not replicated for men. Nations being codified in rhetoric as female has a long history, and in Ireland this can be seen through two lenses. As Ryan among others have highlighted, women as emblems of the nation, while not unique to Ireland, was certainly a feature of nationalist rhetoric, such as Erin, Hibernia, Cathleen and Róisín Dubh and in 'the blurring of boundaries between representations of the people and the country, these allegorical women stood for both Ireland and Irishness'.[15]

In a rhetorical sense, women as evocative of a pure Ireland followed the image of Mary in being both maternal and chaste. In Werner-Leggett's analysis, the Virgin Mary was used as a role model to prepare women for motherhood due to her role in healing and promoting the welfare of children.[16] This discourse was problematic for women who did not fit this mould, in particular single women. There was a 'connection in the minds of many in Catholic Ireland of the 1920s, 30s and 40s between the state of singleness and the state of sin'.[17] Women who crossed the boundaries of sexual propriety were offered a different, more problematic religious icon: Mary Magdalene. Institutions appropriating her name were established first within the Protestant faith and then more widely by the Catholic Church in Ireland, exemplifying local iterations of an international movement having its 'origins in the tradition of evangelical women's philanthropic endeavours throughout the nineteenth century' in America and elsewhere.[18] If Ireland was worried about its depleting population, it certainly did not want the deficit to be made up by illegitimate births. Indeed as Ryan has argued, while women were national symbols of positive attributes, this also made them signify 'national weakness, vulnerability and susceptibility

Amendment Acts (1880–5) and Juvenile Prostitution which was set up in June 1930 to investigate whether changes were needed in the current Criminal Law Amendment Act. **14** Gayatri Spivak, 'In a word: interview with Ellen Rooney' in *Outside in the teaching machine* (New York, 1993), pp 1–24. **15** Louise Ryan, *Gender, identity and the Irish press, 1922–1937: embodying the nation* (Lewiston, 2002), p. 1. **16** Aenne Werner-Leggett, *Being Mary?: Irish Catholic immigrant women and home and community building in Harold Hill Essex 1947–1970* (The Hague, 2012). **17** Redmond, '"Sinful singleness"?', pp 455–6. **18** Jennifer Redmond, 'In the family way and away from the family: examining the evidence in Irish unmarried mothers in Britain, 1920s–40s' in Elaine Farrell (ed.) *'She said she was in the family way': pregnancy and infancy in modern Ireland* (London, 2012), pp 163–85, p. 165. For more on the US context of this movement, see Regina G. Kunzel, *Fallen women, problem girls: unmarried mothers and the professionalisation of social work, 1890–1945* (New Haven, 1993).

to corrupting foreign influences' or 'the threat of immorality or impurity'.[19] Thus great attention was paid in parish sermons and Lenten pastorals, published in detail in national and religious newspapers, to dissuade parents from allowing their sons, but most particularly their daughters, too much freedom in their personal lives lest immorality could occur.

Reports of the views of the Catholic hierarchy were published in full, without comment or critique. While this may imply fear of censure or a lack of open critique of the views of the Church, it may also indicate an acceptance of such statements and values. As might be expected, the religious press published the views of the hierarchy, and opinion pieces on the morality (or otherwise) of emigration, more frequently than the secular press. The *Irish Catholic* newspaper published frequent exhortations to girls to stay in Ireland to avoid the temptations and pitfalls of life in Britain, referring in 1936 to the 'disastrous consequences' that 'usually' befell Irish girls who had not previously been away from home.[20] The euphemistic 'disastrous consequences' surely references sexual impurity, such coded language being easily understood by a readership accustomed to moralistic journalism of this kind. It also reported views of the hierarchy in Britain, such as an editorial on the warning from the Most Revd Dr Downey of Liverpool that girls were in peril from answering 'innocent-looking advertisements' if they didn't use the services of moral welfare organisations to vet them first.[21] The issue being highlighted was the threat of 'a kind of mild slavery or even worse' that could lead a girl to suffer 'degradation and dishonour'.[22] This dramatic language is clearly synonymic for sexual danger, the propriety of the publication being too strict to use clearer language, although another article on the same theme referred to 'unmentionable purposes'.[23] This language is also evident in the prominent reporting of the Lenten pastorals of 1937 in the *Irish Independent* in which emigration featured as a conspicuous, and gendered, theme. Archbishop of Tuam, Dr Gilmartin, railed against the 'terrible risks to soul and body' young girls going to England faced if they went without job or family to meet them, while Dr MacNamee of Ardagh and Clonmacnoise referred to jobs 'where modesty and virtue may be exposed to great dangers'.[24] The body is overtly and implicitly expressed in these statements as at risk, of endangering spiritual and moral purity, of being the

19 Ryan, *Gender, identity and the Irish press*, p. 2. See also Breda Gray and Louise Ryan, '(Dis)locating "woman" and "women" in representations of Irish nationality' in Anne Byrne and Madeleine Leonard (eds), *Women and Irish society* (Belfast, 1997), pp 517–34. 20 'Keep your daughters at home', *Irish Catholic*, 8 August 1936. 21 'Notes and comments', Editorial column, *Irish Catholic*, 15 August 1936. 22 Ibid. 23 'A fearful evil: archbishop's warning to Irish girls', *Irish Catholic*, 15 August 1936. The article is carried in the main body of the paper and mentioned in the editorial column. 24 Report on Dr Gilmartin's Lenten Pastoral, *Irish Independent*, 8 February 1937. For

site of sin committed against the girl. This idea of Irish women being targeted was a frequent theme in the *Irish Catholic*, often quoting Catholic welfare organisations such as the International Catholic Girls' Protection Society on the dangers of travel: 'We also solemnly warn all intending emigrants to be on their guard against the agents of the white slave traffic, who, we have good reason to believe, are always trying to carry on their nefarious work on most of the outgoing transatlantic liners'.[25] Although 'all emigrants' are referred to here, the Society only dealt with female emigrants, as did their counterparts in Britain, and the danger from such gangs was solely in terms of women's entry into prostitution.

Concomitant to the newspaper rhetoric, the state enacted a series of laws that restricted knowledge about sexual matters and family planning, introduced compulsory retirement of women on marriage in the civil service and primary school sectors, limited women's access to the higher echelons of the civil service, took women's automatic right to serve on juries away, banned contraceptives, regulated women's employment in factories and enshrined and valorised a maternal, domestic role for women in the 1937 Constitution. In this era, political parties, despite their bitter Civil War rivalries, appeared united and women found few allies in parliamentary circles or the public sphere in general. Emigration provided a break from this community and parental censure, a feature that worried many and provoked much verbiage on the moral problems of leaving Ireland. As most Irish men and women migrated before the age of twenty-five for much of this period and were unmarried, the problem of confining sex within the marital state was one explicitly associated with migrants who could no longer be influenced by societal and community norms and might, it was feared, become reckless through life in English cities. Yet there are some distinct gender differences that must be borne in mind; an analysis of newspaper commentary reveals that while alcohol was thought to be the root of sin for men, for women it was sexual behaviour. Both practices are associated with the body and had, in contemporary discourses, deleterious effects on physical, moral and spiritual welfare. However, while reform could be hoped for men who fell into alcoholism and its attendant problems of homelessness and isolation, what hope was there for women who besmirched their and their family's name through sex outside marriage? Was this not a permanent stain on their soul? The newspapers, journals and pamphlets of the time might certainly suggest so, and the high rates of literacy and availability of national and local newspapers at this time have been suggested by Ryan as reasons why we should

further analysis of Lenten pastorals, see Ryan, *Gender, identity and the Irish press*, p. 111. 25 'Catholic girl emigrants: fine work of protection society', *Irish Catholic*, 24 May 1930.

take their messages seriously in analysing the formation of the new state, revealing the 'conflicting and competing discourses' they contained.[26] There was, as might be expected, little variation in catholic newspapers of the period as their narratives were informed by church teachings and religious principles with a heavy emphasis on morality. These are not included in Ryan's study of Irish journalism but are quoted here to broaden the analysis of discourses current in post-independence Ireland. The impact printed sermons or journalism had on women's sense of self, or even their decision to migrate, is impossible to know, and the point must be made that we cannot uncritically assume that the powerful hegemony attempted to be asserted by governments and the Catholic Church was passively accepted. As Conway, Bourque and Scott argue:

> To complicate the picture, institutions do not always succeed in their task of inculcating culturally acceptable conduct or conventional behavior [sic]. Individuals do not seem to simply accept or reflect normative designations. Rather, their notions of their own gender identity and sexuality are manifested in their refusals, reinterpretations, or partial acceptances of the dominant themes.[27]

This may have been understood well at the time, and church and state leaders appear to have interpreted the large numbers of women leaving Ireland through the first decades of independence as rejecting the 'dominant themes' that were posited as ideal for women citizens.

Furthermore, continued questioning of women's sexual behaviour as a motivator for emigration, either to hide pregnancy or to embrace 'modern' sexual mores, was in complete contrast to the resounding silence on Irish men's behaviour, as emigrants or otherwise. Women were problematised as emigrants according to sexual double standards that saw them either as temptresses or victims, but either way paying the ultimate price through illegitimate pregnancies. Women's bodies were central to this thinking: they were the site of sin, the literal embodiment of transgressive sexual behaviour through pregnancy, and thus control of them was essential in the eyes of many in order to diminish what was seen as a significant moral problem.

Ferriter has cautioned as to the complexity of the sexual history of Ireland and questioned whether we can assume a national sexual morality or characteristics of sexual behaviour.[28] Inglis' examination of sexuality in Irish

26 Ryan, *Gender, identity and the Irish press*, p. 6. 27 Jill K. Conway, Susan C. Bourque and J.W. Scott, 'Introduction: the concept of gender', *Daedalus*, 116:4 (Fall, 1987), pp xxi–xxx, at p. xxiii. 28 Ferriter, *Occasions of sin: sex and society in modern Ireland* (London, 2009), p. 2.

history has outlined discourses that were shaped by Catholicism as the church rose to power throughout the long nineteenth century.[29] Inglis draws attention to the reductionism in this paradigm, focusing on sexual morality, as opposed to pleasure, and resulting in 'a classification of who could do what to whom, when, where and how'.[30] Effectively this created conformists and non-conformists, the latter included 'the unmarried mother, the homosexual, the lesbian, the fornicating bachelor farmer' who were 'excluded from society and put into convents, homes and asylums', or, in my analysis, out of sight on the boat to England.[31] This 'policing' of bodies in a sexual context created a society that saw private sexual behaviours become in some ways an issue between government and citizen while being shrouded in silence and shame. Although Ferriter rightly points to 'dissent, different opinions, double standards and a more complex sexual identity and practice' than he feels Inglis' analysis allows for, in the early years of independence the evidence does suggest that suppression was more powerful than dissension.[32]

The discourses that constituted sex as an 'obsession' extended to those citizens who left its shores. Opinions on women's sexual practices as emigrants were often based on evidence of the phenomenon of unmarried mothers and the experiences of religious and charitable institutions in Britain that found themselves assisting in 'hiding Ireland's shame'. As the Commission on Emigration and Other Population problems noted, dealing continually with problem cases may have skewed the views of such groups in their reporting to the newspapers as they dealt with a problematic cohort of the emigrant population, rather than the population as a whole.[33] One such example is evident in a 1923 letter from the National Vigilance Association (NVA) in Britain to the Irish High Commissioner, Mr James McNeill, in which he was urged to address the problem of Irish women coming to Britain.[34] Such women were stated to be often without money, luggage or a job, or, alternately, completely unfit for jobs they were accepted for and thus they quickly lost. Mr Sempkins, head of the NVA, pointed out that although many women were helped in their travel arrangements by the International Catholic Girls' Protection Society in Cork and Dublin, he:

> … would suggest that the girls for whom special protection is most needed are not the girls who seek the help of these two Societies; but are

29 Tom Inglis, 'Foucault, Bourdieu and the field of Irish sexuality', *Irish Journal of Sociology*, 7 (1997), pp 5–28. 30 Ibid., p. 5. 31 Ibid. 32 Ferriter, *Occasions of sin*, p. 3. 33 Commission on Emigration and Other Population Pproblems, Majority report, chapter 7, part 2, paragraph 319, p. 137, National Archives of Ireland, DT s14249/Annexe. 34 James McNeill (1869–1938) acted as High Commissioner from 1923 and was later Governor General of the Irish Free State,

> rather those girls who either come over in entire ignorance of the dangers and difficulties awaiting them, or those who think they are quite capable of taking care of themselves.[35] (Emphasis in original)

Women thinking they were 'quite capable of taking care of themselves' is clearly problematic in this analysis. This may not be unexpected given the emphasis of their work and the influence of dealing with problematic migrations leading perhaps to a tendency to see *all* migrant women as problematic. The class, as well as the gender, aspects to this kind of rhetoric are latent but strong; moral philanthropic work was not aimed at female doctors, for example, but rather domestic servants and other unskilled workers.

Archival evidence suggests the attitude expressed by the NVA above infused many Catholic organisations that interacted with them. The Catholic Girls' Society ran a London hostel that provided cheap accommodation for Catholic girls in a spiritual environment. Their 1938 report also detailed their work with 365 girls not living in the hostel but having been brought to their attention (by whom and for what reason is not elaborated upon, although local priests are acknowledged as providing 'help and encouragement').[36] The report thanks the NVA for their cooperation (again unspecified), and highlights three examples of their work with young girls, two of which relate to Irish girls:

> An Irish girl of sixteen was found working in North London, in very undesirable surroundings, she was persuaded to leave and brought to the hostel, where she worked until her return to Ireland. In answer to an appeal from the Lady Almoner of one of the big hospitals, our visitor befriended a young Irish girl of eighteen whose parents were abroad. She was escorted to various interviews with prospective employers till she found suitable work.[37]

In these examples, girls are specifically sought out in order to provide help and guidance they are thought to be lacking. While it may appear helpful and benevolent, it is also the case that this kind of activity was confined to women, and furthermore, the assumption is clear that as working-class women they

replacing Timothy Healy in 1928. 35 For more on the International Catholic Girls' Protection Society and the network of emigrant philanthropy organisations in Ireland and Britain see Jennifer Redmond, 'Safeguarding Irish girls: welfare work, female emigrants and the Catholic Church, 1920s–1940s' in Christina Brophy and Cara Delay (eds), *Women, reform, and resistance in Ireland, 1850–1950* (New York, 2015), pp 79–106. Letter from Mr Sempkins to Irish High Commissioner in London, dated 10 August 1923, 4NVA/04/02 BOX FL098, Women's Library, London. 36 Catholic Girls' Protection Society, *Annual report 1938*, Westminster Diocesan Archives, Hi. 2.215 Miscellaneous Societies. 37 Catholic Girls' Protection Society, *Annual report 1938*.

should accept such offers of help unquestioningly. There is evidence also that the Westminster Diocese was particularly active in their moral welfare work and given the high numbers of Irish migrants to London, it is unsurprising that they interacted with Irish women.[38] However, the degree of control displayed by the Moral Welfare Committee of the diocese again calls attention to the degree to which immorality, or the suspicion of such, was thought justification for interference in the lives of emigrant women.

The body was the site of success or failure for female emigrants, for as I've argued elsewhere: 'failed emigrants were to be found in maternity homes; successful emigrants sent money home to their mothers'.[39] The perception that emigrant behaviours were reflective of national traits was shared by the Irish government and the Catholic Church, thus immoral sexual activity cast an air of profligacy and licentiousness on the Irish 'character' as a whole. Although there is far less commentary in the Protestant *Church of Ireland Gazette* on emigrants' behaviour, newspapers in particular appear to have been fascinated by this topic and were largely responsible for creating the impression that emigrants lapsed in their moral standards in Britain. Whether or not the newspaper headlines can be believed as delivering an accurate picture of public opinion, or whether these stories had any impact on emigrants is not as important to consider as the fact that the persistence of immorality stories created the space for a version of 'truth' in describing emigrants in Britain.

A Department of External Affairs memorandum in 1947 constructed the migration of women, in contrast to that of men, as lonely and unsafe. Furthermore, they were unprotected in their workplace environments:

> ... there is a significant difference between male and female emigrants: the former usually proceed in groups to factory or building work where arrangements are made for their moral and religious welfare and often for the maintenance of an Irish atmosphere, whereas the bulk of the female emigrants who are engaged in domestic service or allied work take up employment individually and are scattered singly throughout Great Britain, the moral atmosphere of which young and inexperienced girls are only too often unfitted to withstand.[40]

38 This is evident in the Westminster Diocese Moral Welfare Committee's involvement in setting up the Repatriation Scheme to return Irish emigrant women who had become pregnant in Ireland (as opposed to Britain). For more on this see Lindsey Earner-Byrne, *Mother and child: maternity and child welfare in Dublin, 1922–60* (Manchester, 2007), Redmond, 'In the family way', and Lindsey Earner-Byrne, '"Moral repatriation": the response to Irish unmarried mothers in Britain, 1920s–1960s' in Patrick Duffy (ed.), *To and from Ireland: planned migration schemes, c.1600–2000* (Dublin, 2004), pp 155–74. 39 Redmond, '"Sinful singleness"?', p. 467. 40 Memorandum for

This assessment denies the fact that while some women may have emigrated singly, they did so within a wider nexus of family and social support. As Lambert has noted, family links and support were crucial to the emigration process.[41] However even if this were the case, it is problematic to accept this analysis that the sole emigrant female body was as weak as posited here – did women, uniquely, require a certain 'moral atmosphere' in order that their bodies comply with social strictures? If Irish women were imbued with religion throughout their lives before emigration, why were they so vulnerable in Britain? Irish female emigrants were, on the one hand, protected from sexual knowledge through censorship and a lack of open discourse, yet at the same time symbolically marked as sources of sexual knowledge and desires that would get them 'into trouble' upon leaving the country. In reality, it seems that the overriding experience of Irish women, at home and in Britain, in relation to sexual matters was a mixture of ignorance and dread.[42] These testimonies suggest that the evidence base for moral panic over the sexual activities of single Irish girls was probably vastly overestimated. However, the very fact that this was an issue of major concern suggests that women in general, and single girls in particular, were a disturbing cohort, especially when they left Ireland.

CONCLUSION

Inglis has posited that the 'practices of postponed marriage and permanent celibacy became associated with a perception of the Irish being a sexually repressed, priest-ridden people who sublimated their libidinal drives in religion and alcohol'.[43] If this perception was shared by those in post-independence Ireland, is this perhaps a reason why emigrants were accused of seeking sexual pleasure through migration? If so, this still fails to explain why women were castigated as having this motive while men were not. It does, however, fit with Butler's theorisation of the body as appearing, enduring and living 'within the productive constraints of certain highly gendered regulatory schemas'.[44]

Theoretical insights can be helpful to the historian in trying to understand the complex and competing discourses about Irish sexuality in the past and how issues of sex were discussed in the public sphere. Bourdieu refers to the

the Government from the Department of External Affairs, 4, 30 August 1947, Department of Foreign Affairs files, National Archives of Ireland, DFA 402/25, p. 6. 41 Redmond, '"Sinful singleness"?', pp 465–6. 42 For example, the testimony of Mary Walker (a pseudonym), who talked about fear as a contraceptive is typical of many oral history accounts in their explanations of sexual knowledge and behaviour in twentieth-century Ireland, in Catherine Dunne, *An unconsidered people* (Dublin, 2003), p. 104. 43 Inglis, 'Foucault, Bourdieu', p. 7. 44 Judith Butler, 'unquestioned social conceptions' which he 'refers to as doxa' and this concept neatly encapsulates the attitude to female emigrants in many quarters during this period.[45] It appears to have been an unquestioned belief that women embodied sinful sexual behaviour, either being the instigator or victims of transgressions. In my analysis this was not simply dogma preached by the Catholic Church and followed to the letter by a slavish population. Attitudes to female sexuality were reflective of wider cultural and social mores in which the protection of family lines of inheritance were as much at stake as personal reputations and moral judgements on sexual behaviour, a conclusion that accords with and with Inglis' analysis of modern Ireland.[46]

The collaboration between the Catholic Church and the state in regulating women's bodies was a feature of successive governments in the post-independence period. While this system may also have been restrictive to men in Ireland who did not fit with hegemonic norms of masculinity and sexuality, as emigrants they were discursively free of moral censure with regard to sexual behaviour, unlike their female counterparts. Theoretical approaches, particularly psychoanalytic conceptions of identity, have led historians into explorations of

> ... the relationship between history and individual psyches, and into what might be called the politics of sexual identity. It suggests that sexual identities are not biologically rooted, but instead continually pursued, and that this pursuit, whether heterosexual or homosexual, is made possible in contexts at once political and personal.[47]

An examination of archival material, public statements and newspapers reveals that female emigrants and their bodies were part of the sexual politics of the time.

The agency of young women in migrating to Britain in the twentieth century is perhaps also at the heart of the moralistic concerns over their behaviour, for their propensity to migrate alone or with other single women highlighted, for some, their sexual availability, unprotected by marital or family status: 'If more female emigrants to England or elsewhere had been married or had moved in family groups, it is doubtful whether there would have been such curiosity, vitriol or debate about them.'[48] This is perhaps attested to best by the lack of concern over female seasonal workers. Even when commentary on their conditions of work and accommodation became prominent after the Kirkintilloch tragedy in 1937 in which several young men died in a fire in their

Bodies that matter: on the discursive limits of 'sex' (New York, 1993), p. xi. 45 Inglis, 'Foucault, Bourdieu', p. 8. 46 Ibid., p. 13. 47 Conway et al., 'Introduction', p. xxvi. 48 Redmond, '"Sinful accommodation, moral concerns over sexual behaviour did not emerge in public rhetoric despite the close contact young men and women had with each other in this line of work.[49] It was because women were working within groups controlled by men and alongside relatives and neighbours that concern for their moral welfare was not evinced in the same way it was for domestic servants, for example, who were framed in many analyses as wayward.

Ryan's work on newspapers in Ireland in the 1920s and 1930s importantly reveals that women's bodies were repeatedly referred to in the context of emigration in national and regional contexts.[50] In her analysis, it is women's bodies that are symbolically representative of population failure, economic stagnation, morality, Irishness, Catholicism and, most viscerally, the 'threat of rural depopulation, low marriage rates and falling birth rates'.[51] By reifying purity and morality in women's bodies in the new state, church and state leaders cast their hopes on the success of the new nation also in women's behaviours. When these women left, it may have seemed like hope for the future nation left with them.

singleness"?', p. 458. 49 For more on the Kirkintilloch tragedy see Brian Coghlan, *Achill Island, tattie-hokers in Scotland and the Kirkintilloch tragedy, 1937* (Dublin, 2006). 50 For further analysis of newspaper journalism in Ireland, see Mark O'Brien and Felix Larkin (eds), *Periodicals and journalism in twentieth-century Ireland* (Dublin, 2014). 51 Ryan, *Gender, identity and the Irish press*, p. 112.

CHAPTER 7

Intersex in Ireland: a legal history from ancient times to the present day

Tanya Ní Mhuirthile

This chapter examines the impact of the law's changing conception of corporeality about people with intersex bodies.[1] In medieval and renaissance times, the law recognised three types of bodies as conferring legal status: male, female and hermaphrodite. Contemporaneous to increased specialisation in medical knowledge about hermaphroditic conditions during Victorian times, the laws governing the registration of persons were introduced. Intersex is notable in its absence from these legal provisions. This chapter analyses this coincidence of events, and argues it signals the beginning of the erosion of intersex from legal consciousness. Examining the case law that directly addressed the categorisation of bodies as either male or female strengthens this analysis as it reveals the disappearance of intersex from legal consciousness. The continuing simultaneous importance of the birth certificate as a historical 'snapshot' of events at a particular moment and as a crucial and current identification document becomes apparent. Arguing that adherence to a binary understanding of gender actively discriminates against intersex people, this chapter considers the re-emergence of the historical paradigm of self-declaration of gender identity for intersex people and what this means for the realisation of their human rights.

INVESTIGATING INTERSEX

How best to determine a person's legal gender has been regularly considered in Ireland in recent times. There have been two High Court decisions, a Declaration of Incompatibility with Ireland's obligations under the law of the European Convention on Human Rights (ECHR), an advisory group report to the government, two private members bills introduced in the Oireachtas and

1 The author would like to acknowledge funding from the Irish Research Council under the COALESCE Scheme 2019.

a Joint Oireachtas Committee report, ultimately resulting in the introduction of the Gender Recognition Act 2015.[2] Analysing these developments reveals that, currently, the law categorises bodies as either male or female. This categorisation continues to be true notwithstanding the fact that the Gender Recognition Act 2015 enables movement between these categories. The existence of intersex in the natural world is commonly accepted. There are many plant and animal species that exhibit intersex traits;[3] that there are also intersex people is unsurprising.

As a term, 'intersex' is becoming more familiar yet it is often misconstrued as referring to ambiguous sexual orientation, the transition period between one gender and the other for transgender people, or as being synonymous with a non-binary gender identity. The term 'intersex' has nothing to do with either sexual orientation or gender identity, rather it is a term that refers to a person's body. Intersex people are born with sex characteristics (including genitals, gonads and chromosome patterns) that do not fit typical binary notions of male or female bodies.[4] It is not always immediately apparent when a body is intersex. While some intersex bodies are identified in early childhood due to ambiguous genitalia, others are recognised at a later stage in development such as at puberty, when experiencing fertility difficulties or even on autopsy.

When discussing intersex, language becomes loaded. Therefore, it is appropriate to pause to explain the linguistic choices taken in drafting this chapter. Historically the term 'hermaphrodite' was employed, however due to the associations with the myth of Hermaphroditus and consequent resonance of fantasy, this term has fallen out of favour. Thus 'intersex' is preferred.[5] The linguistic difficulty with the term 'intersex' is that it presupposes that there are two defining sexes and that this third category is a hybrid that exists between the two. This kind of assumption is limited and eschews recognising the complexity of sex, gender and identity. Since 2006, the term 'disorder of sexual

2 *Foy v. An t-Ard Chlaraitheoir & Ors* [2002] IEHC 116 (9 July 2002) (http://www.bailii.org/ie/cases/IEHC/2002/116.html); *Foy v. An t-Ard Chláraitheoir & Ors (No. 2)* [2007] IEHC 470 (19 Oct. 2007) (http://www.bailii.org/ie/cases/IEHC/2007/H470.html); *Report of the gender recognition advisory group*, Gender recognition advisory group (Dublin, 2011); Gender Recognition Bill 2013; Legal Recognition of Gender Bill 2013; *General scheme of the Gender Recognition Bill 2013*; *Report on the general scheme of the Gender Recognition Bill 2013*, Joint Oireacthas Committee on Education and Social Protection (Dublin, 2014) (https://data.oireachtas.ie/ie/oireachtas/committee/dail/ 31/joint_committee_on_education_and_social_protection/reports/2014/2014–01–16_report-on-the-general-scheme-of-a-gender-recognition-bill-2013_en.pdf). 3 P.E. Howard and D.E. Bjorling, 'The intersexual animal: associated problems', *Problems in Veterinary Medicine*, 1:1 (1989), pp 74–84. 4 United Nations for LGBT Equality, 'Fact sheet intersex' (https://www.unfe.org/wp-content/uploads/2017/05/UNFE-Intersex.pdf) (15 February 2022). 5 Richard Goldschmidt, 'Intersexuality and the endocrine aspect of sex', *Endocrinology*, 1:4 (1917), pp 433–56.

development' (DSD) has been used in addition to, or in place of, intersex for the very reasons outlined above.[6] DSD is contested as it presumes an underlying disorder: that there is something intrinsically wrong with the intersex body requiring it to be fixed as either male or female.[7] Some argue that using this term perpetuates, the medicalisation and problematisation of something that is not inherently medically problematic.[8] Generally, this chapter will use the term 'intersex' save where it is more appropriate, particularly in a historical context, to employ another term such as 'hermaphrodite'.

HISTORICAL HERMAPHRODITES

Intersex is not a new or recent phenomenon. There have always been intersex people in human society. Through an exploration of how society, the law and the medical profession have interacted with intersex people throughout the ages, the repositioning of hermaphrodites, largely unnoticed and unremarked in history as, from the time of the Enlightenment, objects for scrutiny, will be highlighted. Increased interest caused hermaphrodites to be treated as curios both for the paying public at shows and fairs, as well as for the medical community.[9] This visibility contrasts sharply with the virtual invisibility of intersex people in the twentieth century until the advent of the intersex advocacy movement in the mid-1990s. In relating the history of hermaphrodites this chapter attempts to tease out why these changes in visibility occurred.

THE AGE OF ANTIQUITY

The word hermaphrodite originates from the story of Hermaphroditus. This story was told by Ovid in his book Metamorphoses. When the nymph Salmacis saw Hermaphroditus, the son of the gods Hermes and Aphrodite, swimming

6 Christopher P. Houk, Ieuan A Hughes, Peter A. Lee, S. Faisal Ahmed and in collaboration with the participants in the International Consensus Conference on intersex organised by the Lawson Wilkins Endocrine Society and the European Society for Paediatric Endocrinology, 'Consensus statement on the management of intersex conditions', *Pediatrics*, 118:2 (2006), p. 753. 7 Milton Diamond and Hazel Beh, 'The right to be wrong: sex and gender decisions' in Sharon E. Sytsma (ed.), *Ethics and intersex* (Dordrecht, 2006), pp 103–13; Elizabeth Reis, 'Divergence or disorder?: the politics of naming intersex', *Perspectives in Biology and Medicine*, 1:4 (2007), pp 535–43. 8 G. Boulos, 'The DSD: letter to the editor in response to Houk et al.' (http://adc.bmj.com/cgi/eletters/91/7/554); Alice D. Dreger and April M. Herndon, 'Progress and politics in the intersex rights movement: feminist theory in action', *GLQ: A Journal of Lesbian and Gay Studies*, 15:2 (2009), pp 199–224. 9 The Bearded Lady of circus sideshow fame is an example of hermaphrodites

in her lake she fell rapturously in love with him and implored the gods that they never be separated. The gods, with their usual sardonic sense of humour, took her at her word and their two bodies were fused into one: 'They two were two no more, nor man, nor woman – One body then that seemed neither and both'.[10] Hermaphrodites were more than mere myths. Hippocrates, the father of western medicine, held that a uterus had seven cells. If a foetus gestated in one of the three cells on the left it would be a male. If it developed in one of the three cells on the right it would be a female. Finally, if it developed in the middle cell, it would be a hermaphrodite and combine traits of both males and females. Therefore, Hippocrates considered that hermaphrodites were a third sex in a spectrum of sexes.[11] Contrastingly, Aristotle viewed males and females as opposites without any intermediate forms. His explanation for the existence of hermaphrodites was as follows: extra sexual organs, like extra fingers or toes, result from an excess of generative matter, too much for one embryo and not enough for two.[12]

MEDIEVAL AND RENAISSANCE ATTITUDES

In medieval and renaissance times being either a man or a woman affected one's legal status in society. Men were entitled to own property and to vote, women were not. On the issue of the hermaphrodite, Henry de Bracton, in the 1200s, wrote that mankind could be classified as male, female or hermaphrodite and that a hermaphrodite is classified as male or female according to the predominance of the sexual organs.[13] This was still the legal position during Renaissance times when Lord Coke, writing on succession laws, noted: 'Every heire is either a male, or female or an hermaphrodite, that is both male and female. And an hermaphrodite (which is also called Androgynous) shall be heire, either as male or female, according to that kind of the sexe which doth prevaile.'[14] Maimonides, a Jewish rabbi, doctor, theologian and lawyer, provided a detailed diagnostic procedure for determining whether a person was a man, woman or a hermaphrodite. A hermaphrodite could become betrothed to marry

treated as curios. While in the medical community, in 1888, Fancourt Barnes famously presented his 'living specimen of hermaphroditism' at a meeting of the British Gynaecological Society. See Alice Domurat Dreger, *Hermaphrodites and the medical invention of sex* (Cambridge, 2000). 10 Ovid, *Metamorphoses*, trans. A.D. Melville (Oxford, 1986). 11 Geoffrey Ernest Richard Lloyd, *Science, folklore and ideology: studies in the life sciences in ancient Greece* (1999). 12 Aristotle, *On the generation of animals*, trans. A.L. Peck (Cambridge, MA, 1979). 13 Henry de Bracton, *On the laws and customs of England* (Cambridge, MA, 1968). 14 Sir Edward Coke, *The first part of the institutes of the law in England* (Philadelphia, 1853).

either a man or a woman. Such an engagement, being suspect, would require a judgment before the marriage could take place.[15]

In theory this appears inclusive, as if it would enable a hermaphrodite to declare himself male, for example, and then to live his life without interruption from the State. The reality for hermaphrodites could be different. Daston and Park recount the tale of Marie/Marin from Renaissance France.[16] Raised as a female, in her late teens Marie began living as a man named Marin and became engaged to a fellow maidservant Jeanne. Both were tried and convicted of female sodomy, with Marin prosecuted for the additional crime of usurping male dress. Initially sentenced to execution, Marin's sentence was commuted to four years of dressing as a woman and refraining from sexual intercourse with anyone, when medical evidence was adduced that what had previously been considered a clitoris ejaculated a thick masculine semen following extensive rubbing. Ten years after the trial Marin was spotted wearing men's clothes and sporting a thick beard.[17]

If, as indicated by the dicta of de Bracton, Coke and Maimonides, hermaphroditism was accepted in society why was Marie/Marin brought before the court when s/he had chosen to marry in the male role and presumably intended to live in that role? Examining the alternative sentences handed down at the original trial and once the evidence of the post-trial examination had been adduced to court sheds light on the matter. At the original trial evidence of Marie's menstrual cycle was deemed sufficient to determine her sex as female. Thus, the proposed marriage was between two women and hence sufficiently offensive to the law to mandate a death sentence. However, the court considered the additional evidence of ejaculation sufficient to call into question Marie/Marin's sex and therefore, potentially, the relationship between the accused persons was uncontroversially heterosexual. Considered thus, it was Marie/Marin's suspected lesbianism, not her hermaphroditism, which was the cause of societal concern.[18] An alternative reading of the case could consider Marie/Marin's gender performance rather than her sexual orientation as the cause for concern. Regardless, once the anxiety concerning gender/sexuality transgression was eliminated, the punishment was reduced significantly.

15 Maimondies, *The code of Maimonides, book 4, the book of women* (New Haven, 1972). 16 Lorraine Daston and Katherine Park, 'Hermaphrodites in renaissance France', *Critical Matrix*, 1:5 (1985), pp 1–19. 17 For more on the interpretation of masculinity in the Marie/Marin case amongst others see Cathy McClive, 'Masculinity on trial: penises, hermaphrodites and the uncertain male body in early modern France', *History Workshop Journal*, 58:1 (2009), pp 45–68. 18 Patricia Simons, *The sex of men in premodern Europe: a cultural history* (Cambridge, 2011); Margaret Schaus (ed.), *Women and gender in medieval Europe: an encyclopedia* (New York, 2006).

THE NINETEENTH CENTURY AND THE AGE OF THE GONADS

The publication of Darwin's *On the origin of species* greatly perturbed society in the nineteenth century.[19] His theory of evolution held that males and females existed purely for procreative purposes and were naturally selected to ensure the survival of the fittest and the continuation of the species. The polarisation of males and females is the foundation on which life itself was based. The heterosexual male and female were prioritised by society as the highest form of humanity as, uniquely, they were able to ensure the survival of the species through procreation.[20] It is arguable that the primacy of a binary gender paradigm in an organised and intentional manner dates from this time. It was during the Victorian era that the recording of statistics relating to the births, marriages and deaths of the population was put on a statutory footing. The first definition of marriage as something exclusively the preserve of heterosexual men and women was handed down by a court. The law outlawing sodomy was restated afresh and reinterpreted as a prohibition on homosexuality and although the death penalty was removed as a punishment, the crime was punishable by up to life imprisonment.[21]

Simultaneously, doctors were beginning to specialise, and gynaecology, which previously had been almost exclusively the preserve of the midwife, was becoming a specialisation in its own right.[22] Doctors began to discover and report in medical journals several physically hermaphroditic subjects. This can partly be attributed to the rise of gynaecology and as Dreger argues, 'anxiety of sex roles probably also contributed to the rapid rise in medical reports of hermaphrodites by making physicians sensitive to their patients' sexual identities, anatomies and practices'.[23] To curtail hermaphroditism lest it amplify the social sexual confusion, biomedical experts sought a stable definition of male and female. In 1896, Blacker and Lawrence published an article in which they argued that the gonadal tissue is the true indicator of an individual's sex, regardless of any other anatomical factor.[24] This argument received widespread acceptance by

19 Charles Darwin, *On the origin of species* (London 1859; 2018 ed.). 20 For a discussion of homosexuality and Darwin see Jerome Barkow, *Darwin, sex, and status: biological approaches to mind and culture in Darwin sex status* (Toronto, 1989). 21 Registration of Births and Deaths Acts 1863; *Hyde v. Hyde*, [1866] L.R. 1 P. & D. 130; Offences Against the Person Act 1861; Criminal Law (Amendment) Act 1885. 22 The Obstetrical Society of London was founded in 1854, the breakaway society the British Gynaecological Society was founded in 1884. Eventually, these two societies merged in 1929 to form the British College of Obstetricians and Gynaecologists. The College was granted the title 'Royal' in 1938 but did not receive its royal charter until 1947. 23 Alice Domurat Dreger, 'A history of intersex: from the age of gonads to the age of consent' in Alice Domurat Dreger Domurat (ed.), *Intersex in the age of ethics* (Hagerstown, MD, 1999). 24 G.F. Blacker and T.W.P. Lawrence, 'A case of true unilateral hermaphroditism with ovestesis

the medical community. A person who possessed testes would be labelled a male-pseudo-hermaphrodite regardless of how feminine they might be. This led to some cases of extreme social nonsense, such as that of L.S., a Parisian fashion model with testes, who was described as 'frankly homosexual' by doctors because she exclusively sexually desired men.[25]

All people could be labelled as male or female even if 'apparently and falsely' hermaphroditic. It was only upon microscopic inspection of the gonads by many teams of experts that an individual could be declared a 'true hermaphrodite'. Given that biopsies and exploratory surgery were extremely rare occurrences, in practice the only true hermaphrodite tended to be the dead and autopsied hermaphrodite.[26] Hence far fewer people met the criteria for diagnosis as a hermaphrodite regardless of what other 'apparently' hermaphroditic traits they might possess. Thus, the erasure of the hermaphrodite from society began.

SURGICAL SOLUTIONS

With the advent of live biopsies in the early twentieth century a gonadal definition of sex was no longer sustainable. Bell advanced the idea that when determining the sex of an apparent hermaphrodite, each case should be considered as a whole, and the focus should not be exclusively on the gonads. He suggested that in addition to determining the sex of an individual with ambiguous biology, doctors should help that diagnosis along: 'surgical procedures should in these special cases be carried out to establish more completely the obvious sex of the individual.'[27]

Surgeons began to 'disappear' intersex individuals from society by surgically altering their physical appearance such that it more closely resembled the appearances of males or females. Advances in medicine, particularly surgical techniques and hormonal treatments, made it possible to eradicate the external evidence of intersexuality and to 'make' an individual either male or female. The most prolific proponent of this approach was Dr John Money, who specialised in the psychology of sex at the Gender Identity Clinic of Johns Hopkins Hospital in Baltimore, Maryland. He believed that in the nature versus nurture debate, the latter is paramount. Sexual identity is not a matter of biology, but rather a learned process. Any child can be taught to have a male or female

occuring in a man, with a summary and criticism of the recorded cases of true hermaphroditism', *Transaction of the Obstetrical Society of London*, 38 (1896), pp 265–317. 25 Dreger, *Hermaphrodites and the medical invention of sex*. 26 Alice Domurat Dreger, 'A history of intersex: from the age of gonads to the age of consent'. 27 William Blair Bell, 'Hermaphroditism', *Liverpool Medico-Chirurgical Journal*, 35 (1915), 272–92, p. 291.

identity, regardless of biological fact. When treating an intersex child, the assignment of sex is inconsequential, so long as the child is raised clearly and unequivocally as either male or female. Surprisingly his argument was largely based on the study of one individual known as the John/Joan case.[28]

John, an identical twin, was born in 1965 and lost his penis during a surgical accident when he was eight months old. As there was no possibility of repairing the damage, Dr Money suggested a gender change. In 1967, John became Joan. Her parents were under strict instruction from the medical team to keep her original sex a secret lest it undermine the effect of the surgery. Money monitored both Joan and her brother annually. In 1972, acknowledging Joan was a tomboyish girl, Money reported the success of this intervention as proof that nurture trumps nature. The existence of Brian, Joan's twin – an identical genetic control – who was a typical boy, convinced doctors that gender was a societal fiction.[29] No other experiments were conducted to confirm the accuracy of this finding, yet medical and surgical interventions on intersex bodies became the standard treatment. No follow-up studies were ever done on adult intersex people who underwent such interventions as children.

In the late 1990s, researchers attempting to challenge Money's theories began to search for Joan, whom Money had reported was 'lost to research'. It was the publication of the eventual outcome of the John/Joan story that caused some practitioners to begin to reconsider the accepted medical management of intersex.[30] The boy who was raised as a girl was now living as a man. In 2006, the Chicago consensus statement explicitly identified the need for multi-disciplinary teams to manage intersex conditions, now renamed DSDs. Care should centre on the patient, acknowledging the child's evolving capacity. Recognising the increased importance of children's rights, the 2016 updated consensus statement emphasised the need for sharing knowledge, including uncertainties, with patients and families to enable fully informed decision making.[31]

28 John Money and Anke A. Ehrhardt, *Man and woman, boy and girl: differentiation and dimorphism of gender* (Baltimore, 1973); John Money, *Sex errors of the body and related syndromes: a guide to counselling children, adolescents, and their families*, 2nd ed. (Baltimore, 1994), p. xvii, p. 132; Milton Diamond and H. Keith Sigmundson, 'Sex reassignment at birth: long-term review and clinical implications', *Archives of Pediatrics & Adolescent Medicine*, 153:3 (1997), 298–304; John Colapinto, *As nature made him: the boy who was raised as a girl* (New York; Toronto, 2006). 29 Ibid. 30 Milton Diamond and H. Keith Sigmundson, 'Management of intersexuality: guidelines for dealing with persons with ambiguous genitalia', *Archives of Pediatrics & Adolescent Medicine*, 151:10 (1997), pp 1046–50. For an introduction to the various methods of medical management see Tanya Ní Mhuirthile, 'Realising gender recognition: rendering the vulnerable visible or further vulnerabilising the invisible?', *UCD Working Papers in Law, Criminology and Socio-Legal Studies*, 41/2010 (2010) (https://papers.ssrn.com/sol3/papers.cfm?abstract_id=1680899). 31 Houk et al., 'Consensus statement on the management of intersex conditions'.

INTERSEX IN MODERN IRELAND

Rarely has intersex been the subject of official discussion since the creation of the Irish State. Prior to 2009 there was no mention of either intersex or hermaphrodite in any official text or sources from any public body. Where intersex had been mentioned it was cursory at best. The first mention of intersex was in a case before the High Court, *S v. An Bord Uchtála*, in 2009.[32] Here, the Adoption Board was ordered to amend the gender marker for a child with an intersex variation on the Register of Intercountry Adoptions. This was the desired outcome for the litigant family but as there was no written judgment, the case does not establish a strong legal precedent. Thus, it is uncertain whether the legal recognition afforded to S would extend to another intersex person. It is less clear whether it might encompass someone who identifies outside the binary male/female gender paradigm.

The only legal cases to consider the parameters of legal gender identity in Ireland have occurred in the context of a transgender woman seeking to have her birth certificate altered to reflect her preferred identity as female. Dr Lydia Foy lost her first case in 2002, the court emphasising the importance of the register of births as a historical record, a snapshot of a moment in time.[33] Subsequently, a unanimous decision from the European Court of Human Rights, in the case of *Goodwin v. UK*, found the persistent failure of English law to recognise the preferred gender identity of a transwoman amounted to a violation of her right to respect for her private and family life under Article 8 of the European Convention on Human Rights (ECHR).[34] Dr Foy brought fresh proceedings. Dr Foy won her argument that, based on Goodwin, Irish law violated her European Convention right to respect for her private life. The ruling of the court was historic as it was the first time that an Irish court had issued a Declaration of Incompatibility between Irish law and the State's legal obligations flowing from the ECHR.[35]

The Foy case adopted into Irish law the decision of the English High Court as to how legal gender ought to be determined. In *Corbett v. Corbett* (1970) it was held that the legal gender of an individual was determined by the congruence of the chromosomes, gonads and genitals at birth. This test has both biological and temporal aspects. In cases where this congruence is not present at birth the judge held that the genital sex ought to be determinative.[36] Given the importance of the birth moment in determining legal gender such a preference for genital

32 *S v. An Bord Uchtála*, unreported, (December 2009). 33 *Foy v. An t-Ard Chláraitheoir & Ors* [2002] IEHC 116. For more on this case see chapter 15 in this volume. 34 *Goodwin v. UK*, EHRR 588 (2002), p. 588. 35 *Foy v. An t-Ard Chláraitheoir & Ors (No. 2)* [2007] IEHC 470. 36 *Corbett v Corbett (Otherwise Ashley)*, [1970] 2 All ER 33, [1970] 2 All ER 33.

appearance is reductive as it may restrict the gender category available to an intersex person whose condition emerges later in life or who does not identify with the gender the genital appearance might suggest. Consequently, in *W v. W* (2000), the English High Court was willing to develop the Corbett test to find that advances in medical technology would enable Mrs W to be accepted as female in modern times, given she had asserted a female identity since the time she was able to choose her gender and this ought to be acknowledged.[37] The Irish court in the Foy cases was silent on whether this variation on the Corbett test might be applicable in the context of Irish intersex individuals, although, given the practical resolution of the S case, it is reasonable to presume it would be persuasive if advanced in legal argument.[38]

The first mention of intersex people from a non-curial official source in Ireland was contained in the Report of the Gender Recognition Advisory Group published in 2011 on how best to introduce gender recognition legislation to Ireland.[39] The Group declined to recommend acknowledging intersex lived experience within any proposed legislative scheme as this was beyond its remit, requiring more research and medical expertise than was available to it. The report amounts to a knowing refusal to engage with the complex challenge intersex poses for the law. Passing mentions of intersex appear in Seanad debates on the introduction of the Criminal Justice (Female Genital Mutilation) Act, 2012. Commenting on the defences available in section 2(2)(a) of that Act the Minister for Health stated: '[t]he exemption referring to the protection of mental health refers to the possible need for surgery for gender reassignment, intersex conditions or congenital malformations.'[40] Thus, the Minister was giving his imprimatur to medical and surgical interventions on intersex people.

Matters began to pick up pace in 2013 with the introduction before the Oireachtas of two private members' bills both adopting a self-declaration model for a change in legal gender recognition.[41] These bills proposed a return to the historical method of self-declaration as evidence in the writings of Coke in the 1600s. Such a self-declaration model is in accordance with best practice in international human rights discourse.[42] In contrast, the government-sponsored

37 *W v. W (Physical Inter-sex)*, [2001] 1 FLR 324. 38 For a more in-depth discussion of the *Foy* cases and the introduction of gender recognition legislation in Ireland see Tanya Ní Mhuirthile, 'Legal recognition of preferred gender identity in Ireland: an analysis of proposed legislation' in Máire Leane and Elizabeth Kiely (eds), *Sexualities in Irish society: a reader* (Dublin, 2014), pp 127–48. 39 *Report of the gender recognition advisory group*. Although there had been some mentions of intersex aquatic life in Dáil debates concerning water quality in 2005/6. See 'Dáil debate: written answers parliamentary question', 2005. 40 'Criminal Justice (Female Genital Mutilation) Bill 2011: Second Stage (Resumed)', 2011 (https://www.oireachtas.ie/en/debates/debate/seanad/2011–06–02/11/). 41 Gender Recognition Bill; Legal Recognition of Gender Bill. 42 *Gender identity law* 2012 (https://globaltransaction.files. wordpress.com/2012/05/argentina-gender-

General Scheme for the Gender Recognition Bill would require applicants (who must be at least eighteen years of age) to provide a supporting statement from their primary treating physician confirming that they have transitioned or are transitioning to their 'acquired gender.'[43] In restricting the ambit of the recognition rights to those over eighteen, the government's proposed scheme would exclude intersex children from amending their official identification documentation, which was the very defect the S case was brought to address. It was the lacuna leaving intersex children out of the ambit of the potential rights under the proposed legislative scheme outlined by the government that prompted most discussion on intersex inclusion therein. The Report of the Joint Oireachtas Committee on their examination of the scheme identified these concerns repeatedly.[44] It noted the concerns raised by the Ombudsman for Children's Office (OCO) in its report to the Committee. The OCO report detailed the State's obligations under international human rights law in this regard and concluded that any right to recognition enjoyed by an adult under Article 8 of the ECHR extended equally to children.

As a result of these investigations the Committee recommended that the age limit for applicants be reduced to sixteen years with provisions to address the day-to-day concerns of those under that age. It also recommended reconsidering the criterion concerning evidence of transition to ensure that it does not stigmatise applicants.[45] Although the recommendations of the Committee did not specifically address intersex, read together with the discussions contained in their report, they did suggest a more inclusive acknowledgment of the reality of intersex lives than existed in previous government-sponsored discourse. The final text of the bill as published in December 2014 ignored the suggestions of the Committee.[46] It continued to restrict the availability of the mechanisms of gender recognition to those who are over eighteen years of age. It appeared to have taken an even more stringent approach to medicalisation by requiring under s9(1)(g) that the applicant have a written certificate from a medical practitioner that, based upon medical evaluation, the applicant had transitioned gender and fully understood the consequences of the decision to live permanently in the preferred gender. It was the introduction of the phrase 'medical evaluation' that indicated this requirement had shifted from a supportive statement under the general scheme to something more akin to formal diagnosis and thus represented a retrograde step towards the insertion of medical practitioners as

identity-law.pdf); Gender Identity, Gender Expression and Sex Characteristics Act 2015 (https://legislation.mt/eli/cap/540/eng/pdf). 43 *General scheme of the Gender Recognition Bill 2013*, at Head 6(vi). 44 *Report on the general scheme of the Gender Recognition Bill 2013*. 45 Ibid., p. 37. 46 Gender Recognition Bill (as initiated), 2014 (116 of 2014) (https://data.oireachtas.ie/ie/oireachtas/bill/2014/116/eng/initiated/b11614d.pdf).

gatekeepers of legal rights. It is important to note that by not requiring a specific medical diagnostic label to access these rights, the medical criterion would enable intersex people to use the mechanism contained within the bill to change their gender of legal recognition.

Eventually, the government removed the medical criterion from the Gender Recognition Legislation in favour of a self-declaration model. Now, section 10 of the Gender Recognition Act, 2015, requires that the applicant be eighteen years of age; furnishes the Minister with their name; address; PPS number and contact details; the name and surname by which they wish to be known; proof of identity and proof of birth; and, where applicable proof of adoption or registration of foreign birth in the relevant register. In addition, applicants must swear a statutory declaration that they have a settled and solemn intention of living in the preferred gender for the rest of their life, that they understand the consequences of changing their recognised gender and that they make this decision of their own free will. For those who had reached the age of majority, a full self-declaration model was introduced. This was hailed as 'an incredible shift', enabling Ireland's trans community to step out of the shadows.[47]

A second significant change in the legislative scheme as enacted was the introduction of a mechanism for recognition of mature minors. This reflects the increased importance given to the rights of children flowing from the referendum to insert Article 42A into the Constitution which aimed to inculcate awareness and respect for children's rights in law. Those between the ages of 16 and 17 could apply to the Circuit Family Court for an exemption to the minimum age criterion. While the facilitation of young people was welcomed, the evidence necessary to ground an exemption application was the subject of criticism.[48] Under s12 of the 2015 Act, an application may only be made with the consent of the parents or legal guardians of the child. Applications must be accompanied by certification in writing by the child's primary treating physician (defined in the legislation as a person's primary treating endocrinologist or psychiatrist) and an independent endocrinologist or psychiatrist that the child has the necessary maturity to make the decision to apply for gender recognition; that they are aware of, have considered and fully understand the consequences of that decision; that they make the decision freely and independently; and that they have transitioned or are transitioning. Thus, the exemption process for those under eighteen, while welcome in principle, continues to be of limited practical use given the medical evidence required and the lengthy delays in

47 Sara Philips, chair of Transgender Equality Network Ireland, quoted in Dan MacGuill, '"A historic moment" – Oireachtas signs off on gender recognition bill', *TheJournal.ie*, 15 July 2015 (https://www.thejournal.ie/ireland-transgender-recognition-bill-2218956–Jul2015/). 48 Ibid.

accessing the necessary specialist practitioners who can provide the evidence. Those under the age of sixteen remain excluded from the recognition process. These limitations were critiqued in a report from the National Trans Youth Forum, which recommended that the lower age limit be abolished, that a self-declaration model of gender recognition for children and young people be introduced, that the 2015 Act be amended specifically to include recognition of intersex identities and that legislation be introduced to protect intersex infants from medically unnecessary surgeries.[49]

The issue of the explicit inclusion of intersex within the gender recognition legislation was referred to the review group for the legislation established by the Minister for Employment Affairs and Social Inclusion in 2017.[50] Following extensive public consultation and a series of hearings with experts, including those living with transgender and intersex conditions, the Review Group agreed that 'any measures introduced in future to improve the legal gender recognition of transgender people or people who are non-binary, would also be of benefit to people who are intersex and whose preferred gender is neither male nor female.'[51] However, the review contains no recommendations regarding medical and/or surgical interventions without the express consent of the intersex person.

This absence highlights the inherent and most important limitation as regards legal recognition of intersex in Ireland. While Irish law now recognises the existence of intersex people and their right to gender recognition, it does not explicitly engage with the most pressing human rights issue intersex raises: non-consensual medical interventions. While the Criminal Justice (Female Genital Mutilation) Act, 2012 could be read to provide such protection, given its focus on named body parts, this is undermined by the inclusion of 'mental health' in the exemptions grounds, thus enabling the continuation of medical and/or surgical interventions on intersex bodies without expressly requiring the consent of the person prior to intervening.

LIVED EXPERIENCE OF INTERSEX IN IRELAND

In March 2022, an extensive report on the reality of life with an intersex variation in Ireland was published.[52] The Intersex Mapping Study gathered data via an anonymous online survey and a series of in-depth interviews with people with intersex variations living, or who had lived, in Ireland. The report found

49 Peter Dunne and Cearbhall Turraoin, *'It's time to hear our voices': National Trans Youth Forum report 2015* (Dublin, 2015) (https://www.tcd.ie/equality/assets/docs/TimeToHearOurVoices.pdf), p. 22. 50 *Review of the Gender Recognition Act 2015*, Gender Recognition Act 2015 Review Group (Dublin, 2018) (https://www.gov.ie/en/press-release/6b7814–review-of-the-gender-recognition-act-2015–report-to-the-minister-for/). 51 Ibid., p. 84. 52 Tanya Ní Mhuirthile, Maria Feeney,

that intersex people are a very hidden population in Ireland. They are a diverse group with equally diverse needs in terms of their health and welfare. Moreover, they are a vulnerable population.[53] This is not an unusual finding. A study by the World Bank revealed that 93% of the intersex participants are 'never or rarely open about their identity' while merely 2% 'reported that they are completely open about their gender identity of being intersex'.[54] Participants reported engaging in very careful self-management to feel safe as intolerance is high, acceptance is low, and discrimination is 'either fairly common or very common'.[55] This invisibility comes with a cost in terms of access to services of all sorts. This chapter considers this cost from the perspective of one human right, the right to the highest attainable standard of health.

Precisely what is meant by this fundamental human right which was elaborated in the UN Committee on Economic, Social and Cultural Rights, issued as 'General Comment No. 14' from 2000, where it notes that it is not a right to be healthy but rather there is the right to control one's health and body and the right to be free from interference, such as torture or non-consensual medical treatment.[56] In the context of intersex people the Parliamentary Assembly of the Council of Europe noted vindication of this right includes 1) providing all intersex people with healthcare offered by a specialised, multidisciplinary team taking a holistic and patient-centred approach and comprising not only medical professionals but also other relevant professionals such as psychologists, social workers and ethicists, and based on guidelines developed together by intersex organisations and the professionals concerned; 2) ensuring that intersex people have effective access to healthcare throughout their lives; 3) ensuring that intersex people have full access to their medical records; and 4) providing comprehensive and up-to-date training on these matters to all medical, psychological and other professionals concerned, including conveying a clear message that intersex bodies are the result of natural variations in sex development and do not as such need to be modified.[57]

Mel Duffy and Anthony Staines, *Mapping the lived experience of intersex in Ireland: contextualising lay and professional knowledge to enable development of appropriate law and policy* (Dublin, 2022), available to access at https://doras.dcu.ie/cgi/users/home?screen=EPrint%3A%3AView&eprintid=26873). 53 Ibid., chapter 7. 54 World Bank, *Life on the margins: survey results of the experiences of LGBTI people in south-eastern Europe* (2018), p. 118 (http://documents1.worldbank.org/curated/en/12365153851 4203449/pdf/130420–REPLACEMENT-PUBLIC-FINAL-WEB-Life-on-the-Margins-Survey-Results-of-the-Experiences-of-LGBTI-People-in-Southeastern-Europe.pdf, (accessed 4 January 2021), p. 2). 55 Ibid., p. 34. 56 UN Committee on Economic, Social and Cultural Rights, 'General comment no. 14: right to the highest attainable standard of health E/C 12/2000/4', 2000. 57 Parliamentary Assembly of the Council of Europe, 'Promoting the human rights of and eliminating discrimination against intersex people. Resolution 2191', 2017.

A major theme that emerges in the Mapping Study is this issue of access to appropriate, informed and educated healthcare. The study found that, in so far as paediatric practice is concerned, Ireland adopts an approach consistent with international best practice.[58] However, a chief concern noted by the Study is the lack of joined-up services for adults with intersex variations. The Study identifies three issues in relation to healthcare provision: aging out, stepping out and turning out. The study notes that the healthcare professionals who practice in this space remarked that healthcare provision for intersex people in Ireland is imperfect. Additional support is needed to enable the delivery of lifelong, coordinated, informed and expert healthcare. In the same way that much of the academic literature on intersex is focused on the experiences of children, so too a focus on paediatrics dominates medical practice. The Study identifies as its first concern that people 'age out' of coordinated healthcare provision.[59] It quotes one of the healthcare professionals interviewed who describes the issue of transition planning for adult healthcare as 'messy'[60] noting that one patient may require several different services offered in various different hospitals by different specialists, with no easy way to prioritise which service is the most important. The visceral impact this can have on the lives of individual intersex people was described by one of the participants, 'Claire', who explained that when seeking psychiatric support for suicidal ideation the consultant's secretary could not see past her intersex and transgender identity:

> I called them again and they were like 'you are intersex and transgender' and I'm [like] 'I know, just trying to see you about antidepressants' ... and they said 'No, we won't see you here, you need to go to [National Gender Clinic]' ... They refused to see me while I was suicidal.[61]

The inability to consider intersex people holistically, because of being 'blinded' by an intersex diagnosis, results in the denial of much-needed medical support.

The second theme to emerge from the Study relating to medical issues was that of stepping out. Healthcare professionals disclosed that adult patients can become 'lost to follow-up' because of the lack of coordinated adult services.[62] Therefore, when people do re-emerge in the healthcare system, there is a need to be particularly sensitive on the part of healthcare professionals. However, given the traumatic previous experiences some adults had with healthcare provision it is unsurprising that they refuse to engage with it until, in Alan's words, they are 'forced into it'.[63] Alan recounts frustrations experienced seeking

58 *Mapping the lived experience*, p. 154. 59 Ibid., p. 156. 60 Ibid., p. 157. 61 Ibid., p. 157. 62 Ibid., p. 159. 63 Ibid., p. 160.

medical help from 'medical people who only listen to medical people. They don't listen to the patient.'[64] He felt strongly that the average appointment time in the public sector was insufficient for professionals to fully understand his medical history and present needs, and consequently they 'default' to responses that are inappropriate for his situation. Emma's experiences echo this and she recounted the need to consult a few healthcare providers before being able to identify one who would engage with her as she wished. However, she also notes that this option was only possible as she has been able to afford to access healthcare privately.[65]

The final theme identified by the study relating to healthcare provision was that of turning out. This relates to those circumstances where an intersex person has had to look outside of Ireland to access the healthcare services they needed. Healthcare professionals interviewed referred to the low 'footfall'[66] and the need to travel abroad to access specialised procedures not routinely offered in Ireland. This ensures that Irish intersex people can access the best available medical support. However, accessing this support abroad comes with its own complications and costs. Gina reported that accessing healthcare abroad compounded their health challenges by adding layers of physical, emotional and financial stress. A large element of this stress was the sense that this was not something that could be shared with family and friends. She told how she would book time to travel for healthcare appointments abroad as annual leave at work, describing it as 'an absolutely horrendous experience'.[67] The data from the Mapping Intersex Study reveals that due to aging out, stepping out and turning out those living with intersex variations are not enabled to exercise their rights, such as the right to the highest attainable standard of health, in a manner equivalent to others in Irish society.

CONCLUSION

This chapter has traced the evolving response of law to the existence of intersex individuals. It demonstrates that, historically, law acknowledged the legitimacy of hermaphrodites. The chapter argues that as medical knowledge and interest in regulating bodies and sexuality increased, intersex identity was rendered illegitimate. The requirement in birth registration legislation that all children be declared to the state as being either male or female shortly after birth caused the law to be complicit in the erasure of intersex from legal and social consciousness. Cases such as S and W demonstrate that a practical and

64 Ibid., p. 163. 65 Ibid., p. 161. 66 Ibid., p. 165. 67 Ibid., p. 168.

pragmatic approach by the courts can alleviate the difficulties of a system of gender recognition stymied by the prioritisation of the moment of birth as definitive in the determination of a person's legal gender. Nonetheless, it is in legislation that the truly transformative potential of the law lies. Intersex identity was delegitimised by the introduction of birth registration legislation, and it is through the introduction of rights-realising legislation that intersex bodies can be re-legitimised. The data in the Intersex Mapping Study proves that at present Irish law does not actively protect or ensure the vindication of the rights of intersex people. While the ability to correct registration records to reflect one's preferred gender identity is welcome, it is of limited practical benefit when law continues to enable medical and surgical interventions without the express consent of the person undergoing them and healthcare service provision for adults in Ireland is patchy at best. Access to the highest attainable standard of health is a fundamental human right. It is an inherent part of the right to dignity. As Zeid Ra'ad Al Hussein, then UN High Commissioner for Human Rights, opening an intersex expert meeting in September 2015, stated: 'All human beings are born equal in dignity and rights … regardless of our sex characteristics'.[68]

68 Zeid Ra'ad Al Hussein, 'Opening remarks by Zeid Ra'ad Al Hussein, United Nations High Commissioner for Human Rights at the Expert Meeting on Ending Human Rights Violations against Intersex Persons' (United Nations Office of the High Commissioner, 2015), (http://www.ohchr.org/EN/NewsEvents/Pages/DisplayNews.aspx?NewsID=16431&LangID=E).

CHAPTER 8

Strip-searches, sexual violence and feminism during the war in Northern/Ireland

Theresa O'Keefe

Feminist scholarship and practice have been instrumental in the recognition of sexual violence as a weapon of war. Work on the gendered logics and strategic use of sexual violence in conflict zones burgeoned from the 1990s onwards and demonstrated the prevalence of such violence across many jurisdictions and contexts.[1] Northern/Ireland is one of the most researched conflicts, yet when we speak of wartime sexual violence rarely do the 'Troubles' get a mention.[2] To some extent, this can be explained by the erroneous assumption that sexual violence was not weaponised on this island. It also relates to the racialisation of the perpetration of sexual violence and the persistence of a hierarchy of harms that misshapes the analysis of sexual violence in war. Perhaps one of the more curious reasons for the lack of attention to conflict-related sexual violence is feminist divergence in the north on the issues arising out of the war and its associated violence. An historical unwillingness existed within cohorts of the north's feminist movement to name as sexual violence some of the practices weaponised by the state against women from republican communities. Thus, it is not the absence of sexual violence, but the lack of attention afforded it which has helped to mask its prevalence in unsettled times.

1 See, for example, Jelke Boesten, *Sexual violence during war and peace: gender, power, and post-conflict justice in Peru* (New York, 2014); Janie Leatherman, *Sexual violence and armed conflict* (Cambridge, 2011); Aisling Swaine, 'Beyond strategic rape and between the public and private: violence against women in armed conflict', *Human Rights Quarterly*, 37 (2015), pp 755–86, at p. 755; Turshen Meredeth, 'The political economy of rape: an analysis of systematic rape and sexual abuse of women during armed conflict in Africa' in Caroline O.N. Moser and Fiona C. Clark (eds), *Victims, perpetrators or actors? Gender, armed conflict and political violence* (London, 2001), pp 55–68; E.J. Wood, 'Sexual violence during war: toward an understanding of variation' in Laura Sjoberg and Sandra Via (eds), *Gender, war, and militarism: feminist perspectives* (Santa Barbara, CA, 2010), pp 124–37.
2 'The Troubles' is a euphemism for the violent conflict that erupted in Northern Ireland between 1968 and 1998. Though pockets of violence still occur, it is generally accepted that the Troubles ended with the signing of the Good Friday Agreement on 10 April 1998. 'Northern Ireland' is a contested term used to refer to the six counties of Tyrone, Fermanagh, Antrim, Armagh, Down, Londonderry/Derry. This term is rejected by some communities, including some Irish republicans and Irish nationalists, who oppose the partition of Ireland. I therefore

One of the most observable forms of wartime sexual violence in the north of Ireland was the practice of strip-searching. Used in Northern Irish jails, detention and interrogation centres as a 'security mechanism', these often-violent searches became an over-arching feature of prison life for incarcerated women during the Troubles. Strip-searches were a technology of violence and control that were less to do with prison security and more to do with the gendered criminalisation and containment of republicanism, which included the disciplining of politicised women deemed unruly and transgressive. Before 1973, the number of women political prisoners incarcerated in the north was low, with 1–2 women in Armagh prison, then the main women's prison, at any given time. This changed, however, with the reintroduction of internment in 1971, when men and women from nationalist communities across the six counties were pulled from their homes or streets, arrested and in many cases tortured before being incarcerated and held for long periods of time without appearing before a judge or jury.[3] Initially, only men were targeted but this changed with the internment of Liz McKee on New Year's Day 1973.[4] As women in republican communities became more politicised, they were increasingly targeted and incarcerated, with the number growing from two in 1971 to 120 republican women by 1975.[5] The conditions in Armagh, a Victorian prison built in the 1780s, where the first women interned were held, were poor. As the prison population grew throughout the Troubles, it became very overcrowded, with prisoners forced to share cells meant for one.[6] It was cold and damp with inadequate sanitation facilities. The prison also drew international condemnation for its treatment of republican women prisoners. A report by the civil liberties organisation Statewatch declared it had found 'overwhelming

use 'Northern Ireland', 'Northern/Ireland,' 'the north' and 'the six counties' interchangeably to acknowledge this rejection of the border on the island of Ireland. 3 Internment is the incarceration of people without trial. In Northern Ireland it was orchestrated by the British and unionist governments and carried out by the British army through mass incarceration, interrogation, and torture. For more see the CAIN: Conflict Archive of Northern Ireland website https://cain.ulster.ac.uk/events/intern/sum.htm#:~:text=Internment%20refers%20to%20the%20arrest,until%20Friday%205%20December%201975, accessed 1 November 2023. 4 This internment of women mirrors their politicisation. Women organised rent strikes in response to the internment of men. They also organised street protests and thus many became politically active for the first time. When Liz McKee was arrested she was participating in a bin lid protest, a form of protest popularised by women wherein metal lids of rubbish bins are banged off the ground repeatedly. See Joe McCann, 'Fifty years on Liz McKee has her conviction squashed', *Andersonstown News*, 31 December 2020, https://belfastmedia.com/liz-mckee-internment-50-years-ago. 5 Christina Loughran, 'Armagh and feminist strategy: campaigns around republican women prisoners in Armagh jail', *Feminist Review*, 23:1 (1986), pp 59–79. 6 Mary Corcoran, *Out of order: the political imprisonment of women in Northern Ireland, 1971–1998* (Cullompton, 2006), p. 21. See also Raymond Murray, *Hard time: Armagh gaol, 1971–1986* (Dublin, 1998).

evidence' of 'torture, inhuman and degrading treatment' wielded by prison wardens between 1976 to 1981 and the practice at the centre of this was the strip-search.[7]

Strip-searches, or 'full searches' as described by the UK Ministry for Justice, can take a number of forms and can be conducted by any number of people working in the prison and, until contemporary times, of any gender. Strip-searches can be carried out on those incarcerated as well as prison visitors, something that was not uncommon for family visits during the Troubles. On paper, a strip-search resembles a clinical search of the body, hair, genitals, and clothes with provisions for 'modesty' sheets to partially cover the lower or top half the body as the other half is fully exposed and searched. Sometimes these searches would also include body cavity searches, an invasive probing of the anus, mouth and vagina conducted by a prison officer using gloved hands. If women did not consent, they were physically restrained by staff, handcuffed and their clothing forcibly and fully removed to facilitate the completion of the search. This also included inspection of sanitary towels.[8] Until subsequent changes in UK penal policy, such searches, including body cavity searches, could be conducted by men and women. While strip-searches are a normalised yet gendered security mechanism operational in many prison systems, when the political climate of the six counties is considered, strip-searches come into view as an instrument of war and a form of sexual violence. Prisons were a central part of the criminalisation, normalisation and containment policies adopted by British government in relation to Northern Ireland.[9] Indeed, the interrogation procedures and treatment of prisoners and detainees had come under scrutiny from the European Court of Human Rights, Amnesty International and others concerned with human rights abuses.[10] Through the incarceration of combatants, 'suspected subversives', and people living in republican communities, prisons became institutions explicitly used to fight the war in the North of Ireland and unequivocally comprised part of the battleground during the conflict. Prison workers became, in effect, incidental combatants and were regularly targeted by the IRA. The overwhelming majority of security forces and

7 Corcoran, *Out of order*, pp 51–4; Phil Scraton, 'I am sir, you are a number': Report of the Independent Panel of Inquiry into the Circumstances of the H-Block and Armagh Prison Protests 1976–1981 (Coiste na nIarchimí, 2020) https://www.statewatch.org/media/1396/ni-report-inquiry-h-block-armagh-prison-protests-10-20.pdf. 8 Prisoners' statement, 'Women republican prisoners of war, Maghaberry prison, strip-searching ... violence against women', *Women's News* (Belfast, September 1986), p. 11; Sharon Pickering, 'Engendering resistance: women and policing in Northern Ireland', *Policing and Society: An International Journal*, 11: 3–4 (2001), pp 337–58, at p. 351. 9 Brian Gormally, Kieran McEvoy and David Wall, 'Criminal justice in a divided society: Northern Ireland prisons', *Crime and Justice*, 17 (1993), pp 51–135. 10 See Fr Denis Faul and Fr Raymond Murray, 'Violations of human rights in Northern Ireland, 1968–1978' (n.d.),

prison authorities came from Protestant backgrounds and communities, and membership in the Orange Order was common. Many prison officers in Armagh were also ex-soldiers from the British military. Consequently, there was an inevitable hostility within prisons where republicans were held. Strip-searches were thus part of the ecology of conflict, and they afforded an opportunity for reprisals against republicans in the wake of ongoing threats and attacks.

Prison conditions in Armagh worsened in 1979. In April, Agnes Wallace (aged 40), a prison officer, was shot dead outside Armagh prison in an INLA gun and grenade attack. Three of her co-workers, all women, were injured. A new governor also took command of the prison and, according to prisoners and observers, ushered in a harsher approach to running the prison.[11] Within weeks of his instalment, women prisoners became victims of a reportedly unprovoked attack by prison guards in riot gear. Many women were beaten and left with lasting injuries, and it was used as an occasion to taunt and torment women individually and collectively.[12] Women were locked in their cells, denied access to the toilets, and prohibited from slopping out.[13] When their chamber pots became full, women began to empty them through the spy holes in the doors of their cells, which were then nailed shut by prison authorities. This sparked the protracted no-wash protest in Armagh, wherein women smeared their excrement, including menstrual blood on the walls of their cells.[14] Though the dominant republican narrative implied that women joined the no-wash strike in solidarity with their male counterparts in Long Kesh, women were organising against their own prison conditions.[15] The strike lasted a full year and included a hunger strike by three women: Mary Doyle, Mairéad Nugent and Mairéad Farrell. The no-wash strike concluded at the command of republican leadership, who insisted focus should be placed entirely on the second, now infamous, hunger strike undertaken by men in the H-blocks of Long Kesh in 1981.[16] After the hunger strikes, some concessions were afforded to republican men housed

pamphlet, p. 5. 11 National Council for Civil Liberties (NCCL), *Strip-searching: an inquiry into the strip-searching of women prisoners at Armagh prison between 1982 and 1985* (London, 1986). See also Scraton, 'I am sir, you are a number', p. 47. 12 Scraton, 'I am sir, you are a number', p. 48. 13 Prisons lacked basic sanitation facilities. Prisoners had no toilets in their cells and were forced to use buckets or chamber pots instead. 'Slopping out' refers to the emptying of buckets, usually done first thing in the morning. 14 Evelyn Brady, Eva Patterson, Kate McKinney, Rosie Hamill and Pauline Jackson, *The footsteps of Anne: stories of republican women ex-prisoners* (Belfast, 2011), p. 202; Theresa O'Keefe, *Feminist identity development and activism in revolutionary movements* (London, 2013), pp 98–9. 15 Long Kesh was an internment camp on the outskirts of Belfast, that became a prison in 1972 used to incarcerate republican and loyalist prisoners. In 1976 the purpose-built, maximum security 'h-blocks' were opened adjacent to the cages in Long Kesh and this is where sentenced political prisoners were incarcerated until it was closed in 2000. 16 See Theresa in Long Kesh, including the cessation of mirror searches.[17] In Armagh, however, strip-searches were expanded, intensified and became more brutal.[18] Where previously they had primarily been used when entering and leaving prison, from October 1982 strip-searches were routinised and regularised through the introduction of strip-searches for women on remand, who travelled to court often on a weekly basis.[19] Women, regardless of age or health, whether they were menstruating, pregnant or had just given birth, were all searched on a regular basis. This was taking place alongside the denial of sanitary protection for women in Armagh and its use as a disciplinary mechanism.[20]

A few months later, in March 1983, the number of strip-searches in Armagh increased significantly.[21] Random searches were introduced and weaponised against non-sentenced prisoners. Prisoners could be subjected to arbitrary strip-searches at any point in time, with no notice or justification. Some read the arbitrariness as a gendered punishment for the forced concessions in Long Kesh, and it allowed prison authorities to show they still had leverage in Armagh.[22] Random searches were terrorising for women. Coupled with the use of regular searches on women on remand, strip-searches became a mechanism to instil fear in women and signalled to them that they could be subject to a search without notice and under an array of conditions. As a result difficulty sleeping was a common complaint among incarcerated women at the time. Additionally, strip-searches were not just confined to republican women incarcerated in UK jails on the island of Ireland. Martina Anderson and Ella O'Dwyer suffered over 400 strip-searches while incarcerated in Brixton prison between 1984 and 1985.[23] Martina Anderson, speaking of her time in Brixton, stated that she was regularly and excessively subjected to strip-searches and on one occasion suffered a total of six searches in a matter of hours, including one within minutes of another.[24]

O'Keefe, *Feminist identity*, pp 98–9. **17** Mirror searches involved the naked prisoner standing spread eagled over a mirror so as to facilitate the inspection of the anal cavity. For more information on the abuses that accompanied such searches when carried out on republican prisoners, see Scraton, 'I am sir, you are a number', pp 30–1. **18** Brady et al., *The footsteps of Anne*; Corcoran, *Out of order*, p. 183. **19** Linda Moore and Phil Scraton, 'Women's imprisonment, conflict and transition' in Linda Moore and Phil Scraton (eds), *The incarceration of women* (London, 2014), pp 72–97. **20** See Theresa O'Keefe, 'Menstrual blood as a weapon of resistance', *International Feminist Journal of Politics*, 8:4 (2006), pp 535–6. **21** HC Deb., 9 February 1984, vol. 53, cc1041–112, available at: https://api.parliament.uk/historic-hansard/commons/1984/feb/09/maze-prison-hennessy-report. See also Begoña Aretxaga, 'The sexual games of the body politic: fantasy and state violence in Northern Ireland', *Culture, Medicine and Psychiatry*, 25:1 (2001), pp 1–27, at p. 7. **22** Corcoran, *Out of order*, p. 183. **23** Loughran, 'Security or subjugation', p. 5. **24** *Slí na mBan* interview with Martina Anderson, October 1999. http://www.tallgirlshorts.net/marymary/martina.html, accessed 23 February 2024.

STRIP-SEARCHES AS WARTIME SEXUAL VIOLENCE

In 1986, Armagh prison closed and the remaining women were moved to Maghaberry prison, near Lisburn, Co. Antrim. They were placed in Mourne House, a unit described by Phil Scraton as a 'jail within a jail' with state-of-the-art surveillance technologies.[25] Though the archaic conditions of Armagh were not missed in this new purpose-built high security prison, the aggressive strip-searches were carried forward as the Mourne unit was policed by a harsh, violent regime that targeted republican women prisoners and included forced strip-searches.[26] It was also the site of a violent, unexpected and unprecedented mass strip-search in 1992 during a time, as anthropologist Begoña Aretxaga notes, of escalating tensions on the outside and relative calm inside the prison.[27] On 2 March, the week of International Women's Day (8 March), men and women dressed in riot gear, bearing shields and batons, stormed the unit housing republican prisoners to conduct an unannounced wing and cell search, accompanied by strip and body searches that lasted the entire day and evening, with pauses only for dinner and supper. First-hand accounts from prisoners recount how women were forcibly pulled from their cells one by one and dragged through the wing, sometimes by their hair.[28] Many had their clothes partially stripped and were beaten, kicked and punched. Prisoners reported that the wardens who conducted the search smelled of alcohol and sang 'Happy Days Are Here Again' as they commenced the search.[29] During the searches women were jeered at and taunted, with sexual comments and gestures directed at them and their bodies by attendant guards, including those who watched. As each individual search was conducted, the remaining women prisoners listened to the screams of those being searched as they awaited their turn.[30] There were reports of remarks against Catholics, laughter, sexual jokes, and rape threats while women screamed and cried in terror.[31] Those who were subjected to the strip-search referred to the attack as rape. One of the women prisoners interviewed by Aretxaga about the incident recalled:

25 Phil Scraton, 'Bearing witness to the "pain of others": researching power, violence and resistance in a women's prison', *International Journal for Crime, Justice and Social Democracy*, 5:1 (2016), pp 5–20, p. 11. 26 Linda Moore, '"Nobody's pretending that it's ideal": conflict, women, and imprisonment in Northern Ireland', *The Prison Journal*, 91:1 (2011), pp 103–5, at p. 104. 27 Aretxaga, 'The sexual games of the body politic', p. 8. 28 Ibid., p. 7; Statewatch, report: *NI: mass strip-search at Maghaberry*, 1 May 1992. Available at: https://www.statewatch.org/statewatch-database/ni-mass-strip-search-at-maghaberry/, accessed 23 February 2024. 29 Aretxaga, 'The sexual games of the body politic', p. 9. 30 Republican women prisoners, 'Strip-searches in Maghaberry jail', *Women's News* (May/June 1992), p. 5. 31 Aretxaga, 'The sexual games of the body politic', p. 11.

> At one stage I watched a male screw making sick and disgusting sexual remarks. I cannot describe what it is really like to watch women being trailed off the window bars to be sexually assaulted and to listen to their cries and screams – it's a nightmare.[32]

Based on her interviews with formerly incarcerated women who lived through this violent search, Aretxaga also makes the case that it constituted 'a *mise en scène* of military mass rape'.[33] This view of strip-searches as a form of rape is echoed in women's own accounts of not just the Maghaberry mass search but of all forms of strip-searches carried out during the entirety of the Troubles.[34] Women who experienced searches reported being 'frightened of getting torn down there or getting hurt down there … you were terrified of them [the prison officers] really hurting you, you know hurting your internal organs'.[35] Much akin to other forms of sexual violence, women refer to living with the residual trauma brought on by strip-searches, 'I concentrate on trying to block out this trauma. It's no use. I'm embarrassed, I'm degraded, I'm ashamed! Why should I be ashamed? The shame is on them'.[36] Many who endured strip-searches lost weight, developed panic attacks, and stopped menstruating.[37] Similarly, former prisoner Mairead Farrell, who was subsequently killed in Gibraltar by British security forces, delivered a speech at the gates of Maghaberry in 1987 as part of an event to mark International Women's Day wherein she classed strip-searchers as 'a form of state legalised rape'.[38]

The 'strip-search', the act of being stripped, is itself viscerally violent. Discursive connotations of 'strip' include the common usage 'to rob' or 'take from' while its etymological origins derive from 'make bare', 'plunder', and 'despoil', all of which can be inferences to acts of violence. Indeed, the descriptions of the 1992 Maghaberry attack are hauntingly familiar to the stories of torture that emerged from Abu Graib prison in 2003, which included the weaponisation of nakedness, among other forms of abuse, as a means to humiliate, torture and traumatise prisoners.[39] Perhaps one of the more telling

32 Ibid., p. 10. 33 Ibid., p. 18. 34 Niall Gilmartin and Margaret M. Scull, 'Republican women and Catholic Church responses to the strip-searching of female prisoners in Northern Ireland, 1982–92', *Women's History Review*, 31:5 (2022), pp 721–40; Azrini Wahidin, *Ex-combatants, gender and peace in Northern Ireland: women, political protest and the prison experience* (New York, 2016). 35 Wahidin, *Ex-combatants, gender and peace in Northern Ireland*, p. 121. 36 Republican prisoner in Armagh as cited in Christina Loughran, 'Security or subjugation', *Women's News* (December 1984), pp 4–5, at p. 5. 37 Scraton, 'I am sir, you are a number', p. 55. 38 Mairéad Farrell, 'Strip-search degradation/ International Women's Day (Maghaberry gaol 1987) [1:09]' https://www.youtube.com/watch?v=2yw_FrYCbM4, accessed 2 February 2024. 39 See Melanie Richter-Montpetit, 'Militarised masculinities, women torturers, and the limits of gender analysis at Abu Ghraib' in Annick T.R. Wibben (ed.), *Researching war: feminist methods, ethics and politics* (London, 2016), pp 92–116.

aspects of the use of strip-searches in Northern Irish prisons is that as the conflict progressed, the use of strip-searches in the manner in which they were instrumentalised was not only excessive but also unnecessary due to technological advances in security; strip-searches persisted and, in the case of Maghaberry, increased in severity despite these advances. The ever-present threat of random and possibly violent searches meant that even those conducted within the letter of the law had to be read as a potential site of danger for republican women as the tenor of the search could change at any point in the process. Thus, when we consider carceral strip-searches in Northern/Ireland, the lack of consent and subsequent forced searches conducted by hostile state forces, the practice must also be understood as a form of conflict-related sexual violence. Based on the testimonies of women who experienced strip-searches, and indeed other sexualised encounters with state forces, strip-searching was a form of sexual violence, existing on a continuum of violence alongside other forms of intimidation experienced by women in their everyday lives at the hands of security forces.[40]

If we turn to feminist scholarship on wartime sexual violence, we see many similarities between the Northern Irish case and sexual violence that occurs in other conflict zones. Feminist work on war has reshaped considerations on conflict-related violence and brought forth a legal framework for the classification of wartime sexual violence. Feminist accounts of deeply divided societies have demonstrated the prevalence of reliance on sexual violence as a weapon of war, deployed for reasons which include male bonding, ethnic cleansing, humiliation of the enemy and the policing of women deemed transgressive. Though not disconnected from the gender-based violence that occurs outside the confines of conflict, wartime sexual violence has been weaponised by combatants in state and non-state military forces as a 'mechanism of political terror' as described by Cynthia Cockburn.[41] Michele Leiby argues acts of sexual violence during conflict are 'not merely the unavoidable consequence of the chaos of war, but rather part of an explicit or implicit strategy to defeat the armed opposition'.[42] Leiby's work on political prisoners in El Salvador and Peru documents how sexual violence perpetrated by state armed actors in detention centres was used as a form of punishment against

40 Helen Harris and Eileen Healy (eds), *Strong about it all: rural and urban women's experiences of the security forces in Northern Ireland* (North West Women's/Human Rights Project Publications, 2001). 41 Cynthia Cockburn, 'The gendered dynamics of armed conflict' in Caroline O.N. Moser and Fiona C. Clark (eds), *Victims, perpetrators or actors?: gender, armed conflict and political violence* (London, 2001), pp 13–29, p. 22. 42 Michelle Leiby, 'Sexual violence against political prisoners: an examination of empirical evidence in El Salvador and Peru' in Alissa Ackerman and Rich Furman (eds), *Sex crimes; transnational problems and global perspective* (Columbia, 2015), pp 129–42, p. 13.

suspected subversives and was part of the arsenal to advance the interests of the state.[43] Ruth Seifert suggests wartime rape, especially gang rape and systematic rape, serves the purpose of male bonding and solidarity among combatants[44] and this speaks well to Aretxaga's analysis of the Maghaberry attack outlined above.

A striking observation about the Northern Irish case is that women's prison conditions, including violence, were a flashpoint for the feminist movement. As republican women tried to draw attention to prison conditions and the violence of strip-searches, solidarity from some feminist quarters was not forthcoming. Many feminist and women's groups in the north were reticent to support any prison struggles undertaken by republican women, especially during the years of the no-wash strike. For some it was borne out of a fear of being associated with republicanism, especially IRA violence, and to a certain extent this was contextualised within a feminist rhetoric of non-violence. Some went so far as to suggest women were only in prison because they had 'emotionally followed their men'.[45] There was also a desire to hold the space of the middle-ground, to not infer support for one side of the war or to be perceived as showing support for nationalism over unionism, to instead champion the role of bridge-building across the divide.[46] Still others outright refused to comprehend as violence the carceral punishments visited upon republican women and argued that feminists who support the Armagh campaigns should instead fight violence against women.[47] This left a movement divided in Northern/Ireland, with some quarters unable to draw the parallels between ongoing feminist demands for bodily autonomy and the right not to be forcibly stripped and body searched by a hostile, patriarchal prison regime. As the campaign intensified after the routinisation of strip-searches and international feminist solidarity gained momentum, more left-wing groups, including trade unionists and some previously unaligned feminists, rowed in.

Given that one of the central tenets of feminism has been the right to bodily autonomy for women, the conflicted position on prison violence is curious. To understand this divergence, we must look to the feminist tensions and subsequent developments that arose as a result of differently positioned groups

43 Leiby, 'Sexual violence against political prisoners'. 44 Ruth Seifert, 'War and rape: a preliminary analysis' in Alexandra Stiglmayer (ed.), *Mass rape: the war against women in Bosnia Herzegovina* (Lincoln, NE, 1995), pp 54–71, p. 59. 45 Address by Bernadette Devlin to the International Women's Day picket at Maghaberry, 5 March 1989, reprinted in *Women's News*, 42:11 (May/June 1989). 46 Theresa O'Keefe, 'Bridge-builder feminism: the feminist movement and conflict in Northern Ireland', *Irish Political Studies*, 36:1 (2021), pp 52–71; Fidelma Ashe, 'The virgin Mary connection: reflecting on feminism and Northern Irish politics', *Critical Review of International Social and Political Philosophy*, 9:4 (2006), pp 573–88. 47 Loughran, 'Armagh and feminist strategy', p. 64.

in relation to the Troubles. During the 1970s, feminism in Northern Ireland was very much a product of the wider conflict that raged across the north. A series of rows and splits in relation to what was euphemistically referred to by many as the 'constitutional issue' impacted the development of a large-scale, unified feminist movement.[48] On the one hand, some feminists sought to sidestep issues that divided communities in the north and place emphasis on the traditional bread and butter concerns that were assumed to unite all women. Others argued that it was not possible or prudent to ignore the conflict and its associated human rights abuses and injustices as the effect of the conflict on women's lives was profound. One of the largest groups, the Northern Ireland Women's Rights Movement (NIWRM), was founded in 1975, and from its infancy adopted a 'check your label' at the door policy, with the hope of minimising arguments in relation to the conflict, primarily between women from republican and loyalist communities. From the beginning, the group was plagued by tensions that arose in relation to its position or indeed silence around conflict-related issues, especially as they pertained to women.[49] When the matter of Armagh arose, feminists were divided over whether it warranted feminist support; the NIWRM and its splinter group, the Belfast Women's Collective, refused. This ambivalence or position of 'no position' was interpreted as opposition to the prison campaign, and instead read as support for the union.[50]

Loughran argues that two distinct feminist factions emerged during this time – one that sought parity of rights with the UK for women in Northern Ireland and the other, oriented around anti-imperialist feminism, that rejected any extension of UK policy or legislation to Northern Ireland for fear of further establishing British state power and colonialism on the island of Ireland.[51] While groups like the Belfast Women's Collective wished to orient their focus on recognised feminist issues like abortion, they too suffered from internal splits over Armagh. In 1979 they organised a series of 'unity meetings' out of a desire to minimise division but it resulted in more consternation and the subsequent withdrawal of anti-imperialist feminists from further meetings. Discontented with the lack of focus on the situation in Armagh, Women Against Imperialism (WAI) formed in 1978 after a series of splits within socialist feminist groups and began to organise pickets outside Armagh jail to demand that feminists across the island make Armagh a feminist priority. Though the severity of strip-

48 This euphemism usually refers to the constitutional partition of Ireland and the subsequent imposition of what eventually became a policed border between the six counties of Northern Ireland and the Republic of Ireland. This partition meant that those living in the six counties would remain under British rule while the remaining twenty-six counties would form the Republic, often referred to by Northerners as the 'Free State'. 49 O'Keefe, 'Bridge-builder feminism'. 50 Christine Loughran, *Women's News* (Summer 1985), issue 11. 51 Ibid.

searches and the campaign to stop them intensified after the 1981 hunger strikes, WAI had been forcing the issue onto the agenda since they organised a series of pickets outside Armagh, most notably on International Women's Day. At the first picket in 1978, 11 women were arrested, two of whom went to jail when they refused to pay the fines levied against them. One of the women included noted anti-war activist and artist, Margaretta D'Arcy.[52] The following year on International Women's Day (8 March 1979) close to 500 women picketed outside Armagh, a remarkable feat even in settled times. The pickets continued as the prison struggles intensified and the conflict escalated. However, WAI dissolved in 1981 as members took strategic decisions on how best to focus their actions. Some wished to prioritise prison struggles and joined Relatives Action Committees, which came to replace the Stop Strip-Searches campaign; others went on to form a Women's Department within Sinn Féin, in the belief that it would be the best vehicle to achieve change for women. In one of the last statements issued by the group they quipped it was easier to 'feminise republicans than republicanise feminists'.[53]

LEGACY OF FEMINIST FIGHT AGAINST STRIP-SEARCHES

The struggle against strip-searches impacted republicanism, the wider women's movement in Northern Ireland and UK penal policies. The women of Armagh and Maghaberry chose to resist strip-searches, and in doing so were subjected to further violence. They engaged in this act of resistance on their own terms and in the face of limited support from the republican leadership. Much of the focus around prison struggles had been directed at the men in Long Kesh and their campaign for political status. This was compounded by the fact that republican leadership was squeamish about women's involvement in any prison struggles for fear of negative publicity. According to patriarchal gender norms that were commonplace at the time, a woman's place was in the home and men were their 'protectors'; women's prison struggles threatened the republican battle for hearts and minds. In some circles, women's prison protests were considered detrimental to the republican cause because they detracted attention from men.[54] Women's resistance to strip-searches also caused friction in relationships with men for some incarcerated republican women, as their partners, fathers or brothers questioned the necessity of resisting the practice.[55] Despite this frosty

52 Margaretta D'Arcy, *Tell them everything: a sojourn in the prison of her majesty Queen Elizabeth II at Ard Macha (Armagh)* (London, 1981). 53 Nell McCafferty, *The Armagh women* (Dublin, 1981), p. 90. 54 Richard O'Rawe, *Blanketmen: an untold story of the h-block hunger strike* (Dublin, 2005), p. 102. 55 Gilmartin and Scull, 'Republican women and Catholic Church responses', p. 9.

reception from republican leadership, their comrades and family, republican women prisoners were able to garner international attention and condemnation for strip-searches with the support of anti-imperialist feminists. Support for the campaign came from the UK, New Zealand, the United States, Palestine, Cuba, and those who were especially concerned with anti-imperialist struggles.[56] WAI, despite its brief life, succeeded in bringing feminist solidarity to the gates of Armagh and in getting strip-searches on the agenda within republicanism thereby making women's prison struggles visible. Women prisoners, republican and anti-imperialist feminists and those who lent their solidarity to the campaign in the north of Ireland, forced international attention onto the conditions women endured in prison. This, in turn, brought international condemnation for regular strip-searches and prison conditions more generally. An inquiry was undertaken by the UK's National Council for Civil Liberties to examine the practice of strip-searches in UK-run prisons from 1982 to 1986, and it concluded that the routinisation of searches 'amounted to an ill-considered attempt to maintain authority in the prison … We are not convinced by the security arguments. Nor can we find a convincing justification for its continued enforcement'.[57] This was echoed by other human rights organisations including Amnesty International and Statewatch.[58] The UK government was forced to abandon random strip-searches in Armagh because of international pressure, however they resumed upon transfer to Maghaberry whereby the distinction between random and routine searches became artificial.[59] Controversies over strip-searches in women's prisons continue to persist and the UK government continues to come under fire for what is viewed as the inappropriate, unnecessary and excessive use of strip-searches, including on the handful of incarcerated republican women.[60]

The struggle against strip-searches and prison conditions thus irrevocably shaped the wider feminist movement in the north of Ireland in positive and negative ways. International feminist solidarity came as a surprise to those feminists in the North who did not see Armagh as a feminist issue and placed internal pressure on the feminist movement. This made it difficult to not

56 D'Arcy, *Tell them everything*; Norma Hashim and Yousef M. Aljamal, *A shared struggle: stories of Palestinian and Irish hunger strikers* (Belfast, 2020); Brodie Nugent and Evan Smith, 'Intersectional solidarity? The Armagh women, the British left and women's liberation', *Contemporary British History*, 31:4 (2017), pp 611–35. 57 National Council for Civil Liberties, *Strip-searching*. 58 Ibid.; Amnesty International 1986: 4; Murray, *Hard times*. 59 Corcoran, *Out of time*. 60 See for example: Irish legal news, June 2023, https://www. irishlegal.com/articles/northern-ireland-strip-search-law-should-be-re-written-to-include-reasonable-suspicion-test; Conla Young, 'Forced strip-searches at Maghaberry raised in Dáil', *Irish News*, 11 November 2022, https://www. irishnews.com/news/northernirelandnews/2022/11/11/news/forced_strip_searches_at_maghaberry_raised_in_dail-2901953/; Dáil Éireann debate, 25 October 2016, vol. 926, no. 1. https://www.oireachtas.ie/en/debates/question/2016–10–25/50/, accessed 23 February 2024.

support the campaign: 'all of a sudden the anti-imperialist feminists were the ones who became the feminists. There was no way you could say anything more complicated than support for the political prisoners. There was no forum for it'.[61]

While the fissures around the prison struggles have left a legacy of a divided movement that has not yet entirely healed, on the other hand, the strip-searches and prison campaigns politicised a large number of women who had no prior history of feminist activism or engagement. Through feminist solidarity, both international and local, many women were introduced to feminist theories of domination, sexuality, bodily autonomy and feminist histories of struggle, and they subsequently came to identify as feminist. WAI's work helped to foster a coherent republican feminism, which articulated why strip-searches were a form of sexual violence and indeed a feminist issue worthy of feminist solidarity. Their dispersal into the Relatives Action Committees and the Sinn Féin Women's Department ensured this carried forward after their demise. A distinct republican feminism emerged as a consequence and firmly placed gender equality on the republican agenda.[62]

The weaponisation of strip-searching and all forms of sexual violence that occurred in relation to the Troubles still needs to be reckoned with. Though the feminist movement has become more unified in more recent times as evidenced in the emergence of campaigns against sexual violence and in favour of abortion rights, wider conversations regarding conflict-related sexual violence have yet to occur in any organised fashion. This is a legacy of the Troubles itself and the polarisation of the feminist movement that occurred in the 1970s. While there has been growing academic interest in gender and prison violence during the Troubles, there is little by way of an established body of work that examines at its core the gendered violence utilised by the security forces and its resultant trauma. The Northern Irish case also necessitates a wider conversation on the practice of strip-searches used in ordinary times and on so-called ordinary prisoners. This raises questions not just in relation to the incarceration of political prisoners but also in terms of the use of strip-searches more generally both in times of conflict and relative peace. Strip-searches have become a normalised feature of prison life in many jurisdictions. Prisoners are often searched upon entry into a prison and can be subject to random searches at any time. For survivors of sexual violence, they can be especially traumatic and triggering, and some women have attempted or committed suicide as a

61 Interview conducted by Christine Loughran for *Women's news* (summer 1985), issue 11.
62 Theresa O'Keefe, *Feminist identity development and activisms in revolutionary movements* (London, 2013).
63 Zoe Tidman, 'Autistic girl "tried to kill herself after police strip-search while she was menstruating"', *The Independent*, 24 May 2023. https://www.independent.co.uk/news/uk/crime/

consequence.[63] As celebrated academic and former political prisoner Angela Davis notes, jails and prisons are designed to break people and as patriarchal institutions they do so in ways that violently police gender. Strip-searches must therefore be read as a mechanism used by the state to enforce a gender regime.[64]

teenage-girl-strip-search-met-police-b2085886.html, accessed 23 February 2024. **64** Angela Y. Davis, *Are prisons obsolete?* (New York, 2011).

CHAPTER 9

'Women to blame': Irish feminism's story of backlash and resistance, 1979–92*

Sinéad Kennedy

The writer Anne Enright (b. 1962) was a young woman in the Ireland of the 1980s. Reflecting on this experience several decades later, Enright writes of a country fractured by the various taboos it had created for itself around sexuality and gender, fusing the country's history with her own personal narrative and that of her contemporaries:

> Ireland broke apart in the eighties, and I sometimes think that the crack happened in my own head. The constitutional row about abortion was a moral civil war that was fought out in people's homes – including my own – with unfathomable bitterness. The country was screaming at itself about contraception, abortion, and divorce. It was a hideously misogynistic time ... Many of the people I knew at college left the country in the eighties. The newspapers said that people emigrated for jobs, but most of the ones I knew left because they could not breathe any more. They left because the place did not make sense. They ran away. As, finally, did I.[1]

Enright identifies an aspect of Ireland's experience of emigration that is rarely acknowledged, suggesting that a key reason many young people left Ireland in the 1980s was not simply to escape the broken economy and mass unemployment, but to eschew the repression and silence that characterised life in Ireland.[2] This chapter will explore this Ireland of the 1980s through the lens of gender, not as a rider to that decade but as integral to understanding the social/cultural changes that were transforming Ireland. Bookending the chapter are two defining events in Irish social and political history: the 1979 papal visit and the 1992 X case. These events offer a framework to understand the 'backlash'

* The title is a reference to journalist Nell McCafferty's book on the Kerry babies case: *A woman to blame* (Dublin, 1985). 1 Anne Enright, *Making babies* (London, 2005), p. 194. 2 For a detailed discussion on 1970–80s Irish emigration see Russell King and Ian Shuttleworth, 'Ireland's new wave of emigration in the 1980s', *Irish Geography*, 21:2 (1988), pp 104–8.

that occurred in response to the modest gains of the early feminist movement, which continued to operate as a significant presence even in the face of open hostility and repression. Instead, as Linda Connolly argues, it 'transformed from within and continued to mobilise in new movement centres'.[3] This activism, often grassroots and independent in nature, laid important groundwork for the 1990s, which would prove to be a transformative decade for women, and indeed the Irish state, even if many of the necessary legislative and cultural changes would take several more decades to materialise.

In late September 1979, Pope John Paul II made the first ever papal visit to Ireland. An estimated 2.7 million people greeted him in a whirlwind tour over three days with, what the *Irish Times* described as, 'outpourings of joy and fervour'.[4] More than 1.2 million people assembled in the Phoenix Park in Dublin for an outdoor Mass, around 300,000 young people attended a youth Mass in Ballybrit racecourse in Galway, and hundreds of thousands of people lined roads and streets to greet him as he toured the country.[5] Writing about the Pope's visit in 1979, the journalist Mary Holland remarked that 'from the moment it was announced that the highlight of Pope John Paul II's itinerary … would be a visit to Knock, most of us had a shred of suspicion that the Virgin Mary was about to make a comeback into Irish politics'.[6] However, as she also argues, few could have foreseen 'just how strongly the emotions would be stirred … reaching a crescendo at Limerick with his appeal to Irish women and young girls to embrace the vocation of motherhood and to ignore siren voices telling them that there might be more to life than rearing children'.[7]

The scale of the planning, organisation and operation of the visit was enormous, involving state, religious and community co-ordination. A committee was established with representatives from the Department of Foreign Affairs, the Irish tourism board, Bord Fáilte, the national broadcaster, RTÉ, and various national transport bodies, including Aer Lingus. The Mass at the Phoenix Park involved 10,000 stewards who were recruited from parishes, local organisations and the GAA. Two-thirds of the Garda Síochána were involved in security and 1,500 priests were used to distribute communion to attendees.[8] The cost to the state was estimated between £2.5 and £3 million with the Catholic Church contributing close to £2 million, which was raised through a national collection and corporate donations.[9] The economics of the event were significant

3 Linda Connolly, *The Irish women's movement: from revolution to devolution* (Dublin, 2003), p. 156. 4 *Irish Times*, 1 October 1979. 5 RTÉ 'Papal visit to Ireland', 30 September 1979. http://www.rte.ie/archives/exhibitions/681–history-of-rte/705–rte-1970s/289832–papal-visit-to-ireland/. 6 Mary Holland, 'Mary the mother and her impact on Irish politics', *Irish Times*, 19 October 1979. 7 Ibid. 8 Daithí Ó Corráin, 'Why did Pope John Paul II visit Ireland?: the 1979 papal visit in context', *British Catholic History*, 35:4 (2021), p. 476. 9 Ibid., pp 477–8.

considering that Ireland was in the middle of a severe economic crisis precipitated by 1973 oil embargo. Reflecting on the visit twenty years later, Siobhán Kilfeather argued that 'the national interest in and excitement over the visit seemed to confirm Ireland's self-imagined role as the most devout Catholic country in Europe. Yet with hindsight it now looks like the last moment when there was some assured consensus that the majority of Irish people were cleaving to the faith of our fathers'.[10]

The visit is usually understood as a high point for Catholicism and church–state relations before growing social change and a series of systematic abuse revelations in the early 1990s would forever alter the Irish religious landscape. Within the second half of the twentieth century, the long-term processes of social change that were evident throughout Western Europe began to be felt in Ireland too. These processes of transformation may be understood, sociologist Tom Inglis argues, as connected to 'the rise of individualism and a shift from self-denial to self-indulgence, the sexualisation of love, the informatisation of social relations' and a gradual shift in 'the balance of power' in relationships between men and women.[11] Given the nature of the Irish state and the public role played by Catholicism, these changes were evident in Ireland much later than in other European countries. For much of its history the Irish state was characterised as homogeneous in ethnic and religious makeup and remarkable for its intense religiosity. The evidence that exists suggests that, until the late 1950s at least, weekly Mass attendance reached 100% in rural areas and not far off that in cities.[12] This all began to change in the 1960s as Ireland found itself unable to resist the growing influence of modernity and secularisation. The Catholic hierarchy began to understand themselves as particularly vulnerable to what Pope John Paul II characterised during his 1979 papal visit as a 'pervading materialism' that 'imposes its dominion … with an aggressiveness that spares no one'.[13] An information booklet prepared by the Church in advance of the visit was candid about the 'immense challenges' facing the Church, referencing a survey of university students that revealed that one in seven no longer regarded themselves as Catholic, a particularly alarming figure given that a quarter of the population at the time were under twenty-five.[14] Therefore, for the Catholic bishops, and those in political power who relied upon the Church to support the social and economic status quo, the papal visit represented an opportunity to at least forestall the further erosion of Catholic influence in Ireland. The

10 Siobhan Kilfeather, *Dublin: a cultural history* (Oxford, 2005), p. 223. 11 Tom Inglis, *Truth, power and lies: Irish society and the case of the Kerry babies* (Dublin, 2003), pp 128–9. 12 Brian Girvin, 'Church, state, and society in Ireland since 1960', *Eire-Ireland*, 43:1 (2008), pp 74–98, p. 74. 13 P. Connolly, 'The Church in Ireland since Vatican II', *The Furrow*, 30:12 (1979), p. 757. 14 Ó Corráin, 'Why did Pope John Paul II visit Ireland?', p. 467.

emerging women's movement of the early seventies was certainly not the only threat to the Church's position but given that a key exhibitor of that power was its role as arbiter of sexual morality and promoter of the social regulation of sexual conduct, it was significant.

Between 1971 and 1983, the number of women in the formal workforce grew by 34%. The number of married women in the workforce increased by 425% over the same period.[15] In 1973 Ireland joined the EEC and in March 1976 the European Commission made its directive on equal pay binding on the Irish government, which had attempted to obtain an exemption from its provisions. The Civil Service (Employment of Married Women) Act was removed in 1973, ending the employment and promotion bar that had long been a significant obstacle to married women's employment. Between 1980 and 1994, births declined by one-third, and between 1975 and 1995 the probability of female marriage declined by one-third, from 90 to 60%.[16] This shift was certainly facilitated by the McGee case of 1973, when the Supreme Court established that marital privacy was protected under the Constitution and that the law prohibiting the importation of contraceptives even for private use by married persons infringed that privacy and was thus unconstitutional. These changes also had other consequences, namely the development of women's self-awareness and confidence. Irish women were struggling to break free from the language of Catholicism with its emphasis on motherhood and self-denial and to discover a new language, a new way of thinking, writing, and talking about themselves. Women began to form groups, to counsel and advise themselves, and to set up their own education courses. They were beginning to reflect critically about themselves, and the families, communities, and society in which they lived.[17]

These developments were not without controversy, as evidenced by social legislation and policy as well as the norms and regulations of social clubs and organisations. In the 1980s, the American writer Susan Faludi coined the term 'backlash' to describe the opposition to women's newly acquired political and social rights.[18] Faludi's research concentrated on the United States, where the concept first emerged on the fringes of the Christian evangelical right in the 1970s, but it swiftly became more mainstream as opposition to women's rights gained political and social acceptance. This moment, according to Faludi, was a specific backlash – not simply a continuation of society's long-standing opposition to women's rights – but because these attacks are never random, rather, they are provoked by the idea, accurate or not, that women are making

15 Sinéad Kennedy, 'Irish women and the Celtic tiger economy' in Colin Coulter and Steve Coleman (eds), *The end of Irish history?* (Manchester, 2003), pp 95–109, p. 96. 16 Ibid. 17 Inglis, *Truth, power and lies*, p. 140. 18 Susan Faludi, *Backlash: the undeclared war against American women* (New

advances. In other words, Faludi contends, the feminist backlash is provoked 'not by women's achievement of full equality' but by the increased possibility that they might succeed.[19] Faludi also offers a further insight; a backlash against women's rights succeeded to the degree that it appeared *not* to be political, not to be a struggle at all.[20]

'Backlash' in 1980s Ireland would play out broadly in the terms outlined by Faludi. The 1981 general election increased the number of Dáil seats available from 148 to 166, thereby widening opportunities for women and leading to what Frances Gardiner termed 'a new type of feminist candidate, without political kinship networks, [who] pioneered a novel pathway to parliament via leadership in the women's movement'.[21] The results of the 1981 election saw eleven women elected to the Dáil and nine to the Seanad, almost doubling the number of women legislators, although in real terms they were still a tiny minority, just 7% of the total legislature.[22] This, combined with the advances discussed previously, contributed to the perception at least that women's equality in Ireland was progressing, even if in reality the gains made were modest as the majority of women remained marginalised in low-paying, precarious roles with limited participation in public life.[23] Within weeks of the election, the campaign to insert a constitutional prohibition on abortion – effectively equating the life of a pregnant woman with that of a foetus – intensified.

The 1970s was not the first decade in which an Irish women's movement had made transformative gains. Over five decades earlier, as part of the struggle for Irish independence, women had played a crucial role. The historian Senia Pašeta, in her work on feminism and nationalism, argued that the feminists of the period consistently 'highlighted' and 'insisted' upon a 'guarantee of the equality' promised in the 1916 Proclamation, maintaining that it must be central to the newly proclaimed Republic.[24] Yet very quickly, following the foundation of the new Irish state in 1922, and a counter-revolutionary civil war, women's hopes for an equal and inclusive independent Ireland would be crushed. Very quickly the new state began erasing women from public life curtailing their political, economic and reproductive rights so severely so 'as to make it clear and explicit

York, 1991), p. 11. **19** Ibid., p. 13. **20** Ibid., pp 13–14. **21** Frances Gardiner, 'The women's movement and politicians in the Republic of Ireland, 1980–2000' in Angela Bourke et al. (eds), *The Field Day anthology of Irish writing: volume 5: Irish women's writing and traditions* (Cork 2002), p. 230. **22** Ibid. **23** Despite the many legal changes that had taken place by 1979 only 7% of senior positions in the civil service and local authorities were held by women despite a high concentration of women workers; 2 out of 43 district justices were women; there were no female judges in the High Court or the Supreme Court; there was only one woman in cabinet; only 5 women out of 148 TDs, and of 795 members of county councils and county borough councils, only 32 were women. See Pat Brennan, 'Women' in revolt,' *Magill*, April 1979, pp 34–46. **24** Senia Pašeta, *Irish nationalist women, 1900–1918* (Cambridge, 2013), pp 191–2.

that women were … barred from claiming for themselves a political subjectivity, a public identity'.[25]

Shortly after the papal visit, conservative figures, this time among the laity, began discussions about how to advance a Catholic social agenda that many felt had gone into retreat. The ultimate result of this was the 1983 referendum to insert a so called 'pro-life' amendment into the Constitution. The amendment was a product of both the historical Catholic origins of the Irish State, and an attempt by the conservative right to manage and contain the political and social instability of the Irish state at the beginning of the 1980s.[26] The campaign emerged when several small conservative Catholic groups, fearing that abortion could become legal in Ireland at some point in the future, sought to enshrine Catholic teaching on abortion in the Constitution. This concern was aggravated by several factors. First, the legalisation of abortion in Britain following the introduction of the 1967 Abortion Act saw Irish women silently, and often covertly, travel in their thousands every year to access terminations; a fact largely and conveniently ignored by the campaign to introduce the anti-abortion constitutional amendment.[27] Second, the decision by the United States Supreme Court in 1973 to legalise abortion shocked conservative forces in Ireland. They were particularly concerned by the legal reasoning behind *Roe v. Wade*, the 1973 case that legalised abortion in the US.[28] The US Supreme Court stated that a constitutional right of privacy was 'broad enough to encompass a woman's decision whether or not to terminate her pregnancy'.[29] The ruling was an extension of the 1965 US Supreme Court privacy ruling on the right to contraception. It was feared by those in conservative circles that at some point a case would arise with the Irish Supreme Court and that the court would decide the right to privacy in marital affairs not only included a right to contraception – as the Irish Supreme Court ruled in the 1978 McGee case[30] – but a right to abortion as well. It was determined that what was therefore required was a provision in the Constitution that would ban abortion outright, making it impossible for the Supreme Court to ever interpret a right to abortion within the Constitution.[31] Finally, the agenda of the conservative movement was

25 Maryann Valiulis, 'Defining their role in the new state: Irishwomen's protest against the Juries Act of 1927', *The Canadian Journal of Irish Studies*, 18:1 (1992), pp 43–60, p. 43. 26 See Emily O'Reilly, *Masterminds of the right* (Dublin, 1992). 27 Between 1968 and 1983 at least 30,560 Irish women travelled to Britain to obtain an abortion with numbers climbing steadily year by year. See Lindsey Earner-Byrne and Diane Urquhart, *The Irish abortion journey, 1920–2018* (London, 2019). 28 *Roe v. Wade*, 410 U.S. 113 [1973]. 29 See Carol Sanger, *About abortion: terminating pregnancy in twenty-first century America* (Cambridge, MA, 2017), p. 5. 30 *McGee v. The Attorney General* [1974] IR 284. The McGee case resulted in the limited legalisation of contraception with the 1979 Family Planning Act, which permitted only married couples access contraception with a prescription while allowing doctors and pharmacists the right to 'conscientiously object'. 31 See

from the outset much broader than just contraception and abortion which were considered 'one front in a wider religious war'.[32] Conservative forces had already attempted to mobilise on a number of fronts: they organised against the formation of a multi-denominational primary school in Dalkey in 1976 arguing that it was a fundamental challenge to the Catholic dominance of the Irish education system; a group calling themselves the League of Decency organised a series of public campaigns against 'immoral' TV shows and family planning clinics, and opposed a small state grant that was given to the Dublin Rape Crisis Centre.[33] However, it was around the issue of abortion that they got the most traction and so in 1981 they set up the Pro-Life Amendment Campaign (PLAC). Following two-and-a-half years of campaigning from January 1981 to September 1983 and a divisive referendum, a constitutional prohibition on abortion, known as the Eighth Amendment, was signed into Irish law. The campaign was bitter on both sides with debate constructed largely in abstract moral terms or by utilising medico-legal arguments.

The proposed amendment did not go unopposed; feminist groups, left-wing activists and other progressives did form an organised opposition, but they faced unique challenges. Abortion in Ireland was not understood or prioritised as a critical feminist issue in the way that it had been by the women's movement in Europe and North America. While abortion was discussed and debated in some left-wing sections of the movement in the 1970s, it was decided tactically, amid the political struggle around contraception at the time, that to also begin advocating for abortion would risk a conflation of abortion and contraception.[34] The reality of abortion in Ireland was rarely discussed despite it being a real, if unacknowledged, aspect of women's lives.

In 1979 a group calling themselves the Women's Right to Choose Group (WRCG) began politically agitating around abortion and offering support to women who needed referrals to British abortion clinics through the Irish Pregnancy Counselling Centre.[35] Shortly before the launch of PLAC, they held a packed meeting in Liberty Hall, Dublin. The meeting was invaded by the anti-abortion group, the Society for the Protection of Unborn Children (SPUC), who shouted and abused the speakers and attendees.[36] Activist and founding member of the WRCG, Mary Gordan, wrote of the 'unnerving' nature of the experience for the group:

Stephanie Lord, 'The Eighth Amendment: planting a legal timebomb' in Catherine Conlon et al. (eds), *The abortion papers Ireland: vol. 2* (Cork, 2015), pp 90–4. 32 Fintan O'Toole, 'Why Ireland became the only country in the democratic world to have a constitutional ban on abortion', *Irish Times*, 26 August 2014. 33 Ibid. 34 Linda Connolly and Tina O'Toole, *Documenting Irish feminisms: the second wave* (Dublin, 2005), pp 68–70. See also chapter 13 in this volume. 35 See Ruth Riddick, *The right to choose: questions of feminist morality* (Dublin, 1990). 36 SPUC (an offshoot of the British

> It made us realise that we were not going to be allowed to continue to operate unhindered. SPUC had been set up in Ireland in June '80 … but until the Liberty Hall meeting, we had not actually experienced them in operation. We had tended to reject them as arch catholic fanatics, but it was now becoming clear that they were very well organised and that their message had strong appeal. They were using the existence of our group to create the illusion of a serious threat against which the up-to-now latent anti-abortionism of Irish society need to be mobilised.[37]

The launch a month later of PLAC, and the willingness with which Irish politicians appeared to be acquiescing to their demand for a referendum, took feminist activists by surprise and forced them into a reactive position from which they never managed to escape. Official opposition to the amendment was organised around a group called the Anti-Amendment Campaign (AAC). However, given the conservative and reactive political climate of the period, the group did not advocate for abortion rights. Instead, the central tenet of the AAC campaign was that women's lives would be put at risk (health was rarely mentioned), and though women would lose their lives because of the amendment, their arguments simply did not possess enough weight to capture public opinion. By the end of the intense campaign '[t]he only result was that the vision of babies being killed in the womb was stronger in the minds of the Irish than the potential danger in which the amendment would put women'.[38] The voices and experiences of women who had abortions were completely ignored. Indeed, so taboo was the subject that the word abortion was largely absent from the debate with both sides using the term 'the substantive issue' instead of abortion.[39] Support for the amendment was unambiguous with two-thirds of the electorate supporting it, albeit with a low voter turnout.[40]

The amendment, which became Article 40.3.3 of the Irish Constitution, stated that: 'The State acknowledges the right to life of the unborn and, with due regard to the equal right to life of the mother, guarantees in its laws to respect, and, as far as practicable, by its laws to defend and vindicate that right'. No mention of the word 'abortion' is included but by subordinating the life of a pregnant woman to that of the foetus she is carrying, it rendered abortion illegal in all circumstances, except where a termination of pregnancy is

organisation of the same name) was a radical anti-abortion group that operated on the frontlines of anti-abortion campaigning in Ireland for many years. 37 Mary Gordan, 'Fighting for control – the ongoing struggle for reproductive rights', *The Irish Feminist Review 84* (Dublin, 1984), pp 7–37, p. 11. 38 Crystal Hug, *The politics of sexual morality in Ireland* (London, 1999), p. 154. 39 Sophie Cacciaguidi-Fahy, 'The substantive issue and the rhetoric of the abortion debate in Ireland' in Anne Wagner et al. (eds), *Contemporary issues of the semiotics of law* (London, 2005), pp 141–64. 40 The referendum was passed by a 66.9% majority with a voter turnout of 53.6%.

considered medically necessary to save the life of the woman. It is an amendment Ivana Bacik argued that is 'uniquely misogynistic' due to manner in which it 'expressly sets up the right to life of both the pregnant woman and the foetus that she carries in conflict – anticipating that a time would come when somebody would have to decide between them'.[41] Furthermore, the feminist legal scholars De Londras and Enright observe how at first glance the amendment may appear 'innocuous or merely aspirational' and indeed could potentially have been interpreted in a variety of different ways. Instead, in the context of a deeply conservative and misogynistic society, it resulted in 'a near-absolute prohibition on abortion in Irish law'. While this was certainly the intention of those who advocated for its inclusion in the Constitution, it was not inevitable.[42] De Londras and Enright suggest that had Eighth Amendment been interpreted as 'protecting life in all its richness and depth' instead of just 'the bare condition of being alive' pregnant women may not have experienced 'drastic intrusions' into their lives that became characteristic of abortion law in Ireland. However, to understand the amendment in these terms would have required a very different political climate, one where women and their experiences of pregnancy and sexuality was understood in a far less hostile manner.

Emboldened by the referendum victory, conservative campaigners switched their focus to the question of information and canvassed for prosecutions against organisations providing abortion advice or information such as Students' Unions and women's clinics. As one anti-abortion activist put it at the time: 'in order to defend the right to life of the unborn, we must close the abortion referral agencies which are operating in Dublin quite openly and underneath the eyes of the law'.[43] This led to a series of prolonged and expensive legal cases that ultimately would be decided by the European courts. In these circumstances, the right to choose could never be a viable option for abortion campaigners who were forced to concentrate on ensuring women had access to the necessary information so they could travel to Britain for abortions. It would not be until the 1992 X case that the Courts would have to make a specific judgment about abortion and the Constitution, and it would be a further twenty-five years before the amendment was removed and abortion legalised.

The reality of life in Ireland for women during this period was crystallised in the stories of several women, whose private experiences became the subject of fierce public debate: Anne Lovett, Joanne Hayes, Eileen Flynn,[44] and Lavinia

41 Ivana Bacik, 'Legislating for article 40.3.3', *Irish Journal of Legal Studies*, 3:3 (2013), pp 18–35, p. 22. 42 Fiona De Londras and Mairead Enright, *Repealing the 8th: reforming Irish abortion law* (London, 2018), p. 3. 43 Hug, *The politics of sexual morality in Ireland*, p. 157. 44 Eileen Flynn was a teacher who was sacked from a second-level school in Wexford on the basis that her lifestyle contradicted the Catholic ethos of the school. Eileen Flynn was unmarried and pregnant at the time of her

Kerwick.[45] These cases are noteworthy not simply because of the position that they occupied in the public imagination at the time but for the powerful evidence they offer of how conservative, indeed misogynistic, images of femininity were that continued to shape and overshadow the lives of women in Ireland at the time. These women offered 'profoundly disturbing glimpses of Irish society' when they found themselves 'forced into positions in which sexuality and reproduction determined their lives – and … deaths'.[46] Ursula Barry and Clair Wills suggest that one of the key reasons the stories of these women acquired an extraordinary resonance, both at the time and subsequently, was their 'ordinariness'; none were part of a movement, and so could be understood as representing only themselves.[47] Two of these stories – that of Ann Lovett and Joanne Hayes – resonate particularly with the arguments in this essay.

The death of Ann Lovett in January 1984 has become, journalist Rosita Boland remarked, a story that is 'impossible to unknow or, to forget'. On the 31 January 1984, a 15-year-old girl named Ann Lovett left school early. She did not return home; instead, she disappeared into the grotto beside the graveyard that overlooked her hometown of Granard in Co. Longford. There, on the cold, damp ground of the grotto, exposed to the elements, she gave birth alone to a baby boy. Later in the afternoon, three young boys spotted her schoolbag lying at the entrance to the grotto and she was discovered unconscious with a pair of scissors that she had brought with her to cut the umbilical cord. Both she and her baby son both died. Her death provoked national outrage, where her tragic silence around her pregnancy could not but be interpreted in the context of the silencing of women's experiences of unwanted pregnancies during the referendum the previous year. Yet, the local papers carried no reference to her death and, were it not for an anonymous call from an individual in Granard to the national *Sunday Tribune*, the story may never have been known. A young reporter, Emily O'Reilly, was asked by the news editor, Brian Trench, to confirm the story. In her account O'Reilly explained that there was considerable debate among the newsroom and the paper's editor, Vincent Browne, as to whether Ann Lovett's name should appear in the story. O'Reilly remembered remarking that

dismissal. Her partner, the father of her child, was a separated, but married man (he was unable to obtain a divorce in Ireland). She appealed her dismissal to the High Court. Her appeal was rejected.
45 On New Year's Eve, 1990, 19-year-old Lavinia Kerwick was brutally raped by her boyfriend of five months, William Conry, who eventually pleaded guilty to the rape. Despite his guilty plea the judge suspended his sentence in full. In response, Kerwick went public about the assault, pleading for Irish society to take the crime of rape seriously. In so doing, she broke from the protection offered by an 'in camera' court appearance, becoming the first publicly declared rape victim in Ireland. 46 Ursula Barry and Clair Wills, 'The Republic of Ireland: the politics of sexuality, 1965–2000' in Angela Bourke et al. (eds), *The Field Day anthology of Irish writing: volume 5*, p. 1411. 47 Ibid., p. 1412.

'no one would remember an anonymous child, but that everyone would remember the name Ann Lovett'.[48] O'Reilly recollects that there was considerable debate between her and Trench as to how the story should be framed. Trench wanted the first sentence to read that the police were investigating the death of a young girl; O'Reilly disagreed, arguing instead that the story was the girl and her young son had died in tragic circumstances: 'to me', O'Reilly recalled, 'the Garda investigation was incidental'.[49] The paper ran the story front page with the headline 'Girl, 15, dies giving birth in a field' on Sunday 4 February 1984, five days after her death. The headline was read out on the Saturday night television show, *The Late Late Show*, which traditionally concluded with a summary of the front pages of the Sunday newspapers. *The Late Late Show* was a national institution fronted by the much-loved figure in Irish broadcasting Gay Byrne.[50] After a stony pause, Byrne cast the newspaper to the ground adding 'Nothing terribly exciting there'.[51]

The people of Granard argued that Ann Lovett's story was sensationalised but a more accurate description is put forward by journalist Rosita Boland in her assessment of the impact of Lovett's death on Ireland twenty years later: 'Ann Lovett's death was not sensationalised by the media. Her story was itself sensational and, in 1984, it acted as a key that unlocked Pandora's box of many other of Ireland's dark and previously untold, stories'.[52] In addition to his televised show, broadcaster Gay Byrne had a daily morning radio programme with an enormous national listenership consisting largely of women. In the days after the Ann Lovett story broke, women, young and old, began writing anonymously to Byrne, of their experiences of the silence, shame and trauma of an of unplanned pregnancy in Ireland, leading Byrne to devote an entire radio programme to her death. The programme consisted of actors reading the correspondence sent to Byrne. Summarising the many letters received Byrne commented: 'time and time again they make the point that being able to write it all down is a relief. They thank Ann Lovett for giving them the courage to express what they have kept secret. Her sacrifice was not in vain, is their point'.[53] Reflecting on the significance of the Ann Lovett story two decades later, O'Reilly, the journalist who broke the story, noted how 'incredibly, nothing

48 Emily O'Reilly, 'O'Reilly recalls the immediate storm that followed her report of the death of Ann Lovett', *Irish Times*, 31 January 2004. 49 Ibid. 50 Colm Toibín, 'Gay Byrne: Irish life as cabaret', *The Crane Bag*, 8:2 (1984), pp 65–9. For a more recent assessment of *The Late Late Show* in the context of the history of Irish broadcasting see Christopher Morash, *A history of the media in Ireland* (Cambridge, 2012), pp 174, 179, 207. 51 RTÉ, *Scannal*: 01 Ann Lovett. Broadcast 27 September 2004. 52 Rosita Boland, 'Death at the grotto', *Irish Times*, 31 January 2017. 53 Byrne quoted in Róisín Ingle, 'The Ann Lovett letters: sorrow, shame, anger and indignation', *Irish Times*, 31 January 2017. The article includes a selection of the letters read on the Gay Byrne Show on

more has been added to the details of the story amassed in those first few days'. She argued that 'in the absence of photographs, of interviews with family members or of anybody who could shed light on what had happened', Ann Lovett's story 'became a blank canvas on which everyone sketched their own political, cultural, religious, bias'.[54]

The story of Joanne Hayes, who also dominated the headlines in the Ireland of the 1980s, was very different. Instead of the bodies of a dead girl and her baby son on to which people could graft their own ideals about sacrificial motherhood, a young woman emerged, who appeared to be antithetical to the image of the good Irish mother. A baby's body was discovered on a beach close to Caherciveen in south Kerry on 14 April 1984. The infant's body bore several stab wounds. Two weeks later, Joanne Hayes and her family were interrogated in relation to the murder. They resided in Abbeydorney, a small village outside of Tralee in north Kerry, more than 75 kilometres away from where the baby's body was discovered. Joanne acknowledged being pregnant, initially claiming to have experienced a miscarriage, but then acknowledged giving birth to a boy at home on the night of 12–13 April in a field on the family farm. She said that she had left the baby in a pool of water on the farm.[55] The gardaí could not find the body and refused to allow her to show them where she had left the baby. Later that evening she admitted killing the baby with a bath brush and stabbing it with a knife. Other family members made similar, but conflicting statements, admitting to throwing a baby's body into the sea on the west Kerry coast. Joanne was charged with the murder of the Caherciveen baby and remanded to Limerick prison, only for the body of her own baby to be found on the farm. Instead of releasing her, the gardaí concocted a bizarre story claiming that she had had twins by two different fathers and murdered both babies. It would be six months before reason prevailed and the charges were dropped on the advice of the Director of Public Prosecutions. In January 1985 a Tribunal of Inquiry was established to investigate how Joanne and her family came to confess in detail to the murder of the Caherciveen baby. The tribunal quickly turned from an investigation into Gardaí misconduct and into a trial of Joanne herself, lasting eighty-two days, becoming known as the Kerry Babies' Tribunal. The nature of the inquisition endured by her was summed up by journalist Nell McCafferty in her book *A woman to blame*:

RTÉ Radio One, 23 February 1984. **54** Moira Maguire, 'The changing face of Catholic Ireland: conservatism and liberalism in the Ann Lovett and Kerry babies scandals', *Feminist Studies*, 27:2 (2001), pp 335–58, at p. 350. **55** Joanne Hayes' own account of these events, *My story*, co-written with the journalist John Barrett, was published in 1985.

> The legal men and a succession of male doctors, psychiatrists and police officers – 43 in all – spent six months probing the young woman's mind and body. A doctor gave the dimensions of her vagina during a previous birth. Ordnance survey maps were used to pinpoint the exact locations of the places where she had sexual congress with her married lover. The question was asked, 'Did she love this man or what was he and other men prepared to do with her?' It was medieval, but it happened in 1985. The probing of the woman's sexual history brought the men gathered around her to such a fever pitch that she collapsed.[56]

Hayes was not 'the classic Irish single mother'. She did not hide or give up her baby; in the Ireland of the 1980s she was 'a bold and transgressive figure' and sexually transgressive women could be easily isolated, marginalised, and oppressed.[57] If the Lovett case was understood as an illustration of the complexities of women's experiences of pregnancy outside the permitted parameters of heteronormative marriage, the Joanne Hayes case could be read as the logic of state intervention in the aftermath of the 1983 referendum, where the state assumed the role of policing women's bodies and sexuality. If the story of Ann Lovett provoked an outpouring of grief and an attempt by Irish women to punctuate the silence and shame with similar anonymous stories of concealed pregnancies, the inquisition of Joanne Hayes drew more explicit gestures of solidarity and identification, as women sent her Mass cards and flowers. Over the course of the eighty-two days of the Tribunal, feminists, local women's groups and supporters gathered outside to express their support for Joanne Hayes and to protest the treatment she was receiving. Many of the women carried yellow flowers and Hayes was frequently photographed after leaving the witness box carrying yellow flowers. On 23 January 1985, more than forty locals from her home village staged a picket outside the tribunal offices carrying placards declaring 'Abbeydorney supports Joanne'. The following day, Judge Lynch, the Tribunal chairman, had to receive a Garda escort as hundreds of protesters, mainly women, descended, as he, along with Garda witnesses and lawyers, emerged from the tribunal, in an action co-ordinated by feminist groups from across Ireland, including the Tralee Women's Action Group.[58] The chairman described the feminist protesters as 'raucous, ignorant, urban dwellers', threatening them with contempt and imprisonment.[59] The implicit suggestion in his threats was that the women had come from places like Dublin, Cork and

56 McCafferty, *A woman to blame*, p. 98. 57 Inglis, *Truth, power and lies*, pp 223–4. 58 See McCafferty, *A woman to blame*, pp 107–27. For an account of the often forgotten or unacknowledged support Joanne and the Hayes family received see also Mary McAuliffe's discussion of this point on the *Irish Times* podcast: *In the news*, 25 March 2023. 59 McCafferty,

Belfast and even the local town of Tralee and had no right to support the cause of a single mother from a farm in rural Ireland who was being attacked by the forces of the state.

The experiences of Ann Lovett and Joanne Hayes would prove to be a watershed for women in Ireland. The Kerry babies case, in particular, exposed in full view how men dominated Irish society – symbolically, socially, economically, politically and legally. Furthermore, the case, Inglis argues, revealed how Irish men, particularly those with power, perceived and understood a woman like Joanne Hayes, and, by extension, all women in Ireland.[60] The next decade would prove to be a very different one for Irish women, although it would take several more for the many injustices of the 1980s to begin to be addressed. The first signs of this shift could be found in the election of Mary Robinson as the first woman president of Ireland in November 1990. Robinson as a feminist, a senator, and a constitutional lawyer had actively fought against the misogyny of the Irish state and its conservative allies, most notably in the areas of contraception and abortion. As Chrystel Hug remarks, when watching and listening to Robinson during and after her election it was 'enough to sense that something momentous was happening; a distinct euphoria was palpable, and so was the sense of being at the crossroads'.[61] In February 1992, a year and a half after Robinson's election, the issue of abortion would return to the headlines with the X case. But this time the reaction was very different, and the case became the catalyst for the emergence of a very different type of Ireland. The X case, once again, involved a young girl facing the entire force of the Irish legal and judicial system. But this time, the reaction was very different; this time, there would be no 'woman to blame'.

The X case involved a 14-year-old rape victim known only as Miss X whose parents attempted to take her to Britain for an abortion. The Gardaí were contacted by the girl's parents to see if DNA from foetal tissue could be submitted as evidence against her rapist, who was contesting the charges. When the Gardaí sought legal clarification on the admissibility of the tests, the Attorney General, Harry Whelehan, obtained a High Court injunction against Miss X and her parents prohibiting them from leaving the jurisdiction. Justice Costello, granting the injunction, argued that the risk posed to Miss X's life by requiring her to continue the pregnancy was 'much less and of a different order of magnitude' than the risk to the life of the unborn.[62] When the story broke in the Irish media some days later, there was a public outcry with thousands of

A woman to blame, p. 128. 60 Inglis, *Truth, power and lies*, p. 236. 61 Hug, *The politics of sexual morality in Ireland*, p. 6. 62 Sunniva McDonagh, *The attorney general v. X and others* (Dublin, 1992), p. 89.

people taking to the streets in a series of spontaneous protests, expressing shock and horror at the treatment of the young woman. The protesters demanded not only that Miss X should be allowed to travel abroad for an abortion but that she should be allowed to have an abortion in Ireland. This was a dramatic shift in public opinion for a country that less than nine years previously had voted to enshrine in its Constitution a foetal right to life. Psychologically overwhelmed at the prospect of being compelled by the state to carry her rapist's baby to term, Miss X became suicidal. The government, concerned at the growing level of protests erupting across the country in support of Miss X, encouraged her parents to appeal the injunction to the Supreme Court, offering to pay the court costs. The Supreme Court heard the case and uncharacteristically handed down their verdicts within days, voting, by a majority of four to one, to remove the injunction. The details of the judgment illuminated the legal complexity the X case had created for pregnant women and girls in Ireland: all five justices held that the young woman had a constitutionally protected right to an abortion if there was a 'real and substantial' risk to her life and this, they ruled, included a risk of suicide. However, two of the five judges noted that Article 40.3.3 did not permit a woman to travel abroad for an abortion. Legal clarity required another referendum but this time the character of the debate would be very different. In November 1992, the electorate voted in favour of the right to travel abroad for an abortion and in favour of the right to abortion information. However, they rejected the government's attempt to reverse the X case ruling excluding suicide as grounds for an abortion. The presence of the Eighth Amendment in the Constitution meant that abortion was still illegal in most circumstances in Ireland. Nevertheless, the X case had irrevocably changed the nature of the debate about abortion and about women. It was the beginning of the end for Catholic Ireland. Things would never, could never, be the same again.

SECTION FOUR

WOMEN AND WORK

CHAPTER 10

Taking the pledge: women and pawnbroking in Ireland, 1850–1922

Antonia Hart

In the late nineteenth century, the heart of commercial Dublin was Sackville Street, and the heart of Sackville Street was the tram terminus at Nelson's Pillar. A passenger alighting at Nelson's Pillar might have boarded a tram outside the city, perhaps in Howth, or Kingstown, planning to shop, meet a friend for lunch, or go to the theatre. A fifteen-minute stroll down Lower Sackville Street to the river Liffey, turning left at the bridge on to Eden Quay, left for Marlborough Street, and left for North Earl Street completed a loop back to the Pillar. This circuit, little more than half a mile even with meandering, took the shopper past all kinds of businesses. Lower Sackville Street was lined with luxury establishments: smart hotels like the Imperial and the Metropole; Clery's department store; and specialist shops like confectioners Lemon's and Noblett's, high-end cigar shops, Butler's Medical Hall, Elvery's waterproofers, and Eason's subscription library. At the river, Eden Quay's travel theme showed in marine businesses, parcels offices, hotels, a navigation school and the Seamen's Institute. In Marlborough Street everyday shops like dairies, grocers, newsagents and tobacconists rubbed shoulders with larger companies, including Alexander Thom and Co., who published the *Directory* in which all these businesses can be found.[1] The bell of St Mary's Pro-Cathedral provided the soundtrack for Marlborough Street businesses, including its neighbour the First-Class Pawn Office, owned for 25 years by Margaret Lowry. Along these streets over 300 businesses operated at street level, and women ran just under 10% of them. It is worth reflecting on how the presence of that 10% affected the experience of those who walked this short route. Over fifteen minutes, they passed at least 29 visible businesses run by women, averaging one every thirty seconds. If women business owners were so readily visible here, in the smartest, busiest streets of the capital, those passers-by might easily have guessed, if they thought about it at all, that women were in business in the lesser streets too, and in other cities, and in towns and villages around the country.

1 *Thom's official directory of the United Kingdom of Great Britain and Ireland for the year 1894* (Dublin, 1894).

In Ireland, female entrepreneurship has benefited from fifty years of gathering speed in scholarship on Irish women's history. In 1987 Imelda Brophy surveyed 50 businesswomen listed in the *Dublin Directory* of 1800; in 2000, Catherine Cox looked at women and business in eighteenth-century Ireland; and in 2015 Therese Moylan's PhD thesis examined female business owners in the first fifty years of the State.[2] Related detailing of the female working experience includes Mary Cullen's work on women's contributions to rural labouring households; Joanna Bourke has examined Irish women's transition from agricultural to domestic labour, while Maria Luddy has looked at activities such as prostitution, philanthropy and political activism.[3] Recently, Laura Kelly has studied Irish women in medicine, and Maeve O'Riordan has researched women of the 'Big House'.[4] Elsewhere, full explorations have been made of women's business activities, but Ireland has not so far seen a dedicated study.[5]

There is no single archive for women in business, and primary sources must therefore be collected and collaged from various record sets. Sources include directories, census entries, advertising, and newspaper articles, but imbalance can result from reliance on any one of these. Directories quickly went out of date, and often retained an entry's historic male name; census entries frequently elided women's occupations; advertising was taken out only by those who could afford it; newspaper reports could be inaccurate. Industry-specific official publications include detailed reports on pawnbroking and liquor licensing, and there are some administrative records for these sectors too.[6] Legal records in the

2 Imelda Brophy, 'Women in the workforce' in David Dickson (ed.), *The gorgeous mask: Dublin, 1700–1850* (Dublin, 1987), pp 51–63; Bernadette Whelan (ed.), *Women and paid work in Ireland, 1500–1930* (Dublin, 2000); Therese Moylan, 'Women entrepreneurs and self-employed business-owners in Ireland, 1922–1972' (PhD, NUIG, 2015). 3 Mary Cullen, 'Breadwinners and providers: women in the household economy of labouring families, 1835–6' in Maria Luddy and Clíona Murphy (eds), *Women surviving: studies in Irish women's history in the 19th and 20th centuries* (Dublin, 1989), pp 85–116; Joanna Bourke, *Husbandry to housewifery* (Oxford, 1993); Maria Luddy, *Prostitution and Irish society, 1800–1940* (Cambridge, 2007); Maria Luddy, *Women and philanthropy in nineteenth-century Ireland* (Cambridge, 1995). 4 Laura Kelly, *Irish women in medicine, c.1880s–1920s: origins, education and careers* (Manchester, 2013); Maeve O'Riordan, *Women of the country house in Ireland, 1860–1914* (Liverpool, 2018). 5 Edith Sparks, *Capital intentions: female proprietors in San Francisco, 1850–1920* (Chapel Hill, NC, 2006); Susan Ingalls Lewis, *Unexceptional women: female proprietors in Albany, 1830–85* (Columbus, OH, 2009); Hannah Barker, *The business of women: female enterprise and urban development in northern England 1760–1830* (Oxford, 2006); Alison C. Kay, *The foundations of female entrepreneurship: enterprise, home, and household in London, c.1800–1870* (London, 2009); Jennifer Aston, *Female entrepreneurship in nineteenth-century England: engagement in the urban economy* (London, 2016). 6 *Report of the commissioner appointed to inquire into the laws of pawnbroking in Ireland* (House of Commons, 1868). *Minutes of evidence taken before the royal commission on liquor licensing laws (Ireland)* (House of Commons, 1898). Publicans' Licences Register County Dublin, 1896–1903, Crown and Peace Office Files 1C-40–58, National Archives of Ireland. *Return from the marshal of the city of Dublin of the pawnbrokers of Ireland, for the year*

form of judgments and court reports are always useful, and the Public Record Office of Northern Ireland holds individually catalogued files of the bankruptcy and arrangement petitions of businesswomen in Antrim and Down, which reveal financial details and sometimes inventories of material assets, giving plenty of colour to individual stories. Wills, letters, and recorded property transactions offer other opportunities to study particular women's businesses. The digitised records of the Property Losses (Ireland) Committee contain claims made by proprietors to cover loss of or damage to stock and premises, and by customers for lost or looted items which had been left in for repairs, or in pawn.[7] It is also possible to glimpse women's commercial relationships by studying the records of businessmen. The account books of Richard Walsh's Westport pub and shop include boarding-house keeper Mary Casey's account over six years, showing what and when she bought, and how often she settled up.[8]

The records indicate that thousands of women across the island operated their own businesses. Many of them worked in hospitality, running boarding-houses, hotels, and public houses. A few operated large distilleries, producing whiskey under still-recognisable names like Bushmills and Locke's. Women were numerous in retail, from front-room shops to department stores, like the famous Monica Duff's of Ballaghaderreen. They owned and ran regional newspapers, sawmills, medical halls, laundries, dairies, and employment agencies, set up as shoemakers, fleshers, cabinet-makers, tobacconists, newsagents, chair manufacturers, mineral water manufacturers, legal scriveners, musical instrument importers, and coal merchants. It is not just these entrepreneurial roles which are interesting, but the women themselves: who they were, how and with what skills and experience they came into business, how and with whom they worked. Using pawnbroking as a sample sector, this chapter explores women's commercial roles and lives.

Pawnbroking was everywhere, and available to everyone, facilitating the nineteenth-century credit economy through a fundamentally open-access lending approach. If you were poor, or a woman, or otherwise marginalised, and unable to access credit through the banking system, you could walk into a pawnshop with personal property in your hand, and out again with cash in your pocket. Credit was at the heart not just of commerce, but of everyday life, and women exercised agency on both sides of the pawn counter, both as clients converting goods to ready money, and as brokers issuing collateralised loans. Pawnbroking

ending 31 December 1844 (House of Commons, 1845). 7 1916 (PLIC) series, PLIC/1, National Archives of Ireland. 8 Ledger of Walsh's, Westport, BRS Mayo 17/1 BC4, National Archives of Ireland.

provided a good living to those who could clear the barriers to entry, and it was a sector in which women's business lives could be fully enmeshed with men's.

Margaret Keyes, born McGrath, had been widowed once already when in 1883 she married Dublin pawnbroker Laurence McNally, and became Margaret McNally. In 1891 Laurence died, and Margaret assumed control of his Marlborough Street shop, the First-Class Pawn Office. In January 1894 she changed her name for the third and last time, when she married Edwin Lowry.[9] Margaret Lowry could not run the First-Class Pawn Office without being a licensed broker herself. There was no bar to women becoming brokers: the relevant legislation used explicitly gender-inclusive language in relation to a would-be pawnbroker's certificate of 'his or her fitness to be entrusted in carrying on the said business'.[10] Subsequent legislation, stating that 'each and every pawnbroker … shall be at liberty to employ any one of said four auctioneers, for the sale of his or her pledges when forfeited', echoed this language.[11] It was envisaged that both men and women would apply for pawnbroking licences, and both men and women would run pawnbroking businesses.

The licensing process was cumbersome, regardless of an applicant's gender. As part of her application, Margaret Lowry had to get references from five reputable citizens, confirming her fitness to carry on the business of a pawnbroker. She was required to put up a bond of £1,000, and submit the names of three people who would provide sureties of £300 each.[12] As her business was in Dublin, once licensed she had to contribute £100 annually to the running costs of the Dublin Metropolitan Police. A receipt for her payment of this levy in 1898 survives, as do her 1895 and 1903 receipts for the additional optional costs of plate and tobacco licences. There were ongoing burdens too, such as sending monthly returns, with an accompanying shilling, to the regulator, the Dublin City Marshal.

In 1867, mother and daughter Jane Moore and Ellen Jane Gilchrist finalised the details of a pawnbroking business transfer and partnership agreement. The surviving memorandum of agreement gives effect to the wishes of Downpatrick widow Mrs Moore, to make provision for an unmarried daughter, Elizabeth. The mechanism was to make over 'certain stock in Trade fixtures and other necessaries for carrying on the Trade or business of a Pawnbroker' to her married daughter Ellen Jane.[13] Ellen Jane paid her mother £150 and promised £80 to her sister Elizabeth. Partnership with your mother might seem like an

9 For simplicity the name Margaret Lowry is used throughout. 10 Pawnbrokers Act, 1786, 26 Geo. 3, c. 43 (Ir.). 11 Pawnbrokers Act, 1788, 28 Geo. 3, c. 49 (Ir.). 12 *R v. Woodlock* [1883] QB 178. 13 Memorandum of agreement re. pawnbroking business, D366/874, Public Record Office of Northern Ireland.

easy route to business, but Ellen Jane Gilchrist had to produce £230, as well as the cost of her own licence, while reserving some capital with which to issue loans. Being the daughters of a pawnbroker gave Ellen Jane, and Elizabeth, who also worked in the shop, the valuable opportunity to watch and listen, and begin to learn the trade. Paul O'Brien writes that Jane Lane-Joynt, whose widowed mother took over the family pawnbroking business in Limerick, was exposed to 'basic bookkeeping and business management – hardly surprising in view of her widowed mother's management of the business'.[14] In Enniskillen, the daughters of pawnbroker John Bigham were in business together. In addition to a skills transfer, the proximity of the trade in action enabled women like Ellen Jane Gilchrist, Elizabeth Moore, and Mary and Eliza Bigham to make an informed decision about entering it, knowing what pitfalls and rewards it entailed. In Margaret Lowry's case, the close-quarters observation was of her husband, and the business she inherited came complete with existing customer base and good reputation. This reduced risk: she could be almost sure of recouping the costs she incurred in maintaining her licence and complying with regulation. The business name, the First-Class Pawn Office, was gender-neutral and owner-neutral, but she made sure, after she had remarried, that when she reprinted the business's pawn tickets with her new name on them, they also retained Laurence McNally's name.[15] This may have been in the knowledge or hope of certain reputational benefits that would continue to flow even after his death. Financial investment, capitalised connections, and financial literacy all point to a level of privilege that had to exist before entry to the pawnbroking industry could be considered. Privilege and advantage came in many forms: inheriting a ready-made business; amassing enough capital to invest; education; and family members on hand with loans and business advice. However it was manifested, privilege smoothed the route to business, while its absence ensured that pawnbroking's model was a profitable one: its success pivoted on the existence not of privilege but of the precarity of those forced to depend on the rapid credit solution the pawnshop offered.

In addition to the licensing costs, and the ongoing costs imposed by the regulator, there were the usual business overheads of salaries, rent, rates, fit-out, and other bills to consider. Dublin pawnbroker John Byrne, whose wife ran his Lombard Street business in his absence, employed four clerks, a foreman and an assistant.[16] Even with an existing house, conversion to commercial use could be time-consuming and costly, and Byrne explained such a conversion in 1869:

14 Paul O'Brien, *The Glynns of Kilrush, County Clare, 1811–1940* (Dublin, 2019), p. 59. 15 PLIC/1/6210, National Archives of Ireland. 16 *Minutes of Evidence*, 5734–5.

> The front portion, what originally constituted a parlour and a hall, were thrown into one; a portion of the parlour and the hall constitute the place where the public are; the other place, at the back of the fire-place, my office and that of my assistants, but it is no longer in the form of a hall, it is an open shop ... The hall still partly exists, a portion of the partition stands, and a large opening has been made in the partition in which there are two folding doors, which are open from half-past 8 to 7.[17]

Like Byrne, Margaret Lowry needed help in the business, and for at least seventeen years she employed a manager, licensed broker Henry Cunningham. On his salary Cunningham supported six children, and employed two domestic servants, and lived in some comfort in Ballsbridge. In both the 1901 and 1911 census returns, there are three male pawnbroker's assistants living over Margaret Lowry's shop at 85 Marlborough Street, along with a female housekeeper. If all three assistants were working for Margaret Lowry, including Cunningham, she provided employment for at least four men, and given that the youngest male assistant in 1911 was only 14, it seems likely that her business provided young men, at least, with a training option too. Her ownership of the business also appears to have influenced the career of her third husband, Edwin Vincent Lowry. It had been Lowry, an accountant, who furnished Glasnevin Cemetery with the details of Laurence McNally's death in 1891, pointing to a prior relationship with one or both of the McNallys.[18] When Margaret Lowry was prosecuted in 1899 for failing to provide her monthly returns, Edwin Lowry was one of her fifteen co-defendants, suggesting that he had also become a licensed pawnbroker, perhaps to help with his new wife's business.[19]

For a woman to be sustaining men's careers in pawnbroking was not new. Twenty years before Margaret Lowry inherited the First-Class Pawn Office, Margaret Farrell was de facto divisional auctioneer, the only person authorised to auction unredeemed pledges for pawnbrokers in her quarter of Dublin. Margaret Farrell had for some years substituted for her husband Charles while he was ill. After his death, though she was not legally permitted, as a woman, to be given this, or any public appointment herself, a group of men with whom she had already worked devised a strategy to keep her in the job, cognisant that she was the most skilled, experienced, and capable person. Her extraordinary situation was summed up before a commission of inquiry:

17 *Copy of minutes of the evidence taken at the trial of the Dublin city election petition* (House of Commons, 1869), 5746. 18 Register of Glasnevin Cemetery, 41/1891. 19 *Daily Express*, 20 May 1899.

> Mr Gray was appointed [divisional auctioneer] ... Mrs Farrell ... is the real deputy. Mr Fitzgerald is an assistant of hers, and his name is used to get over the difficulty of having a female deputy auctioneer. She, however, advertises and carries on the business in her own name.[20]

Gray knew nothing about auctioneering, nor claimed to, remarking of the auction room: 'it would be ruin if I worked it myself'.[21] There were mutual dependencies: the men needed Margaret Farrell to do the job, she needed them to keep her in it. Her work created salaries for at least five men, including two auctioneers, two clerks, and Fitzgerald, whose job was to look after the money, but who had 'no power or authority in the room'. Farrell also contributed to male incomes through employing accountants Kidd and Reid, as Margaret Lowry did later by her use of solicitors Casey, Clay and Collins.

Somewhat subtler, both to define and to navigate, than financial and practical issues, were issues of respectability. Managing the risks to respectability was unavoidable if you were aiming for the rewards of a career in pawnbroking. A preoccupation with respectability was not exclusive to brokers. In the 1888 advertising book *Industries of Dublin*, nine of the 24 women's businesses raised respectability as a selling point. Those women who didn't use the word respectable used words like tasteful, influential, best, genteel, prominent, first-class, first-rate, select, honourable, reputation, esteemed: words chosen to demonstrate their absolute respectability, from which flowed desirability.[22] Could a pawnbroker offer similar reassurances, or were they really on the fringes of respectability? Respectability was not necessarily the main concern of a customer who needed money in a hurry and knew that pawnbrokers provided a more-or-less no-questions-asked route to ready cash for goods. But respectability was something of which all pawnbrokers had to be aware, particularly if they were women, whose respectability was more easily dented. Just as the businesses in *Industries of Dublin* advertised themselves repeatedly as 'respectable', pawnbrokers frequently specified respectability when recruiting: 'Wanted, a respectable Young Girl, who understands the above business, as an Assistant'; 'Wanted, a respectable Lad as an Apprentice; must be good writer'.[23]

Laurence McNally, and later Margaret Lowry, sought to define the standing and respectability of the pawnshop through branding it the First-Class Pawn Office. An early recruitment advertisement sought a 'respectable, intelligent' young man who wrote 'an expeditious hand'.[24] The business Margaret Lowry inherited was one habitually billed as high-end. Newspaper advertisements

20 *Report on pawnbroking, 1868*, p. 52, National Library of Ireland. 21 Ibid., p. 65. 22 *Industries of Dublin* (Dublin, 1888). 23 *Belfast Telegraph*, 11 February 1882; *Belfast Telegraph*, 2 September 1881. 24 *Irish Times*, 20 February 1878.

describing forfeited pledges show that rather than sacrificing a few flimsy essentials, many clients who came to 85 Marlborough Street pawned what they could afford to do without: a box of good cigars, a sealskin jacket, shares in the tram company. But dealing in diamonds and oil paintings did not necessarily indemnify Margaret Lowry against questionable respectability.[25] Respectable people didn't want a pawnbroker's shop nearby. In 1883 a licence was initially refused because the proposed shop would 'cause a nuisance, and seriously deteriorate the value of property' in Upper Gardiner Street, at that time still mainly though not exclusively residential.[26] This echoed an earlier case in which the residents of Fitzwilliam Square objected to their smart square being polluted by Elizabeth Perry's medical boarding-house.[27]

A pawnshop in Philadelphia maintained a separate entrance for women, but a pawnbroker could 'only do so much to shield customers from each other, or, more to the point, from their own shame'.[28] The idea that pawning comes wrapped in shame and degradation appears frequently in nineteenth-century fiction.[29] For some commentators, the pawner in such literature teeters on the brink of a moral or sexual fall, and the pawned item 'hovers between home and marketplace as a symbol of a character's uncertain fate'.[30] If the act of pawning was interpreted as an act twinned with sexual shame, moral shade must also have been cast on the facilitating broker. For a woman considering entering the business, any lingering doubts over whether pawnbroking was an appropriate occupation for a respectable woman may well have been cancelled out by the promise of at least supper on the table, and at best healthy profits. For customers, their knowledge of the cycle of pawning must have told them that though one day brought surrender, subsequent days held the possibility of even a temporary redemption.

A sensitive broker met the possibility of shame with the promise of discretion. In 1895 Margaret Lowry's customers could send parcels from 'all parts of the Kingdom' and have the full value sent by return. 'Strictest privacy observed', she reassured potential clients, for whom it must have been a relief to know that they need not frequent their local pawnshop.[31] Sometimes clients attended in person and still concealed their real identities. Twenty years after Margaret Lowry placed the 'strictest privacy' advertisement, Thomas Malone borrowed money from the First-Class Pawn Office using the name 'Mr

25 *Freeman's Journal*, 18 July 1874; *Evening Telegraph*, 3 November 1881. 26 *R v. Woodlock*. 27 *Pembroke v. Warren* [1896] 1 IR 76. 28 Wendy A. Woloson, *In hock: pawning in America from independence through the great depression* (Chicago, 2009), p. 68. 29 Jennifer Tate Becker, 'Round the corner: pawnbroking in the Victorian novel' (PhD, Washington University, 2014). 30 Elizabeth Coggin Womack, 'A pledge out of time: redemption and the literary pawnshop', *Victorian Literature and Culture*, 40:12 (2012), pp 451–67. 31 *Irish Times*, 15 August 1896.

Cosgrove'. Two months later, amid the chaos of the 1916 Rising, the First-Class Pawn Office was looted. Malone's pawned jewellery was taken, and he had to come clean. 'The goods were pawned by me in name on ticket', he wrote on the pawn ticket, submitting it in support of his compensation claim.[32] The respectability issue, raised but not resolved in the Gardiner Street case, dogged pawnbrokers. Public misgivings about the trade arose in relation to profits made from the poverty of others, the trade's association with crime and with public health problems, sparked by the circulation and recirculation of textile goods. Through the second half of the nineteenth century, as the state began increasingly to take responsibility for the health of the general population, there were public health campaigns against various communicable illnesses, including scarlet fever, smallpox, typhus and cholera.[33] Awareness developed of pawnshops as breeding grounds of disease, and discussion of the issue clarified the low status of pawnbrokers:

> the class of the community, above the rank of operatives, who suffer most are those who are brought by business into direct communication with the affected, such as victuallers, pawnbrokers, undertakers and small shopkeepers.[34]

Other businesses were problematic from a public health perspective, too. Dealers in second-hand goods sold infected textiles, cab drivers drove passengers on infected upholstery, and boarding-house keepers put guests to sleep in bedding which, even if it had been washed, was not disinfected. Dairies and butchers sold tubercular milk and meat. Through the conduit of the pawnbroker, anyone who held goods on a temporary basis, and might end up pawning them in extremis, represented a risk. The owner of a newly-made suit of clothes or repaired pair of boots might never think that the tailor or cobbler might have found it expedient to pawn them to cover some short-term crisis. Public health legislation introduced penalties against the careless, and courts imposed them.[35] Esther Ryan was prosecuted for having pawned for 6*d.* in a North King Street pawn office 'the robe of an infant who died in a house in which typhus and smallpox had occurred'. The defendant argued in vain that 'it was not the robe of a child that died from the smallpox', and she was fined 40*s.*[36]

Some pawnbrokers risked tainting their reputations with criminal wrongdoing, or ended up accused of it. In Ballybricken, in the six years from

32 PLIC/1/6300, National Archives of Ireland. 33 Catherine Cox, 'Health and welfare, 1750–2000' in Eugenio F. Biagini and Mary E. Daly (eds), *The Cambridge social history of modern Ireland* (Cambridge, 2017), pp 263–311, p. 269. 34 *British Medical Journal*, 7 April 1866. 35 Public Health (Ireland) Act, 1878, s. 142. 36 *Freeman's Journal*, 13 February 1897.

1854, pawnbroker Eleanor Grannon was in court repeatedly, usually to answer charges of failing or refusing to deliver pawned goods to their owners 'though the money lent and interest thereon is paid to said Defendant'.[37] Most of the charges were unsuccessful, but Eleanor Grannon had to deal with each one as it arose, and take time away from running her pawnshop, either closing it or paying someone to mind the shop, to make an appearance in court and respond to the charges. Nor was this always in respectable company: in August 1854 the five other defendants entered on the same page as Grannon were all pleading guilty to public drunkenness; in 1859 her fellow defendants were all accused of assault. Despite most of the charges going nowhere, Grannon's repeated presence in court (or, on the occasions she did not appear, the reading aloud of her name, trade and address) in the company of the drunk and the violent cannot have done much for her respectability or reputation.

The goods mentioned in conjunction with Grannon's court appearances were mainly second-hand clothes, suggesting that her shop was a modest one.[38] Negative publicity generated by brushes with the law was also an issue for higher-end brokers like Margaret Lowry. Fencing stolen goods was a significant problem, and, given the possible fines, disruption to work and damage to reputation that an incident with stolen goods could involve, responsible pawnbrokers remained alert. By 1899, Margaret had employed Henry Cunningham to manage the First-Class Pawn Office. His competence was essential to the protection of her brand, and fortunately he was experienced in spotting and turning away stolen property. He stopped some stolen golf trousers that year, and in 1909 was immediately suspicious of three boxes of furs, which turned out to have been stolen from McBirney's, the smart department store across the river. The problems persisted, though, and it must have seemed to some brokers as if there was always some issue to be dealt with, as Margaret Lowry and her third husband Edwin, co-defendants in the 1899 returns case already mentioned, knew only too well. The charges went nowhere, but their names had already been published in the newspaper.[39] In 1901, Inspector John Roe, a DMP detective, told an inquiry that his 'pawn office men' had to 'go round the pawn offices every day. It is disagreeable, dirty work'.[40] Police oversight was one of the reasons that Dublin pawnbrokers were required to contribute £100 per year. This charge was not differentiated. It had to be paid whether you were starting out or established, whether your business was extensive or modest, and was 'a very serious impediment to beginners and to

37 18/01/1856, National Archives of Ireland. 38 27/01/1854; 10/02/1854; 18/01/1856; 29/02/1856; 20/08/1856; 08/07/1859, National Archives of Ireland. 39 *The Daily Express*, 20 May 1899. 40 *Report of the committee of enquiry on the Dublin Metropolitan Police, 1901* (House of Commons, 1902), p. 10.

those who wish to do business on a small scale, and thus it produces an artificial monopoly in favour of those who have an extensive or long established business'.[41]

Sample figures from 1867 indicate that contributions from pawnbrokers (men and women) constituted over 5% of the DMP's annual budget.[42] The fact that women's earnings went into supporting policing the capital shows with absolute clarity that women in business had a direct effect on the society in which they lived. Tackling the Gordian knot of the returns was a headache for administration after administration. Often, it was all officials could do to keep returns coming in, and chasing recalcitrant brokers was time-consuming and often fruitless. Pawnbrokers universally detested the monthly drag of preparing returns and having them receipted and certified, on top of their everyday work, and resented the monthly shilling fee. In 1866, 624 licensed brokers operated nationally, and business was booming. The 537 brokers who made returns showed an aggregate of almost 14 million tickets issued in twelve months, almost £2 million issued in loans.[43] That year, 87 brokers, 13%, did not meet their obligation to make returns, suggesting a sizeable number of transactions and loans left unreported. By June 1870 the regulator had travelled to Enniskillen five or six times to compel Mary Bigham to complete her returns. She wrote to him dismissively:

> Mr Hayes –
> Yours to hand. I will send returns every six months. I will not send returns for 1869, and I hope you will come and look for them. You will fare I promise you as well as you did on the last occasion.
> Yours,
> Mary Bigham.[44]

In the sympathetic opinion of the *Belfast Morning News*, the monthly returns 'must inflict great trouble and expense on pawnbrokers … the nation would not suffer much if the Act were erased from the Statute-Book'.[45] Certainly Mary Bigham was sick of the process; nor was she going to be told what to do by the City Marshal.

The office of the regulator was not above reproach, which did not help enforcement efforts. In fact, it was a model of corruption, lax administration and absence from office, described mildly as 'a very unsatisfactory state of affairs'.[46] Throughout the nineteenth century successive marshals borrowed

41 *Report on pawnbroking, 1868*, p. 345. 42 *Account of receipt and expenditure of Dublin Metropolitan Police* (House of Commons, 1867). 43 *Report on pawnbroking, 1868*, p. 33. 44 *Evening Freeman*, 16 June 1870. 45 *Belfast Morning News*, 20 June 1870. 46 *Report on pawnbroking, 1868*, p. 20.

money from pawnbrokers, extracted additional fees from their own assistants, and did not bother either to check brokers' books nor attend sales of forfeited goods. If the marshal himself could ignore regulation, so could the brokers, particularly if it meant saving money, or generating a little extra. Shops were opened out of hours, pawnbrokers gave loans without getting names and addresses, exceeded the statutory maximum, and operated unlicensed premises.[47]

Despite the barriers to entry, and the risks involved, there was no shortage of women entering pawnbroking. Nor did ongoing reputational problems stop women from being able to make plenty of money. The prospect of making money may have overridden concerns about reputation. Respectability, and even social advancement, were objectives too, and both Margaret Farrell and Margaret Lowry must have been pleased that their pawnbroking careers were successful enough to support lives outside the noise and dirt of the city centre. Farrell lived in Clarinda Park in Kingstown (now Dun Laoghaire); Margaret Lowry lived in Bayswater Terrace in Sandycove, a house whose long seaside garden stretched down to a private swimming spot. Meanwhile, Henry Cunningham took care of the Marlborough Street shop, and dealt with administrative issues, even the tricky ones like compensation claims. Money and property alone did not confer respectability. On Lowry's first marriage certificate, her father described himself as a 'gentleman', but much of respectability was bound up in how other people saw you, rather than in how you wanted to be seen. Women whose comfortable lives were made possible on the profits of pawnbroking may well have been regarded with a similar contempt to 'common publicans' in a novel of 1878, who were the 'laughing-stock of Dublin for vulgarity', even though they had made enough money to move into one of the smart city squares.[48]

Pawnbrokers' shops were a kind of crossroads at which people from different social strata, business sectors and geographical areas might meet. The business permeated many areas of life, meaning it was ever-present for people, but usually in the shade cast by problems, and, if you were a pawnbroker, it was likely that everyone would have an opinion on your business. The nature of the business was problematic: even if every pawnbroker played a straight bat, clients were in difficult financial circumstances and did not necessarily want to be seen going in to the shop. The discretion of the pawnbroker, and the privacy in which the client could do business, were essential to a customer who might be conscious of not wanting his or her personal circumstances to be deduced by passers-by.

47 House of Commons debates, 21 July 1890, 347 c356; House of Commons debates, 12 July 1898, 61 cc 670–1670; *Saunders's News-Letter*, 27 November 1824. **48** May Laffan, *Hogan, MP* (London, 1876), p. 31.

Although all these problems nudged pawnbroking closer and closer to the periphery of respectability, at the same time a certain amount of privilege was required for starting off. It was easier then, as now, for those with structural privilege to access education, accumulate property and money, get credit, and have recourse to the law (to recover debt, say, or to compel performance of a contract). Even one businesswoman in the family could make a difference, as is evidenced by Jane Lane-Joynt's pawnbroker mother passing on skills of bookkeeping and business management; Ellen Jane Gilchrist's mother Jane Moore bringing her into partnership with her; and Mary Bigham going into business with her sister.

An individual was in a privileged position if they had a family member with a business which might be transferred on or before their death, or if they were a child of a broker and could learn the skills of the business through close quarters observation. If a person could fulfil the specific requirements of the licensing regulations, then that pointed to privilege too. Not everyone had money to invest, nor a network of capitalised connections who could vouch for them and risk a surety. Not everyone had the financial literacy to run a brokerage day-to-day and prepare returns for submission once a month. Pawnbroking's particular situation between privilege and the importance of reputation on one side, and questionable respectability on the other, seems to have created a space women could occupy, while providing a service to those in financial precarity.

Although both Farrell and Lowry may have begun their working lives under the influence of men, they finished them by exercising their own influence over the men who worked with and for them. Initially both women carried on their husbands' careers, but it was their own work which subsequently bolstered and facilitated the careers of men, as well as paying the professional fees and salaries that between them made up the livings of at least ten men. While an existing network of powerful men was always useful, the benefits flowed both ways. Margaret Farrell's singular expertise, acknowledged by her male supporters, kept a sprawling, complicated business afloat and paid men's salaries. Margaret Lowry employed, housed, and trained male apprentices, employed a male manager supporting a large family, and probably brought her third husband into the business. Even in her husband's lifetime it was Margaret Farrell who kept the work flowing and the business going. When, after his death, a strict interpretation of the law meant she had to operate behind a curtain, the curtain was merely a scrim, and lit from behind. Everyone knew what was going on. The men who put their names to the arrangement that kept her in charge did so in the expressed knowledge that she was the best and most experienced person for the job. In all the discussion about this arrangement there is no mention of any man being worried about any adverse consequences for himself, nor any sanctions. The evidence, so far as it is possible to tell from the transcript, was heard and accepted by a commission of inquiry, which scarcely turned a hair. This reinforces the argument that women in business were a common feature of nineteenth-century Ireland, even in the context of their having been specifically ruled out of positions.

These profits, these salaries, these luxurious homes were not just generated by women's hard work. The money came from interest payments on loans to the needy, and the resale of unredeemed goods, in an industry linked with dirt, disease and crime, regulated by an office brought repeatedly into disrepute. Women in pawnbroking were required not just to roll up their sleeves, but to stand face to face with those who would never have enough to live on without having recourse to moneylenders and living in a cycle of debt. The precarity imposed by poverty, want and impossibly low wages fuelled most of the transactions which kept the pawnbrokers in business.

CHAPTER 11

'Provided the family is not neglected': women's work, maternity leave and childcare in Ireland, 1969–81*

Deirdre Foley

In 1974, a Mrs Kiernan interviewed for a dental receptionist position in Louth. She was offered the job, but this offer was rescinded on the same day by letter from one of the practices' dentists. He wrote:

> ... Having had more time to think of it in relation to your married status with as yet no children at the moment balanced against the difficulty of training someone into the intricacies of the position I regret that I feel that it would not be satisfactory and I would constantly be wondering if you would come to me and say you're leaving because you were pregnant, and I would then be faced with the problem of finding someone else and the difficulty of retraining ...[1]

Mrs Kiernan forwarded the letter to the Department of Labour, claiming discrimination on the hypothesis of a future pregnancy. Her situation, while inequitable, was perfectly legal in 1974.

The letter was written after the publication of the final report of the Commission on the Status of Women, assessed by Mary Robinson as a 'charter for women in the modern Irish state'.[2] The Commission, the Republic of Ireland's first state-sponsored investigation into gender inequality, was formed in 1970 after an *ad hoc* committee of women's organisations lobbied the government for its establishment from 1967. The Commission's final report was a comprehensive examination of the issues affecting women in Ireland, such as the marriage bar, equal pay, education, social welfare, childcare, and maternity leave. To oversee the implementation of the report's findings, the Council for

* For the source of the quotation in this chapter's title see note 20, 'Cork town ICA response'. 1 McDermott Dental Surgeons to Mrs Kiernan, Dundalk, Co. Louth, 3 December 1974. National Archives of Ireland (NAI), Department of Labour papers, 2007/109/6. 2 Mary Robinson, 'Women and the new Irish state' in Margaret MacCurtain and Donncha Ó Corráin (eds), *Women in Irish society: the historical dimension* (Dublin, 1979), p. 65.

the Status of Women, an umbrella group of over 30 women's organisations, was formed, and campaigned for the implementation of the Commission's recommendations throughout the 1970s. Two statutory bodies also emerged after the Commission's report: the Women's Representative Committee (1974), and the Employment Equality Agency (1977). Recommendations made by the Commission are connected to many changes in legislation during the 1970s. It recommended the removal of the civil service marriage bar, which occurred in 1973. On the publication of the Commission's report in 1973, it was a relief for many to see detailed evidence of women's inferior legal and social status distilled into one document. Gemma Hussey recalled: 'Now, at last, the facts of discrimination were laid bare for all to see; forty-nine recommendations formed the nucleus around which women lobbied politicians.'[3] The report was an asset for women's groups for years to come, because the government accepted and pledged to implement its forty-nine recommendations.[4]

The current occlusion of women's paid labour from Irish economic history limits our capacity to understand the impact of women's enormous transition from the home to the labour market. As Scott argues, 'a sex-segregated labour market is part of the process of gender construction'.[5] A historical analysis of the changes in women's working lives can reveal the dynamics of changing gendered identities in Ireland at the level of lived experience. This chapter makes an initial intervention into this absence by exploring the changing legislation associated with the increasing entry of women – particularly married women and mothers – into the Irish labour market. Drawing on a large body of official and media sources, the papers of various women's groups and oral history, it traces the development of maternity leave and childcare for working women in Ireland, and public opinions arising from discussion of these issues. This chapter reveals not only social and legal change, but also the voluntary work, activism and public discourse associated with this change. While opportunities were widening for women in the workplace, the historical dominance of the male breadwinner model limited the scope of what was possible for all women. However, this limitation was particularly acute for working mothers.

MATERNITY LEAVE

The Commission's report outlined the extremely limited system of maternity leave available to Irish women in 1972. The near-ubiquitous nature of the

3 Gemma Hussey, *Ireland today: anatomy of a changing state* (Dublin, 1993), p. 422. 4 Women's Political Association flyer re: 'Capsule Course in Politics', UCD Archives (UCDA), Gemma Hussey papers, P197/33. 5 Joan Scott, 'Gender: a useful category of historical analysis', *The*

marriage bar, which imposed retirement on married women, meant that most Irish employers had little impetus to grant maternity leave to female employees. The long duration of the marriage bar was closely connected to the male breadwinner ideal and the wider system of narrowly defined gender roles in Irish society, which a practically non-existent system of maternity leave also helped to preserve. The bar was both a legal provision in the civil service, and an observed custom in many other workplaces. The habitual retirement of many women upon marriage, and the treatment of unmarried mothers as a national social problem, confined the agency and earnings of working mothers for decades. Shifting social attitudes and a younger average age of marriage meant that the marriage bar was gradually giving way to what the Commission called a 'maternity bar' from the 1960s.[6] An increasing number of women remained at work after marriage, but were far less likely to continue after having a child. According to a survey of nearly fifty major employers carried out by the Commission, including Bank of Ireland, Cadbury and Shannon Airport, there was little if any pressure from employees for the grant of maternity leave, either paid or unpaid.[7] However, it was not determined by this survey whether this perceived lack of pressure from female employees was due to fear. There was no guarantee of employment for mothers upon return to work. No statutory protection was in place to prevent dismissal for pregnancy until 1977.[8]

Irish social insurance provided for 'maternity benefit', a cash grant of £4 'payable in respect of each confinement.'[9] If a woman wasn't formally employed outside the home, the grant could be claimed against her husband's social insurance. If both parents were employed (and if they were married), two grants could be claimed. For women who did not qualify, either through their own or their husband's contributions, a means-tested maternity grant of £8 per birth was available.[10] A separate maternity 'allowance' was also payable to working women, ostensibly for the purpose of maternity leave from employment. The allowance of £5.55 for 12 weeks was paid for six weeks both before and after the birth.[11] The payment could also be claimed by women who had not been in employment for some time but had kept their social insurance contributions updated by credits.[12] Women could be disqualified from this allowance 'if, during the period for which the allowance is payable, she engages in any occupation other than domestic duties in her own household'.[13] Such arrangements did not

American Historical Review, 91:5 (1986), p. 1068. 6 Commission on the Status of Women, *Report to Minister for Finance* (Dublin, 1972), p. 231. 7 Commission on the Status of Women, *Report to Minister for Finance*, p. 112. 8 Unfair Dismissals Act 1977, s. 6 (f). 9 Social Welfare Act 1952, s. 19; Commission on the Status of Women, *Report to Minister for Finance*, p. 112. 10 Health Act, 1970, s. 64. 11 Commission on the Status of Women, p. 112. 12 Mary Daly and Sara Clavero, *Contemporary family policy in Ireland and Europe* (Dublin, 2004), p. 27. 13 Statutory Instrument equate to any right to maternity leave from employment for women. The Commission did not find any instance in its survey where paid maternity leave was granted by an employer. Two semi-state bodies, RTÉ and Aer Lingus, had recently enacted regulations facilitating the retention of married women and the grant of unpaid maternity leave for up to twelve weeks.[14]

An entitlement to maternity leave for all working women was recommended by the Commission, the provisions for which were devised to match what was already available under Irish social insurance. The Commission proposed at least twelve weeks of maternity leave, with a further optional four weeks during which they would not be entitled to social welfare benefit, and the prohibition of dismissal on the grounds of pregnancy. These proposals allowed for a woman to return to work when her baby was, at maximum, two-and-a-half months old. No suggestion was made for companies to provide paid maternity leave, or for any increase in state maternity benefits. The Commission's discussion of the employment of married women acknowledged 'a very marked change in attitudes in recent years'.[15] There was an increasing number of married women at work and an increasing demand for their labour, which was cheap. Women's choices in the labour market were expanding as the average family size was contracting. The growing availability and use of birth control, and a lowering average marriage age, signalled that mothers were increasingly returning to paid work after the birth of their final child at a relatively young age. However, the Commission also expressed a certain level of support for traditional gender roles in Irish society: 'it is still the case that the vast majority of married women continue to devote the greater part of their time to their traditional role within the family and none of the recommendations set out below is intended to reflect on this position'.[16]

This position associated women with the bulk of practical family responsibilities. Despite the Commission's statement that married women who chose to work should not have to face 'obstacles which can and should be removed', no suggestion was made in the report that men should integrate themselves more fully with domestic or family tasks.[17] The Commission also referred to an Economic and Social Research Institute (ESRI) survey. Of the women respondents to this survey 74% approved of married women working outside the home, but mostly under certain conditions: 'that the woman should have no young children to look after or that she should be in a position to get help with children'.[18] The male breadwinner model was reinforced by women as

no. 375, 1952: Social Welfare (Maternity Allowance) Regulations, 1952. 14 Ibid. 15 Commission on the Status of Women, *Report to Minister for Finance*, p. 124. 16 Ibid. 17 Ibid., p. 25. 18 Brendan M. Walsh, 'Aspects of labour supply and demand, with special reference to the well as men. Former chair of the Council for the Status of Women, Anne Kavanagh, recalled: 'there was some women who believed a woman's place was in the home and that they should be there for the children. Oh, there definitely was'.[19]

The Irish Countrywomen's Association (ICA), Ireland's largest women's organisation, conducted a survey of its guilds (branches) in 1973 to record opinions of the Commission's recommendations. Many responses expressed similarly entrenched attitudes regarding gender roles. Cork town ICA responded that part-time work was 'to be encouraged for married women, provided the family is not neglected'. ICA Kildare stated that married women should only be permitted to work should their husbands become ill or unemployed.[20] The Gormanston Guild agreed that married women should be allowed to work 'provided that their children were not neglected', stating that it was advisable, if possible, for women to stay at home for the first five years of their children's life.[21] Similarly, ICA Mitchelstown recorded: 'Married women should not work. Circumstances, however, may have occasion to alter this'.[22] ICA Skerries submitted their 'concern about latch key children' in the event of mothers being at work.[23] In this sense, for many women, family responsibilities remained strictly gendered between parents. The ESRI survey also found that 34% of 'non-farm husbands' disapproved or would disapprove of their wives engaging in paid work. The 'non-farm' distinction is a significant reminder that many farmers' wives were certainly engaged in agricultural labour. Despite this fact, many married farming women were repeatedly enumerated on census returns as 'engaged in home duties', a gendered category indicative of the belief that women were best suited to the domestic sphere.[24]

EMPLOYMENT EQUALITY?

The civil service marriage bar was removed in 1973 under new legislation that allowed married women to apply for new posts in state employment. Women who had already retired were not entitled to direct reinstatement.[25] In addition

employment of women in Ireland' (1971), cited in Commission on the Status of Women, *Report to Minister for Finance*, p. 124. **19** Author's interview with Anne Kavanagh, 20 September 2021. **20** 'Cork town ICA response to survey re *Report to Minister for Finance*'; 'Kildare ICA response re: Commission on the Status of Women, received 19 Mar. 1974', National Library of Ireland (NLI), Records of the Irish Countrywomen's Association (ICA), MS 39,866/4. **21** Reply to ICA Survey from Gormanston Guild, 1974, NLI, ICA MS 39,866/4. **22** Replies to ICA Survey from Cork Guilds, 1974, NLI, ICA MS 39,866/4. **23** Reply to ICA Survey from Skerries Guild, 1974, NLI, ICA MS 39,866/4. **24** Catríona Clear, *Women of the house: women's household work in Ireland, 1926–1961* (Dublin, 2000), p. 15. **25** Civil Service (Employment of Married Women) Act 1973.

to the state's acceptance of the recommendations of the Commission on the Status of Women, this legislation was an obligation for Ireland to comply with the Treaty of Rome shortly after it became an EEC member state on 1 January 1973. Later, and again for Ireland to comply with European directives, the Employment Equality Act, 1977 extended the legal definition of discrimination to include sex and marital status, and prohibited marriage bars in the private sector.[26] The Unfair Dismissals Act, 1977 included a limited clause on pregnancy and dismissal, leaving plenty of loopholes for employers.[27] For example, if a pregnant employee was unable to do adequately the work for which she was employed, an unfair dismissal could not be alleged.

While married women and mothers were among those most particularly discriminated against in the workplace, all women faced low pay. In 1970, women's hourly earnings in manufacturing industries averaged 55% of men's.[28] The minimum rates of pay for women prescribed by Joint Labour Committees (appointed by the Labour Court, comprising equal numbers of employer and worker representatives) in 1969 were, on average, just two-thirds of those prescribed for men.[29] The Anti-Discrimination (Pay) Act, 1974 was introduced to comply with Ireland's new obligations under European legislation, as well as the recommendations of the Commission on the Status of Women. A co-operative feminist campaign was necessary for this act to be implemented in full after the government's attempt to delay its application in 1975.

The act introduced an equality clause into all contracts of employment whereby women became entitled to equal pay with men (or vice versa) when employed for 'like work', defined as where the work was identical or interchangeable; of a similar nature, with differences occurring only infrequently; and 'equal in value … in terms of the demands it makes'.[30] In a claims-based approach, applicants under the act were required to have a comparator of the opposite sex with whom to compare work and pay, narrowing the pool of potential applicants. Irish workplaces were highly segregated; it was frequently impossible for women to find a male comparator. Both applicant and comparator had to be employed in the same place (a city, town or locality), under the same employer. Mary Maher flagged the limited nature of the legislation:

26 Employment Equality Act 1977. 27 Unfair Dismissals Act 1977. 28 Irish Congress of Trade Unions, *Submission by Irish Congress of Trade Unions to the Commission on the Status of Women* (Dublin, 1970), p. 7. 29 Citizen's Information, 'Joint Labour Committees' http://www.citizensinformation.ie/en/employment/employment_rights_and_conditions/industrial_relations_and_trade_unions/joint_labour_committees.html, accessed 2 March 2019; Irish Congress of Trade Unions, *Submission by Irish Congress of Trade Unions to the Commission on the Status of Women* (Dublin, 1971), p. 7. 30 Anti-Discrimination (Pay) Act 1974, s. 3.

> Consider the woman working in an all-woman textile factory owned by a small employer. She may be doing similar work to men in factories all over Ireland, but she has no grounds for an equal pay claim. Consider the shop assistant working for a large chain store. In her shop, only women may be employed; though she's doing the same work as men working for the same boss in other shops, she cannot submit an equal pay claim. Consider the hairdresser or waitress in one place where only women may be employed, watching hairdressers and waitresses in another shop win equal pay because men also worked on their premises. Even if the work is identical, even if the same boss pays all, women in the all-female establishment have no claim to equal pay.[31]

The act was due to come into force on 31 December 1975, but the government attempted to delay its application until 1977 due to an economic downturn. Oil prices quadrupled due to the Arab-Israeli conflict; Ireland relied on the Middle East for 90% of its oil. Consequently, public sector borrowing rose from 8.6% of GNP in 1972–3 to 12.9% by 1976–7.[32] As the Irish economy declined, the Federated Union of Employers (FUE) lobbied in 1975 to allow deferral of equal pay. The Taoiseach, Liam Cosgrave, made a televised appeal for a pay pause in December 1975.[33] On 17 December, Cosgrave announced that the Act would be amended to provide for 'the position of industries that would experience unemployment as a result of the implementation of equal pay', such as manufacturing and retail.[34] Companies such as Magee Clothing and Williams Supermarkets had made repeated representations to the Taoiseach on the matter.[35] While the 1974 legislation was drafted with European regulation in mind, a new EEC directive published in February 1975 (75/117/EEC) came to ensure its eventual enforcement.[36] This directive was drawn up to force member states to legislate for the practical application of Article 119 of the Treaty of Rome, which underscored the principle of equal pay for equal work of equal value.[37]

A large protest was mounted after the Irish government's attempt to defer. In January 1976, women's liberation group Irish Women United occupied the

31 *Irish Times*, 26 March 1974. 32 Ciara Meehan, 'Towards a "modern progressive society": the National Coalition and social reform, 1973–7', *Irish Historical Studies*, 38:151 (2013), pp 457–75, p. 472. 33 Ibid. 34 Garry Sweeney, *In public service: a history of the Public Service Executive Union, 1890–1990* (Dublin, 1990), p. 222. 35 H.L. Temple, chairman, Magee Clothing, to the Taoiseach, 27 September 1974, NAI, Taoiseach papers, 2008/148/331; J.J. Quinn, chairman, H. Williams & Company Limited, to the Taoiseach, 8 December 1975, NAI, Taoiseach papers, 2008/148/331. 36 'Council Directive 75/117/EEC of 10 February 1975 on the approximation of the laws of the Member States relating to the application of the principle of equal pay for men and women', https://eur-lex.europa.eu/legal-content/en/ALL/?uri=CELEX%3A31975L0117, accessed 10 February 2021. 37 Deirdre Curtin, *Irish employment equality law* (Dublin, 1989), p. 106.

FUE headquarters, demanding 'the full and immediate implementation' of equal pay.[38] Trade unions and women's organisations collected over 36,000 signatures to the Promotion for Equal Pay *ad hoc* Committee petition, calling on the government to implement the legislation without delay. Signatures were collected outside shopping centres, through trade unions and women's organisations.[39] Prominent names attributed to the petition, printed at the top of each copy, included Nuala Fennell, Hilda Tweedy, Margaret MacCurtain, Catherine McGuinness and Gemma Hussey.[40] Women's organisations such as the Council for the Status of Women (CSW) and the Dublin University Women Graduates' Association wrote to the Taoiseach and the President of the European Commission, expressing deep disappointment at the attempted delay. In February Hilda Tweedy, CSW chair, travelled to Strasbourg to lobby the European parliament against any postponement of equal pay for equal work in Ireland. Anne Kavanagh of the CSW explained:

> Hilda went to Brussels to make sure that the government couldn't get derogation. Mary Robinson was most helpful … she was able to give us the legal reference number [of the EEC directive], when we were writing, to be able to quote that, that they had no right to derogation.[41]

Similarly, the Irish Congress of Trade Unions sent a submission to the EEC. The government's request to delay the implementation of equal pay legislation was denied by the EEC in April 1976.[42] From this point, the Anti-Discrimination (Pay) Act had force. The act did not eradicate pay differences between men and women. 1993 figures show that women's hourly earnings were 69% of men's, while women's weekly earnings were only 60.7% of men's. Disparity is greater in terms of weekly pay because this figure includes overtime and bonus payments, more commonly accrued by men.[43] Another significant reason why the legislation did not eradicate differences in pay was the deeply segregated nature of the labour market, a fact underscored by how relatively cheap female labour was, particularly in industrial settings.[44]

Despite the legal and cultural restrictions placed on married women's ability to work after marriage, and stark official census returns, it has nevertheless been

38 *Irish Press*, 22 January 1976. 39 *Irish Times*, 28 January 1976. 40 Promotion for Equal Pay *ad hoc* Committee, 'Equal Pay Now' petition, January 1976, NAI, Taoiseach papers, 2008/148/331. 41 Author's interview with Anne Kavanagh, 20 September 2021. 42 Ciara Meehan, *A just society for Ireland? 1964–1987* (London, 2013), p. 123. 43 European Foundation for the Improvement of Living and Working Conditions, 'Anti-Discrimination (Pay) Act 1974', https://www.eurofound.europa.eu/efemiredictionary/anti-discrimination-pay-act-1974, accessed 20 January 2021. 44 Helen Russell, Frances McGinnity and Philip J. O'Connell, 'Gender equality in the Irish

observed that many women engaged in casual, undocumented paid labour in the domestic sphere.[45] Married women were entering employment in increased numbers even before the civil service marriage bar was removed. Women's labour force participation rates rose from 5.2% in 1961 to 7.5% in 1971. While the overall participation rate of Irish women remained static between 1971 and 1977, the rate for married women essentially doubled – rising from 7.5% to 14.4%.[46] The impact of this change in wider society and within the family was more gradual, as much of this work was part-time. Work for married women, particularly married mothers, was envisioned, ideally, as flexible, and as a means of generating supplementary income for the home. Advertisements for private sector jobs increasingly emphasised this. Notices seeking candidates for retail, hotel, and factory positions often entailed flexible shift work, specifically seeking 'girls and married women'. Taking examples from 1974, Jacob's biscuit factory sought 'girls and married women 18–35'; Hayden's Hotel in Ballinasloe sought 'married women for casual work'; Dunnes Stores advertised 'vacancies for married women' on a flexible shift pattern; and Celtic Toys, Cork, advertised: 'Girls and Married Women Required for full-time or part-time work.'[47]

The rate of employment for married women was comparatively low by European standards. While the rate of marriage remained high, there was no statutory scheme of paid maternity leave for full-time employees in the private sector until 1981.[48] The end of the civil service marriage bar prompted a demand for a scheme of maternity leave in the civil service and semi-state bodies. In May 1974 the (entirely male) Labour Court was asked to investigate a claim by the Local Government and Public Services' Union for maternity leave.[49] In 1975 the Labour Court recommended for maternity leave with full pay to be granted to staff at RTÉ.[50] By 1975, maternity leave for civil servants granted twelve weeks of leave with full pay, and four additional weeks of optional unpaid leave.[51] The Maternity Protection of Employees Act, 1981 eventually entitled female employees to a minimum of fourteen weeks' leave, the right to return to work after such leave, and to time off from work for antenatal and post-natal care. Four weeks had to be taken before the birth, and four after. Up to four weeks of additional unpaid leave was also made available. The act applied to all women who worked eight hours or more per week, with no service qualification. Under

labour market, 1966–2016: unfinished business?', *The Economic and Social Review*, 48:4 (2017), p. 413. 45 Mary E. Daly, 'Women in the Irish workforce from pre-industrial to modern times', *Saothar*, 7 (1981), pp 74–82, p. 76. 46 Tim Callan and Brian Farrell, *Women's participation in the Irish labour market* (Dublin, 1991), p. 18 and p. 30. 47 *Evening Herald*, 11 September 1974; *Evening Herald*, 3 April 1974; *Connacht Tribune*, 5 April 1974; *Evening Herald*, 9 March 1974; *Cork Examiner*, 9 September 1974. 48 Maternity Protection of Employees Act 1981. 49 *Irish Times*, 17 May 1974. 50 The Labour Court, *Annual Report 1975* (Dublin, 1975). 51 Women's Representative Committee, *Second progress* the Social Welfare (Amendment) Act, 1981, a new pay-related maternity allowance scheme was introduced. Maternity benefit was now payable for fourteen weeks at a level corresponding to take-home pay.[52] In the first year of the scheme, 4,603 women claimed maternity benefit, rising to 10,727 in 1985.[53] A crude calculation shows that this represents just over 17% of live births in 1985.[54]

CHILDCARE

Childcare was examined by the Commission on the Status of Women as a factor to facilitate the employment of married women, albeit largely only in situations of economic necessity. Shortly after the Commission was announced by the Taoiseach, Jack Lynch, a memorandum was sent to him by the Civics Institute of Ireland (CII), flagging the need for greater state funding and regulation of childcare 'to ensure high standards of responsible personnel and suitable premises'.[55] Founded in 1914 by a group interested in improving Ireland's urban areas, the CII was a voluntary organisation with the objective of publicising 'social problems and opportunities and the promotion of ideas and measures which it hopes will be taken up and developed by the special bodies which are best able to handle them'.[56] Similarly, an objective of the *ad hoc* committee of women's organisations, which lobbied from 1967 for the creation of the Commission on the Status of Women in Ireland, was the registration and inspection of nursery schools.[57]

For most of the twentieth century, state funding of childcare was almost non-existent. The CII ran two day nurseries in Dublin city centre, St Joseph's on Rutland Street, and St Brigid's on Mountjoy Square, with 'partial support' from the Dublin Health Authority.[58] Initiated in 1940 by the ladies' committee of the CII, St Brigid's nursery was intended for the pre-school children of local women who, as one fundraising notice stated, were 'obliged to work for their living ... these children would otherwise be left to look after themselves during

report on the implementation of the recommendations of the Commission on the Status of Women (Dublin, 1978), p. 49; *IPCS News*, February 1975. 52 Department of Social Welfare, *Social Welfare (Amendment) Bill 1981: Explanatory memorandum* (Dublin, 1981). 53 Department of Justice, 'Maternity Protection of Employees Act, 1981: representations', NAI, 2015/81/2. 54 Department of Health, 'Report on vital statistics 1985', https://www.cso.ie/ en/media/csoie/releasespublications/documents/ birthsdm/archivedreports/P-VS_1985.pdf, accessed 20 October 2021. This report counted the number of births, but not birth mothers. 55 The Civics Institute of Ireland, 'Memorandum on the registration of day nurseries, in connection with the proposed Commission on the Status of Women', 25 November 1969, NAI, Taoiseach papers, 96/6/184; *Irish Times*, 13 November 1969. 56 Francis Douglas, *The history of the Irish Pre School Playgroups Association, 1969–1994* (Dublin, 1994), p. 21. 57 The Civics Institute of Ireland, 'Memorandum on the registration of day nurseries'. 58 Ibid.

their mothers' working hours'.[59] In addition to fulfilling the practical need for day care, this and other childcare initiatives were founded as an educational intervention to prepare and socialise young children from disadvantaged backgrounds for primary school.[60] A teacher in Rutland Street stated in 1971 that the nursery was focused on engaging children in 'pre-number, pre-reading and pre-writing activity ... so that they won't be handicapped when the time comes to go to school'.[61]

The Rutland Street nursery was set up by the Department of Education and the CII in 1969 with financial assistance from the Bernard van Leer Foundation, catering for 180 children.[62] The concentration of these schemes, both of which were set up with assistance from independent voluntary groups, in working-class areas of inner-city Dublin again serves as an example of the then commonly held view that women could only be facilitated by the state to work outside of the home in cases of severe financial necessity. This reveals how the marriage bar had a varying impact on women according to social class. It was certainly incumbent on many married women to find work if their husband's wage could not look after the family. The male breadwinner model was primarily a social aspiration rather than a universal reality. The Commission on the Status of Women visited the Rutland Street nursery, citing it as 'an example of the type of high standard which should be aimed at in pre-school care due to its provision of meals for children, small group numbers, appropriate equipment and trained staff.'[63]

The CII was associated with a newer group, the Irish Pre-School Playgroups Association (IPPA). This association was formed after a series of talks run by the CII, as well as a residential study weekend held in association with the ICA on the subject of pre-school playgroups. The CII's secretary, Máirín Hope (an architect who designed St Brigid's Nursery on Mountjoy Square in 1940), was founding chair of the IPPA in 1969.[64] As informal playgroups and nurseries for

59 Pamphlet available at https://stbrigidsnursery.ie/wp-content/uploads/2021/03/StBridgets-oldphoto.jpg, accessed 3 September 2021. 60 Dr Barnardo's Irish Division, *Working with pre-school children: the development of community playgroups in Dublin 1 and Tallaght* (Dublin, 1985), p. 17. 61 RTÉ Archives, 'Experimental schooling in Rutland Street, 1971' https://www.rte.ie/archives/2016/0121/761828–rutland-street/, accessed 3 September 2021. 62 Ibid. The Bernard van Leer Foundation was founded in 1949, and from 1965, focused on the improvement of 'opportunities for all young children, especially the millions of young children growing up in circumstances of socio, economic and environmental disadvantage around the world', https://bernardvanleer.org/about-us/, accessed 20 September 2021. 63 Commission on the Status of Women, *Report to Minister for Finance*, p. 133. 64 The Civics Institute of Ireland, 'Memorandum on the registration of day nurseries'; Dublin City Council, 'Mountjoy Square Park: Conservation plan & historic landscape study, July 2014', http://www.dublincity.ie/sites/default/files/content/RecreationandCulture/DublinCityParks/NewsEvents/Documents/MountjoySquareConservationPlan

children in private homes were growing in popularity, members of the IPPA were concerned about adequate training, supervision, and registration. They were influenced by increasing trends in child psychology which demonstrated the benefits of group play for pre-school children, as well as various international reports, such as Tessa Blackstone's *Pre-school education in Europe* study for the Council of Europe's 'Permanent Education' project, and the Plowden report on children's education in England. Furthermore, as more mothers were staying on at work, an increasing number of families needed childcare.

The IPPA's 1972–3 report noted an increasing number of enquiries about facilities for pre-school children from community groups wishing to open nurseries. Many consultations with the IPPA took place, and visits were arranged to the CII nurseries in Dublin city centre.[65] In 1972 the IPPA furnished the Commission with information on the running costs of nurseries and the names of those using the facilities of the Institute.[66] The Commission suggested in 1972 that legislation 'requiring all existing and new playgroups to register with the local authority' was necessary. It made the case for state investment in the IPPA, an entirely voluntary organisation, recommending that a small grant be made available to them 'towards the cost of publishing annually a register of playgroups recognised as conforming to its code of standards and for which planning permission has been obtained'.[67]

While not all children of working mothers were in day care, and not all mothers of children in day care were working, the Commission focused on the sentiment that mothers should engage in paid work only out of necessity while their children were very young:

> ... we wish to stress that we are unanimous in the opinion that very young children, at least up to 3 years of age, should, if at all possible, be cared for by the mother at home and that as far as re-entry to employment is concerned, the provision of day care for such children must be viewed as a solution to the problems of the mother who has particularly strong reasons to resume employment.[68]

Immediate large-scale state investment in childcare for children under four years of age was ruled out by the Commission due to high cost. A further recommendation was made with special regard for women who were unable to remain in the home full-time for financial reasons:

HistoricLandscapeStudy.pdf, accessed 31 May 2019. 65 The Civics Institute of Ireland Limited, Mountjoy Square Park North, Dublin 1, *Annual Report 1972/3* (Dublin, 1973). 66 Ibid. 67 Commission on the Status of Women, *Report to Minister for Finance*, p. 233. 68 Ibid., p. 130.

> Where new housing schemes are being erected, provision should be made for the building of crèches or day-nurseries and the provision of facilities of this nature should be a condition for the grant of planning permission for such housing schemes where many women may have an economic necessity to take up part-time work.[69]

This was never implemented, but alongside ongoing private childcare in the home, the number of crèches funded by the health boards was growing; 31 in 1975, and 66 in 1978. The matter of regulation was examined by a task force on childcare, set up by the Minister for Health in 1974. There was no legal action in this regard until 1991, when the Child Care Act provided for the regulation of pre-school services.

CONCLUSION

Statutes can serve as an implicit endorsement of gender roles, a cue for what is and is not possible. The slow passage of legislation to regulate maternity leave and childcare, and the consequent intervention of voluntary groups into childcare, shows the deep legacy of the male breadwinner model in this state. Ireland was the last country in the EEC to make legal provision for maternity leave. The state's reluctance to intervene in this field should be viewed against the comparatively late and gradual entry of Irish women into the labour market. Worth and Paterson have established that for working mothers, 'organisational labour' has been a third responsibility in addition to both paid and domestic work, highlighting 'the interrelationship between women's caring roles and labour market participation'. They define organisational labour as part of the gendered burden on mothers; 'the means by which women managed working and mothering in the home and the workplace', such as the negotiation of part-time jobs and childcare.[70]

Inequality persisted in terms of differing perceptions of male and female careers, especially within marriage and after childbirth. Despite the Commission's insistence that women should be enabled to work for either 'economic or psychological' reasons, the argument that women should work outside the home only in cases of severe economic necessity still had a strong foothold in Irish society when its report was published. This hardly differed from the ideal enshrined in Article 41.2 of the 1937 Constitution which pledges

69 Ibid., p. 232. 70 Eve Worth and Laura Paterson, '"How is she going to manage with the children?" Organisational labour, working and mothering in Britain, *c.*1960–1990', *Past & Present*,

that the state will 'endeavour to ensure that mothers shall not be obliged by economic necessity to engage in labour to the neglect of their duties in the home'.

When the Maternity (Protection of Employees) Act was passed in 1981, the rhetoric returned to economic necessity when Eileen Lemass stated that 'for economic reasons there always has been and always will be a need for some women to go out to work'.[71] However, both Gemma Hussey and Mary Robinson emphasised how basic and essential a reform it was, agreeing that policy-makers should approach the question on the basis of *parental* leave.[72] At this time, a homogenous cultural acceptance of the increasingly dynamic role played by women outside of the domestic sphere had not fully been realised. This contextual understanding opens up the agenda for further research on the position of women in 1980s Ireland, a vista which was increasingly conservative and repressive.

246:15 (2020), p. 318. **71** 'Maternity Protection of Employees Bill 1981: second stage', *Dáil debate* 327, no. 1, 24 February 1981. **72** Ibid.

SECTION FIVE

THE SEXUAL POLITICS OF DEBATE AND ACTIVISM

CHAPTER 12

Culture wars in Ireland, 1996–2021: sex education debates

Elizabeth Kiely

The first formal programme on Relationships and Sexuality Education (RSE) was introduced into the Irish schooling system from the mid 1990s.[1] In 2018, the Minister for Education and Skills requested a programme review to be conducted by the National Council for Curriculum and Assessment (NCCA). The introduction of the RSE programme in the 1990s stimulated media coverage and an active debate in the public sphere. Its review and the consultation that stemmed from it, also prompted coverage and public debate, albeit not as intense as in the 1990s. This chapter contributes to the existing literature on 'culture wars' in diverse country contexts.[2] Both sides of the debate are utilised to explore continuities in each, but also changes in socio-cultural attitudes to the governance of child and youth sexualities over time in Ireland. The coverage of the debate suggests a higher level of support in recent years for more comprehensive sex education provision than when the RSE programme was first introduced.

The letters page in the print media was a key site, which facilitated the expression of public opinion on RSE when it was first introduced in the 1990s and again after the programme review was announced in 2018. The letters pages of two national newspapers, the *Irish Times* (1 January 1996–31 December 2002) and the *Irish Examiner* (1 July 1997–31 December 2002), provides one body of material for analysis in this chapter.[3] The second body of material is provided by letters pages of the same two newspapers (1 April 2018–31 October 2021). Initially each letter was coded in accordance with whether it expressed opposition to or support for the introduction of the programme. However,

1 Government of Ireland, *Report of the expert advisory group on relationships and sexuality education* (Dublin, 1995). 2 See, for example, Janice M. Irvine, 'Doing it with words: discourse and the sex education culture wars', *Critical Inquiry*, 27:1 (2000), pp 58–76; Judith Peppard, 'Culture wars in South Australia: the sex education debates', *The Australian Journal of Social Issues*, 43:3 (2008), pp 499–516. 3 I commenced the search from the date each online newspaper archive was launched, hence the different starting date for each newspaper search. After finding and reading a number of other letters on RSE on microfilm held in the library in University College Cork, the different starting

evident in the fusion of sexuality and schooling prompted by the introduction of RSE and its review was an opportunity for programme opponents and proponents to elaborate their own set of views and regulatory ideals as they related to children/students, key figures in the production of the nation. In articulating RSE programme opposition or support, competing discourses or understandings of four different sites (child/student, family, school and nation) were put forward. These are the four themes, that following a brief description of the Irish societal context, structure this chapter with consideration as to how the contours of the debate were similar or different in the two timeframes.

IRELAND: AN EXEMPLAR OF SOCIAL PROGRESS?

In 2013 Ireland was characterised as a country undergoing '… radical and dynamic change moving from a place of troubles and trauma to one of renovation and rebirth'.[4] Undoubtedly, some of this change had its genesis in the 1990s, when Ireland was enjoying the kind of prosperity afforded by the Celtic Tiger economy. There was the ceasefire in Northern Ireland and the signing of the Belfast/Good Friday Agreement in 1998. The first female president Mary Robinson was elected in 1990 and the second, Mary McAleese, in 1997. Female students (at 56% participation) were outnumbering males in third level education participation rates.[5]

Homosexuality was decriminalised in 1993; divorce was legalised and use of artificial contraception less taboo. Of all marriages in 1995, 6% were civil marriages[6] and births outside marriage increased from 4% in 1978 to 28% by 1998.[7] The numbers entering the clergy persistently declined and the first sex shops opened in the 1990s.[8] At the same time, numerous high profile child abuse scandals were coming to light.[9] Tribunals and inquiries to investigate child abuse and other matters of public concern occurred through the 1990s and 2000s and the ongoing Catholic Church control over education, health and women's bodies troubled notions of unidirectional progressive social change.[10]

By 2018, Irish society was emerging out of a period of austerity politics that followed the severe economic recession of 2008. Any notion that clerical sexual abuse was a problem exposed and finished with was belied by the Ryan Report

dates did not seem to raise any issues worthy of consideration. 4 C. Rees, *Changes in contemporary Ireland: texts and contexts* (Newcastle-upon-Tyne, 2013), p. 15. 5 Central Statistics Office, *That was then, this is now. Change in Ireland, 1949–1999* (Dublin, 2000). 6 Ibid., p. 53. 7 Ibid., p. 30. 8 Tom Inglis, 'Origins and legacies of Irish prudery: sexuality and social control in modern Ireland', *Éire–Ireland*, 40:2 (2005), pp 9–37. 9 Kevin Lalor, *The end of innocence: child sexual abuse in Ireland* (Cork, 2001). 10 Helen Buckley and Caroline O'Nolan, 'Recommendations from child abuse inquiries in 2009 as its recommendations relating to events in the past were considered highly relevant.[11] A Children's Referendum in 2012 built on a series of discursive, legislative and policy measures promoting children's voice, participation and rights, paving the way for a constitutional amendment setting out child-specific rights. Notions of Ireland as no longer a Catholic backwater but rather an exemplar of social progress were invoked nationally and internationally with the passing of the Marriage Equality Referendum 2015 allowing for the legalisation of same sex marriage and the passing of a referendum, in 2018, making way for legalised abortion provision.[12] Indicators were strong that the time was opportune for a progressive re-imagining of the sex education curriculum. Despite debate intensifying about Catholic domination of education provision particularly at primary level in an increasingly secular and diverse society, and a report recommending divestment of religious patronage from some Catholic schools to offer greater choice to non-Catholic families, minimal progress was made.[13] Any narrative that Irish society had freed itself of its Catholic past continued to be troubled.

After 2017, RSE was back on the political agenda in Ireland for different reasons. The Citizens' Assembly on the Eighth Amendment (the constitutional provision that gave equal right to the unborn and to the pregnant woman) report submitted to government in 2017 recommended improved sexual health education.[14] The fallout from a Belfast rape trial in 2018 generated public discourse about issues pertaining to rape and sexual consent as well as sexism and misogyny in Irish sexual culture.[15] The UN Convention on the Elimination of all Forms of Discrimination against Women (CEDAW) put a direct spotlight on the need for more comprehensive school RSE provision.[16] From 2017 onwards, sexual consent workshops and bystander interventions were being

and their impact on policy and practice' *Children's Research Digest*, 2:1 (2015), pp 5–10. **11** *The report of the commission to inquire into child abuse* (The Ryan Report), 2009. **12** Aoife Neary, 'Civil partnership and marriage: LGBT-Q political pragmatism and the normalisation imperative', *Sexualities*, 19:7 (2016), pp 757–79. **13** John Coolahan, et al., *The forum on patronage and pluralism on the primary sector: report of the forum's advisory group* (Dublin, 2012); Irish Human Rights and Equality Commission, 'Ireland needs sanctions for breaches of anti-racism commitments.' (Press Release, 2021), https://www.ihrec.ie/ireland-needs-sanctions-for-breaches-of-anti-racism-commitments/, accessed 22 February 2024. **14** The Citizens' Assembly, *The first report and recommendations of the Citizens' Assembly: the Eighth Amendment of the Constitution* (Dublin, 2017). **15** The Belfast rape trial happened in 2018. It involved a young woman, who alleged she had been raped and sexually assaulted at a party by four men, two of whom were high-profile male rugby players, who faced charges ranging from rape and sexual assault to perverting the course of justice and withholding information. The four men involved were found not guilty. See Susan McKay, 'How the "rugby rape trial" divided Ireland', *The Guardian*, 4 December 2018. **16** UN CEDAW, Concluding observations on the combined sixth and seventh periodic reports of Ireland, /C/IRL/Co/6–7, 2017, https://www.ohchr.org/en/documents/concluding-observations/cedawcirlco6–7–concluding-observations-combined-sixth-and-seventh (accessed 22 February 2024).

rolled out on Irish college campuses in response to concerns about incidences of sexual violence among students. Solidarity/People Before Profit politicians introduced the 'Provision of Objective Sex Education Bill' in 2018, seeking to prevent Catholic schools from using religious ethos as the reason for not providing a more comprehensive sex education curriculum in their schools, but it was a bill that was not signed into legislation. Students increasingly reported that while they received RSE, for the most part it was minimal or deficient; at times poorly taught and key aspects were not discussed or addressed too late to be beneficial.[17] Undoubtedly, momentum continued to build and in April 2018, it was announced that the outdated school RSE programme was to be reviewed.

THE RELATIONSHIPS AND SEXUALITY EDUCATION PROGRAMME

Prior to the introduction of RSE in the mid-1990s, no definitive action was taken by any Irish government on the issue of school-based sexuality education despite calls for such provision inside and outside government.[18] RSE aimed to help students to 'understand and develop friendships and relationships'.[19] It set out to advance their 'understanding of sexuality' and to promote 'a healthy attitude to sexuality and to relationships'. It sought to progress students' 'knowledge of and respect for reproduction' and to enable them 'to develop attitudes and values towards their sexuality in a moral, spiritual and social framework'.[20] Compulsory, in so far as it had to be included in the school timetable, schools were allowed to choose what to teach from a set of resource materials organised by student age and in accordance with each school's ethos and individual RSE policy.

Very carefully steered from the beginning by programme planners, the introduction of the programme and its implementation involved trade-offs and resource commitments to keep religious bodies and educational stakeholders on board with it. For instance, an opt out clause was afforded to parents, who did not wish their children to participate and to teachers, who conscientiously objected to teaching it.[21] An extensive and costly in-service teacher training

17 See Evelyn Ring, 'Students' experience of sex ed "Terrible"', *Irish Examiner*, 2 May 2018; Sandra Roe, *Life skills matter – not just points: a survey of implementation of Social, Personal and Health Education (SPHE) and Relationships and Sexuality Education (RSE) in second-level schools* (Dublin, 2010); Youth Work Ireland, 'Make sex education inclusive. Young people say it's time for better and inclusive sex education in Irish Schools', 2018. 18 K. Kiernan, 'School sex education in Ireland – towards a feminist perspective' (M.Phil. thesis, Trinity College Dublin, 1992); Department of Education, *Education for a changing world* (Dublin, 1992), p. 131. 19 Government of Ireland, *Report of the Expert Advisory Group*, 1995, p. 17. 20 Ibid. 21 Elizabeth Kiely, '"Sexing the curriculum":

course and a sophisticated support infrastructure aided RSE implementation.[22] As the programme was rolled out throughout the education system from the late 1990s onwards, it generated debate, much of which was played out in Irish media.

To review RSE as requested by the Minister, the NCCA embarked on a consultation process and produced its report in December 2019.[23] In January 2019, a Government Joint Committee called for major reform of RSE in its report.[24] In 2021, pre-empting NCCA progress on the production of a more secular and wide-ranging curriculum, the Irish Bishops Conference, co-operating with the Catholic Primary Schools Management Association, produced a Catholic RSE resource entitled *Flourish* for use in all classes of Catholic primary schools.[25] Controversial statements in this programme when plucked from it and publicised generated public debate on the issue of RSE teaching, particularly in Catholic-controlled schools.

DESCRIPTION OF THE LETTERS

Letters to newspaper editors when researched have been shown to provide 'ordinary' citizens, albeit more often those who are older, with higher education, income and security, with a platform to share their opinions, even if these opinions are subjected to editorial selection and editing or rejection.[26] Their use as a yardstick to assess wider public opinion is perceived limited but their longstanding role in organised campaigns or as a mode of strategic communication is recognised.[27] Of the total number of letters printed in the *Irish Examiner* on the subject of RSE (1 July 1997–31 December 2002), twenty-five were written in opposition to the programme and seven published were in support of the programme's introduction. Of those in opposition, a number were written by individuals, who acknowledged their Christian organisational

a poststructuralist interrogation of the politics of Irish sexuality education 1960–2002' (PhD, University College Cork, 2004). **22** John Walsh, *A new partnership in Irish education: from consultation to legislation in the nineties* (Dublin, 1999). **23** National Council on Curriculum and Assessment, *Report of the review on relationships and sexuality education (RSE) in primary and post-primary schools* (Dublin, 2019). **24** Houses of the Oireachtas, *Joint Committee on Education and Skills report on relationships and sexuality education*, 32/ES/20, 2019. **25** Catholic Primary Schools Management Association, *RSE primary resource–Flourish* (Maynooth, 2021). **26** Steve Pasternack, 'The open forum: a study of letters to the editor and the people who write them', paper presented at the annual meeting of the Association for Education in Journalism and Mass Communication, 2–5 July 1988, https://files.eric.ed.gov/fulltext/ED298501.pdf, accessed 22 February 2024. **27** Ibid.; Lori A. Roessner, 'The voices of public opinion: lingering structures of feeling about women's suffrage in 1917 U.S. newspaper letters to the editor', *Journalism History*, 46:2 (2020), pp 124–44; Bill Reader, 'Who's really writing those "canned" letters to the editor?', *Newspaper Research Journal*, 26:2–3 (2005), affiliation (Positive Action for Children PACh, Parents and Teachers for Real Education PATRE, the Christian Democrats, the National Parent and Teacher Alliance and the National Party). In contrast, of the supporting letters, only one was written by an individual on behalf of a Dublin-based reproductive rights group. Most of the letters were printed in the *Irish Examiner* in the latter half of 1999, which may be explained by intensifying RSE programme activity in this period.

In the *Irish Times* (1 January 1996–31 December 2002) there were nearly as many letters (16) categorised as having been written in support of the programme as in opposition to it (20), though many of the contributions challenged opinions or points made by other letter writers without directly articulating support or otherwise for the programme. This indicates the extent to which the programme served as a vehicle for competing views about Irish society past and present. There were two letters written from individuals opposed to the programme representing Christian organisations (PATRE, the Irish Family League) and one letter in support of the programme from the CEO of the Irish Family Planning Association. A number of letter writers (parents, teachers, priests, psychologists, school principals and doctors) for and against RSE cited their credentials. The majority of the contributions were made in the years 1997 and 1998, which coincided with the most concentrated attention being given by journalists writing on RSE in the *Irish Times*, an intensive programme of in-service teacher training (1996–8) and the staging of many information sessions/public meetings on RSE (1997–8).[28]

In the period extending from the announcement of the review of RSE (1 April 2018–31 October 2021), nine letters printed in the *Irish Examiner* and fourteen letters printed in the *Irish Times* on the topic of RSE were accessed. In the *Irish Examiner*, six were written in favour of comprehensive RSE, in opposition to Catholic interference or control of RSE and three of these were specifically opposing the introduction of the Catholic-inspired RSE, *Flourish*. Three letter writers supported a Catholic informed RSE or opposed the introduction of a more comprehensive RSE. In the *Irish Times*, eleven letters favoured a more expansive curriculum, or they expressed opposition to the *Flourish* initiative or Catholic control of schooling. One letter writer, opposing *Flourish*, was a member of Education Equality, an organisation which, he explained, was advocating for children's right to the same experience of school irrespective of their families' beliefs.[29] One letter writer advocated for the Catholic *Flourish* programme and one other evaded straightforward

pp 43–56. 28 See Kiely, 'Sexing the curriculum', p. 228. 29 *Irish Times*, 24 May 2021.

categorisation as pro- or anti-RSE, merely pointing out that religious ethos was only one of many contextual barriers to school RSE.[30]

COMPETING DISCOURSES ON THE CHILD/STUDENT

A key assumption in letters opposing RSE in the 1990s was that primary school students (approximately 4–12 years) were innocent and did not need sex education. RSE would, according to one letter writer, 'rob our children of their childhood' or 'rob our youth of their innocence', according to another.[31] That the 'innocence of children' would be sacrificed did not abate as it was also held by a letter writer in 2019.[32] Sex education's potential to awaken prematurely a presumed latent sexuality, which then became disordered and dangerous, was at issue. For instance, B. wrote: 'Many children have already experienced shock, embarrassment and even trauma by insensitive and ill-timed sex instruction' and N. drew attention to 'conclusive evidence worldwide, to prove that classroom sex education had horrendous effects on children particularly in the latency period between six and twelve years of age'.[33]

That sex education should not be given to innocent children is a longstanding discourse in Irish society. It was evident in public opposition to *Stay Safe*, an Irish school based child abuse prevention programme introduced in the early 1990s and in the 2000s, in popular and official discourses concerned with the 'sexualisation' of children.[34] As in other contexts, RSE opponents sought to scare parents as to what children would learn.[35] This was evident in letters published in the 1990s and again in 2019 when W.D. criticised plans to update RSE so that it would have 'explicit sexual content' such as 'the benefits and correct use of pornography'.[36]

In contrast to RSE opponents, supporters tended to construct children as sexual subjects. For instance, T.C. wrote that receiving sex education 'was merely an acknowledgment of the fact that we are all sexual beings'.[37] Some letter writers argued that childhood innocence kept children ignorant and vulnerable. Births to teenagers and HIV incidence among children in the 1990s were sufficient reasons for H. to question if it was right 'to keep young people in the dark'.[38] S. also claimed that 'modesty will not protect our children. They must

30 *Irish Times*, 24 May 2019. 31 *Irish Times*, 14 May 1997; *Irish Times*, 10 March 1999. 32 *Irish Examiner*, 19 October 2019. 33 *Irish Examiner*, 29 April 1999 and *Irish Times*, 30 March 1998. 34 See Kiely, 'Sexing the curriculum', 2004 and Elizbeth Kiely, et al., *The commercialisation and sexualisation of children: an exploratory study* (Dublin, 2015). 35 See Irvine, 'Doing it with words' and Peppard, 'Culture wars in South Australia'. 36 *Irish Examiner*, 19 October 2019. 37 *Irish Times*, 8 August 1997. 38 *Irish Examiner*, 14 March 2000.

be given the skills and the appropriate language to report immediately such instances [of sexual abuse]'.[39]

In the 1990s, RSE proponents were more likely than their counterparts to construct children as sexual citizens in their contributions, albeit only extending to them a restricted kind of sexual citizenship in the form of access to information and skills for their protection against exploitation and their responsible conduct. Calls for a more expansive, up-to-date RSE in schools more inclusive of difference were evident in a number of letters printed post-2018. For instance, SMcK claimed that students who 'do not conform to the Judeo-Christian heterosexual model of gender alignment' would be 'comprehensively rejected' in Catholic schools and he urged the government not to permit such schools to discriminate.[40] This suggests that among RSE proponents there was a stronger perception that all students should have a sex education curriculum capable of addressing their needs and interests, irrespective of their beliefs.

COMPETING DISCOURSES ON THE FAMILY

In a background paper for the *Commission on the Family Report,* Tony Fahey identified two contrasting policy paradigms, one which he called 'patriarchal familism', the dominant model up to the 1950s in Ireland. The other was 'egalitarian individualism' which, according to Fahey, emerged in the 1950s and subsequently became ascendant.[41] Patriarchal familism, as he defined it, rested on the cultural ideal of family as a solidaristic mini-community, a foundation of social order and individual welfare. Family members' roles were well defined, differentiated, complementary and hierarchically structured by gender and generation. In Fahey's analysis, public policy decisions and Catholic social and moral teaching were significant in elevating this patriarchal model of family life in twentieth-century Ireland. In contrast, with the emergence of egalitarian individualism the importance accorded to family roles was reduced and greater significance attributed to the needs, rights and obligations of individuals within families. According to Fahey, a mix of liberalism, secularism, humanism and feminism provided ideological underpinnings for this new model, as gender equality and children's rights became matters for public policy. In the 1990s egalitarian individualism gained ground in family policy in Irish society, but the patriarchal familist model retained appeal and influence.[42]

39 *Irish Examiner,* 20 October 1998. 40 *Irish Times,* 1 May 2021. 41 Tony Fahey, 'Family policy in Ireland: a strategic overview background paper for the Commission on the Family', *The Commission on the Family: final report for the Minister for Social, Community and Family Affairs, Strengthening families for life* (Dublin, 1998), pp 384–403. 42 Fahey, 'Family policy in Ireland', p. 386.

Assumptions and ideals related to the family and state–family relations underpinning patriarchal familism were propagated in anti-RSE contributions. The anti-statist dimension was evident in DD's argument that by introducing RSE, 'the state in quiet collusion with select groups and interests has taken a deal of responsibility away from parents'.[43] Ní C. claimed that the cross-curricular feature of RSE delivery undermined the parental opt out clause and essentially made 'a mockery of parents' rights'.[44] O'F's anti-RSE letter constructed children as the property of their parents when she wrote: 'Remember parents, your children are yours and yours alone. You try to give them food for their bodies, remember their minds are much more important'.[45] For W. the RSE programme signalled a move too far away from familism towards individualism as reflected in the statement 'the notion of [parental] care and protection has almost gone in favour of the fatal illusion of children's autonomy together with state protection'.[46] The patriarchal family based on marriage was idealised in contributions critical of RSE for not placing enough emphasis on marriage and for not being sufficiently condemnatory of lifestyles and practices falling outside of the patriarchal familist domain. MacK (1997) argued that the unwanted outcome of RSE would be 'mums, unmarried, loads of' and O'S urged educators to 'teach more about marriage and the full-time care babies need, not just how to get pregnant'.[47] Patriarchal familism was also invoked by contributors post-2018. In 2019 W.D. reminded parents of their right to withdraw their children from RSE classes noting that they comprised the 'majority voice' and not the organisations making submissions to the NCCA.[48] This letter writer asserted that parents should continue to be the 'main influencer' of their children on the 'sensitive area of sexuality and relationships'.[49]

Proponents of RSE in the 1990s put less faith in parents' abilities to carry out their sex education responsibilities and they were much less likely to positively romanticise Irish family life. T. rather sarcastically responded to C.'s letter, writing that she hoped 'the sun always shines for her, up in *Seventh Heaven* on *Walton's Mountain*' but that RSE was needed by families in the real world.[50] While some highlighted teenage pregnancies as evidence of parents' failings as sex educators and as justification for schools' role in RSE, others thought it important that RSE be imparted sensitively and respond to the needs of children and respect each child's family unit, regardless of its form.[51] Pro-RSE

43 *Irish Examiner*, 5 February 2000. 44 *Irish Times*, 8 May 1997. 45 *Irish Examiner*, 19 September 1999. 46 *Irish Times*, 24 October 1998. 47 *Irish Times*, 23 June 1997; *Irish Examiner*, 23 March 1999. 48 *Irish Examiner*, 19 October 2019. 49 *Irish Examiner*, 19 October 2019. 50 *Irish Examiner*, 29 April 1999; *Irish Examiner*, 6 May 1999. 51 *Irish Times*, 30 May 1997; *Irish Examiner*, 20 October 1998.

advocates, unlike RSE opponents, tended not to argue for a revitalisation of patriarchal family values, though in the 1990s they were not necessarily signalling their support for alternative family forms either. Opposition to Catholic control of schools was a stronger theme in letters post-2018. In this context, the increasing number of secular marriages was reported as evidence that the Catholic management of schools was no longer appropriate.[52]

RSE proponents in the 1990s viewed RSE as a more reliable and superior education than that provided in families. They claimed that it potentially made up for the parents failing in their duties because its delivery in schools provided a captive audience. Notwithstanding their concern about programme deficiencies and its outdated curriculum in 2018, pro-RSE letter writers did not want its removal from schools, just its improvement. For example, E.S. bemoaned the 'woefully inadequate standard of sex education'. S.N.D. deemed RSE 'not fit for purpose' while M.R. (2019) asserted students' right to an '… evidence-based relationships and sexuality education curriculum'.[53]

SCHOOL: AN APPROPRIATE SITE FOR SEX EDUCATION?

That school is an appropriate site for sex education generated contested views. Letter writers opposed to the RSE programme in the 1990s articulated their resistance to any sex education being in school. For instance, T. wrote: 'There is no right way to give explicit sex education in a classroom setting'.[54]

RSE opponents tended to valorise the common-sense knowledge of parents and their intimate relationship with their children to argue that sex education should stay within the private family domain. K. asserted that sex is not such 'a complicated matter that it takes the whole 13 years of school life to impart it', rather, she argued, it could be done expediently and practically if left to parents.[55] One contributor highlighted that teachers' expertise was in imparting discrete subject knowledge and that 'teachers just don't want to spend their time in a classroom discussing sex with children'.[56] In a 2019 letter, W.D., a former teacher, principal and parent, claimed that inviting '… unnecessary trauma, confusion or distress into our classrooms' could be avoided, if [oppositional] parents could assist in writing the RSE curriculum'.[57] This letter writer urged those who shared her concerns to use the consultation process to make their views known to the NCCA.

52 *Irish Times*, 24 June 2020. 53 *Irish Times*, 20 April 2018; *Irish Times*, 6 August 2019. 54 *Irish Times*, 20 March 1999. 55 *Irish Times*, 18 August 1997. 56 *Irish Times*, 28 August 2000. 57 *Irish Examiner*, 19 October 2019.

In the 1990s, pro-RSE contributors identified positive features of the classroom setting for sex education. For instance, T.C. argued that in contrast to the limitations of the family, 'the group setting of a school is ideal for reinforcing standards and utilising peer support'.[58] RSE proponents cast doubt on parents' abilities to consistently respond to children's sex education needs. They frequently validated teacher knowledge, professionalism and competence above that of parents, who were at times constructed as ignorant, incompetent or careless. C. asserted that 'not all children are fortunate enough to have clear-headed parents, who are completely comfortable with all aspects of sexuality'.[59]

Responding to the Catholic bishops' *Flourish* RSE resource in 2021, one letter writer opined that the Catholic Church should be building bridges with what's left of its community due to its legacy of sexual abuse, rather than intervening in the RSE curriculum.[60] Pro-RSE letter writers advocated for the RSE curriculum to be 'scientific' 'modern' 'evidence-based' 'gender-diverse' 'comprehensive', 'objective' and 'factual', the latter two terms mirroring the language adopted in the Solidarity/People Before Profit proposed sex education legislation.[61] Indeed, one RSE proponent stated that it was time to put RSE online so that the teacher could be replaced by a trusted young online celebrity figure, who, armed with up-to-date information and effective communication skills, could demystify and normalise the subject.[62] Teacher employment of defensive teaching techniques, seeking to avoid parent upset or controversy in an area like sex education, has been documented in the literature on sex education.[63] Presumably in the event that programme withdrawal, their ultimate goal, was not achieved, anti-RSE contributors in the 1990s sought to exercise some control over teachers' use of resources, their scripts and classroom interactions. Notwithstanding the many different issues impacting on RSE implementation, it is reasonable to assume that publicity garnered by the relatively small number of RSE opponents exercised at least some impact on the management and teaching of RSE in schools throughout the 2000s.

COMPETING DISCOURSES ON THE NATION

Discursive differences were evident in the letters' pages in the late 1990s and early 2000s, which related to the perceived origins of the RSE programme and the

58 *Irish Times*, 8 August 1997. 59 *Irish Times*, 30 May 1997. 60 *Irish Examiner*, 29 April 2021. 61 *Irish Times*, 28 April 2021; *Irish Times*, 6 August 2019. 62 *Irish Examiner*, 11 May 2021. 63 See, for instance, Davina Cooper, 'Governing troubles: authority, sexuality and space', *British Journal of Sociology of Education*, 18:4 (1997), pp 501–17; Bonnie Trudell, *Doing sex education: gender politics and schooling* (New York, 1993); and Louisa Allen and Moira Carmody, '"Pleasure has no passport":

success (or otherwise) of similar programmes in other jurisdictions. These generated another competing discourse about the 'imagined community' of Ireland, as articulated by pro- and anti-RSE proponents.[64] RSE opponents presented the programme as a creation of the International Planned Parenthood Federation and its affiliate, the Irish Family Planning Association. Ní C. claimed that the Minister for Education was 'helping to further the agenda of International Planned Parenthood', an organisation which 'supported abortion, contraception, sterilisation and perverted sexual practices'.[65]

Proponents of RSE contested the notion propagated by opponents in the 1990s that RSE was not an organically Irish programme. For instance, F. welcomed the programme, viewing it as the co-creation of different representative bodies in Irish education.[66] Anti-RSE contributors presented themselves as protectors of an Irish way of life, which they perceived to be threatened by the introduction of 'foreign' secularist programmes like RSE. Ní C. posed the question in her letter on RSE: 'Now that we have entered the post-Christian era in Ireland, must we be apologetic for being grateful and proud of our Irish Christian heritage?'[67] O'M. railed against the convergence of culture and lifestyle characteristic of a more globalised world, of which RSE was yet another marker: 'It seems that Americanism has completely swamped our people so that all we do, say and think in the big cities and towns is under American influence'.[68] Anti-RSE proponents identified countries with longstanding sex education programmes such as the US and Britain as having active, excessive, promiscuous and dangerous sexualities, issuing apocalyptic warnings as to what would happen in Ireland. O'F pleaded with parents in Ireland to familiarise themselves with RSE because 'so many other countries where this type of programme has been introduced have found themselves with an increase in crime, violence, promiscuity, teenage pregnancies, venereal diseases etc.'.[69] By equating the 'outside' with the proliferation of social problems, the 'inside' or the familial nation of Ireland was constructed as the space of heterosexual normalcy needing protection. This was not a feature of the letters post-2018. Indeed, W.D. opposed widening the RSE curriculum, urging Irish parents to follow the example of English parents, who when 'outraged' by school sex education 'took to the streets in protest' and chose 'to home school' their children.[70]

Letter writers supporting RSE in the late 1990s countered arguments that school-based sex education produced disastrous results in other countries. T.C., a

re-visiting the potential of pleasure in sexuality education', *Sex Education*, 12:4 (2012), pp 455–68. 64 Benedict Anderson, *Imagined communities: reflections on the origins and spread of nationalism* (London, 1983). 65 *Irish Times*, 8 May 1997. 66 *Irish Times*, 3 May 1997. 67 *Irish Times*, 8 May 1997. 68 *Irish Times*, 5 June 1997. 69 *Irish Examiner*, 10 April 2000. 70 *Irish Examiner*, 19 October 2019.

dual American and Irish citizen, advocated for the programme on the basis of the perceived benefits of American school sex education: 'In the US … the schools near us do an admirable job of giving students the understanding needed to make them morally responsible teenagers'.[71] The 'imagined community' of Ireland constructed in anti-RSE contributions at that time was challenged. The social problems projected on to other countries were not particular to them according to P., who cited Irish statistics in evidence: 'With 60 teenagers under 16 giving birth and 26 cases of HIV in children under 12, we simply cannot afford not to give our youngsters sex education'.[72] References to clerical abuse and sexual abuse within families in pro-RSE contributions exposed Irish society's underbelly, countering assumptions that Irish society was morally superior any time in its history. Binary oppositions in anti-RSE letters of insider/outsider, safety/dangerousness, health/disease, sexual normalcy/sexual abnormality were challenged and disrupted by pro-RSE letter writers in the 1990s.

RSE opposition arguments had shifted in letters post-2018. Instead, there were invocations for majority rule in a democratic society. Advocating for a Catholic approach to the teaching of RSE in 2021, one letter writer queried how it could be 'fair' in a democracy for the majority 'to be forced to abandon their preferred ethos, on account of the presence of a few children from some other backgrounds'.[73] N.F. challenged 'RSE lobbyists' in 2021, who they perceived as seeking to impose their 'ideology' on students in a country 'with some element of democratic process'.[74] Indeed, the Catholic approach to life was propagated by these letter writers as offering a much better alternative to the 'ideology' they perceived to be pervasive in the contemporary world and which 'casualises sex, relationships and even life itself'.[75] Those writing letters expressing their opposition to *Flourish* did so on the basis that they perceived it to be a Catholic RSE framework, running contrary to a modern and 'inclusive Ireland'.[76]

CONCLUSION

As shown in this chapter, RSE in Ireland generates surges in public debate. The letters pages of newspapers provided in the late 1990s an obvious target for anti-RSE proponents to garner public attention and to galvanise any opposition to the programme that could be present in the wider society. Opposition never

71 *Irish Times*, 28 May 1996. 72 *Irish Examiner*, 16 December 1999. 73 *Irish Times*, 7 June 2021. 74 *Irish Examiner*, 16 December 2019. 75 *Irish Times*, 7 June 2021. 76 *Irish Times*, 1 May 2021; *Irish Times*, 28 April 2021.

succeeded in forcing programme withdrawal. Anti-RSE contributions prompted reaction from those who took issue with arguments made and who succeeded in ensuring that pro-RSE arguments also found their way into the public repertoire to exert influence.

As reflected in political culture and in the media, the problematisation of children and young people's sexualities shifted from unplanned teenage pregnancies and sexually transmitted infections in the 1990s, to the sexualisation and pornification of youth culture via the internet and social media networking and to youth perpetrated sexual violence in 2018.[77] However, also evident was a shift in adult/parent support for RSE over time from that which saw students and their sexualities solely as problems (of unwanted pregnancy, abortion, sexually transmitted infection) to one which saw students as a diverse constituency with rights and needs to be recognised in the teaching of RSE. Children and young people have been increasingly viewed and treated as rights holders, even if the re-imagining and realising of what this means in both relational and concrete terms still falls short.[78] While students' voices and advocacy on their own behalf, assisted through organisations and research findings, were not so evident in the media coverage and public debate in the 1990s, this had significantly changed pre- and post-RSE review as many students took opportunities to articulate what they wanted and needed from RSE.

No letter in the first corpus analysed (late 1990s/early 2000s) showed signs of the emergence of a radical counter-discourse, capable of dramatically transcending limits set by either anti-RSE or pro-RSE contributions. For example, there was nothing favourable to the programme's introduction to suggest that anything other than nominal regulatory improvements were envisaged due to programme participation. In letters advocating for RSE in the late 1990s and early 2000s, increased sexual knowledge was considered important to reduce sexually transmitted infections and unintended pregnancies among young people. Dominant constructions of sexuality for the most part remained uncontested and there was no indication that the programme's value was perceived in its potential to open spaces for students to explore limited sexual subjectivities and their associated practices. The consistent message from both sides of the RSE debate was that sexually responsible, heterosexual citizens had to be produced, even if perspectives on their production varied. Certainly by 2018, calls in letters for RSE to be more comprehensive and inclusive of difference reflected the impact of social movements, changing gender roles and

77 See Kiely, et. al., *The commercialisation and sexualisation of children.* 78 Aoife Daly and Catherine O'Sullivan, 'Sexuality education and international standards: insisting upon children's rights', *Human Rights Quarterly*, 42:4 (2020), pp 835–58.

extended sexual citizenship for minorities. The way was being paved for the programme to embrace a broader conception of students' sexual citizenship, but without a licence to adopt critical approaches to norms and constructions of normality, characteristic of inclusive, anti-discriminatory sex education in some contexts.[79]

Peter Taubman argued that in countering the moralistic and religious investments of conservative critics of sex education, 'progressives' in a neoliberal climate resort to science, evidence and standardisation of the sex education curriculum.[80] This is also evident in the Irish public's 'progressive' contributions calling for an evidence based, objective, science-based curriculum on sex education, from 2018. The implications of this are such that the RSE curriculum will possibly continue to rely on an inventory of lessons and topics, which adults/parents perceive children should learn and from teachers, in a relatively cautious and sanitised way in the classroom. It possibly means that spaces where teachers move out of their comfort zones and facilitate messy, complicated and shared learnings about sexualities, are still avoided. It is not yet evident if there is sufficient momentum to shift school sex education from being overwhelmingly health focused and concerned with problem prevention to being more sex positive in its orientation and responsive to student-articulated relational needs.

The letters reviewed in the post-2018 period show a similar gulf as evident in the 1990s between on the one side, a constituency seeking a more scientifically informed, secular, and comprehensive sex education programme (in a predominantly publicly funded but Catholic controlled Irish school system) and on the other, a small Catholic constituency, seeking to do all it can to ensure a restrictive, catechetically framed and informed RSE programme endures. Irish sex education is likely to remain a contested terrain for some time to come.

79 Jenny Bengtsson and Eva Bolander, 'Strategies for inclusion and equality – "norm-critical" sex education in Sweden', *Sex Education*, 20:2 (2020), pp 154–69. 80 Peter M. Taubman, *Teaching by numbers: deconstructing the discourse of standards and accountability in education* (New York, 2009).

CHAPTER 13

The struggle for abortion rights in the Republic of Ireland

Mary Muldowney

Research into pro-choice activism in Ireland between 1983 and 2018 suggested that the changes in Irish attitudes to abortion during those years were significant and the approach to abortion access was of a very different nature in 2018 than it had been in 1983. An earlier version of this chapter, published in 2015,[1] presented extracts from oral history interviews with people who participated in the Anti-Amendment Campaign in 1983, the widespread protests about the X case in 1992 and the campaigns associated with the 1992 and 2002 Referenda, as well as campaigns on other 'hard cases' and various initiatives to promote the inclusion of abortion in reproductive health services in Ireland. Those interview extracts are not included in this chapter, which will be based on documentary sources, considering why those attitudinal changes took place, and how they led to repeal of the Eighth Amendment to the Constitution (Bunreacht na hÉireann) in September 2018. This was after a referendum was held in May 2018 that resulted in a landslide vote in favour of repeal, which would allow the Oireachtas to legislate for abortion.[2] It is widely acknowledged that breaking the silence around abortion was one of the most influential elements of the 2018 campaign in securing a 'Yes' vote for repeal of the Eighth.

THE EIGHTH AMENDMENT TO THE CONSTITUTION (ARTICLE 40.3.3)

The 1983 Referendum on abortion followed nearly a quarter century of unprecedented economic, political and social change in Ireland although it was not until the 1970s that Ireland began to see the pace of social change really start to speed up. Women's reproductive rights, however, were not high on many agendas.

1 Mary Muldowney, 'Breaking the silence: pro-choice activism in Ireland since 1983' in Jennifer Redmond, Sonja Tiernan, Sandra McAvoy, Mary McAuliffe (eds), *Sexual politics in modern Ireland* (Dublin, 2015), pp 127–48. 2 Turnout for the vote on 25 May 2018 was 64.1%; the total valid poll was 2,153,613 (64.1% of the electorate) with 1,429,981 (66.4%) voting Yes to repeal the Eighth

Many anti-Amendment activists had previously been involved in campaigns for the legalisation of contraception, among other social justice issues. The legal situation forced the adoption of a range of imaginative measures to get around the law. In 1971, members of the Irish Women's Liberation Movement (IWLM) travelled by train from Belfast to Dublin in the so-called 'Contraceptive Train' initiative so that they could consciously break the law and draw attention to the issue. Contraceptives that were illegal in the Republic of Ireland could be legally purchased across the border in Northern Ireland. In 1979, Charles Haughey was Minister for Health when he introduced the Health (Family Planning) Act 1979 that made contraceptives available (by medical prescription only) 'for the purpose, bona fide, of family planning or for adequate medical reasons'.[3] It gave physicians and pharmacists who had moral objections to contraception the right to refuse to write prescriptions or to fill them.

The process of industrialisation in Ireland in the second half of the twentieth century was accompanied by increasing urbanisation and demographic change. The growth of modern media (particularly television) improved communications, increased foreign travel, greater employment opportunities for women and expanded education all contributed to major cultural change.[4] The forces that influenced the holding of the 1983 Referendum and the embedding of the anti-abortion position in the Constitution have often been portrayed as the assertion of traditional values in the defence of Irish culture. The role played by the Catholic Church and its devotees was an intrinsic element of that defence.

The background to the Referendum owed much more to the politics of government than to any groundswell of opinion in favour of a constitutional change. The early 1980s were years of political upheaval, with mounting national debt, massive emigration, a housing crisis, unemployment, and the volatile situation in Northern Ireland all preoccupying the parties. There were three general elections between June 1981 and November 1982, in which Fianna Fáil under Charles Haughey was locked in battle with Garret FitzGerald's Fine Gael on several fronts, not including women's rights. Labour, under Frank Cluskey, was ready to support Fine Gael, and Tomás MacGiolla and the Workers Party, as the next biggest grouping, was rooted in opposition.

Abortion was already illegal under the terms of the 1861 Offences Against the Person Act. However, in 1981 the Pro-Life Amendment Campaign (PLAC) secured pre-election promises from Ireland's biggest political parties, Fianna Fáil

Amendment and 723,632 (33.6%) voting against. 3 This is a quotation from the long title of the Health (Family Planning) Act, 1979 – Number 20 of 1979. 4 J.P. O'Carroll, 'Bishops, knights – and pawns? Traditional thought and the Irish abortion referendum debate of 1983', *Irish Political Studies*, 6 (1991), pp 53–71.

and Fine Gael, to amend the Constitution to ensure that abortion could not be introduced either by legislation or by the courts. In the November 1982 election, a Fine Gael and Labour coalition was successful and in March 1983 they announced that a referendum would be held later that year, in fulfilment of their pre-election promise. Despite those promises, abortion does not seem to have been an issue in any of the three elections.[5] The 1983 pro-amendment campaign was conducted on emotive lines that played effectively to an electorate that was still operating within a framework shaped by the Catholic Church's influence on the legislature. The anti-Amendment campaigners were portrayed and for the most part saw themselves as the harbingers of a more open, liberal society in which traditional authority figures would be replaced by political representatives who thought outside the old certainties of nationality and religion. The text of the proposal is indicative of the status of women in Ireland in the 1980s, when pregnant women would have no more than an equal right to life with the fertilised egg, embryo or foetus that they were carrying:

> The state acknowledges the right to life of the unborn and, with due regard to the equal right to life of the mother, guarantees in its laws to respect, and as far as practicable, by its laws to defend and vindicate that right.[6]

The Anti-Amendment Campaign (AAC) was a broad-based campaign, made up of groups, organisations and individuals of widely differing, social, religious and political beliefs who were united in their opposition to the proposed amendment. It was founded in 1982 after Charles Haughey's announcement of his intention to hold a referendum. Their founding statement said that the proposed amendment to the Constitution would do nothing to solve the problem of unwanted pregnancies in Ireland. The amendment would allow for no exceptions, even in cases where pregnancy severely threatened a woman's health or where pregnancy resulted from rape or incest. The amendment sought to enshrine in the Constitution the teaching of one religious denomination. Leaders of Protestant churches and the Jewish Community expressed grave reservations about the matter. The statement also noted that at a time of severe unemployment, when one-third of the population was living on or below the poverty line, the proposed amendment was an irresponsible waste of public funds.

5 Brian Girvin, 'Social change and moral politics: the Irish constitutional referendum 1983', *Political Studies*, 34 (1986), pp 61–81. 6 Text of the Eighth Amendment to Bunreacht na hÉireann, the Constitution of Ireland.

The AAC was not united on the substantive issue and there was reluctance among some members to discuss abortion openly. Open Door Counselling had been offering advice and referrals to abortion clinics in England since 1980[7] but there was no clear demand for abortion rights and the focus of the AAC was simply on securing a rejection of the Eighth Amendment, in which it was notably unsuccessful.[8] However, they were sadly prescient in their predictions for the outcome of inserting such a dangerous amendment in the Constitution. In a document entitled *This Amendment could kill women*, their warnings about what it could mean for pregnant women were vindicated by later events:

> It could be disastrous. Doctors who now treat a woman suffering from high blood pressure, severe kidney disease or toxaemia by terminating the pregnancy may now be prevented from acting to save her life ... If she has cancer, like cancer of the breast or leukaemia, and is being treated with cell-destroying drugs or radiation she will not be treated while she is pregnant. This is because such treatment will seriously damage or kill the foetus.[9]

The referendum result in 1983 suggested that an overwhelming majority of those who voted rejected abortion, which had been presented to them as inherently evil, anti-Catholic and there were even suggestions that it was anti-Irish. A 1981 banner featured the slogan 'the abortion mills of England grind Irish babies for blood that cries to the Heavens for vengeance', reinforcing the impression of Irishness as encompassing moral rectitude, from which women were tempted to stray by alien forces.

The turnout for the September 1983 Referendum on the Eighth Amendment (The Right to Life of the Unborn) was 53.7% of the electorate, of whom 66% were in favour of the proposal, almost identical to the percentage of the valid poll 35 years later that voted to repeal it. Nevertheless, given the deference to the Catholic Church that was still a feature of Irish society at the time, that means there was a very significant minority who chose to defy the Catholic bishops' instructions to vote for the Amendment. Table 13.1 shows the final results.

7 In the early 1980s Open Door Counselling took over the operation of the Irish Pregnancy Counselling Centre (IPCC) which had been set up in 1979 to offer non-directive pregnancy counselling and referral to Britain for legal abortions there. In 1980 the Director of Public Prosecutions confirmed that this was legal under the criminal law. The IPCC had financial difficulties and Open Door was set up in 1983. 8 Nearly 67% of the valid poll (53.67% of the electorate) voted for the Eighth Amendment. 9 Extract from *This Amendment could kill women*, published in 1983 by the AAC.

Table 13.1. 1983 Referendum Results, 7 September 1983

Total electorate	Total poll	Percentage poll	For the proposal	Against the proposal	Spoiled votes
2,358,651	1,265,994	53.7	841,233	416,136	8,625

It is clear from research subsequent to the 1983 Referendum that at that time Irish women had been travelling to England in significant numbers to access the abortion services made available by the passing of the 1967 Abortion Act.[10] Nevertheless, discussion of the issue was not encouraged and when it did occur, it was often in an atmosphere that was not conducive to open debate. The Workers Party produced a leaflet in 1983 advocating a 'No' vote in which abortion was not mentioned once. Even more significantly, neither were women mentioned.

Some individuals and groups tried to raise public consciousness about abortion in the context of women's rights. They believed that the 1983 Referendum offered the opportunity to make arguments that might not otherwise be possible. A pamphlet entitled *No more chains: why you should oppose the constitutional ban on abortion* was published in 1983, despite its authors knowing that such a document was in contravention of the law, specifically the laws on censorship, which prohibited discussion of the issue.[11] The authors believed that they were going to lose the referendum but they should use the opportunity to get accurate information about abortion into the public domain.

After the passing of the Eighth Amendment, pro-choice groups continued to use the tactic of provocation. This was done to help women with crisis pregnancies as much as it was to challenge the law. Activists in Cork also believed it was important to publicise information about abortion clinics and how to access them. The information was incorporated into *Censored: Ireland's abortion reality – including a guide to services for Irish women.* Various initiatives were undertaken in the years between 1983 and 1992 to get information out to women who needed it, most publicly by handing out leaflets in Dublin city centre, weekly for several years, containing information with the telephone number for the Women's Information Network where anybody could phone up and could

10 The United Kingdom Department of Health releases statistics each year on the number of women and girls who gave Republic of Ireland addresses at abortion clinics in England and Wales. 11 *No more chains: why you should oppose the constitutional ban on abortion* (Belfast and Dublin: A People's Democracy Pamphlet, 1983).

arrange to meet someone, to get non-judgemental, hard information on all the options available to them.

THE X CASE AND THE 1992 REFERENDUM

In 1992 a 14-year-old girl was the victim of rape by a neighbour and became pregnant. Her parents arranged to bring her to England for an abortion because she was suicidal at the prospect of going through with the pregnancy. They asked the Garda Síochána (the police) if the DNA from the foetus could be used in evidence against the rapist. The Gardaí asked Attorney General Harry Whelehan for advice and he secured a High Court injunction against her leaving the country, on the grounds that it would be in breach of Article 40.3.3 of the Constitution. This judgment was appealed to the Supreme Court who ruled that the injunction was a breach of the girl's right to life if she were to kill herself. The Supreme Court judges ruled four to one that the girl should be permitted to travel for an abortion in England. She miscarried before the procedure could be carried out.

The response to the X case in 1992 illustrated perhaps the most dramatic change in public perception of abortion in the extent to which ordinary people took to the streets to register their support for the young girl at the centre of the case. The activists who were involved in organising the big demonstration in Dublin in February 1992 were taken by surprise by the numbers of people who appeared on the streets and the number of protest marches that took place in Ireland and around the world demanding compassion for the young girl at the centre of the X Case. The appeal to traditional values that was so successful in 1983 was now tempered by the consciousness that the issue was not as clear cut as had been claimed. The fact that a 14-year-old was at the centre of the controversy was hugely significant because the amendment had been sold on the basis of protecting children and here was a child who was suffering because of that amendment and the state's insistence on upholding it.

After the Supreme Court delivered its judgment on X and the young girl at the centre of the case was given permission to travel to England for an abortion, the government was under pressure to make constitutional change in recognition of the complex situation that now existed because of the X Judgement.[12] Another outcome of the X case was its impact on the determination of some activists to start openly demanding the right to abortion and be absolutely clear about their message.

12 After 1992, successive governments failed to legislate on foot of the X case because the Supreme Court judges argued that it was a specific case and could not be the basis for permitting

The 1992 Referendum campaign was dogged by confusion, not least because there were three propositions (the Twelfth, Thirteenth and Fourteenth Amendments) and the campaign also coincided with a general election. The first proposal (Twelfth) was intended to reverse the X Judgement while the second (Thirteenth) and third (Fourteenth) referred to the right to travel from Ireland, including to have an abortion abroad, and the right to secure information and counselling about abortion in Ireland, respectively. By 1992 the PLAC had evolved into the Pro-Life Campaign (PLC) and continued to work against any possibility of relaxing the ban on abortion. They found themselves arguing for a rejection of the Twelfth Amendment but on diametrically opposed grounds to those put forward by the pro-choice advocates. They rejected the government's wording because they said it would leave the assessment of risk to the life of the mother to doctors and they believed that some doctors might give in to the temptation to carry out abortions.

Youth Defence emerged after a split in the anti-choice movement. They were mainly young people who believed that the PLC was not militant enough in its approach to campaigning. They launched themselves publicly on the radio show presented by a Roman Catholic priest, Father Michael Cleary, who used it as a platform to oppose the liberalisation of Irish society.[13] Youth Defence consistently adopted confrontational and provocative approaches to campaigning, resulting in increasing distance being placed between it and other anti-choice groups. They used extreme forms of rhetoric in well-funded advertisements and were involved in referendum and election campaigns under the banner of related organisations such as Cóir and the Mother and Child Campaign. In 1992 Youth Defence mobilised their first 'Rally for Life' which brought 10,000 people on to the streets of Dublin, most of them from areas outside the city.

In the event the Referendum result was a victory for the pro-choice side in that the attempt to overturn the Supreme Court ruling on X was voted down and the rights to travel and obtain information were accepted and later enshrined in the Thirteenth and Fourteenth Amendments to the Constitution. Table 2 sets out the results of the 1992 Referendum. The turnout was much higher than it had been for the 1983 Referendum, suggesting that the nature of the X case had undermined the certainties postulated in the earlier campaign

abortions to be carried out. 13 Michael Cleary was a Catholic priest who had a very high national profile in the 1970s and 1980s, partly on account of his development work in Dublin's inner-city communities, where he raised the issue of poverty but also because of his frequent appearances on radio and television. After his death it was revealed that he had fathered two children with his housekeeper who had been seventeen when their relationship commenced. The first child was adopted, and the second one was raised by the couple without Cleary and many voters had been shaken by the effect that the Eighth Amendment could have in practice.

Table 13.2 1992 Referendum results, 25 November 1992

Twelfth Amendment of the Constitution Bill (Referendum on Right to Life) 1992

Total Electorate	Total poll	Percentage poll	For the proposal	Against the proposal	Spoiled votes
2,542,841	1,7333,309	68.2	572,177	1,079,297	81,835

Thirteenth Amendment of the Constitution Bill (Right to Travel) 1992

Total Electorate	Total poll	Percentage poll	For the proposal	Against the proposal	Spoiled votes
2,542,841	1,733,821	68.2	1,035,308	624,059	74,454

Fourteenth Amendment of the Constitution Bill (Right to Information) 1992

Total Electorate	Total poll	Percentage poll	For the proposal	Against the proposal	Spoiled votes
2,542,841	1,733,433	68.1	992,833	665,106	74,494

HARD CASES AND DESPERATE STRAITS

There was a relatively muted public response to the C and D Cases in 1997 and 2007 respectively when again two young women were faced with the might of the state refusing them the right to travel abroad for an abortion. The C case involved a 13-year-old girl who was raped. She was placed in the care of the Local Authority and a successful court case was taken on her behalf to seek permission for her to travel to Britain for an abortion, on the grounds of her suicidal state. The D case also involved a young girl (aged seventeen) who became pregnant while in the care of the Local Authority. Her foetus was diagnosed as anencephalitic with no chance of surviving outside the womb and again the court ruled that she should be permitted to travel to Britain for an abortion because she was suicidal.[14]

The apparent lack of concern seems to have been due to the belief that the courts would 'do the right thing' and permit the young women to leave the country, which, of course, was what happened. This confidence in the safety

acknowledging him as his son. 14 Anencephaly is a serious birth defect in which a baby is born without parts of the brain and skull. There is no known cure or standard treatment for valve offered by abortion services in other countries was also evident in the response to the Women on Waves initiative mounted by a coalition of pro-choice activists in 2001.[15] Despite the media frenzy when it was announced that a Dutch ship would be bringing a portable surgery to Ireland in which abortions could be carried out in international waters, the event had very little impact on national sensibilities. Given that more than 300 women called the helplines organised by the Irish activists requesting termination of crisis pregnancies and that those women were clearly prepared to go on board a ship to be taken to international waters for that procedure, the level of desperation evident in those calls was strangely unacknowledged.

THE 2002 REFERENDUM

The role of the Catholic Church has come under particular scrutiny in recent years in the aftermath of the paedophile scandals and the reaction of the Irish episcopate to revelations of their role in covering up abuse of children. The influential role it played in 1983 was impossible to repeat in 2002 when the Fianna Fáil/Progressive Democrat coalition tried to overturn the X judgment. The evolution of the anti-choice position in line with developments in public sympathy manifested quite dramatically during the 2002 Referendum campaign, when the PLC's support for the government's proposition required them to concede that abortion might actually be necessary in some cases. The pro-choice side was represented by the Alliance for a No Vote, who argued against the proposal because it would remove even the limited protection offered by the X Judgement for suicidal pregnant women.

Table 13.3 25th Amendment (Protection of Human Life in Pregnancy Bill) 2001, 6 March 2002

Total Electorate	Total poll	Percentage poll	For the proposal	Against the proposal	Spoiled votes
2,923,918	1,254,175	42.9	618,485	629,041	6,649

anencephaly. Almost all babies born with anencephaly die shortly after birth. 15 Women on Waves was set up in 1999 in The Netherlands by Dr Rebecca Gomperts with the aim of preventing unsafe abortions and unwanted pregnancies by providing sexual health services including early medical abortions with pills, on board a Dutch ship outside the territorial waters of countries where abortion is illegal. They were invited to Ireland and came in June 2001, but the Dutch government said that the ship would not be licensed as a medical facility and any medical procedures that took place on board would not be covered by Women on Waves' insurance.

The voter turnout was roughly 50% in the 1983 Referendum, in the high 60s in 1992 and much lower in 2002, varying between 48% in Dublin and as low as 37 and 38% in Connacht and Ulster. The CEO of one of Ireland's largest family planning clinics, who was involved in policy development around reproductive health, was convinced that the Irish government's inconclusive interventions in the European Court A, B, and C cases and in submissions to the United Nations Convention on the Elimination of Discrimination against Women were evidence of their ambivalence and the intention to allow abortion by default, rather than initiating legislation.

In 2005 three women, known as A, B and C, challenged Ireland's restrictive abortion laws at the European Court of Human Rights. All three women had been forced to travel abroad for abortions. In December 2010 the court unanimously found that Ireland's failure to provide life-saving abortion services was a breach of Ms C's human rights. She had found she was pregnant while she was receiving treatment for cancer. The court ruled that all three women had experienced stigma and isolation, and that the necessity to travel to the UK for abortions caused them significant psychological, financial and physical hardship. The court also found that there had been an interference with the rights of Ms A and Ms B under the European Convention on Human Rights.

The government responded to the European Court's ruling by appointing an Expert Group to study the options[16] but the outraged national and international response to the tragic death of Savita Halappanavar on 28 October 2012 forced the issue.[17] The Irish abortion ban and the failure of successive governments to legislate for abortion as required by the X Judgement left doctors with no legislative framework for dealing with complications in a pregnancy that threatened the life of the mother.

In 2013, twenty years after the Supreme Court delivered the X Judgement, the Fine Gael/Labour government delivered the Protection of Human Life in Pregnancy Act 2012, as their solution to the legislative lacuna that had led to the death of Savita Halappanavar. In contrast to the changed attitude to

16 The Expert Group was tasked with resolving three central issues: 1) to examine the A, B and C v Ireland judgment of the European Court of Human Rights; 2) to elucidate its implications for the provision of healthcare services to pregnant women in Ireland; and 3) to recommend a series of options on how to implement the judgment, taking into account the constitutional, legal, medical and ethical considerations involved in the formulation of public policy in this area and the overriding need for speedy action.

17 Savita Halappanavar was a young Indian woman living in Galway with her husband when she became pregnant. When she developed sepsis the medical staff at Galway University Hospital would not terminate the pregnancy as requested by the couple because a foetal heartbeat could still be heard. Savita died shortly afterwards. When the story broke in the national and international media, it was followed by mass protests in Ireland and other countries, including India.

abortion among the general public, evidenced by successive opinion polls, some of the arguments posed by opponents of the 2013 Act had not changed since the early 1980s. They did not reflect at all the much more nuanced approach adopted by so-called 'ordinary people' concerning the role of abortion in women's reproductive health choices in Ireland. Many of the people involved in the PLC were later active in opposing divorce, the legalisation of homosexuality and marriage equality among other issues. Table 13.4 outlines the ballot results from the four Referenda related to abortion that were held in Ireland between 1983 and 2018.

Table 13.4. Comparison of voting patterns in abortion referenda, 1983–2018

Year	Referendum title	Turnout in numbers and as percentage of electorate	Percentage in favour of the proposal	Percentage against the proposal
1983	The right to life of the unborn	1,265,594 (53.7)	66.4	32.9
1992				
(i)	Right to Life	1,733,309 (68.2)	33.0	62.3
(ii)	Right to Travel	1,733,821 (68.2)	57.7	35.9
(iii)	Right to Information	1,732,433 (68.1)	57.3	38.4
2002	Protection of Human Life in Pregnancy	1,254,175 (42.9)	49.3	50.2
2018	Health (Regulation of Termination of Pregnancy) Act 2018	2,153,613 (64.1)	1,429,981 (66.4)	723,632 (33.6)

Following the signing into law of the Protection of Life During Pregnancy Act in 2013, there were a number of abortions carried out in Irish hospitals. The criminalisation of abortion was maintained, except on the narrow grounds of the X Judgement when there was a risk to the life of the pregnant woman. There was particular concern about the adequacy of the law when a young immigrant woman, pregnant as a result of rape, in 2014 was refused permission for an abortion on the grounds of being suicidal and had her baby delivered by caesarean section. Ireland's abortion law was criticised by the United Nations Human Rights Commission and the UN Committee on Economic, Social and Cultural Rights.[18] A number of Private Members' Bills legislating for abortion were put before the Dáil but were overwhelmingly defeated on each occasion.

18 Joan McCarthy, Katherine O'Donnell and Louise Campbell et al., 'Ethical arguments for access to abortion services in the Republic of Ireland: recent developments in the public

In July 2016, the Irish government established a Citizens' Assembly with a remit to deliberate on the Eighth Amendment to the Constitution, prior to further consideration of potential legislative change. In April 2017, the Citizens' Assembly recommended by an overwhelming majority (87%) that Article 40.3.3 (the Eighth Amendment) of the Irish Constitution should not be retained in full. Fifty-six per cent of Assembly members voted that Article 40.3.3 should be replaced or amended, and 57% voted for a replacement of Article 40.3.3 with a constitutional provision authorising the Oireachtas to legislate. Sixty-four per cent of Assembly members voted in favour of access to abortion with no restriction as to reason. In addition, a majority recommended twelve situations in which abortion should be lawful. These included risk to the life of the woman; risk to the health of the woman; pregnancy that results from rape; foetal abnormality (including non-fatal); socio-economic reasons.[19]

In August 2017, the United Nations Committee against Torture accused the Irish government of causing 'severe physical and mental anguish and distress' to women and girls as a result of the State's policies on abortion. The Joint Committee on the Eighth Amendment of the Constitution was appointed by the government to consider the recommendations of the Citizens' Assembly with regard to abortion and the repeal of the Amendment. The Joint Committee met regularly between June and December 2017, considering evidence presented by national and international experts on abortion care, reproductive health and human rights. Their report was published on 20 December, recommending that abortion should be lawful in Ireland where the life or the physical or mental health of the woman is at risk, or in cases of fatal (as distinct from non-fatal) foetal anomaly and on a woman's own indication of up to 12 weeks pregnancy, provided that the termination is carried out in a clinical setting.

Following debate in the Dáil between 17 and 25 January 2018, during which 80 speakers contributed in 17 hours of statements about the Joint Committee's recommendations, Minister of State David Stanton summarised their position:

> The main conclusion of the committee is that change is needed to extend the grounds for lawful termination of pregnancy in the State. In order to effect that change, the committee recommended that Article 40.3.3 should be removed from the Constitution. The committee then went on to make recommendations on the grounds on which the termination of pregnancy should be permitted in Ireland if Article 40.3.3 was repealed. It

discourse', *Journal of Medical Ethics* 44 (2018), pp 513–17. 19 *First report and recommendations of the Citizens' Assembly. The Eighth Amendment of the Constitution.* Downloaded from 2016–2018. citizens assembly.ie, on 16 December 2021.

> recommended extending the law on abortion to cover cases where the health of a woman was concerned, cases of fatal foetal abnormalities and a broader legal regime that allows abortions where a woman seeks it from her medical practitioner for pregnancies of under 12 weeks' gestation.[20]

It had taken thirty-five years and unimaginable distress and hardship for tens of thousands of Irish women for politicians to finally stop avoiding the issue of abortion and a woman's right to bodily autonomy. Agreeing to call a Referendum was not the end of the battle, as the proposal to Repeal the Eighth Amendment was only the first step in securing a full reproductive health service, assuming that the electorate supported it in the first place. This could certainly not be taken for granted, as the anti-choice forces were very well resourced. As in previous Referendum campaigns on abortion, both sides formed umbrella organisations to carry out the task of persuading the electorate to their point of view. 'Together for Yes' spearheaded the campaign for a 'Yes' vote and it was noticeable from an early stage in the movement that there was a significant difference in how the issue was posed to voters. In the aftermath of Savita Halappanavar's death, many of the groups that formed to demand the right to choose abortion in their own country were not disguising their anger at the way women had been treated. Many women were prepared to tell their stories publicly, breaking the silence and stigma that had shadowed the issue of crisis pregnancies for so long. This was to be a critical tool in persuading the undecided, and even some opponents of abortion to change their minds and trust women to make their own choices about their health.

As the directors of the Together for Yes campaign noted in their thank you message to the 1,429,981 people who voted for repeal of the Eighth Amendment:

> Without the massive support of people in every county in Ireland this momentous vote would not have been possible … We thank all those who shared their stories and everyone who spoke out for the need to change. We thank the thousands of volunteers across the country who campaigned tirelessly for a better Ireland, now and over many decades.[21]

Following the Referendum on 25 May 2018, the Eighth Amendment was formally removed from the Irish Constitution and replaced with a new Article

20 Statements on the Report of the Joint Committee on the Eighth Amendment of the Constitution, Thursday, 25 January 2018, www.oireachtas.ie, accessed 16 December 2021.
21 Message posted on the Together for Yes website by Grainne Griffin, Ailbhe Smyth and Orla O'Connor, Directors of Together for Yes, www.togetherforyes.ie, accessed 17 December 2021.

40.3.3 which stated that provision may be made by law for the regulation of termination of pregnancy by the Thirty-Sixth Amendment of the Constitution Act 2018. On 20 December 2018 the Health (Regulation of Termination of Pregnancy) Act was signed into law by President Michael D. Higgins. Sadly, while it is an improvement on the previous situation, it continues to curtail women's rights in Ireland: 'It established a needlessly cumbersome regime that remains grounded in a criminal law framework and incorporates barriers that have no grounding in medical evidence'.[22]

The Health (Regulation of Termination of Pregnancy) Act 2018 demands a three-day 'cooling off' period for abortion on request, hardly abortion on demand as the opponents of choice liked to claim. Are there any other medical procedures where such a delay is required? Abortions are only lawful up to 12 weeks of pregnancy, regardless of the circumstances. In the horrific case where a pregnant woman is told her foetus has been diagnosed with a fatal foetal anomaly, the death of the foetus must be expected before or within 28 days of birth. While the legislation offers free abortions to Irish citizens and women living in Ireland permanently, this is a grey area for asylum seekers and refugees who are housed in direct provision and likely to have both restricted capacity to travel and limited incomes. The legislation does not decriminalise medical or other personnel who assist a woman with an abortion outside the limitations imposed by it, although it does at least remove the previous criminalisation of women who terminated their own pregnancies.

The Minister for Health, Stephen Donnelly, announced a review of the law in early December 2021, on the third anniversary of its enactment. The review was led by Barrister Marie O'Shea, whose report was issued in April 2023. The government referred it on to the Joint Committee on Health, for consideration of the review findings and recommendations. O'Shea noted that several key elements of the law are contrary to best medical practice in countries where reproductive healthcare is not treated as a bizarrely separate category from other treatments. It also suggests a level of distrust in women that is worryingly consistent with the anti-female discrimination that drove the creation of the Eighth Amendment in the first place.

22 Anna Carnegie and Ruth Roth, 'From the grassroots to the Oireachtas: abortion law reform in the Republic of Ireland', *Health and Human Rights Journal*, 21(2), December 2019, pp 109–20.

SECTION SIX

PERSONAL REFLECTIONS AND NEW DIRECTIONS

CHAPTER 14

The Cork LGBT Archive and lesbian activism in Cork, 1970–2000

Orla Egan

Cork has a rich history of lesbian activism, dating back to at least the 1970s. Cork lesbian activists were agents of change, involved in lesbian, feminist, peace, environmental, social change activism. Cork lesbians established groups, organisations and centres, campaigned for legislative, political and social change, reached out to those who were isolated, and through their actions, changed the lived reality for lesbians in Cork. They also created multiple opportunities for fun and for the creation of lesbian spaces and lesbian culture. There is a thread of activism and community continuing from the 1970s through to current times. During the 1970s a small group of lesbians socialised with gay men in a number of Cork city pubs known to be gathering places for the LGBT community – The Imperial Hotel, Le Château, The Green Room, The Steeple Bar, Hill's Bar and Stripes. When the Gay Centre opened at No. 4 MacCurtain Street in 1976 they would go dancing at the Club held there at the weekends. As one woman commented: 'It was brilliant, a great place to go. It was great fun.' She recalled a great sense of community there.[1] Around the same time several Cork lesbians were involved in the Cork Women's Collective (CWC), set up in late 1978/early 1979, following two public meetings in Cork on feminist issues. The CWC campaigned on various issues, including contraception, abortion, rape, politics, and nationalism. According to founding member Joan McCarthy, there was very strong lesbian involvement in the CWC and there was good support for issues of concern to lesbians.[2]

On 30 January 1978 a group of Cork lesbians gathered in the Gay Centre at No. 4 MacCurtain Street. The purpose of the meeting was to try and set up a specifically lesbian social scene in Cork, as outlined by Marian Barry in the 1978 edition of *Sapphire* newsletter:

> Since the formation of the Cork Branch of the Irish Gay Rights Movement (IGRM) the gay women of this city have been considering

1 Author interview with Bernie O'Leary, September 2016. 2 Author interview with Joan

> setting up a social scene for themselves. Now that the facilities of the club have been made exclusively available to us for one night a week, I will try with your assistance to get this underway. The first women's meeting will take place on Monday 30th January, 1978 at 8p.m., and hopefully will continue on each subsequent Monday at the same time. Looking forward to your support.[3]

Following the meeting the group of lesbians headed off to a nearby pub. This pattern continued for a while, with weekly meetings, until eventually the women instead began to meet up each week in the Steeple Bar near Shandon, run by LGBT ally Claire O'Sullivan.

The opening of the Quay Co-op in May 1982 provided the space and impetus for the further development of lesbian activism and social scene in Cork. The Quay Co-op was established as a workers' co-operative bringing together gay men and lesbians, women's groups, left-wing organisations, environmental and anti-nuclear groups. The building housed a café, bookshop, food co-op, and meeting rooms that were used by various 'alternative' groups in the city and was a hive of political activism in 1980s Cork. Additionally, a Women's Place was part of the Quay Co-op, with two rooms at the top of the building housing a library and drop-in space. This Women's Place provided a base for a number of groups including a Women's Action Group, the Cork Women's Collective, the Cork Rape Crisis Service, the Women's Health Group, Anti-Nuclear and Disarmament Groups as well as lesbian groups and activities. A lesbian discussion group began meeting in the Women's Place in the Quay Co-op in November 1983 – this was an important visible lesbian group: facilitating discussions on a wide range of issues of interest to the community. An article in *Women's Place News* outlined the reasons for establishing the group, 'It was felt that there was a need for lesbians to get together to combat isolation and provide support'.[4]

One Cork activist commented that, prior to the establishment of this alliance, 'there was no identifiable lesbian scene or group at the time'.[5] She described how she and a lesbian friend would be sitting in Loafers Bar, looking over at two other women, wondering if they were dykes, while the other women were sitting there, looking over at them, wondering the same thing! The lesbians gradually did get organised: 'It was on the 17 November 1984 that we Politico-lesbians organised what we thought was the first Lesbian group. We had fifteen women at our first meeting. I remember it well the amazing feeling that there

McCarthy, August 2014. 3 Marian Barry in *Sapphire*, Cork IGRM Newsletter, 1:1, Jan.–Feb. 1978. 4 *Women's Place News*, Cork (undated but probably September 1984). 5 Interview with activist, were so many of us and we were all so different'.[6] The Lesbian Discussion Group met on Thursday nights in the Quay Co-op. Following the meetings, women would head to Loafers Bar, thus beginning the tradition that Thursday night was the night that Cork lesbians met in Loafers, a tradition that continued for decades.

Loafers Bar on Douglas Street was opened in 1983 by Derrick Gerety and operated until 2015, making it one of the longest-running gay bars in Ireland. Loafers became an important social meeting space for the LGBT community as well as for people involved in 'alternative' groups and lifestyles in the city and for those involved in the Quay Co-op. The back bar in Loafers was reserved for women only on Thursday evenings. This provided an important regular public meeting space for the Cork lesbian community, facilitating social support and engagement as well as political discussions. This availability of public social venues was very important for the emerging lesbian community in Cork. As Lapovsky Kennedy and Davis note in their study of lesbian bar culture in Buffalo in the 1930s and 1940s, public bars can play an important role in terms of lesbian community formation and assertion:

> By finding ways to socialise together, individuals ended the crushing isolation of lesbian oppression and created the possibility of group consciousness and activity. In addition, by forming community in a public setting outside of the protected and restricted boundaries of their own living rooms, lesbians also began the struggle for public recognition and acceptance.[7]

Of course, there were also lesbian parties in the living rooms of various homes, often after the Loafers gatherings!

Many Cork lesbians were very active in a wide range of social change movements, including the campaign against the 1983 anti-abortion amendment (Eighth Amendment), campaigns for contraception and divorce, HIV/AIDS activism, as well as in peace and anti-nuclear movements. In addition to the political activism there has always been a sense of playfulness in the Cork lesbian community, a recognition of the importance of creating spaces for fun, dancing and forming community. It was in this spirit that the Cork Women's Fun Weekend began. The first Cork Women's Fun Weekend was held 13–15 April 1984. The Fun Weekend is still running, usually held during the first weekend

September 2016. 6 Deirdre Walsh, 'My personal lesbian history of Cork', *Linc, Cork's Lesbian Magazine*, 1:1 (November 2000), p. 6. 7 Elizabeth Lapovsky Kennedy and Madeline D. Davis, '"I could hardly wait to get back to that bar": lesbian bar culture in Buffalo in the 1930s and 1940s' in Brett Beenyn (ed.), *Creating a place for ourselves: lesbian, gay and bisexual community histories* in May each year. It is a social weekend with a mixture of dancing, music, workshops, sporting events and an infamous pub quiz. A number of Cork women's bands were formed in the 1980s and they played at the Women's Fun Weekends in the mid-1980s. These included bands called Brazen Bitch and Standing Ovulation. Women would travel from near and far to participate in the Cork Women's Fun Weekend. It helped to forge and foster relationships between women from Cork, Belfast, Galway, Dublin and London. Cork women who had emigrated would return to Cork for the Fun Weekend, bringing friends with them, facilitating connections and cross-pollination of ideas and politics between the Cork community and international lesbian and bisexual communities. Commenting on the beginnings of the Cork Women's Fun Weekend in the 1980s, Helen Slattery said 'there was a lot of heavy-duty political women's conferences and discussions going on, and as an antidote we decided to have a weekend of just fun'.[8] This playfulness can also be seen in the various sporting activities that have played an important role in the Cork lesbian community. Cork queers have competed, and won gold medals, in the international Gay Games since they began in San Francisco in 1982. A Cork lesbian soccer team, Douglas Street, competed in the Women's Soccer league in Cork as an openly lesbian team. Softball, soccer and other sports provided playful competition at the annual Cork Women's Fun Weekend. The Boot Women group organised walking trips in West Cork. There were weekend-long parties with women camping in the gardens of women's houses in the countryside and full-moon skinny dipping at midnight at one of Cork's many beautiful beaches.

The community was also conscious of the need to reach out to others and provide support for those who were 'coming out'. The Cork Lesbian Line began operating on Thursday nights in January 1985. An article in *Out For Ourselves* discussed the impetus behind establishing the Cork Lesbian Line:

> It grew out of an awareness of the problems of isolation and lack of information facing lesbians. The Line aims to counteract this by providing support and contact and giving a positive image of lesbians. Women contact the line for a lot of different reasons. The variety of enquiries range from calls from women who are first coming out, women unsure of their sexuality, to lesbians wanting to contact other lesbians and find out what social events are happening … A lot of the women who ring up are in a very isolated position and feel themselves to be the only one in the

(New York and London, 1997), p. 27. 8 Deirdre Walsh interview with Helen Slattery in *Linc, Cork's Lesbian Magazine*, 2 (May 2001).

> world. We stress that they are not alone and we aim to give them a positive view of themselves and of lesbians.[9]

One of the main problems facing the Lesbian Line, and the men's helpline Gay Information Cork, was how to advertise the service they were providing. The main local newspapers, the *Cork Examiner* and the *Evening Echo,* refused to carry advertisements for the Lesbian Line and Gay Information Cork, claiming that it would be illegal to do so. A letter from the Chief Executive of the *Cork Examiner* in 1986 claimed that 'the type of activity referred to is illegal and, accordingly, any advertisement referring to same is also illegal and, as such, we must decline publication'.[10] This presumably refers to the fact that gay male sexual activity was still criminalised in the 1980s. Lesbians were not covered by that legislation, but the Lesbian Line advertisements were still refused. Despite interventions on behalf of the information lines by politicians, trade unions and health professionals, the newspapers continued to refuse to carry the advertisements. The telephone lines did succeed in having their numbers placed in the telephone directory. Helen Slattery recalls: 'We were brave for our time. I remember going in to put the listing in the telephone directory for the Lesbian Line. It was all done in a very strained silence, with a lot of pointing to the offending word "lesbian". It felt like a great victory that they accepted it'.[11] Despite these challenges the Cork Lesbian Line continued to operate for decades and continues today under the umbrella of the national LGBT Helpline.

In 1987 the Women's Place in Cork and the Women's News Collective in Belfast applied for and received Co-operation North funding to further develop links and exchange skills.[12] The Cork Women taught the Belfast women how to set up and run a Women's Library, while the Belfast women showed the Cork women how to produce a newsletter, leading to the publication of a series of Cork Women's Space newsletters.[13] This was followed by another Co-operation North exchange the following year. In 1988 Co-operation North funded an exchange between the Lesbian Lines in Cork, Belfast, Galway, Derry, Dublin and

9 Article written by the Cork Lesbian Line in *Out for ourselves: the lives of Irish lesbians and gay men* (Dublin, 1986). 10 Letter T.E. Crosbie, Chief Executive, *Cork Examiner,* to Arthur Leahy, Gay Information Cork, 20 November 1986. 11 Deirdre Walsh interview with Helen Slattery in *Linc, Cork's Lesbian Magazine,* 2 (May 2001). 12 Co-operation North was established in 1979 to fund and foster co-operation and exchanges between groups in the Republic of Ireland and Northern Ireland. It is now known as Co-operation Ireland https://cooperationireland.org/our-history/. 13 Women's Space Newsletter in Cork LGBT Archive, https://corklgbtarchive.com/items/show/59, accessed 21 February 2024.

Limerick – essentially an all-Ireland lesbian line network. Commenting on the Co-Operation North exchange one of the participants notes that:

> this exchange offered us a chance as Lesbian Lines to meet with relative ease with each other. It certainly wove a very strong network between us all for the continuation of skills, information and fund raising. It is only because the exchange took place that we were enabled to begin to do many of these things. As isolated groups we have neither enough information, skills or money to get much of the work needed to be done, done. As a larger national network all things are possible.[14]

The Lesbian Lines exchange received an award from Co-operation North; they were joint winners under the Women's Groups projects in the Community Programme, sharing the award with the Dublin Travellers' Education and Development Group and Newry Travellers' Group. However, Hayley Fox-Roberts suggests that there was a 'cover-up' of sorts in relation to the Co-operation North awards: 'These events had previously been public but were held that year in private, with no press, to avoid embarrassment over awards being made to queer-affiliated organisations'.[15]

The 1980s was a decade of activism and development of the Cork lesbian community, with new groups formed, events organised and campaigns fought. However, all was not harmonious. Within the Cork lesbian community in the 1980s there was very little respect or open acknowledgment of bisexual or transgender members of the community. It was to be the 1990s before the development of bisexual and transgender groups in Cork came about. There were also often tensions between lesbian activist and gay male activists in Cork, with issues arising in relation to space and resources. This eventually led to the Women's Place leaving the Quay Co-op at the end of the 1980s.

The opening of The Other Place LGBT Community Centre in Cork in 1991 provided an important base and space for the further development of the community. Of particular importance was the availability of jobs, with people employed under the Community Employment Scheme. The aims of The Other Place were outlined in a leaflet:

> As a focus point for the lesbian and gay community, the centre aims to provide a resource catering specifically to the needs of this community in

14 Geraldine McCarthy 'Co-operation North exchange, Cork Lesbian Line 1988' – paper distributed to participants on the LEA/NOW Introduction to Lesbian Studies Cork, March and April 1997. 15 Hayley Fox Roberts, '"Always keep a lemon handy": a skeletal history of lesbian activism in late twentieth-century Ireland', *The History Review*, 12 (2001), pp 113–27, p. 120.

> a supportive and safe atmosphere. The projects undertaken by the centre are initiated in direct response to the needs of the community and The Other Place aims to rise to the challenge of responding to these needs as the community changes and new requirements emerge.
>
> The provision of support groups, as well as information lines and services, is an integral part of the work of the centre. The drop-in, social space is provided in answer to a crucial need for a safe meeting place where lesbians and gay men can relax and feel comfortable ... Less visible aspects of the Centre's work involve networking with State and voluntary bodies and responding to Government and social issues which affect the lesbian and gay community ... . The Centre is committed to supporting and initiating events which reflect the creativity of lesbian and gay people and our place in the wider community.[16]

Several lesbian and bisexual projects were organised in The Other Place, under the umbrella of LEAP (Lesbians for Employment Against Poverty) – which later became known as CLASS (Cork Lesbian Advice, Support and Self-Help Project). Various self-help groups were set up including a Young Lesbians Group, a Coming Out Group, a Bisexual Group and a Married Lesbians Group. A Lesbian Health Project was established in February 1996. A project leaflet outlined the reasons for setting up the Lesbian Health Project:

> The project was set up out of a recognition that even where there is adequate women's health care in society the needs of lesbians are often overlooked as the clientele are all assumed to be heterosexual. Whether this is in GP practices, ante/post natal care, sexual health (STD clinics), cancer screening, drug and alcohol treatment centres etc., lesbians can find it hard to get a sympathetic ear from health-care professionals who are unaware of the needs (and sometimes of the existence!) of lesbian women.[17]

The Lesbian Health Project organised a Lesbian Drug and Alcohol Recovery Group, ran Lesbians and Safer Sex Workshops, conducted a Women's Sex Survey and organised an annual Lesbian Health Day. The project also developed lesbian specific information on STDs, addictions, bereavement issues, self-help groups, and AIDS prevention.

16 *The Other Place*, lesbian and gay community centre leaflet. 17 *Cork Lesbian Health Project* leaflet [no date].

DEVELOPING LESBIAN SOCIAL SPACES IN CORK

There was a regular Friday night Women's Disco in The Other Place in addition to the mixed club nights held there each weekend. LEAP also organised monthly socials in The Other Place; the idea was to provide an alcohol-free lesbian social space as an alternative to the pub or club scene. The pool table in The Other Place provided a popular hangout spot for Cork dykes. The Cork Lesbian and Gay Film Festival began in 1991, with a range of queer films being screened as part of the annual Cork Film Festival. In 1992 lesbians working in The Other Place organised the first LGBT entry in a St Patrick's Day parade – the first anywhere in the world! It was organised in response to the banning of the ILGO (Irish Lesbian and Gay Organisation) from marching in the St Patrick's Day parades in New York and Boston. It also provided an opportunity for greater visibility for the Cork LGBT community. As this author wrote in an article in *Munster GCN (Gay Community News)* in 1992: 'On Patrick's Day '92 we made history, and we did it in style. Our float was a blaze of colour with balloons, banners, streamers and dancing lesbian, bi and gay people blowing bubbles at the 80,000 people lining the streets of Cork'.[18] It is interesting to note that most of the people involved in organising the St Patrick's Day entry, as well as the majority of those participating, were lesbian. Thirty women, but only five men marched with the LGBT float. In sharp contrast to what was happening to the ILGO in New York, where members were arrested if they stepped off the footpath into the parade, the Cork LGBT float won a prize for the Best New Entrant in Cork in 1992.

In 1992 Joan McCarthy organised a course on Lesbians, Feminism and Philosophy in The Other Place lesbian and gay resource centre. This course provided a wonderful opportunity to explore philosophical questions about being lesbian – What is a lesbian? Do we define 'lesbian' primarily in sexual or political terms? Does its meaning change in different historical periods? Is there such a thing as a 'lesbian community'?[19] The playfulness of the Cork lesbian community can again be seen in the organisation of the annual Lesbian Fantasy Balls, beginning in 1994. The first Ball, billed as Pandora's Box, a Lesbian Camp Drag Fantasy Cabaret Ball, was held in Blackrock Castle on 19 November 1994. It was so amazing to see the courtyard of the castle fill with lesbians arriving to the Ball adorned in a wide variety of costumes. The annual event provided an opportunity for lesbians to dress up and to express, explore and play with our fantasies. It provided a rare opportunity for overt lesbian sexual expression and

18 Orla Egan, 'Historic victory', *Munster GCN*, April 1992. 19 Author's notes from Lesbianism, Feminism and Philosophy course, January–March 1992.

play. It also provided a forum for lesbians to play with notions of gender expression and identity. Emma Bidwell, who was centrally involved in starting the Cork Lesbian Fantasy Ball, commented that it

> is in many ways the Irish lesbian scene and herstory in miniature. There are all kinds: butch, femme, man, boy, girlie, goddess, slut. There are those still finding their nerve to be what they want, those who are pushing the limits of what is acceptable to others, those who will always play safe, those comfortable as they are and the unseen many who are still so scared of being lesbian that they are invisible in this parade.[20]

Cork lesbians also organised in support of Donna McAnallen, who was fired from her job as a lifeguard and fitness instructor in Brookfield Leisure Centre in September 1992, for allegedly kissing another woman in the changing rooms.[21] The Cork lesbian community rallied to support McAnallen and protests were organised at the Brookfield leisure centre with women wearing t-shirts with the slogan 'I wished I had kissed Donna McAnallen.' She took the case to the Irish Labour Court, which found that she had been treated unfairly but that the current Employment Equality legislation did not cover discrimination on the basis of sexual orientation.[22] This case, and the publicity it generated, provided impetus for the inclusion of sexual orientation in the new Employment Equality Legislation enacted in Ireland in the 1990s.

Cork's first lesbian centre opened at 14 George's Quay on 26 April 1999. A small grant (£10,000) was obtained from the EU funded LEA (Lesbian Education and Awareness) project. Several lesbian community meetings were held in Cork (December 1998 and February 1999) and a steering group, operating under the name Cairde Corcaí (Cork Friends), was set up to oversee the establishment of the Lesbian Centre. Several groups operated from the George's Quay lesbian centre. Social and information events were organised. For example, a Health Day was held on 6 November 1999 and a Seminar on Racism and the Lesbian Community was held on 21 November 1999. However, there were challenges due to the lack of resources to employ any staff, which led to limited opening hours. Problems also emerged with the landlord. The lesbian centre moved to Princes Street in 2000 and the name was changed to LINC (Lesbians in Cork). It moved to its current home on White Street in 2002.

20 Emma Bidwell, 'Where have all the dungarees gone?', *Irish Journal of Feminist Studies*, 2:1; Special Issue: Aspects of Irish Feminism (July 1997), p. 60. **21** Know your rights – case study 2: Donna McAnallen and Brookfield Leisure Centre – Orla Egan. FSU and Irish Congress of Trade Unions webinar series June 2022 https://www.youtube.com/watch?v=VHdF32–tBoo, accessed 21 February 2024. **22** Labour Court Order, case EEO 1293, Brookfield Leisure Limited and A

Obtaining funding and being able to employ staff enabled LINC to develop a wide range of groups and activities in support of the lesbian and bisexual communities in Cork.

THE IMPORTANCE OF LESBIAN HISTORY AND ARCHIVES

The preceding brief glimpses into some of the rich history of lesbian activism in Cork would not be possible without access to archival documents and materials. How do we write lesbian history if we can't access information on the lives of lesbians? It shows the importance of queer archives in enabling our history to become more visible. The history of lesbian lives and lesbian activism in Ireland has, too often, been invisible, ignored or deliberately obscured or denied. This is even truer when we talk of the lives and activism of bisexual and transgender women. In order to write this history we need access to historical records and archives, the kinds of records that are rarely found in mainstream archives. This was part of the motivation in creating the Cork LGBT Archive – the desire to gather, preserve and share information about our rich queer history and heritage.

Community archives, such as the Cork LGBT Archive, have challenged the concept that archives are neutral and impartial keepers of our past, and have highlighted the absences and exclusions within traditional archives and museums. Those who do not see ourselves reflected within the archives and museums have created our own and ensured that our history is preserved and shared. These community archives have posed challenges to traditional archives, to the practices of archiving and to our concepts of what is an archive and who is an archivist. Andrew Flinn calls this social movement archival activism, leading to the democratisation of the archives and of knowledge production.[23] Jamie Ann Lee talks about queering the archive:

> I deploy the term queer as a practice and a politics. I use 'to queer' as a verb working on and within the archives as an act of intervention, an upsetting of the normative archival structures that continue to uphold and reproduce the hegemonic power dynamics at work to exclude.[24]

Worker. 23 Andrew Flinn, 'An attack on professionalism and scholarship? Democratising archives and the production of knowledge', *Ariadne*, 62 (2010); www.ariadne.ac.uk/issue 62/flinn/accessed 14 May 2021. 24 Jamie Ann Lee, 'A queer/ed archival methodology: theorising practice through radical interrogations of the archival body' (PhD, University of Arizona, 2015), https://repository.arizona.edu/bitstream/handle/10150/ 556236/azu_etd_13787_sip1_m.pdf?sequence=1, accessed 21 February 2024.

The work of creating community archives is political: it is activism. It seeks to bring about change, not only in the content of our archives and museums, but also in how this work is done and by whom. Through a consideration of the politics of community archives and queer archives, I have come to the position of calling what I do Queer Archival Activism. The Cork LGBT Archive is queer, not just in content, but also in the sense that Lee means when she talks of queering the archives – its existence poses challenges to the politics and priorities of traditional museums and archives.

The beginnings of the Cork LGBT Archive can be traced back to a damp basement in the home of Arthur Leahy, a Cork activist who had the foresight to begin collecting and saving items in relation to the LGBT community and political activism in Cork from the 1970s onwards. It was a treasure trove but was unorganised and some of the material was damaged from the damp and inappropriate storage conditions. This collection forms the core of the Cork LGBT Archive. Initial work on the archive entailed moving the collection out of the damp basement and beginning the process of sorting and cataloguing. This was done on a voluntary basis by community activists, primarily by myself and historian Liz Steiner-Scott. Simultaneously a digital archive, www.corklgbtarchive.com, was created to digitally store and share information about Cork LGBT history. In 2016 the Cork LGBT Archive received its first funding, a grant from the Irish Heritage Council to buy acid-free boxes to properly store the collection. While the grant was small and specific, it was hugely symbolic as a step towards the recognition of Irish LGBT history as an important and valued part of Irish history and heritage. One of the conditions of the funding was that we organise an event as part of Heritage Week, so in August 2016 the first Cork LGBT Archive exhibition was held as part of Heritage Week 2016. The Exhibition was displayed in Camden Palace Community Arts Centre and traced the history of the community from the 1970s to the 1990s, using material from the Cork LGBT Archive. One of the comments left by a visitor to the exhibition sums up its significance: 'Such an important contribution to Irish heritage! Fantastic that this was done, reflecting Cork LGBT history'.[25] The Cork LGBT Archive was awarded a Hidden Heritage Award by the Heritage Council for this work – a hugely symbolic acknowledgment and inclusion of a previously hidden and excluded community history. The archive has also received funding from the Cork City Council Heritage Grants. This funding enabled the publication of a book: *Queer republic of Cork, Cork's lesbian, gay, bisexual and transgender communities, 1970s–1990s*.[26] A Cork

25 Exhibition Comments Book, 2016. 26 Orla Egan, *Queer republic of Cork: Cork's lesbian, gay, bisexual and transgender communities, 1970s–1990s* (Cork, 2016).

City Council Heritage Grant also enabled the archive to print the exhibition on a series of pull-up banners. This makes the exhibition much more portable and has enabled its display in a range of venues in Cork, Belfast and in Berlin.

In 2021 a new Exhibition, Cork Queeros, was created, showcasing photographs of a wide range of Cork LGBT people. It includes community activists, athletes, artists, those who contribute to making the Cork LGBT community colourful, dynamic and vibrant. Participants identify as Lesbian, Gay, Bisexual, Transgender, Queer, GenderQueer, GenderFluid, Feminist, Dyke. The most senior was born in 1945, while the youngest participant was born in 1999.[27] A walking tour was developed in 2019 in collaboration with Cork Pride Festival. The following year, in the middle of the pandemic, this was further developed into an Interactive Walking Tour, with plaques placed on buildings of significance to the LGBT community, with QR codes linking to exhibitions on the Cork LGBT Digital Archive.[28]

In 2021 the Cork LGBT Archive produced a short Cork LGBT documentary, *I'm Here, I'm Home, I'm Happy,* directed by the author. The film uses extracts from oral history interviews and items from the Cork LGBT Archive to bring Cork LGBT history to life and to tell the story of the lives of some LGBT people in Cork in the 1970s and 1980s. It explores how the Cork LGBT community provided a sense of connection, belonging, mutual support and fun to LGBT people at a time of criminalisation, prejudice and discrimination. The participants talk about the community spaces, parties, pubs, clubs and political activism. In 2022 Cork City Library published *Diary of an activist*; this book is a Cork social activism graphic memoir produced through an inter-generational collaboration between Orla Egan and artist Megan Luddy O'Leary.[29] The book draws on items from the Cork LGBT Archive collection to illustrate activism in 1970s, 1980s and 1990s Cork. These are all examples of the variety of ways in which the Cork LGBT Archive strives to animate its content, to bring the history to life and to make it more accessible and engaging to a range of audiences.

In 2023 the author directed a new documentary, *LOAFERS*, marking 40 years since the opening of Loafers Bar in 1983. Using a combination of interviews, archival footage, photographs, illustrations and animation it gives a glimpse into the legend and legacy of Loafers. The documentary explores what Loafers meant to the people who ran it, worked in it and frequented it, and the impact of the loss of such an important safe space for the community. Loafers was

27 'Cork Queeros' page, Cork LGBT Archive, https://corklgbtarchive.com/cork-queeros/.
28 https://corklgbtarchive.com/items/show/348, accessed 21 February 2024.
29 Orla Egan, Megan Luddy O'Leary, *Diary of an activist*, Cork City Library, 2022.

much more than a bar – it was a crucial community space, a home for the weird and wonderful of Cork and a refuge for the Cork LGBT community. Its rooms were filled with love, laughter, dancing, political discussions and activism.

These have been important steps in bringing Cork LGBT history out of the basement and in from the margins of Irish heritage. Another important step was the decision to donate the Cork LGBT Archive collection to the Cork Public Museum in Fitzgerald's Park in Cork. The museum has agreed to complete the task of sorting and cataloguing the collection and will then make it accessible, by appointment, to those interested in accessing the archive. Of huge significance is the commitment to the creation of a permanent Cork LGBT Exhibition in the museum. In recent years the Cork Public Museum has sought to broaden its exhibitions to be more reflective and inclusive of the diversity of Cork's culture and heritage. There is a permanent Traveller Community Exhibition in the museum, and an exhibition about the Cork Jewish Community has also been added. The Cork LGBT Exhibition in the Cork Public Museum will enable greater visibility for this community and ensure its inclusion in the history and heritage displayed in the museum. As well as ensuring preservation of, and access to, the physical collection of the Cork LGBT Archive, it was also essential to ensure the long-term digital preservation of the collection. The Digital Repository of Ireland (DRI) provided the best option for this. The DRI is Ireland's national digital repository for humanities, social sciences, and cultural heritage data.[30] In 2019 the Cork LGBT Archive won the DRI's inaugural Community Archives Award and the Cork LGBT Archive collection has been added to the DRI.[31] The collection has also been added to Europeana, the EU cultural heritage site that enables widespread access to a range of cultural heritage collections.[32]

In 2023 the Cork LGBT Archive received funding from the Heritage Council that enabled us to rent space, for the first time ever. Having a space of our own, even for a few months, made a huge difference to our ability to develop the work of the archive. We had space to work, to display our exhibitions and to host a range of local and international visitors to the archive. Most importantly it enabled us to facilitate a dynamic and enthusiastic group of volunteers. We held weekly Volunteer Evenings, provided training for the volunteers and they then contributed to the work of the archive – a mutually beneficial arrangement. Most of the volunteers are young LGBTQI+ people. In volunteer testimonials they talk about the 'sense of community' they find at the archive, that it is 'a

30 For more see www.dri.ie, accessed 21 February 2024. 31 'Digitally preserving and sharing Cork's LGBT history: new collection published in DRI', https://www.dri.ie/digitally-preserving-cork-lgbt-history, accessed 21 February 2024. 32 Europeana site, https://www.europeana.eu/, accessed 21 February 2024.

place where I can be my authentic self, surrounded by a diverse and supportive community of volunteers and mentors.' So inadvertently the Cork LGBT Archive created a much-needed safe space for young queers, facilitated intergenerational collaboration and connection to their history and heritage.

Much work remains to be done, in particular in terms of adding more materials to the digital archive and increasing the diversity of the collections. However, in many ways this is a tale of the success and impact of queer archival activism. A rich, previously hidden history is being preserved and shared. This work has been acknowledged and supported by Irish heritage organisations, by the Heritage Council and Cork City Council. The inclusion of the Cork LGBT Archive collections in the Cork Public Museum and the DRI ensures their long-term preservation and facilitates greater access to them. It acknowledges the decades of Cork LGBT activism and the bravery and pride of those who refused to accept discrimination and prejudice, those who demanded respect and equality for Cork's lesbian, gay, bisexual and transgender communities.

CHAPTER 15

Out is a very dangerous place: the emergence of the trans movement in Ireland

Sara R. Phillips

On 9 June 2014, *Time Magazine* put actress Laverne Cox on their cover and declared the 'Transgender Tipping Point'. In the ensuing interview, Cox told the reporter, 'More of us are living visibly and pursuing our dreams visibly, so people can say, "Oh yeah, I know someone who is trans"'. Reporter Katy Steinmetz declared that when people have points of reference that are humanising, that demystifies difference.[1] In September, of the following year, 2015, Ireland became only the fourth country in the world to enact gender recognition legislation based on self-determination.[2] This legislation had been the culmination of a 22-year legal battle by Dr Lydia Foy, supported by the trans community and its allies, campaigning for, in both the media and with government to, not only advance the legislation, but to ensure the right to self-determination. For some, it seemed that the transgender community had suddenly appeared from nowhere. This was far from reality.

In 1993, the name Dr Lydia Foy was unknown to most of us, and this was nowhere more evident than in the trans community itself. The premise of her campaign was certainly not on anyone else's agenda. In fact, comments made to me in later years, by some older trans women who knew her, said they thought she was mad to request a change to her birth certificate. 'We were more worried about acceptance, healthcare, transition pathways and most importantly our own safety'. In an Ireland that was ruled by Catholicism, where the 12th Amendment on abortion (to exclude the risk of suicide as grounds for an abortion) had failed in 1992, Mother Theresa had visited President Robinson in Áras an Uachtaráin in June, homosexuality had just been decriminalised that same month, and in Northern Ireland, the Shankill Bombings and Greysteel killings had occurred in October, it was brave or crazy choice to start on a path so public.

1 'The Transgender Tipping Point', *Time Magazine,* 9 June 2014, https://time.com/135480/transgender-tipping-point/, accessed 14 December 2023. 2 By May 2023, 20 countries enacted Gender Recognition Legislation based on self-determination: Argentina, Belgium, Brazil, Chile, Colombia, Costa Rica, Denmark, Ecuador, Finland, Iceland, Ireland, Luxembourg, Malta, New Zealand, Norway, Pakistan, Portugal, Spain, Switzerland and Uruguay.

But Dr Lydia Foy was not just looking for a new birth certificate. She was looking for identity papers to recognise her current gender identity and make life easier to traverse. She realised that the only way to achieve this was to apply for changes to her birth certificate, the fundamental document of identity in Ireland. Her application was responded to by An t-Ard Chláraitheoir (the Registrar of Births), informing her that there was no mechanism in Irish law to achieve such a change but would keep her application on file. Across a series of correspondence over the next few years, Dr Foy was continually refused this new birth certificate by An t-Ard Chláraitheoir.

In May 1996, Dr Foy contacted the Free Legal Advice Centres (FLAC) and received a response from solicitor Mary Johnson, who advised that: 'It was agreed that the issue of seeking to amend your birth certificate is of interest to FLAC by virtue of its human rights dimension'.[3] FLAC agreed to take on Dr Foy's case.[4] Over the next eleven years, through several legal cases, and standing up to the attacks on her person and on her family life by the media, Dr Foy fought to be given respect and recognised for who she was. In 2007, in the High Court, Justice Liam McKechnie found that the Irish state was in contravention of the European Convention of Human Rights 2003. In his summing up Justice McKechnie stated:

> Everyone as a member of society has the right to human dignity, and with individual personalities, has the right to develop his being as he sees fit; subject only to the most minimal of State interference being essential for the convergence of the common good. Together with human freedom, a person subject, subject to the acquired rights of others, should be free to shape his personality in the way best suited to his person and to his life. All persons by virtue of their being are so entitled.[5]

It was to take another eight years and another court case before Dr Foy was to receive her birth certificate recognising her female gender.[6] It also required a strong and dedicated community, led by Transgender Equality Network Ireland (TENI), to advocate for the right to self-determine their gender identity, to remove a divorce requirement from the recommendations, to remove a requirement to be pathologised and to live in role for two years and lastly to prove your identity to a three-person panel.[7] Dr Foy and the community were

3 FLAC, *'A story of great human proportions: Lydia Foy and the struggle for transgender rights in Ireland* (Dublin, 2018), p. 6. 4 Ibid. 5 *Foy v. An t-Ard Chláraitheoir & Ors*, [2007] (IEHC 470 (2007) High Court, Ireland). https://www.casemine.com/judgement/uk/5da052154653d07dedfd55ec, accessed 14 December 2023. 6 *'A story of great human proportions'*, p. 18. 7 2011 Report of the Gender Recognition Advisory Group to Minister for Social Protection, Joan Burton, 15 June 2011,

forthright in their convictions, held true to their beliefs, and, eventually, with the passing of the act, Dr Foy received her new birth certificate in September 2015.

GENDER VARIANCE AND IRELAND

Dr Lydia Foy was certainly not the first trans or gender variant individual from Ireland. Ireland has a rich history dating back into the nineteenth century, with, so far, some scant evidence dating back further. Our current community dates its roots back into the 1970s, at the same time that the gay and lesbian movements were becoming more visible. Irish related trans-archival research provides a rich history of Irish gender variance and transgression throughout the centuries. Names such as Albert Cashier (1843–1915), Dr James Barry (*c*.1789–1865), Edward De Lacy Evans (1830–1901), Patrick McCormack (1821–71), John Murphy (*c*.1800–30), Marianne Weldon (*c*.1863), John Bradley (*c*.1889), Charlotta Gibbons (1849–90), James Walker (*c*.1836), Margaret King (1773–1835) John Coulter (1834–84), Michael Dillon (1915–62) are easily researched but many more exist. Individuals such as Cashier,[8] De Lacy Evans[9], and Dr James Barry[10] had a determined zeal to ensure they lived authentic lives and their stories have been deservedly told many times, although not always with the respect they should be shown. Both Cashier and De Lacy Evans, in latter years, on becoming infirm, were admitted to hospital, one in the US and the other in Australia. Their secret was discovered. They were both made to present and dress as their birth gender. This greatly affected Cashier's mental state. At 67 years old, he passed away on 10 October 1915, his spirit and heart broken. De Lacy Evans tried to continue his life as female unsuccessfully for another twenty-one years and he died of the flu in 1901.

Dr James Barry, a renowned surgeon general in the British army, with a lifetime of service, famous for his work in hygiene in medicine and Caesarean sections, was so determined to keep his identity as that of a man, he requested to be buried in the clothes in which he had died. There was to be no washing or dressing of the body, but that request was not honoured and so his story, his

https://tgeu.org/irish-government-gender-recognition-advisory-group-report-a-missed-opportunity/, accessed 14 December 2023. **8** Rob Sanders, *The fighting infantryman: the story of Albert D.J. Cashier, transgender Civil War soldier* (London, 2020); Lon Dawson, *Also known as Albert D.J. Cashier: the Jennie Hodgers story, or how one young Irish girl joined the Union Army during the Civil War* (London, 2005). **9** The Mysterious Edward/Ellen De Lacy Evans: the picaresque in real life – State of Victoria Library, https://latrobejournal.slv.vic.gov.au/latrobejournal/issue/latrobe-69/t1–g-t9.html, accessed 22 February 2024. **10** Michael du Preez and Jeremy Dronfield, *Dr James Barry: a woman ahead of her time* (London, 2016); Rachel Holmes, *The secret life of Dr James Barry: Victorian England's most eminent surgeon* (London, 2020); Lisa Robinson and Lauren Simkin Berke, then scandalous story, was to be told. Dr Barry clearly wished to secure his legacy and not to deflect from his achievements. In fact, what is lost in the story of Dr Barry is the similarity to the story of Cork-born Margaret King. Both the King and Barry families would have moved in similar circles. King attended college in Jena, Germany, to study medicine, which necessitated cross-dressing and turning up to classes as a man. She later studied with professor of surgery, Andrea Vaccá Berlinghieri of the University of Pisa, and wrote a book of household medicine for the care of babies and children – *Advice to young mothers on the physical education of children by a grandmother* (1835). In her formative years, she had been a favoured pupil of feminist Mary Wollstonecraft.[11] However, when King completed her studies in medicine, unlike Dr Barry, she returned to living as a woman.

In her essay '"It should not be so easy to construct a man": a history of female to male transsexuality in the journal *Urania*', Sonja Tiernan reminded the reader of the words of Michael Dillon. Transsexuals, he noted, 'have the most difficult life of all, for they cannot conceal their forms from curious eyes'.[12] Ironically, Dillon was to do just that, as he was to traverse life, happily for many years, studying, working, socialising and competing in rowing competitions as a man. In 1942, he persuaded a certain Doctor George Foss to give him male hormone pills, and had a mastectomy, and in 1944 had his birth certificate amended, changing 'daughter' to 'son' and his assigned name at birth to 'Laurence Michael'. He entered medical school in Trinity College Dublin in 1945 under his new name. During the long holidays, he had protracted and painful operations at the hospital of the plastic surgeon Sir Harold Gillies to complete the physical changes. Sir Harold Gillies completed the first ever known phalloplasty on Dillon in 1948. In the recently posthumously published book by Michael Dillon, *Out of the ordinary: life of gender and spiritual transitions*, Susan Stryker, in her forward, tells us that:

> While still a medical student in the midst of gender transition in 1946, Dillon authored an obscure and erudite little book, *Self, an essay on ethics and endrocrinology*, which functioned as a cryptoautobiography. Grounded in his self-experimentation with hormones but written in an impersonal voice in spite of his deeply personal, embodied stake in the argument, it laid out from the perspective of the sexological science, a cogent case for the ethical

Were I not a girl: the inspiring and true story of Dr James Barry (London, 2020). 11 Emma Garman, *A liberated woman: the story of Margaret King* (London, 2016). 12 Sonja Tiernan, '"It should not be so easy to construct a man": a history of female to male transsexuality in the journal *Urania*' in Sonja Tiernan and Mary McAuliffe (eds), *Sapphists and sexologists: histories of sexualities*, volume 2

> use of medical procedures to change the sex signifying characteristics of people like himself who experienced a mismatch between their inner and outer realities. Seen through a contemporary transgender lens, *Self* is a prescient account, avant la lettre, of the transexual discourse, that took shape in the mid-20th century.[13]

It is believed that Dillon was the first female to male trans person to use testosterone therapy. Many of Dillon's observations on endocrinology in *Self* are still reflected in today's trans healthcare.[14]

THE MODERN IRISH TRANS MOVEMENT – VISIBILITY AND RIGHTS

By the mid-1960s, Irish trans people were forming and attending trans groups in the UK while still living in Ireland. In late 1977, the first trans group, the Friends of Eon, was formed in Dublin, and named after the Chevalier d'Eon, an eighteenth-century French diplomat, spy, and soldier, and who had famously or infamously lived part of their life as both male and female.[15] But the era in which I grew up was bereft of any positive visibility. Trans people hid in the shadows, stayed in the closet, or decided that this life was not for them. Any evidence to be found was on the pages of the UK tabloids or as the subject of a joke or as a victim in a television programme or film; these were never complementary. In 1977, information about that first trans group was impossible to find. Small adverts were to be found only in the *In Dublin* magazine or in *Hot Press,* the music, culture and politics magazine. National radio and TV presenter, Gay Byrne, and the hugely popular weekly RTÉ TV talk show, the Late Late show, did host British trans woman Jan Morris in May 1975, interviewing her about her book *Conundrum*. Morris was received kindly in the media, with remarks such as 'she had great dignity and courage, she made a good case for humanity, of whatever sex, without hammering home any points'.[16]

However, when the Late Late Show hosted a Friends of Eon representative in February 1979, there was uproar in the media in the days following, led by the then Taoiseach's (Prime Minister) wife Maureen Lynch and Leslie Quelch, president of the Irish League of Decency. A national newspaper, the *Irish*

(Newcastle upon Tyne, 2009), pp 56–7. 13 Michael Dillon, *Out of the ordinary: a life of gender and spiritual transitions* (New York, 2017), p. vii. 14 Michael Dillon, *Self – a study in ethics and endocrinology* (London, 1946). 15 Simon Burrows, Jonathan Conlin, Russell Goulbourne, Valerie Mainz (eds), *The Chevalier d'Eon and his worlds: gender, espionage and politics in the eighteenth century* (London, 2010). 16 *Irish Press,* 10 May 1975.

Independent, led with the headline, 'Storm over Transvestite on RTÉ Late Late'.[17] Claire Farrell, one of the founding members of the Friends of Eon and long-time trans activist, talks about those heady days in an interview she did with me for national LGBTI magazine *Gay Community News (GCN)* in 2020.[18] She explained how it was both a dangerous and exhilarating time to be a trans activist. She spoke of her first outing:

> An event was organised for my first official outing in the rear of a business in Crumlin which was owned by a trans woman known as Alga Campbell. Alga was in fact a founder of a trans group called the Beaumont Society in the UK which she ran from Dublin. The Beaumont Society still exists to this day, long after the passing of Alga.[19]

The Friends of Eon was founded by Farrell and another trans woman called Lola. They set about hosting social events in the Parliament Inn, on Parliament Street, Dublin. Farrell explained that some of the group felt they should connect with the Gardaí (Irish Police) about safety, and RTÉ radio about spreading information. On the Pat Kenny radio show in 1979, it was estimated that there was approximately 1,000 transsexuals and 20,000 transvestites in Ireland.[20] Farrell subsequently appeared on the RTÉ television social affairs program, Summer House, in August 1980, with presenter Áine O'Connor.[21] The Friends of Eon continued to focus on social events but, subsequently, the group split into those who wished to continue the activism and those who wanted social outlets.

By the late 1980s, early 1990s, many individual trans people are found to be working in isolation to improve their lives through medical care, without having to go to the UK or America. Passports and birth certificates are slowly becoming important. It was in this atmosphere that Dr Lydia Foy requested her gender to be reflected on her birth certificate. By 1995, the Department of Foreign Affairs had issued her with a new passport recognising her gender as female.[22] These individuals are rarely connected and very few even knew of each other. Often, even those who knew each other's names, did not want to know each other as friends. However, what did connect them is the need and drive to

17 *Irish Independent*, 12 February 1979. 18 *Gay Community News (GCN)*, 17 November 2020, 'Ireland's first trans group Friends of Eon – Sara R. Phillips of the Irish Trans Archive talks to friend and trailblazing trans activist, Claire Farrell', https://gcn.ie/this-transgenderawarenessweek-we-look-back-at-irelands-first-trans-group-friends-of-eon/accessed 17 November 2023. 19 *GCN*, 17 November 2020. 20 The Pat Kenny Day by Day programme, RTÉ Radio 1, autumn 1979, from the author's personal cassette recording of the show. 21 RTE Archives, Freedom to be yourself, August 1980 – rte.ie/archives/2020/0812/1158815–gender-expression/ 17/11/2023. 22 FLAC, *'A story of great human proportions'*, p. 6.

achieve their rights and access the services they required. They had accepted that society dictated what their identity was to be and in what way they were to be treated. But also, they accepted that they were moving from one gender binary box to another. So, they did what they were told in order to exist, often trying to avoid being on the front of the newspaper in a horrendously written article. Throughout the 1990s, Irish newspaper headlines mirrored those in the UK tabloid press. Headlines such as 'I was always a natural born woman inside,' 'You need to go abroad to get it off', 'Sex changes are costing the state £21,000', 'We are sending men to Britain for sex changes', are just some regular examples of the front pages of Irish newspapers;[23] still marginalised, still victimised, and still misunderstood.

For instance, throughout the late 1980s and into the 1990s, Rebecca (Tallon) de Haviland's story was spread across the pages of the *Sunday World* and other newspapers. de Haviland underwent gender reassignment surgery in Ireland in 1991, one of the first trans women to do so in this country, and her story was never represented as positive but always as sensationalist. Her life and transition were dissected and examined and served up for public consumption. In 1994, I found myself in one such article – horrifically headlined 'Men in dresses'

> The atmosphere was a heady mix of French perfume and cigarette smoke. Sara adjusts her black silver lame jacket and steps from one high heeled foot to another. Her car has been broken into outside the city centre club where she is socialising with her friends and she is clearly upset. It is only when Sara turns and speaks you would really know – The voice is unmistakably that of a man.[24]

Throughout the 1990s, other campaigns, like Dr Foy's, were being activated individually. A new medical clinic began in St Patrick's Hospital in Dublin and provided mental health services and diagnosis for transsexual individuals. Passports became a standard identity document, being issued in ones preferred gender, while the changing of educational documents such as Leaving Certificates and tertiary degrees, and the changing of details in college records was now common. But most of all, into the 1990s, we began to see visibility. Trans people were more willing to speak out in the media and advocate for their rights.

23 *Sunday Independent,* 13 June 1993, 'Rebecca Tallon – I was always a natural born woman inside'; *Sunday Independent,* 24 April 1994, 'You need to go abroad to have it off'; *Evening Herald,* 8 February 1995, 'Anger at cost of sex swaps'; *Irish Independent,* 10 March 1995, 'We are sending men to Britain for sex changes'. 24 *Evening Herald,* 1 October 1994, 'Men in dresses'.

TRANSGENDER EQUALITY NETWORK IRELAND

In 2003, Transgender Equality Network Ireland (TENI) was mentioned for the first time in the media by Diane Hughes, although no organisation had been set up yet. TENI was eventually founded in 2004, following the publication of the Nexus Report on access to healthcare for transgender people.[25] The founding members were Lynda Sheridan, Nik Krievenko, Diane Hughes, Sara Jane Cromwell, Kyra, and Catherine from Waterford. By 2005, many of its founders had left and Sara Jane Cromwell attempted to re-energise the organisation and approached the newly formed Trans Peer Support Group in Dublin. In April 2006, TENI was reformed as we know it today.[26] More and more trans people were able to stand up and support campaigns for equality, for our human rights. TENI became a well organised and effective group seeking to improve conditions and advance the rights and equality of trans people and their families and soon began to make its presence felt.[27] Their focus, in the beginning, was to provide support throughout the country and advocate for the improvement of healthcare services. Over the past number of years, the trans community has become more empowered, more visible, and more active. The demographic of our community has swung from middle age to young adults. As society listens to more of our stories, starts to understand and accept us, many more trans people find the courage to present themselves to the world. And now with the support of their families, friends, schools and work colleagues but also with the support of each other.

By 2008, TENI had started to make inroads into changing Irish societal attitudes. In 2008, they hosted, along with Sara Cromwell, a healthcare symposium in the Mansion House, Dublin, inviting the key healthcare providers and the then Minister for Health, Mary Harney, to provide the keynote speech.[28] Niall Crowley, then chief executive of the Equality Authority, told the meeting that 'a report by his authority in 2004 highlighted the fact that "policy and practice" in meeting the needs of transsexual people is underdeveloped'.[29] They followed this up on 17–18 April 2009 with Transforming Attitudes – a Transgender Human Rights Conference and Educational Seminar in the Law Society of Ireland. The European Council Commissioner for Human Rights, Thomas Hammarberg, provided a video address. In 2010, with funding support from Atlantic Philanthropies, a privately funded foundation which funded health, social, and politically left-leaning public policy causes in Ireland, TENI

25 Eoin Collins and Brian Sheehan (eds), *Access to health services for transsexual people* (Dublin, 2004).
26 Transgender Equality Network Ireland (TENI), https://teni.ie/, accessed 22 February 2024.
27 *'A story of great human proportions'*, p. 19. 28 *Irish Times*, 21 February 2008, 'Transsexual says healthcare is lacking'. 29 Ibid.

became an NGO. This provided an opportunity to build on a platform to educate politicians, the wider public, families, schools, and employers to be more inclusive. TENI, with the support of its allies, could educate government to provide the appropriate services and enact legislation that spoke to the needs of the trans community, legislation that was based on self-determination.

GENDER RECOGNITION

Despite, in 2007, having been declared in contravention of the European Convention on Human Rights, by not providing a mechanism by which transgender people could access recognition, the state appealed the decision to the High Court. However, in October 2009, it dropped the appeal and the Fianna Fáil and Green Party coalition government included in their Programme for Government the sentence, 'we will introduce legal recognition of the acquired gender of transsexuals'.[30] In May 2010, the government set up a Gender Recognition Advisory Group (GRAG) to advise the Minister of Social Protection. This was a group which consisted mainly of civil servants and without any trans representation. The GRAG invited submissions from the public and held meetings with Free Legal Aid Centres (FLAC), TENI, the Irish Human Rights Commission, the Equality Authority, and other interested organisations. In April 2011, after a four-year battle, trans woman and TENI board member, Louise Hannon, won a landmark legal case. Having been dismissed from her employment with First Direct Logistics, Louise took a case to the Equality Tribunal for unfair dismissal. An important precedent had been set in recognising the inclusion of transgender people under the gender ground of equality legislation.[31]

While the GRAG was commissioned in early 2010, their report was not published until July 2011. For the community, it was very disappointing. It did call for gender recognition legislation and, while advising against making gender reassignment surgery a pre-condition for recognition, it proposed a psychiatric diagnosis of 'gender identity disorder' as a basic condition for recognition, despite it being an out-dated term.[32] It also proposed that married trans people must divorce before they could be recognised in their acquired gender – to avoid the possibility of having same-sex marriages.[33] In 2013, two private members bills were lodged in the Irish parliament, the first by Sinn Féin TD, Aengus

30 *'A story of great human proportions'*, p. 11. 31 *Hannon v. First Direct Logistics*, Equality Tribunal of Ireland (29 March 2011). See *'A story of great human proportions'*, p. 51. 32 *International Classification of Diseases 10*, 2013 (approved in 2011). 33 Report of the Gender Recognition Advisory Group to Minister for Social Protection, Joan Burton, 15 June 2011, pp 63–4.

Ó Snodaigh,[34] and the second by then Senator Katherine Zappone.[35] Both these bills set self-determination at their heart. Both also included a process for under 18s. By October 2013, the government through Tánaiste (Deputy Prime Minister) and Minister for Social Protection, Joan Burton, created the heads of Bill and sent it to the Committee for Education and Social Protection for consideration. The committee held public hearings where, unlike during the GRAG hearings, TENI brought together the community, allies in the LGBT community, interested groups and legal experts. All spoke with a unified voice. TENI's lobbying campaign continued throughout 2014, meeting with politicians and civil servants. TENI's campaign 'Positive Visibility Matters' provided a platform for more and more diverse trans voices to be heard. TENI's videos, 'I Am – Positive Visibility Matters' and 'Gender Recognition Matters', had a significant impact.[36] The government received official complaints from the EU Commissioner of Human Rights, Nils Muižnieks, for its lack of movement on the issues, and Amnesty International launched its report 'The State decides who I am' in February 2014, bringing further pressure on government.[37]

Upon the launch of the Bill at the end of 2014, Tánaiste Joan Burton handed responsibility for the legislation to Minister for State, Kevin Humphries. In early 2015 the government brought the legislation to the Houses of the Oireachtas (parliament). The bill eventually passed all stages in the Seanad, disappointingly with only one change, that of a two-year review. By the time it came to the Dáil, TENI had stepped up its campaign. In the space of five days, they contacted, phoned, or met with over 50% of Dáil deputies. In the end 27 deputies, from all parties including both Labour and Fine Gael, informed Minister Humphries of the changes that the trans community were demanding. Having listened to the community and educated themselves, and with very little opposition, the opportunity for the government to do the right thing arose with the passing of the Marriage Equality Referendum in May 2015. With the removal of the divorce clause, the government went one step further and fulfilled the trans community dream of self-determination. Despite being such a progressive act, the Gender Recognition Act 2015 is far from perfect. Currently the Act does not recognise under 16s, non-binary identities and the system is quite onerous for

34 Gender Recognition 2013, Sinn Fein TD Aengus O'Snodaigh, https://www.youtube.com/watch?v=1KstbPsSkrI, accessed 22 February 2024. 35 Gender Recognition 2013, Independent Senator Katherine Zappone, https://www.pila.ie/resources/case-studies/teni-flac-gender-recognition-in-ireland/, accessed 22 February 2024. 36 'I Am – Positive Visibility Matters', https://www.youtube.com/watch?v=OkdVbbr407k, accessed 22 February 2024. 37 'Europe: the state decides who I am: lack of legal gender recognition for transgender people in Europe', Amnesty International. This report included Ireland. https://www.amnesty.org/en/documents/eur01/001/2014/en/accessed 17 November 2023.

16- and 17-year-olds. In 2018, the Act was reviewed by a cross section of departmental representatives, children's experts and representatives of the trans and LGBT communities. However, to date, none of the legislative recommendations have been implemented.[38] In the aftermath of Gender Recognition 2015 and Marriage Equality 2015, we have seen an increase in those coming out. We have, however, also experienced a collapse of our adolescent healthcare services and, with more individuals on the waiting list, there has been an increase in the disrespectful and restrictive nature of our adult healthcare service. Both online social media and mainstream media are creating an environment where it is no longer safe to be trans in Ireland. Globally, we have never been so visible and yet more in danger. We have returned to Janice Raymond's 'the problem of transsexualism would best be served by morally mandating it out of existence'.[39] And more recently, with anti-trans activist Helen Joyce, author of *Trans: when ideology meets reality* (2021), stating that 'the fewer of those people there are, the better, in a sane world that I hope we will reach', trans activism has never been more necessary.[40]

Today, on the internet, especially social media, we experience the huge gap between those who espouse trans rights and those who oppose them. The reasonable, respectful discussions of the middle is cast to the extremes. There are people who misbehave on both sides. Those who refuse to respect people's identity, pronouns and consistently dogpile when a trans person, any trans person, puts their head above the parapet. And on the other side, we see trans activists who behave in despicable ways also, through violent threats and sexual commentary. This does nothing for the advancement of trans rights, the education of the wider public and the understanding of the trans community's needs. It also drowns out those of us who continue to engage and explain and educate on what it means to be trans. The need to fight back, having been constantly attacked, treated with disrespect, and marginalised, is understandable, but we now need to find a new approach, for our allies to step into the breach and elevate trans voices. I am reminded of Michael Dillon's words 'transsexuals have the most difficult life of all, for they cannot conceal their forms from curious eyes'.[41]

38 The Review of the Gender Recognition Act 2015, Report to the Minister for Social Protection, Regina Doherty, 2018; Committee chaired by Moninne Griffith, https://www.gov.ie/en/press-release/43aef0–minister-doherty-publishes-her-report-on-the-review-of-the-gender-re/, accessed 12 October 2023. 39 Janice Raymond, *The transsexual empire: the making of the she-male* (Boston, 1979), p. 178. 40 In an online discussion with gender critical activist Helen Staniland, Joyce stated that trans people were 'damaged' and 'the fewer of those people there are, the better, in a sane world that I hope we will reach', May 2023, https://www.thedailybeast.com/happy-pride-month-trans-people-are-just-trying-to-survive-it, accessed 30 May 2023. 41 Dillon, *Self*, p. 51.

REFLECTIONS ON RESEARCH

Sonja Tiernan reminds us 'that documenting the history of transsexuality is fraught with problems and primary source material is limited'.[42] The sacking of Magnus Hirschfeld's Institute of Sexology, in Berlin, on 6 May 1933, saw the destruction of countless scientific research papers into both healthcare and transition procedures for trans people. This was a huge loss to constructing trans histories. However, widening the language and understanding of gender variance opens more source material to research and allows us to examine histories through the language of the time rather than the current discourse. Throughout history medical expectations on trans people insisted upon assimilating to the gender of transition, moving from one box to the other, resulting in individuals living with a secret and, for many, the need to live in stealth. Websites such as 'Zagria blogspot – A Gender Variance Who's Who' provide extensive data and research on examples of gender variance in history.[43]

Simon Joyce, in his paper, 'Two women walk into a theatre bathroom – the Fanny and Stella trials as a trans narrative,[44] suggests that current discourse 'misreads the historical record' in which people like Fanny and Stella have persistently risked being misidentified on the basis of a diminished understanding of gender identity.[45] Reopening the archive to new scrutiny might be a helpful first step in rethinking a broad LGBT+ alliance, the terms of which have been under-theorised and often poorly articulated. Politically, then, it is crucial to document precursor moments like theirs to forestall conservative objections that the legal discussion of transgender rights is entirely uncharted territory; in this sense, the simple recognition that public discussions of bathroom use or the correct gender pronouns to use in legal cases have occurred before gives weight to the idea, enshrined in a web series documenting trans people in history, that 'We've Been Around'. He further theorises 'the possibilities of a genealogical trans history becoming imaginable once we loosen the presumed connection between figures like Fanny and Stella and the larger narratives of gay male historiography'.[46] What is most interesting about Joyce's theories is that it is possible to trace a link between his thinking and more recent

42 Tiernan, 'It should not be so easy to construct a man', p. 56. 43 'A gender variance who's who: essays on trans, intersex, cis and other persons and topics from a trans perspective … All human life is here', https://zagria.blogspot.com/, accessed 11 October 2023. 44 Simon Joyce, 'Two women walk into a theatre bathroom: the Fanny and Stella trials as trans narrative', *Victorian Review*, 44:1 (Spring 2018), pp 83–98. 45 In London in 1870 Ernest 'Stella' Boulton and Frederick 'Fanny' Park were arrested, charged with 'conspiring and inciting persons to commit an unnatural offence'. Both were wearing women's clothing; 'Women personators – The 1871 trial of Boulton and Park', https://blog.britishnewspaperarchive.co.uk/2020/05/29/the-1871–trial-of-boulton-and-park/ accessed 9 October 2023. 46 Joyce, 'Two women walk into a theatre bathroom', p. 93.

treatment of the trans community, especially trans women. This idea that trans women are purely men 'pretending' to be women and to be successful at it, you need to be, in the medics reasoning, stereotypically, the gender you assume. In the nineteenth century, young trans women were considered to be gay men dressing up to lure other men, and that trans women needed to assume ultimate femininity to be really women. In 1979, the Harry Benjamin International Gender Dysphoria Association,[47] consisting of therapists and psychologists, devised a set of Standards of Care (SOC) for the treatment of gender dysphoria, largely based on Benjamin's cases and studies. These standards of care were heavily influenced by similar theories. Throughout my many assessments by psychiatrists, psychologists, counsellors, every report started with a description of how I presented; whether I could assimilate, whether I could pass. This was an assessment of how I could fit into the social norms of the gender binary. I was very aware of this from the early stages of coming out. 'The more you can look and behave like a woman the more successful you will be in your gender identity' one male psychiatrist said to me in 1992. What did that even mean, a need to fulfil the stereotypically understanding of a man as to what it is to be a woman, all make-up, dresses, and heels? During another assessment in 1997, I was given a booklet, 'Feminine deportment training manual – an instructional course for every aspiring feminine lady', to consider guiding my assimilation. To be the 'perfect woman.'

GENDER IDENTITY AND SEX

Identity is a fundamental core of who we are, whether it is nationality, race, religion, or gender. And to assert the demand to be respected for your identity is a brave and sometimes dangerous thing to do. It certainly leaves one open to criticism, abuse, and possible attack. In an interview with the BBC in 1975 about her book *Conundrum* Jan Morris explains the differences between sex and gender:

> there seems to be no problem defining sex. There are several very well accepted criteria of what sex a person is. There's anatomical sex, there's nuclear sex, there's psychological sex, and there is another one that I've momentarily forgotten. But nobody has really ever defined what gender is, whether you are masculine or feminine. It is quite a different matter altogether. It is the way you move and feel and think and respond. For me

47 The Harry Benjamin International Gender Dysphoria Association, now known as the World Professional Association for Transgender Healthcare (WPATH).

> it is in some way related to the idea, not only of self but even of soul. I think it's a mysterious thing. But that does not make a conviction of gender any less real or any less forceful than the certainty of sex.[48]

However, having been subjected to a barrage of questions on another BBC talk show by several people, she informed them that it was 'arrogant to assume anyone could know what anyone else might feel like. The transexual experience was an inner-music and a quest towards a new reality'.[49] This view clearly understands that when examining histories, we cannot examine it through a present-day lens. In the past, language and opportunity were very different, society was very different. Although we know that many women lived lives presenting as men for economical, educational and advancement purposes, we cannot make assumptions that all individuals did. Whether Dr James Barry identified as male or not, he clearly wanted his life and legacy to remain so, even in death. We should afford him that respect.

However, there is a need to ensure that social causes and heroes like Dr Lydia Foy are documented and remembered, and for the trans community, we must pledge to keep this story alive in the minds of young people, so they know the struggle that has gone before. Having given her life, in a such very personal way to the campaign, Lydia eloquently stated: 'Though I will not let it dominate my life, the facts remain with the scars. The process was much too long – I am now 70 and this struggle has taken up nearly a third of my life!'[50] We should remember the words of Justice McKechnie's judgment in the Foy case in 2007:

> Together with human freedom, a person subject, subject to the acquired rights of others, should be free to shape his personality in the way best suited to his person and to his life.[51]

48 BBC Archive – On this Day 1975 – Jan Morris talked about her autobiography *Conundrum*, https://www.facebook.com/watch/?v=514100019637564, accessed 10 November 2023. 49 Ibid. 50 FLAC, 'A story of great human proportions', p. 38. 51 'Lydia Foy v. Ireland 2007', *GCN*, https://magazine.gcn.ie/articles/164160?article=44–1, accessed 21 November 2023.

Afterword – the lost and not found

Maria Luddy

In November 1935 Patrick Lynch was tried for the murder of Bernard Sheridan, near Kinnegad, Co. Westmeath, on 23 June in the same year. Murder cases, particularly those related to family concerns, can be a very useful way to examine the relationships and interaction of members of that family with each other and their relationship to the wider community. This particular murder provides us with some indication as to how shame worked in a rural Irish society in the mid-1930s. After the shooting Lynch went to the local Garda station and handed in a revolver stating 'I am after shooting Sheridan beyond in Hughes's yard. There is the weapon'. He continued, 'I can't stand it any longer – bringing a man's family into disgrace – I don't care what happens to me now.'[1]

In court Lynch was presented as a hard-working man, assiduous in the support of his family. He, and his wife, had eight children. He had enlisted in the British army in 1915 and had left it physically debilitated, spending months in hospital afterwards, and with a pension of 26*s.* 6*d.* per week. Once his health recovered he set himself up as a house painter, and as his physical health improved he bought a bicycle so that when the painting trade was slack he could go out and find work as a farm labourer. Indeed, his defence asked, 'Could the Free State produce a picture of family life more favourable than that given in this case?' And yet, the defence asked what had brought such a man to court to face a murder charge. The fault was laid at the feet of the state which had not 'received the protective legislation for its children and girls that it should have received'.[2] The Democratic Programme of the first Dáil in 1919 had placed the care of children 'as the first duty of the republic'. That aspiration fell by the wayside. By 1937 the protection of 'the family' had taken precedence, but that concept had little to do with protecting individual children within a family.

1 For reports of the case in the press see, *Irish Press*, 15 November 1935, *Drogheda Independent*, 30 November 1935, *Leitrim Observer*, 16 November 1935, *Meath Chronicle*, 16, 23 November 1935. For the court documents see Central Criminal Court/State Files at Central Criminal Court, Waterford 1934, National Archives of Ireland. 2 This is not strictly the case as under the Criminal Law Amendment Act of 1885, which still applied in Ireland until 1935, it was an offence to have, or attempt to have, carnal knowledge of a girl between 13 and 16 years. See Thomas O'Malley, *Sexual offences* (Dublin, 2013, 2nd ed.), p. 118.

During the trial some details of what had happened to bring shame on the family were revealed. Lynch's 14-year-old daughter had gone into employment as a domestic servant with Sheridan and his mother, and, as was the fate of many hundreds of Irish girls in the same situation, he had 'seduced' her, which was often a euphemism for rape. She became pregnant. She had been sent home by her employer around 14 June, but the girl herself did not understand that she was pregnant.

In his statement to the Gardaí, Lynch said that he had been working for the local parish priest on 15 June and after his conversation with the priest, he suspected that his daughter was pregnant. So it appears that the cleric was aware of the girl's condition before her family was. When he returned home he questioned his daughter as to why she had left her employment and she informed him that Mrs Sheridan had been 'fighting with her' for some time and would not let her work. The father pressed her further and asked her if the son 'had ever done anything to her', and she replied 'he had'. When asked how often this had occurred she said 'a whole lot of times, in the bedroom and in the dining room' and usually on a Sunday when his mother was at Mass. When Sheridan discovered the girl was pregnant he told her that when he went to the fair in Mullingar he would get her medicine 'that would leave her alright'.[3] He did not do so. Her father made the decision that she must 'go away'. A couple of days later her mother brought her to the County Home and 'left her there'.[4] She gave birth on 11 August 1935.

Lynch had been brooding on the matter for about eight days before he shot Sheridan. He believed that his family had been disgraced and that it had been shamed. Lynch also believed that he, and his eldest son, would no longer be able to get employment in the area because of what had happened to his daughter. But Lynch and his family had the support of the local community, and it is evident that though Lynch wanted his daughter away from the area, her 'secret' or the family's shame was widely known in the community. Indeed, the defence stated they were not calling for any evidence as 'the atmosphere of that court was teeming with sympathy for the man in the dock'.[5] For Lynch, issues of family honour, respectabilty, shame and humiliation were enmeshed in his response to his daughter's condition. While he had made a complaint to the

3 No one has studied the full extent of abortions in twentieth-century Ireland and the ways in which men and women had knowledge of how to bring about a miscarriage. Cara Delay notes that thirty-three illegal abortion cases came to court in the south of Ireland between 1900 and 1950. Cara Delay, 'Pills, potions and purgatives: women and abortion methods in Ireland, 1900–1950', *Women's History Review*, 28:3 (2019), pp 479–99. 4 Statement of Patrick Lynch, 21 June 1935 in Central Criminal Court/State Files at Central Criminal Court, Waterford [sic] 1934, NAI. 5 *Meath Chronicle*, 23 November 1935.

Gardaí on 21 June about what had happened to his daughter, it is unclear whether the case was to be followed up and Sheridan prosecuted. If it had been, and the accused denied the charges, then the matter could have come to court and the details of what had happened would come to light. That would have been a very public forum for such a sensitive issue to Lynch's family. Instead, Lynch took matters into his own hands. He shot Sheridan in front of a number of witnesses. For Lynch, the shame of what had happened to his daughter was traumatic. We hear nothing in this case of how his daughter reacted or if she even knew what had been happening to her in Sheridan's house. She certainly did not understand that she was pregnant when she returned home. It is not clear either how her mother felt about the events that had occurred. The authority of the father in this household over his wife and children gave him a very particular power; it was he who made the decision to send the girl away, it was he who decided what revenge he would inflict. He believed that his manly duty was to support and protect his family, and in this situation he could not let the man who had ruined his family's reputation live.

William Carrigan, as Lynch's defence counsel, argued that if the father had come upon Sheridan interfering with his daughter, then Sheridan would be committing a felony, and as the law stood, to protect his wife and children the father could shoot a felon 'out of hand' to prevent the crime. Instead then of the case being one of murder, it would be considered as justifiable homicide. Carrigan further stated that when the girl went to work for the family in 1934 there was no 'Statute passed, which in fact had since been passed, that would have protected her'.[6] Carrigan had been appointed chair of a committee in 1931 to investigate sexual crimes in Ireland.[7] He was aware that cases of illegitimacy and outrages against children had been increasing year by year since the foundation of the state. He wanted the jury to be alert to this context and no doubt to judge Lynch's actions from that perspective.

The prosecution, on the part of the state, was adamant that the jury could not and must not return a verdict of innocence, nor indeed should they return a verdict of manslaughter. That, they argued, would suggest to any man with a grievance against another that it was reasonable to go out and shoot that individual. But it was clear from the trial reports that the judge, Mr Justice

6 The Criminal Law Amendment Act was passed in 1935. It raised the age of consent to 17 years in cases of carnal knowledge cases. 7 The committee's report, known as the Carrigan report, was never published though a number of clerics were given the report for consideration. The Revd Michael Browne of Maynooth noted that the report should not be published as it would show the public that 'religion has failed to neutralise the aphrodisiac influence of cinema, drama and literature to a great number of young people'. Revd M.J. Browne to Geoghegan, 13 November 1932, Department of Justice, H247/41B NAI.

Meredith, was in favour of a manslaughter charge. The judge directed the jury to consider 'what was the effect of the provocation on the mind of the accused at the time he committed the offence?'[8] The jury was absent for an hour and a quarter and returned with a verdict of guilty of manslaughter. The judge sentenced Lynch to three years' penal servitude believing it to be a severe sentence. He took into consideration the extreme provocation that there was in this case and 'the whole life and character of the defendant'.[9]

The perspective of this story is all from the male view; the father, the lawyers, the jurors, the judge, and even the witnesses, were all men. We hear little of the voice of the daughter, and her mother, and the mother of the victim, remain silent. In our own time, if we look only at the final report of the Commission of Inquiry into Mother and Baby Homes we see that, during the period covered, 1922 to 1998, by the inquiry, there were about 56,000 unmarried mothers and about 57,000 children in the homes they investigated. There were about 25,000 unmarried mothers, with more than that number of children, in the county homes not investigated.[10] Lynch's daughter was one of these girls. It is difficult to comprehend such numbers. The majority of women who entered institutions or county homes had no voice, and while the country's shameful history of the abuse of women and children has been aired, many of the survivors still feel they have not been listened to.

The results of these various commissions of inquiry into child sexual abuse, Magdalene asylums and mother and baby homes have thrown up challenges as to how we view Irish history in the twentieth century and the place of women and children in that society. The essays in this collection are linked by the varying ways relationships of power and dominance have shaped Irish society. The history of Irish women in the twentieth century reveals how the ideals of the state, and the Church, shaped the laws of the country to arrange how intimacy was organised in everyday life. From the foundation of the state there was considerable discussion of sexuality in Ireland. The published and unpublished reports of the various investigative committees raised concerns about reading material, films, illegitimacy, unmarried mothers, the apparent spread of venereal diseases, prostitution, levels of sexual crime, deviancy, and the dangers of sociability, particularly reflected in dance halls and the motor car, which appeared to offer possibilities for unrestricted mixing of the sexes.[11]

8 *Meath Chronicle*, 23 November 1935. 9 Ibid. 10 Government of Ireland's Department of Children Equality, Disability, Integration and Youth, *Final report of the commission of investigation into mother and baby homes*, 12 January 2021, available at https://www.gov.ie/en/publication/d4b3d-final-report-of-the-commission-of-investigation-into-mother-and-baby-homes/. 11 Within the sphere of government the printed, but unpublished, 'Report of the inter-departmental committee of inquiry regarding venereal disease' (1926), and the 'Report of the committee on the Criminal

Throughout the 1920s and 1930s there was in essence a moral panic about the perceived sexual immorality evident in the country. Earthy newspaper accounts of sexual crime, the extensive publication of clerical sermons and pamphlets about immorality, and about the dangers of sex, reinforced public concern about sexual morality.[12] The censorship of films act came into force in 1923, and the censorship of publications act in 1929. Both the state and the Church emphatically presented women's place as being in the home and the ideal role of the Irish woman was as mother. But the unmarried mother was a problem that could only be dealt with in an institution.

As many of the essays in this collection reveal, there was concern with the female body at work, and in public life, the emigrant body and the maternal body, particularly in its unmarried condition. The real threat to chastity and sexual morality resided in the bodies of women. Conservative views were tightly held on these issues and shaped how the law evolved in relation to its interaction with female bodies. Many feminists resisted received opinion on women's place in society from the foundation of the state but it was only from the 1970s that success in changing attitudes and the law began to be successful. Not only were female bodies dangerous but also from the foundation of the state women's citizenship was harnessed to fit the moral judgments of Church and state. Restrictions were placed on women's duties as citizens, seen especially in limitations relating to jury service from the late 1920s.[13] The same also happened in relation to women's employment. Alice Kessler Harris argues that most white American men and women shared what she called a 'gendered imaginary' relating to gender, work, family, and rights. In this mindset men were rights-bearing individuals and one of the rights that marked them as men was the right to work. Women, on the other hand, were defined not as persons, but as family members.[14] Their waged work was seen as a family necessity, not individual right. Such views were also held in Ireland.

The right to work, however, did remain a central point of importance to women trade unionists and to women political activists from the foundation of the Free State. Attempts to restrict women's access to employment were strongly

Law Amendment Acts (1880–85) and Juvenile Prostitution (1931)', known as the Carrigan committee report, offer extensive and complex accounts of perceived sexual activity throughout the country and the fears raised by that activity. Other publications include the *Report of the committee on evil literature* (1927) and the *Report of the commission on the relief of the sick and destitute poor* (1927). The Inter-Departmental Ad-Hoc Committee on the Suppression of Prostitution (1947–8), which was again unpublished, provides much information on the 1920s and 1930s. 12 See, for instance, *Irish Times*, 23 April 1931; *Irish Independent*, 24 March 1931; *Evening Herald*, 3 March 1931. 13 Maryann Gialanella Valiulis, 'Defining their role in the new state: Irishwomen's protest against juries act of 1927', *Canadian Journal of Irish Studies*, 18:1 (July 1992), pp 43–60. 14 Alice Kessler-Harris, *In pursuit of equity: women, men and the quest for economic citizenship in 20th century America* (Oxford, US, resisted by women activists. Important campaigns were instigated around the Civil Service Amendment Bill (1924), the Marriage Bar, the Conditions of Employment Bill (1935) and the campaign against the draft Constitution of 1937. Much of women's political activism in the 1920s and 1930s was informed by their understanding of both the 1916 Proclamation and certain articles in the 1922 Constitution. From the 1916 Proclamation the phrase, 'The Republic guarantees religious and civil liberty, equal rights and equal opportunities to all its citizens …', was the standard against which government policy, particularly where it affected women, was measured. Article 3 of the 1922 Constitution, which guaranteed equality to all Irish citizens, strengthened the position outlined in the Proclamation.[15] The simple promise of equality found in these documents held more resonance for women activists than any of the rhetoric of the suffrage campaign, which did not argue for the equality of all women. The Proclamation and the 1922 Constitution gave women activists the power to protest against the discursive construction prevalent in Irish society that all women, whatever their marital status, and whether they were mothers or not, were enmeshed in traditional families.

This collection brings further attention to the political, economic and social significance of the female body in Irish society and culture. It reveals pioneering work on lesbian women in Ireland in the revolutionary period, and later, and the challenges around the archives of those who do not 'fit'. It brings to light activism in the Lesbian community in Cork and explores in particular the creation of the Cork LGBT Archive and the Irish Trans Archive. There is a rich potential within these archives for the study of sexualities and activism in Ireland.

Researchers are all too aware of the great difficulties that have arisen with access to documents used by the various commissions since the 1990s. Indeed, all these documents are closed to researchers. Legal experts, historians and campaigners have fought for the retention of these records and access to them by the individuals who suffered in these various institutions. Those battles continue. The importance of archives cannot be over emphasised.

In the case of Patrick Lynch there is an archival record, but that record gives little voice to his daughter, and no voice at all to his wife, both of whom were part of the unfolding events. But at least they are there. What happens when we have no archives or access to archives? When archives are missing or lost then people are lost too. And the absence of archives brings me to a much more

2003). 15 Article 3 stated that all Irish citizens 'shall within the limits of the jurisdiction of the Irish Free State (Saorstát Éireann) enjoy the privileges and be subject to the obligations of such citizenship'.

personal story. This is another version of shame and its implications within a family. It is a story that never became public in the way that the Lynch story did. But shame was at its centre in a way that the family could and did control.

St Finbarr's Hospital in Cork city was a former workhouse which opened in 1841. The Sisters of Mercy took up nursing duties there in 1871, as they had in a number of other workhouse hospitals around the country. From 1898 the hospital was known as the Cork District Hospital. With the establishment of the Irish Free State the hospital became known as the Cork County Home and Hospital and was responsible for the treatment of medical, surgical and maternity cases, and cases of infectious and contagious diseases.[16]

My paternal aunt was born in county Cork in 1909, the eldest in a family of what would be five children. Her father was a farm labourer. My aunt, whom I never met, passed away in St Finbarr's Hospital in 2002, aged 93 years. She was in her mid-thirties when she went in and had spent 58 years in the hospital. In 2011, I became interested in trying to discover why my aunt had been left in the hospital and under what conditions she had entered it. I knew little of her situation as my father, her brother, never spoke of her but he did disappear once a year on a trip to Cork, which we later discovered was to visit 'Maggie'. Another aunt and cousins also visited her a couple of times a year. My mother did not know of Maggie's existence until about fifteen years into her marriage when an 'American' aunt, Maggie's sister, came home and mentioned Maggie to my mother. My mother never discussed Maggie with my father, and neither did any of his children. We knew when not to ask questions. The only people who had a fragment of information were my cousins and even they knew little. The story they told was that Maggie had been in the Blitz in London and when she came home in the early 1940s took to wandering the roads at night around her family home. By the mid-1940s she had been placed in St Finbarr's by her mother, a formidable woman, and perhaps another member of her immediate family. She never came out.

When she went into the hospital it was considered a county home and many county homes took in ill individuals, chronic cases and looked after the elderly. Perhaps she was ill, but she certainly wasn't elderly. But what illness could keep her there for so long? If she was mentally disturbed why was she not sent to, for example, the Cork District Mental Hospital? The county home also took in unmarried mothers but there is no evidence at all that Maggie was an unmarried mother. If she were, she would more than likely have been sent to the now notorious Bessborough mother and baby home.[17]

16 Sr M. Emmanuel Browne, *A tale of two hospitals, St Finbarr's Hospital/regional hospital* (Cork, *c.*1990).
17 'Survey of hospital archives in Ireland', funded by the Wellcome Trust and undertaken by the

I sent in a Freedom of Information request in August 2011 and it was early October 2011 before any information was forthcoming. I was asked if someone could call me about the case. This happened later in October, and I then discovered that there were no files or written information available relating to my aunt, and the only records the hospital had referred to her final illness when she was an actual patient in the hospital. There were, I was told, one or two elderly women who vaguely remembered Maggie but no one could say why she had been sent to the hospital in the first place. There was not even a record marking her entry. She had received no treatment, there were no case notes and there was nothing, except perhaps any member of her family refusing to take her out, to keep her in the hospital. Apparently, according to the information given to me over the phone, she had a small room in the hospital, and she did a little bit of cleaning around the wards, but was never actually employed by the hospital. The authorities were apologetic that they were not able to tell me more. They just did not have the information. I felt the caller's anxiety and perhaps she thought I was going to make this a very difficult call, but I accepted what was said and am still wondering to this day how someone could have been incarcerated for so long without any record being kept or any information being known of her condition. I do recall my cousin telling me that whenever she went to visit Maggie a lot of the conversation was taken up with Maggie's desire to leave the hospital and to live with a member of her immediate family. That was never to be an option. No one was prepared to look after her. Neither did I ever visit her, and I never considered taking her out. She left the hospital only in a coffin. She was buried in the town nearest to her place of birth, no notice was put in the paper and no one, except my cousin who organised the funeral, knew of her burial.

As a historian who has spent decades working in historical archives I consider myself pretty good at ferreting out information, but this case has me completely lost. No members of Maggie's immediate family are still alive, so there is no one left who knows the reason for the hospitalisation. The family knowledge on Maggie is limited almost to what I have noted above. We cannot even speculate as St Finbarr's was such an odd place for her to have lived for so long. The hospital did have long-stay 'welfare cases' who resided in St Mary's Block, part of the old workhouse, but to be there for 58 years seems incomprehensible.[18] There is no doubt that such a long incarceration must have led Maggie to become institutionalised. And yet, while her circumstances might

National Archives, available at https://www.nationalarchives.ie/wp-content/uploads/2019/03/PRF_106780_SURVEY_OF_HOSPITAL_BOOK_V7.pdf (accessed 22 Mar. 2024), pp 18–22.
18 Browne, *A tale of two hospitals*. For a superb analysis of unmarried motherhood and family secrets see Clair Wills, *Missing persons, or, My grandmother's secrets* (London, 2024).

seem odd, Maggie is also one of the thousands of Irish women who, in the twentieth century, were retained for decades in an institution, and were not allowed to have an ordinary life. This case may be a little different as the institution is not one in which we would expect to find a woman who could not leave. Her story, though we know little of it, forms part of that history of lost Irish women. I fear Lynch's daughter was also lost.

From its foundation the state found its way into intimate life, through family and employment law to criminal law. Limits were placed on reproductive autonomy and contraception. The state and Church have profoundly, often with the willing consent of the population, structured realms of desire, sexual practice, punishment, domestic life, the life of work and politics and the regulation of sexuality and gender. They embedded shame in Irish families and individuals whose lives were subsequently circumscribed by that emotion. Only conformity and secrecy mattered and there were things that were not allowed to be spoken of to anyone outside the family. It took decades to unravel much of the legislation that governed women's lives and their citizenship rights from the foundation of the state. That unravelling allowed many women to hear their own voices. It took decades for women to be heard; the process of recovering their voices is still ongoing and it may take decades more before it is complete.

Select bibliography

A People's Democracy Pamphlet, *No more chains: why you should oppose the constitutional ban on abortion* (Belfast and Dublin, 1983).

Aitken, Jo, 'The horrors of matrimony among the masses: feminist representations of wife beating in England and Australia, 1870–1914', *Journal of Women's History*, 19:4 (2007).

Aretxaga, Begoña, 'The sexual games of the body politic: fantasy and state violence in Northern Ireland', *Culture, Medicine and Psychiatry*, 25:1 (2001).

Ashe, Fidelma, 'The virgin Mary connection: reflecting on feminism and Northern Irish politics', *Critical Review of International Social and Political Philosophy*, 9:4 (2006).

Astley Cooper, J.W., 'The care and control of inebriate men', *The British Journal of Inebriety*, 11:4 (April 1914).

Bacik, Ivana, 'Legislating for article 40.3.3°', *Irish Journal of Legal Studies*, 3:3 (2013).

Barton, Alana, 'Wayward girls and wicked women: two centuries of "semi-penal" control', *Liverpool Law Review*, 22 (2000).

Barry, Ursula and Clair Wills, 'The Republic of Ireland: the politics of sexuality 1965–2000' in Bourke et al. (eds), *The Field Day anthology of Irish writing: volume 5: Irish women's writing and traditions* (Cork, 2002).

Bennett, Judith M.,'"Lesbian-like" and the social history of lesbianism', *Journal of the History of Sexuality*, 9 (2000).

Bidwell, Emma, 'Where have all the dungarees gone?', *Irish Journal of Feminist Studies*, 2:1; Special issue: aspects of Irish feminism, ed. Dolores Dooley and Liz Steiner-Scot (Cork, 1997).

Boland, Rosita, 'Death at the grotto', *Irish Times*, 31 January 2004, http://www.irishtimes.com/news/death-at-the-grotto-1.1304620.

Brady, Evelyn, Eva Patterson, Kate McKinney, Rosie Hamill and Pauline Jackson, *The footsteps of Anne: stories of republican women ex-prisoners* (Belfast, 2011).

Branthwaite, R.W., 'Inebriety: its causation and control', *The British Journal of Inebriety*, 5:3 (January 1908).

Breathnach, Micheál, 'A notable centenary II', *The Irish Monthly*, 827 (1942).

Bretherton, George, 'Irish inebriate reformatories, 1899–1920: a small experiment in coercion', *Contemporary Drug Problems*, 13 (1986).

Burrows, Simon, Jonathan Conlin, Russell Goulbourne and Valerie Mainz (eds), *The chevalier d'Eon and his worlds: gender, espionage and politics in the eighteenth century* (London, 2010).

Butler, Judith, *Bodies that matter: on the discursive limits of 'sex'* (New York, 1993).

Cacciaguidi-Fahy, Sophie, 'The substantive issue and the rhetoric of the abortion debate in Ireland' in A. Wagner, T. Summerfield, S.F. Benavides Vanegas (eds), *Contemporary issues of the semiotics of law* (London, 2005).

Carey, Timothy, *Mountjoy: the story of a prison* (Cork, 2000).

Carnegie, Annie and Rachel Roth, 'From the grassroots to the Oireachtas: abortion law reform in the Republic of Ireland', *Health and Human Rights Journal* (2019).

Cockburn, Cynthia, 'The gendered dynamics of armed conflict' in Caroline O. Moser and Fiona C. Clark, *Victims, perpetrators or actors?: gender, armed conflict and political violence* (London, 2001).

Commission of Investigation into Mother and Baby Homes and Certain Related Matters, *Final report* (2021). Available from: https://www.gov.ie/en/publication/d4b3d-final-report-of-the-commission-of-investigation-into-mother-and-baby-homes/.

Collins, Eoin and Brian Sheehan (eds), Nexus Research: 'Access to health services for transsexual people' (Dubin, 2004).

Connolly, Linda, *The Irish women's movement: from revolution to devolution* (Dublin, 2003).

Connolly, Peter, 'The Church in Ireland since Vatican II', *The Furrow*, 30:12 (1979).

Conway, Jill K., Susan C. Bourque and Joan W. Scott, 'Introduction: the concept of gender', *Daedalus*, 116:4 (Fall 1987).

Corcoran, Mary, *Out of order: the political imprisonment of women in Northern Ireland, 1972–1988* (London, 2013).

Cromwell, Sara Jane, *Becoming myself: the true story of Thomas who became Sara* (London, 2008).

Daly, E.D., 'The struggle between the state and the drunkard', *Journal of the Statistical and Social Inquiry Society of Ireland* (February 1897).

d'Arcy, Margaretta, *Tell them everything: a sojourn in the prison of her majesty Queen Elizabeth II at Ard Macha (Armagh)* (London, 1981).

Darcy, Erin, *In her shoes: women of the eighth* (Dublin, 2020).

Davis, Angela Y., *Are prisons obsolete?* (New York, 2011).

De Londras, Fiona and Mairead Enright, *Repealing the 8th: reforming Irish abortion law* (Bristol, 2018).

Dobash, Russell P. and Pat McLaughlin, 'The punishment of women in nineteenth-century Scotland: prisons and inebriate institutions' in Esther Breitenbach and Eleanor Gordon (eds), *Out of bounds: women in Scottish society, 1800–1945* (Edinburgh, 1992).

Dillon, Michael, *Self – a study in ethics and endocrinology* (London, 1946).

Dillon, Michael, *Out of the ordinary, a life of gender and spiritual transitions* (New York, 2017).

Doan, Laura, 'Topsy turvydom: gender inversion, sapphism and the great war', *GLQ: A Journal of Lesbian and Gay Studies*, 12 (2006).

Doan, Laura and Jane Garrity, *Sapphic modernites; sexuality, women and national discourse* (London, 2006).

Dublin Lesbian and Gay Men's Collectives and Women's Community Press, *Out for ourselves: the lives of Irish lesbians and gay men* (Dublin, 1986).

Dunne, Catherine, *An unconsidered people* (Dublin, 2003).

du Preez, Michael and Jeremy Dronfield, *Dr James Barry: a woman ahead of her time* (London, 2016).

Earner-Byrne, Lindsey, '"Moral repatriation": the response to Irish unmarried mothers in Britain, 1920s–1960s' in Patrick Duffy (ed.), *To and from Ireland: planned migration schemes, c.1600–2000* (Dublin, 2004).

Earner-Byrne, Lindsey, *Mother and child: maternity and child welfare in Dublin, 1922–60* (Manchester, 2007).

Egan, Orla and Megan Luddy O'Leary, *Diary of an activist* (Cork, 2022).

Egan, Orla, *Queer republic of Cork* (Cork, 2016).

Enright, Anne, 'Antigone in Galway: Anne Enright on the dishonoured dead' in Katherine O'Donnell, Maeve O'Rourke and James M. Smith (eds), *Redress: Ireland's institutions and transitional justice* (Dublin, 2022).

Enright, Anne, *Making babies: stumbling into motherhood* (London, 2005).

Faludi, Susan, *Backlash: the undeclared war against American women* (New York, 1991).

Faul, Fr Denis and Fr Raymond Murray, *Violations of human rights in Northern Ireland, 1968–1978* (n.d.), pamphlet.

Ferriter, Diarmaid, *Occasions of sin: sex and society in modern Ireland* (London, 2009).

FLAC, *'A story of great human proportions'; Lydia Foy and the struggle for transgender rights in Ireland* (Dublin, 2018).

Flinn, Andrew, 'An attack on professionalism and scholarship? Democratising archives and the production of knowledge', *Ariadne*, 62 (2010).

Foster, Roy, *Vivid faces; the revolutionary generation in Ireland, 1890–1923* (London, 2014).

Gardiner, Frances, 'The women's movement and politicians in the Republic of Ireland, 1980–2000' in Angela Bourke et al. (eds), *The Field Day anthology of Irish writing: volume 5: Irish women's writing and traditions* (Cork, 2002).

Garman, Emma, *A liberated woman: the story of Margaret King* (London, 2016).

Garrett, Paul Michael, 'Excavating the past: mother and baby homes in the Republic of Ireland', *British Journal of Social Work*, 2 (2017).

Gilmartin, Niall and M.M. Scull, 'Republican women and Catholic Church responses to the strip-searching of female prisoners in Northern Ireland, 1982–92', *Women's History Review* (2021).

Girvin, Brian, 'Social change and moral politics: the Irish constitutional referendum 1983', *Political Studies* (1986).

Godfrey, Barry S. and Paul Lawrence, *Crime and justice, 1750–1950* (Devon, 2005).

Gormally, Brian, Kieran McEvoy and David Wall, 'Criminal justice in a divided society: Northern Ireland prisons', *Crime and Justice*, 17 (1993).

Graham, Ann-Marie, 'Unmarried mothers: the legislative context in Ireland, 1921–79' (M.Litt. thesis, National University of Ireland Maynooth, 2012).

Gray, Breda and Louise Ryan, '(Dis)locating "woman" and women in representations of Irish nationality' in Anne Byrne and Madeleine Leonard (eds), *Women and Irish society* (Belfast, 1997).

Hammerton, A. James, *Cruelty and companionship: conflict in nineteenth-century married life* (London, 1995).

Hamner, Emily, *Britannia's glory: a history of twentieth-century lesbians* (London, 1995).

Harris, Helen and Eileen Healy (eds), *Strong about it all: rural and urban women's experiences of the security forces in Northern Ireland*, North-west women's/human rights project publications, 2001.

Haughton, Miriam, Mary McAuliffe and Emilie Pine (eds) *Legacies of the Magdalen laundries: commemoration, gender, and the postcolonial carceral state* (Manchester, 2021).

Hill, Myrtle, *Women in Ireland: a century of change* (Belfast, 2003).

Holland, Mary, 'Mary the mother and her impact on Irish politics', *Irish Times*, 19 October 1979.

Holmes, Rachel, *The secret life of Dr James Barry: Victorian England's most eminent surgeon* (London, 2020).

Howes, Marjorie, 'Public discourse, private reflection, 1916–70' in Angela Bourke et al. (eds), *The Field Day anthology of Irish writing: volume 4: Irish women's writing and traditions* (Cork, 2002).

Hug, Chrystel, *The politics of sexual morality in Ireland* (London, 1999).

Hunt, Geoffrey, Jenny Mellor and John Turner, 'Women and the inebriate reformatories' in L. Jamieson and H. Corr (eds), *State, private life and political change* (London, 1990).

Ingle, Roisín, 'The Ann Lovett letters: sorrow, shame, anger and indignation', *Irish Times*, 31 January 2017, available at: https://www.irishtimes.com/life-and-style/people/the-ann-lovett-letters-sorrow-shame-anger-and-indignation-1.1673920

Inglis, Tom, 'Foucault, Bourdieu and the field of Irish sexuality', *Irish Journal of Sociology*, 7 (1997).

Inglis, Tom, *Moral monopoly: the rise and fall of the Catholic Church in modern Ireland* (Dublin, 1998).

Inglis, Tom, *Truth, power and lies: Irish society and the case of the Kerry babies* (Dublin, 2003).

Jamison, Anne, *E.Œ. Somerville and Martin Ross: female authorship and literary collaboration* (Cork, 2016).

Joyce, Simon, 'Two women walk into a theatre bathroom: the Fanny and Stella trials as trans narrative', *Victorian Review*, 44:1 (Spring 2018).

Kennedy, Finola, *Cottage to creche: family change in Ireland* (Dublin, 2001).

Kennedy, Robert E., *The Irish: emigration, marriage and fertility* (Berkeley, 1973).

Kennedy, Sinéad, 'Irish women and the Celtic tiger economy' in Colin Coulter and Steve Coleman (eds), *The end of Irish history?* (Manchester, 2003).

Kilfeather, Siobhan, *Dublin: a cultural history* (Oxford, 2005).

King, Russll and Ian Shuttleworth, 'Ireland's new wave of emigration in the 1980s', *Irish Geography*, 21:2 (1988).

Kunzel, Regina G., *Fallen women, problem girls: unmarried mothers and the professionalisation of social work, 1890–1945* (New Haven, 1993).

Lambert, Sharon, 'Irish women's emigration to England: 1922–1960: the lengthening of family ties' in Alan Hayes and Diane Urquhart (eds), *Irish women's history reader* (Dublin, 2004).

Lane, Leeann, *Rosamund Jacob: third person singular* (Dublin, 2010).

Lapovsky Kennedy, Elizabeth and Madeline D. Davis, '"I could hardly wait to get back to that bar": lesbian bar culture in Buffalo in the 1930s and 1940s' in Brett Beenyn (ed.), *Creating a place for ourselves: lesbian, gay and bisexual community histories* (London, 1997).

Lee, Jamie Ann, 'A queer/ed archival methodology: theorising practice through radical interrogations of the archival body' (PhD, University of Arizona, 2015).

Leiby, Michele, 'Sexual violence against political prisoners: an examination of empirical evidence in El Salvador and Peru' in Alissa Ackerman and Rich Furman (eds), *Sex crimes; transnational problems and global perspectives* (Colombia, 2015).

Loughran, Christina, 'Armagh and feminist strategy: campaigns around republican women prisoners in Armagh jail', *Feminist Review*, 23 (1986).

Lord, Stephanie, 'The Eighth Amendment: planting a legal timebomb' in Catherine Conlon, Sinead Kennedy and Aideen Quility (eds), *The abortion papers Ireland: volume 2* (Cork, 2015).

Lucey, Donnacha Sean, *The end of the Irish poor law? Welfare and healthcare reform in revolutionary and independent Ireland* (Manchester, 2015).

Luddy, Maria, 'Sex and the single girl in 1920s and 1930s Ireland', *The Irish Review*, 35 (2007).

Luddy, Maria, 'Moral rescue and unmarried mothers in Ireland in the 1920s', *Women's Studies*, 6 (2007).

Luddy, Maria, 'Unmarried mothers in Ireland, 1880–1973', *Women's History Review*, 20:1 (2011).

Maguire, Moira J., 'The changing face of Catholic Ireland: conservatism and liberalism in the Ann Lovett and Kerry babies scandals', *Feminist Studies* 27:2 (2001).

McAuliffe, Mary, *Margaret Skinnider* (Dublin, 2022).

McAuliffe, Mary and Harriet Wheelock, *The diaries of Kathleen Lynn; a life revealed through personal writing* (Dublin, 2023).

McAvoy, Sandra, 'The regulation of sexuality in the Irish Free State, 1929–1935' in Elizabeth Malcolm and Greta Jones (eds), *Medicine, disease and the state in Ireland, 1650–1940* (Cork, 1999).

McCafferty, Nell, *The Armagh women* (Dublin, 1981).

McCafferty, Nell, *A woman to blame; the Kerry babies case* (Dublin [1985], 2010).

McCormick, Leanne, *Regulating sexuality: women in twentieth-century Northern Ireland* (Manchester, 2009).

McCormick, Leanne, Sean O'Connell, Olivia Dee and John Privilege, *Mother and baby homes and Magdalene laundries in Northern Ireland, 1922–1990* (2021), available from /https://www.health-ni.gov.uk/sites/default/files/publications/health/doh-mbhl-final-report.pdf

McDonagh, Sunniva, *The attorney general v. X and others: judgments of the high court and supreme court. Legal submissions made to the supreme court.* Incorporated Council of Law Reporting for Ireland, 1992.

Marshall, C.F., 'Alcoholism and prostitution', *The British Journal of Inebriety*, 8:1 (1910).

Milotte, Mike, *Banished babies: the secret history of Ireland's baby export business* (Dublin, 1997).

Moore, Linda and Philip Scraton, 'Women's imprisonment, conflict and transition', *The incarceration of women; punishing bodies, breaking spirits* (London, 2015).

Morash, Christopher, *A history of the media in Ireland* (Cambridge, 2012).

Morgan, Sue, *The feminist history reader* (London, 2006).

Morrison, Brownyn, 'Controlling the hopeless: re-visioning the history of female inebriate institutions, *c.*1870–1920' in H. Johnston (ed.), *Punishment and control in historical perspective* (London, 2008).

Muldowney, Mary, 'Breaking the silence: pro-choice activism in Ireland since 1983' in Jennifer Redmond, Sonja Tiernan, Sandra McAvoy and Mary McAuliffe (eds), *Sexual politics in modern Ireland* (Dublin, 2015).

Mulholland, Marie, *The politics and relationships of Kathleen Lynn* (Dublin 2002).

Murray, Raymond, *Hard time: Armagh gaol, 1971–1986* (Dublin, 1998).

National Council for Civil Liberties (NCCL), 'Strip-searching: an inquiry into the strip-searching of women prisoners at Armagh prison between 1982 and 1985' (1986).

Nugent, B. and E. Smith, 'Intersectional solidarity? The Armagh women, the British left and women's liberation', *Contemporary British History*, 31:4 (2017).

O'Carroll, J.P., 'Bishops, knights – and pawns? Traditional thought and the Irish abortion referendum debate of 1983', *Irish Political Studies*, 6 (1991).

Ó Corráin, Daithí, 'Why did Pope John Paul II visit Ireland? The 1979 papal visit in context', *British Catholic History*, 35:4 (2021).

O'Donnell, Katherine, Maeve O'Rourke and James M. Smith (eds), *Redress: Ireland's institutions and transitional justice* (Dublin, 2022).

Ó hÓgartaigh, Margaret, *Kathleen Lynn: Irishwoman, patriot, doctor* (Dublin, 2006).

O'Keefe, Theresa, *Feminist identity development and activism in revolutionary movements* (London, 2013).

O'Keefe, Theresa, 'Menstrual blood as a weapon of resistance', *International Feminist Journal of Politics*, 8:4 (2006).

O'Keefe, Theresa, 'Bridge-builder feminism: the feminist movement and conflict in Northern Ireland', *Irish Political Studies*, 36:1 (2021).

O'Rawe, Richard, *Blanketmen: an untold story of the H-block hunger strike* (Dublin, 2005).

O'Riordan, Ellen, 'Rights of eight mother and baby home survivors breached over report, State says', *Irish Times*, 17 December 2021.

O'Reilly, Emily, *Masterminds of the right* (Dublin, 1992).

O'Reilly, Emily, 'O'Reilly recalls the immediate storm that followed her report of the death of Ann Lovett', *Irish Times*, 31 January 2004

O'Toole, Fintan, 'Why Ireland became the only country in the democratic world to have a constitutional ban on abortion', *Irish Times*, 26 August 2014. Available at: https://www.irishtimes.com/news/politics/why-ireland-became-the-only-country-in-the-democratic-world-to-have-a-constitutional-ban-on-abortion-1.1907610.

Pašeta, Senia, *Irish nationalist women 1900–1918* (Cambridge, 2013).

Pickering, Sharon, *Women, policing and resistance in Northern Ireland* (Belfast, 2002).

Radzinowicz, Leon and Roger Hood, *A history of English criminal law, vol. 5: the emergence of penal policy* (London, 1986).

Raymond, Janice, *The transsexual empire: the making of the she-male* (Beacon Press, 1979).

Redmond, Jennifer, '"Sinful singleness"?: exploring the discourses on Irish single women's emigration to England, 1922–1948', *Women's History Review*, 17:3 (2008).

Redmond, Jennifer, 'In the family way and away from the family: examining the evidence in Irish unmarried mothers in Britain, 1920s–40s' in Elaine Farrell (ed.), *'She said she was in the family way': pregnancy and infancy in modern Ireland* (London, 2012).

Redmond, Jennifer, 'Safeguarding Irish girls: welfare work, female emigrants and the Catholic Church, 1920s–1940s' in Cara Delay and Christine Brophy (eds), *Women, reform, and resistance in Ireland, 1850–1950* (New York, 2015).

Redmond, Jennifer, *Moving histories: Irish women's emigration to England, from independence to republic* (Liverpool, 2018).

Reidy, Conor, *Ireland's moral hospital: the Irish borstal system, 1906–1956* (Dublin, 2009).

Richter-Montpetit, Melaine, 'Militarised masculinities, women torturers, and the limits of gender analysis at Abu Ghraib' in Annick Wibben (ed.), *Researching war: feminist methods, ethics and politics* (London, 2016).

Riddick, Ruth, *The right to choose: questions of feminist morality* (Dublin, 1990).

Robinson, Lisa and Lauren Simkin Berke, *Were I not a girl: the inspiring and true story of Dr James Barry* (London, 2020).

Ruane, Medb, 'Kathleen Lynn' in Mary Cullen and Maria Luddy (eds), *Female activists; Irish women and change, 1900–1960* (Dublin, 2001).

Ryan, Louise, *Gender, identity and the Irish press, 1922–1937: embodying the nation* (Lewiston, 2002).

Sanders, Rob, *The fighting infantryman: the story of Albert D.J. Cashier, transgender civil war soldier* (London, 2020).

Sanger, Carol, *About abortion: terminating pregnancy in twenty-first century America* (Harvard, 2017).

Scraton, Philip, 'Bearing witness to the "pain of others": researching power, violence and resistance in a women's prison', *International Journal for Crime, Justice and Social Democracy*, 5:1 (2016).

Scraton, Philip, 'I am sir, you are a number': Report of the Independent Panel of Inquiry into the circumstances of the H-block and Armagh prison protests 1976–1981 (2020).

Seifert, Ruth, 'War and rape: a preliminary analysis' in Alexandra Stiglmayer (ed.), *Mass rape: the war against women in Bosnia Herzegovina* (Lincoln, 1995).

Smith, Beverly A., 'Ireland's Ennis inebriates' reformatory: a nineteenth-century example of failed institutional reform', *Federal Probation*, 53 (1989).

Smith, James M., *Ireland's Magdalen laundries and the nation's architecture of containment* (Indiana, 2007).

Smith-Rosenberg, Carroll, 'The female world of love and ritual: relations between women in nineteenth-century America', *Signs*, 1:1 (Autumn 1975).

Tiernan, Sonja, '"Engagements dissolved": Eva Gore-Booth, *Urania* and the radical challenge to marriage', Mary McAuliffe and Sonja Tiernan (eds), *Tribades, tommies and transgressives: histories of sexualities: volume I* (Newcastle, 2008).

Tiernan, Sonja, 'It should not be so easy to construct a man; a history of female to male transsexuality in the journal *Urania*' in Sonja Tiernan and Mary McAuliffe (eds), *Sapphists and sexologists: histories of sexualities: volume 2* (Newcastle, 2009).

Tiernan, Sonja 'Challenging presumptions of heterosexuality: Eva Gore-Booth, a biographical case study', *Historical Reflections*, 37:2 (2011).

Toibín, Colm, 'Gay Byrne: Irish life as cabaret', *The Crane Bag*, 8:2 (1984).

Valiulis, Maryann, 'Defining their role in the new State: Irishwomen's protest against the Juries Act of 1927', *The Canadian Journal of Irish Studies*, 18:1 (1992).

Vicinus, Martha, *Lesbian subjects: a feminist studies reader* (Indiana, 1996).

Vicinus, Martha, 'The history of lesbian history', *Feminist Studies*, 38 (2012).

Walsh, Deirdre, 'My personal lesbian history of Cork', *LINC*, Cork's lesbian magazine, 1:1 (2000).

Walsh, Deirdre, 'Interview with Helen Slattery', *LINC*, Cork's lesbian magazine, 2 (May 2001).

Wahidin, Azrini, *Ex-combatants, gender and peace in Northern Ireland: women, political protest and the prison experience* (London, 2016).

Walkowitz, Judith, *Prostitution and Victorian society: women, class and the state* (Cambridge, 1982).

Warsh, Cheryl Krasnick, '"John Barleycorn must die": an introduction to the social history of alcohol' in C.K. Warsh (ed.), *Drink in Canada: historical essays* (Quebec, 1993),

Whyte, J.H., Church *and state in modern Ireland, 1923–1970* (Dublin, 1971).

Zedner, Lucia, *Women, crime, and custody in Victorian England* (London, 1991).

Contributors

JENNIFER REDMOND is associate professor in twentieth-century Irish history at the Department of History, Maynooth University. She is a former president of the Women's History Association of Ireland and researches in the field of women and gender history in modern Ireland. Her book, *Moving histories: Irish women's emigration from independence to republic* (Liverpool, 2018), was long listed for the 2020 Michel Déon Prize. She is the chair of the EU-funded COST Action HIDDEN: History of Identity Documentation in European Nations (2022–6), which examines issues of identity documentation, migration and citizenship from the twentieth century to the present day.

MARY MCAULIFFE is a historian and lecturer in gender studies at University College Dublin (UCD). Her latest publications include (co-authored with Harriet Wheelock) *The diaries of Kathleen Lynn: a life revealed through personal writing* (Dublin, 2023) and *Margaret Skinnider; a biography* (Dublin, 2020). Other publications include (co-edited with Miriam Haughton and Emilie Pine) *Legacies of the Magdalen Laundries: commemoration, gender, and the postcolonial carceral state.* Throughout the Decade of Centenaries, 2012–23, she has been conducting extensive research on the experiences of women during the War of Independence and Civil War and is currently completing her book *Gendered and sexual violence in the Irish War of Independence and Civil War, 1919–1923*. She is a past president of the Women's History Association of Ireland, a member of the Irish Women's Museum Advocacy Group, and a member of the Humanities Institute, UCD.

MAEVE O'RIORDAN is a lecturer in women's and cultural history at University College Cork. She is author of *Women of the Irish country house, 1860–1914* (Liverpool, 2018) and several other pieces on elite women in Ireland. She is currently exploring the experiences of single women. With Dr Leanne Calvert, she chairs RIFNET: Reconstituting the Irish Family Research Network, a network funded by the ESRC and IRC that aims to tell the story of Irish families that sit outside of what we perceive as the 'traditional' norm.

CONOR REIDY is a specialist in Irish penal and criminal history. He is the author of three monographs and numerous chapters and articles. He has lectured at the University of Limerick and Mary Immaculate College, Limerick. He served as a historical researcher with the Commission of Investigation into

Mother and Baby Homes in Ireland. Between 2013 and 2016 he was secretary of the Women's History Association of Ireland. While maintaining his historical research interests, he now works as a freelance professional copy editor, indexer and editorial project manager.

LEANNE MCCORMICK is professor in modern Irish social history at Ulster University. She has published widely in the areas of women's and gender history, history of medicine, sexuality and crime with a focus on Northern Ireland and the Irish diaspora. She is co-creator of the Bad Bridget project, which includes the book, *Bad Bridget: crime, mayhem and the lives of Irish emigrant women,* as well as a podcast and exhibition. She is co-investigator on the AHRC-funded 'Queer Northern Ireland' project and is co-chair of the Truth Recovery Independent Panel on mother and baby institutions and Magdalene laundries in Northern Ireland.

SEAN O'CONNELL is professor of modern Irish and British social history at Queen's University Belfast. He is editor of the journal *Oral History* and has used that method to inform several of his publications, including work on credit unions, moneylending, joyriding, and working-class communities in Belfast. With Leanne McCormick, he was a lead author on *Mother and baby homes and Magdalene laundries in Northern Ireland, 1922–1990 research report* (2021). He is currently co-chair of the Truth Recovery Independent Panel examining mother and baby institutions, Magdalene laundries and workhouses in Northern Ireland.

JOHN PRIVILEGE is research associate at Ulster University and has published on the history of the Catholic Church in Ireland, the foundation of the NHS in Northern Ireland and Jewish refugees from the Third Reich. Along with Dr Livi Dee, McCormick, O'Connell and Privilege researched and wrote the *Mother and baby homes and Magdalene laundries in Northern Ireland, 1922–1990 research report.*

CAITLÍN O'NEILL is a graduate of Maynooth University where she completed her MA thesis on the Sean Ross Abbey mother and baby home. She currently teaches English and history in a secondary school in Dublin. She is interested in the histories of working-class women.

TANYA NÍ MHUIRTHILE is an associate professor of law and body politics at Dublin City University. Her research interrogates the impact of law on the lived experience of the human body. She advises governments, civil servants and national and international NGOs on legislation and public policy in her areas of expertise. Tanya was appointed to the Gender Recognition Act Review Group in 2017. She currently serves as a member of the Drafting Committee for the Council of Europe's Recommendation on the Rights of Intersex People.

THERESA O'KEEFE is a senior lecturer in the Department of Sociology & Criminology and board member of Women's Studies at University College Cork. She has published in leading feminist and gender studies journals and currently serves as a member of the editorial board for *Gender, Work & Organisation.*

SINÉAD KENNEDY teaches in the English department at Maynooth University and is co-ordinator of the MA in Literatures of Engagement. Her most recent book (with Camilla Fitzsimons) is *Repealed: Ireland's unfinished fight for reproductive rights* (London, 2021). She was the co-founder of the Coalition to Repeal the Eighth Amendment and executive member and research head for Together for Yes.

ANTONIA HART currently lectures at Maynooth University and is a visiting research fellow at Trinity College Dublin. She completed her PhD on nineteenth- and early twentieth-century Irish women in business at Trinity College Dublin in 2021, supported by an Irish Research Council Government of Ireland Postgraduate Scholarship. Her book *Business as usual: the commercial lives of Irish women, 1850–1922* is forthcoming from Liverpool University Press as part of its Reappraisals in Irish History series.

DEIRDRE FOLEY is a historian of modern Ireland with a particular interest in birth control, maternity care, and the legal status of women in twentieth-century Ireland. She is currently an Irish Research Council postdoctoral research fellow at Trinity College Dublin and was previously Roy Foster Irish Government Research Fellow at Hertford College, Oxford.

ELIZABETH (LIZ) KIELY is a senior lecturer in the School of Applied Social Studies, University College Cork, whose teaching and research spans social policy, gender and women's studies. Recent publications include (with R.R. Meade and Ó. O'Donovan), 'Cruel optimism in the universities: a discursive deconstructive reading of promising promotional projects of gender equality', *Gender, Work, and Organisation* (2023) and (with E. Swirak), *The criminalisation of social policy in neoliberal societies* (Bristol, 2022).

MARY MULDOWNEY is Dublin City Council historian in residence for the North-West area. A graduate of Trinity College Dublin, she is widely published, frequently using oral history interviews as a primary source in her research. She is a member of the organising committee of the Irish Labour History Society and is co-editor of the Society's internationally recognised journal, *Saothar*. Mary is also a member of the Grangegorman Histories Working Group, and she is directing a pilot oral history project as part of the programme. She is the tutor for the Lord Mayor's Certificate Course in Oral History.

ORLA EGAN is a queer archival activist and founder of the Cork LGBT Archive. Orla is author of the Irish social activism graphic memoir *Diary of an activist*, in collaboration with artist Megan Luddy O'Leary. She is author of *Queer republic of Cork, Cork's lesbian, gay, bisexual and transgender communities, 1970s–1990s* and of the short theatre play *Leeside Lezzies*. She is the director of two Cork LGBT documentaries, *LOAFERS* and *I'm here, I'm home, I'm happy*. She has created a number of exhibitions, including *Cork Queers* and *Art & Activism*.

SARA R. PHILLIPS is a trans activist working globally. She has been involved with trans activism for over 30 years. Sara is the founder, researcher and archivist of the Irish Trans Archive. She is a board member of the National Women's Council of Ireland, co-chair of Transgender Europe and co-chair of International Trans Fund. She is the former chair of the board of directors of Ireland's national trans organisation, Transgender Equality Network Ireland (TENI).

MARIA LUDDY is emeritus professor of modern Irish history at the University of Warwick. She has published extensively on Irish social history and the history of women and gender in the nineteenth and twentieth centuries. Her most recent book, with Mary O'Dowd, is *Marriage in Ireland, 1660–1925* (Cambridge, 2020). She is currently researching the support of illegitimate children in Ireland since 1800.

Index